THEORY AND REALITY
IN PUBLIC INTERNATIONAL LAW

OTHER BOOKS FROM

THE CENTER OF INTERNATIONAL STUDIES

PRINCETON UNIVERSITY

Gabriel A. Almond, *The Appeals of Communism*

William W. Kaufmann, editor, *Military Policy and National Security*

Klaus Knorr, *The War Potential of Nations*

Lucian W. Pye, *Guerrilla Communism in Malaya*

THEORY AND REALITY IN PUBLIC INTERNATIONAL LAW

CHARLES DE VISSCHER

TRANSLATED FROM THE FRENCH BY

P. E. CORBETT

PRINCETON, NEW JERSEY

PRINCETON UNIVERSITY PRESS

1957

L.C. CARD 56-8378

This book is a translation of
Théories et Réalités en Droit International Public,
first published in 1953
by Editions A. Pedone, Paris.
It incorporates most of the changes made
between the first and second French editions,
and thus is substantially the same as the second.

Charles De Visscher's career includes service as counsel and arbiter in international disputes, as minister in and representative of the Belgian Government, as president of the Institute of International Law, and as judge of the International Court of Justice. He is now professor at the University of Louvain. *P. E. Corbett* is research associate in international studies at Princeton University.

Printed in the United States of America
by Princeton University Press, Princeton, New Jersey
ISBN 978-0-691-64933-7

FOREWORD

IN RECENT YEARS a new and highly significant trend has become visible in the literature of international law. The shape of this trend is exhibited in three books written by leading authorities in different parts of the world. These are *Théories et Réalités en Droit International Public* by Charles De Visscher of Belgium (1953), *Legal Controls of International Conflict* by Julius Stone of Australia (1954), and *Law and Society in the Relations of States* by P. E. Corbett of the United States (1951). In order that the full significance of this trend may be made apparent to audiences in the English-speaking countries, the Center of International Studies of Princeton University decided to undertake an English edition of Professor De Visscher's volume. The task of translating was entrusted to Professor Corbett, who is on the staff of the Center, and was carried out with the aid of a grant from the Rockefeller Foundation.

In this volume Professor De Visscher dissects the strengths and weaknesses of the various theories, ancient and modern, that have presented the law of nations as an operative and imperative system governing a ready-made community, as well as those theories that identify law and power. Law in his view is still a normative order, not a mere record of practice. He believes that the international scene is one where legal notions and structures struggle for influence with the still dominant drives of political interests. Development toward an effective world order can proceed only as power is coordinated to the ends of human welfare, and as the need for a universal law and society finds intimate recognition in the minds of men. The legal theory that can accelerate this necessarily slow process must take full account of the findings of contemporary social science, and especially of the recent advances made in the study of international politics. His book offers a masterly appraisal of what has been achieved in the past and a challenge to current writing on law and politics in the international arena.

The Center of International Studies, which has sponsored this enterprise, was established at Princeton University in 1951 for the purpose of promoting research and training in the field of interstate relationships. Its studies, although concerned with all aspects of international affairs, are devoted primarily to analyzing contemporary problems in the foreign policy of the United States. Individual projects are undertaken by members of the Center on their own initiative.

FREDERICK S. DUNN
Director

Center of International Studies
Princeton University
February 1, 1956

TRANSLATOR'S PREFACE

Théories et Réalités en Droit International Public was first published in Paris in 1953. Within a year English-speaking readers were raising the question of its translation. Impressed at once by the depth and by the breadth of the book, they felt strongly that it ought to be made available to a wider range of students than could and would read it in French.

The suggestion was not at once taken up. With some unintended flattery of the international-law fraternity, the objection was raised that the vast majority of those who should master a work of this sort would be quite capable of doing so in the original.

The advocates of translation were not satisfied with the assumption that the language of Talleyrand is still—if indeed it ever was—so common a possession of those who concern themselves with the legal aspects of diplomacy. Even in the century of the Enlightenment, there was apparently justification for an English translation of Vattel's *Droit des gens* within two years of its appearance on the Continent. Nor is this comparison made with any sense of exaggeration. The pages of this volume will show reason for believing that *Théories et Réalités en Droit International Public* may be no less a contribution to the subject in our day than was the *Droit des gens* in 1758.

About the vast contemporary expansion of interest in international relations there can be no doubt; and there will be little debate about the broadening out of participation in the making of foreign policy. However much has been done to spread the knowledge of foreign languages to keep pace with this development, it is clear that a very large proportion of the new audience can be reached in English only. The field of international relations is, par excellence, one where familiarity with foreign thought is essential, if only as an antidote to distortion. So, when any work marked not only by command of all the traditional scholarship, but also by originality, boldness, and objectivity, appears in this field, the case for translation is stronger than it ever was.

Théories et Réalités is such a work. The author, professor at the University of Louvain, has been adviser and representative of the Belgian Government in international negotiations, president of the Institute of International Law, judge of the International Court of Justice, and umpire in international arbitration. This book is the ripe fruit of learning enriched by broad practical experience and a wisdom that grasps things whole. It is much more than a legal treatise; indeed the juristic purist will hardly accord it that title. It is a profound study in their living reality of relations of which law is the formalized pattern. As a documented exposition of the limitations imposed by the present distribution of political power on the operation of legal norms in shaping the external conduct of governments, it is a pioneer work—a work which, by clearing the field of illusions, may serve as the starting point for a more fruitful approach to the vast problem of world order.

Because he sees things whole, Professor De Visscher's belief in the value of law and of the legal techniques never blinds him to the disparity between the best-intentioned formulations of rules and the actual conduct of governments. He is an interested but undeceived witness of movements towards and away from lawlike patterns and procedures in the relations of States. If legal science has not made the contribution to world order that might have been expected of it, the fault is by no means wholly in the perversity of politicians and the nationalistic passions of their peoples. Part of it lies in the jurist's propensity to formal generalization, and the professional prejudice that finds law in two or three approximate repetitions of a way of doing things. If the contribution is to be more significant in future, the jurist must measure accurately the relative roles of the legal and the political as determinants of public policy. He must understand the multiplicity of psychological and social influences that vie with a priori rules in shaping the decisions of the human beings who are the realities behind the construct of State personality. What civil lawyers call "doctrine," and common lawyers "jurisprudence," can no longer wall itself off in its own "pure" world. On penalty of continued barrenness in the international field, it must welcome an invasion of modern social science.

The literature of international law has habitually trimmed off the rough excrescences of international events in an effort to force those events into the pre-established molds of abstract rules. The resulting distortion far exceeds the maximum of disparity that can separate the effective legal norm from the social facts for which it serves as standard. It is Professor De Visscher's considered judgment that law cannot be built upon a heedless sacrifice of reality. Politics, which, though it is by no means an unmitigated search for power, makes the preservation of the State's power a minimum objective, is the dominant factor in international relations. But there are points where interest may lead power into convergence with law, and it is in the discernment of these points and elaboration of the techniques by which the convergence may be sustained and enlarged that the jurist can assist the politician in any conscious move towards world order.

The aggregate of States does not exhibit that minimum of solidarity which would justify regarding it as a community or its tentative and shifting patterns of practice as a legal system. But in areas of interest which governments do not regard as vital the elaboration of rules and the organization of structure for their administration show considerable and promising growth. It is by working with the politician in these areas that the jurist can do most to limit the disruptively individualistic exercise of State sovereignty. But Professor De Visscher does not see development along these "administrative" lines as a process which by itself will gradually conquer the reserved domain where governments continue to demand a discretion unrestricted by any collective obligation. The process, if it is to reach such heights, must be accompanied by a drastic change in men's conceptions of the State and its power. These, pulled down from their present eminence as the supreme goals of political organization, must be subordinated to the ends of the human person. Here we find the essential link between national and international social development; and the prospect is not one to rejoice the heart of the internationalist. For the State's unceasing invasion of all fields of human activity, even in democratic countries, seems to point to the consolidation and increase rather than the subordination of its power. How can the State organization be used to maximize individual welfare and yet be prevented from usurping the position of end in itself? Here, in general terms, is the common problem of contemporary law and politics in the international as in the national sphere.

Without committing himself to any one of the contemporary fads or schools of methodology, Professor De Visscher may perhaps have launched a revolution in the study of international law. In attempting that, he has subjected the procedures and institutions of world politics to an examination which in its breadth and analytical power makes his work as valuable to the general student of international relations as to the specialist in their legal aspects. Out of mature scholarship, knowledge of the world, and rare receptivity to new ideas, he has built a bridge across the chasm of misunderstanding, even antagonism, that has separated the older and more formal from the younger and more roving discipline. This English version of his most recent book is dedicated to the hope that those who cultivate what is essentially one field may henceforth work in productive partnership.

AUTHOR'S PREFACE

THE first world war opened a new era in the doctrine of international law. The war had exposed the bankruptcy of the law in the relations of peoples; the return to peace revealed the changes in the social order. Work in depth, which escaped neither uncertainty nor error, took the place of premature systematization. Slowly, and not without encounters with stubborn prejudices, it began to enrich the substance, transform the methods, and enlarge the horizons of international law.

The positivist school had cherished the hope of reducing international law as a whole to the logical forms of a rigorous system. Its confidence in criteria which it regarded as established bore the marks of a stability and of a tranquil assurance in the value of experimental methods that were characteristic of the nineteenth century. The school had the merit of substituting for the vague suggestions of a deformed natural law an attentive examination of inter-State relations. But its doctrine, voluntarist in its most widely received version, misrepresented reality by reducing law to nothing more than the rules evolving from agreements between States by a method of elaboration believed characteristic of international relations. Remaining in this sense essentially formal, it exaggerated the specificity of international law, separating it off from the moral, social, and political data which form its sphere of application and condition its effectiveness. Though this school's avowed aim was to exclude all political elements from the statement of legal norms, it adopted as the decisive criterion of the validity of such norms the manifestations of will proceeding from political authority. This attitude paralyzed the critical spirit and too often froze the law in positions ill adapted to the profound changes demanded by the times.

Most contemporary authors are conscious of the insufficiency of these methods. More or less clearly, they recognize that the rules of international law are inadequate to meet the conditions and demands of life. Too often an atmosphere of unreality surrounds their ritualistic exposition. This is so whenever the gap between the fact and the rule is so wide as to set up an excessive tension. To this extent law may lose contact with life.

Yet there was no uniformity in the reaction of doctrine to the violent political commotions that marked the first half of our century. The formidable reality of politics made some nostalgic for a closed and complete legal universe, where disembodied law, reduced to a pure logical structure, would operate as sovereign regulator of the relations between abstract conceptions. The aspiration to make law an absolutely autonomous system led to detaching it from its social function and reducing it to the position of a mere intellectual construction.

A larger number of authors, less influenced by abstract analysis, devoted themselves to making international law more effective. With this in view they tried to place it frankly, and without doctrinal preoccupations, in its particular setting, which is still in large measure an unorganized setting. This is the general direction of the present work.

Law has its legitimate and necessary autonomy over against realities, when realities attain that degree of juristic integration and that formal "setting apart" which protect them, at least temporarily, against social and political oscillations. But it is the weakness of neopositivism and the mark of its antihistorical spirit that it approaches the problem exclusively from this point of view; that it sees in the process by which norms are formed only the special procedure that constitutes its last phase and marks its full achievement; that, to satisfy purely logical requirements, it states as a principle a completeness of law that immediately brings all social facts within the legal order.

It is impossible to put such a logical strait jacket on the study of a law still so imperfect as international law, where what has been achieved is small compared with what might reasonably be expected in a society truly integrated in a legal order. The problem is of another order of magnitude. The stake in the sphere of international organization, the great question posed by the minimum demands of international security, is nothing less than the social solidity of the present distribution of power among States. The central problem of the normative order is henceforth much less the legal validity of the formal process of elaborating international law than the obstacles confronting its extension. We must know why and how far certain aspects of the external activity of States, and those certainly the most fundamental, continue to be refractory to law, even at times immune from any common value-judgment, resistant to reasoned analysis and the test of general criteria. We must determine—since object or matter here provides no usable indication—the influence in this state of affairs of the present forms of political power and, still more, of the spirit animating those forms. We must understand in all its profound reality, that is to say at the national level and in the internal order first, what it is in the State that determines that other "setting apart," this time purely political, which in international relations bars the way to more complete legal integration and inspires discretionary decision. Even positive international law itself demands a critical examination of content, first to measure the now constructive, now disruptive influence of power in the formation of norms, and then, using criteria gradually being defined by international case-law, to fix the level of generalization or individualization that must be adopted in the specific application of norms.

Such a program of research (which must in no event neglect the internal organization and operation of power, since these are always closely linked with its external operation) involves a study of the political system within which international relations have been conducted since the beginnings of the modern State, together with a review of the doctrines which the system has inspired and of the experience of the League of Nations (Book I). This study serves as introduction to the analysis of the general relations of power and law from three points of view—the present and still essentially political orientation of power; its ends; and its redistribution through international organization.

The third and much the longest part of this work examines the principal institutions, rules, and practices that make up what is conventionally called positive international law. It has seemed to us that it is in the heart of this law, illustrated in its concrete data by the practice of States, that we must re-establish contact with the realities of every kind that explain its origin, enable us to understand its organization, and foreshadow its future evolution. International law has nothing to fear from this direct confrontation with the real. The vistas that it reveals assuredly lack the intellectual elegance and the dialectical charm of the theories that jealously insist on the autonomy of law. They have one merit: they open upon life. Institutions and norms appear more charged with social substance, richer in human meaning, clear in their very depths with a new light, when they are shown immersed in the element that gave them birth and where they find their daily application.

The fourth part discusses the resistance of politics to the expansion of judicial settlement, and the resources made available for the legal solution of disputes by the one function that can ensure the exact adaptation of rules to the diversity of cases.

AUTHOR'S PREFACE

A normative discipline makes progress only in contact with what resists it. International law cannot gather strength by isolating itself from the political realities with which international relations are everywhere impregnated. It can only do so by taking full account of the place that these realities occupy and measuring the obstacle which they present.

Brussels, September 1, 1953

CONTENTS

ABBREVIATIONS

A.J.I.L.	*American Journal of International Law*
B.Y.B.I.L.	*British Year Book of International Law*
Guggenheim, *Traité*	P. Guggenheim, *Traité de droit international public*
Hackworth, *Digest*	G. H. Hackworth, *Digest of International Law*, 8 vols., 1940-1944
Rec. A.D.I.	*Recueil des cours professés à l'Académie de Droit International de La Haye*, Paris

BOOK I

POLITICAL POWER IN EXTERNAL RELATIONS FROM THE BEGINNINGS OF THE MODERN STATE TO THE PRESENT

CHAPTER I. THE FOUNDATIONS OF THE MODERN STATE

THE INDIVIDUALIST CONSEQUENCES OF THE NEW DISTRIBUTION OF POWER

Section I

The Introduction of State Pluralism and Its First Results

MEDIEVAL society appears so different in structure from that of our day that it is difficult to place or even to imagine in it what we now call international relations. What differentiates it almost everywhere except in England is the fractioning of power—the eclipse, in the political thought of the period, of the Roman notion of the *imperium,* a sovereign power of command concentrated at one point, fountainhead of all the public functions, exercising general and exclusive competence in a defined territorial setting. We find an infinity of powers, but no power structured into a State regime offering in the external order a single and stable point of attachment for rights and responsibilities. For a long time, moreover, life remains purely local, confined within the narrow limits of the feudal seigniory. Nor, finally, is there any uniform principle in the distribution of power; everywhere profound differences appear; princes and lords, very unequal in law and in fact, are entitled to a bundle of personal prerogatives and to special public rights, which are objects of contractual or quasi-contractual relations and deeply imprinted with the patrimonial mark.[1]

True, in striking contrast with these tendencies toward an infinite fractioning of political authority, there was always the majestic conception of the unity of the Christian community—one of the great civilizing ideas that humanity owes to Christianity.[2] If this

[1] Cf. Max Huber, *Die Soziologischen Grundlagen des Völkerrechts,* p. 29; van Vollenhoven, *Le Droit de Paix,* pp. 30-31. The merchant towns of Italy, those called City-States (*Citta Stato, Stadtstaaten*), present another spectacle. Freed by their maritime relations from all authority, they behave to the world outside like independent political entities, thus demonstrating that the existence of an international law (*jus inter gentes*) is dependent on a particular form of power distribution.

[2] P. Vinogradoff, *Historical Types of International Law,* Bibliotheca Visseriana, vol. I, p. 38; Serge A. Korff, *Introduction à l'Etude du Droit international, Rec. A.D.I.,* vol. I (1952), p. 18.

had triumphed, political relations, instead of becoming fixed in juxtaposition, would have assumed the form of a vast federation (*diversum in diversis nationibus*),[3] an organic bond, founded on the divine origin of all power, uniting in one grand hierarchy the whole and the part, the collective and the individual.

Closely associated with the political ideal of a universal monarchy, this doctrine broke, halfway through the Middle Ages, against the historical evolution of political relations, in particular against the resistance of the young national States of the West. Its universalist conception postulated a social organization and an institutional order which, on the temporal plane, brought it into direct opposition to the separatist tendencies working towards particular sovereignties and against universal monarchy. Its high religious and moral inspiration nevertheless had profound influence. It preserved the idea of a Christian community which lies at the origin of international law. It helped to set a term to the scourge of private wars. By saving for the kings, long robbed of the reality of power by their great vassals, the pre-eminence of a divine source of their authority, it provided the principle from which, having become strong again, they would one day, especially in France, derive modern sovereignty.[4] Finally, and above all, by identifying authority with public service and subordinating monarchy itself to law, medieval doctrine built the foundations for a regime of law which through the centuries would oppose to the absolutist and wholly political conception of sovereignty the eminently legal and functional notion of power ordered for human ends.[5]

How was it that from this disaggregation, explained by the temporary incapacity of royalty to guarantee security, power would one day emerge in the form and figure of the State? On what bases would the young States organize their relations?

The first lineaments of the new order are drawn with the establishment of national States in Western Europe: England, France, and later Spain. Achieved immediately in England by the Norman kings,[6] State organization was in France the patient work of the monarchy, which, supported by the *bourgeoisie* of the towns, devoted itself to perfecting little by little those essential instruments

[3] O. von Gierke, *Les Théories politiques du Moyen-Age*, Pange's translation, passim; M. Zimmermann, *La Crise de l'Organization internationale à la fin du Moyen-Age*, *Rec. A.D.I.*, vol. 44 (1933), p. 326.

[4] Cf. Henri Pirenne, *Histoire de l'Europe*, pp. 104-107, 194-195.

[5] O. von Gierke, *op.cit.*, pp. 159-163, 249-253.

[6] G. M. Trevelyan, *History of England*, chap. VIII, p. 123.

of modern government: a permanent administration, sound finances, and an army at the command of central power. Freed in fact from the Empire's tutelage, the kingdoms of Henry II Plantagenet and Philippe-Auguste were already solid political units. With Philippe le Bel, the royal legists trained in the traditions of Roman law and of *raison d'Etat* applied themselves to making the monarchy absolute. "Exclusive consideration of the Crown's interest replaced St. Louis's ideal of justice and charity. With the constant growth of its strength, the royal power no longer had any tolerance for obstacles and justified the means that it used by the ends that it set itself."[7]

The need for security, which always plays a leading role in the formation of political units, after working for the great vassals, from now on supported the centralizing action of the monarchy. Feudalism, impoverished by wars, was everywhere in retreat, while royal prestige made the throne the focus of the first manifestations of nationalist sentiment.[8]

But, while national unity would be only slowly defined, territorial unification was the immediate object of the policy of sovereigns. They had inherited from feudalism an entirely territorial conception of power; the possession of the soil seemed to them the essential basis on which to develop public power. Then came the gradual substitution of sharply defined frontiers for the uncertain and shifting limits of principalities and seigniories. This was the origin of the tendency, so characteristic of the modern State, jealously to wall itself up and to exclude from its jurisdictional preserve any exercise of alien sovereignty.

In the substitution of the plural system for the medieval universalist conception, the territorial principle played a leading role. What doctrine, especially after the Treaties of Westphalia, would call the international community corresponded to an order of things in which territory, framework of a common life and coveted by outsiders, had an essential place. In its turn the exercise of stable political power in a defined territorial setting entailed the participa-

[7] Henri Pirenne, *op.cit.*, p. 277.

[8] In smaller compartments, the evolution took the same course in Italy. The old name "commune" gave place there to "dominion" or "seigniory." This, says Julien Luchaire, "is the mark of the constitutional history of this time; the notion of state clearly replaces that of association; power is clearly stabilized in the hands of those, princes or magnates, who can provide strong assurance of internal tranquility and the unity of the social body." *Les Sociétés Italiennes du XIIIe au XVe Siècle*, 1933, p. 170.

tion of all the inhabitants in historic events, promoted a collective mentality, and made a decisive contribution to national sentiment.[9] Thus out of common memories and a common historical destiny grew the spiritual unity that is the essential element of the modern nation.

In the destruction of the medieval order the Renaissance and the Reformation exercised considerable influence. The Renaissance secularized thought; and the Reformation nationalized religion, making of the Lutheran princes heads of territorial churches whose religion determined that of their subjects. In the economic domain, finally, powerful forces shook the rural economy and social life of feudalism. These forces, in the hands of the monarchy and the towns, became essential instruments of their power; from the fifteenth century on they would have a strong impact upon international relations.[10] The development of the means of communication, the re-establishment of international trade, the growth of the towns—all contribute to the triumph of centralized monarchy over feudalism in France. The same factors in Italy and in Germany promote the transformation of the cities into independent republics. Nascent capitalism finances the warlike enterprises of sovereigns, while seigniors and barons, heavily hit by the economic changes following the advent of urban economy and the geographic discoveries, group themselves around the kings and seek court office. The era of economic competition among nations is about to open. The sovereigns would find in the accumulation of the precious metals a new instrument of power, while the mercantilist policy and the struggle for colonies already foreshadowed the imperialisms of our time.

Such were the various factors that explain the gradual accomplishment of that union of the nation with the central power in which the modern State finds the essential source of its strength and the conditions for its rise to full political maturity. England achieved this union by the end of the thirteenth century—a fact that partly explains the extraordinary continuity of her foreign policy. In France it would be gradually cemented around the mon-

9 It has been said that "this synthesis of the soil and an idea is the very essence of the Nation." G. Burdeau, *Cours de Droit Constitutionnel*, p. 9.

10 This impact was not merely destructive of the established universal order; it was also unifying and constructive, for it fostered the State at a time when the temporal primacy of the Empire was nothing more than the ghost of an idea. By the first half of the sixteenth century the imperial idea had become so feeble that the opponents of Charles V could appeal against him to "the common liberty of Europe."

archy. Upon this union, always more intimate and conscious, would be built in later years the doctrine that makes the sovereign State the personification of the nation and the exclusive support of public authority. The doctrine has its perceptible dangers. Its efficacy, on the other hand, is incontestable, for, placing power above the individuals who exercise it, it goes further than any other to meet the two essential living requirements of political entities, namely permanence for the interests of the collectivity and a single center of function and responsibility.

Among sovereign and equal States, simply juxtaposed henceforth on the new plane of plurality, political rivalries take on a new amplitude. A common error, partly explained by the fame of Machiavelli's work, traces the entire development to the contacts of the West with the Italian tyrannies from the end of the fifteenth century on. This overlooks the fact that, for two centuries before this, central monarchies had been working in France and England to free themselves from all external control and to make the State a unit of autonomous power. Thus the moral and universal order of the Middle Ages had in those two countries been continuously undermined. The support given by the Kings of France to the Papacy against the Empire, their conflicts with the Papacy itself under Philippe le Bel, their clever control of the Pope during the Avignon exodus, the hand taken by France and England in the great schism of the West—these were all enterprises of national policy, contrary to the medieval order and hastening its liquidation.[11] What is true is that in more limited settings Italy knew long before the West the system of plural independent States. It is also true that the interventions of France, Spain, and the Empire south of the Alps helped to spread over Europe, and even to make a system of, the amoral and coldly reasoned practices adopted among the Italian principalities as a sequel to the despotic and violent seizures of power. Italian modernity consisted in part of the pluralism of its political structures and in part of a diplomatic technique based exclusively upon the calculation of forces and applied to their analysis with a lucidity and finesse previously unknown.[12] Such are the lineaments of an

[11] Pierre Dubois's work *De Recuperatione Terrae Sanctae* (1308) is significant in this connection.

[12] Machiavelli's State shows the two essential features of its modern counterpart, namely the conception of the fatherland, which makes for the establishment of the State on the national basis, and the absolute and exclusive character of national sovereignty. Cf. J. P. F. Ancillon, *Tableau des Révolutions du Système Politique de l'Europe*, t. 1, p. 262, which emphasizes the political ferment

evolution which came to completion in the Congress of Westphalia. The Treaties of 1648 confirmed the plural and secular system of a society of independent States, replacing thenceforth the providential and hierarchic order of the Middle Ages.

This exclusively political view of international relations proceeds from the reason of State and leads to balance of power. The State, an end in itself, is free of any moral rein; it seeks unlimited power and answers to no one for what it does. But excessive power evokes formidable coalitions; for want of a better alternative, well-understood interest counsels everyone to stabilize his advantages, and this can be done only by a balance of forces acting as counterweights to one another. Practiced at first quite empirically, raised later to the status of political principle, this balance was to become the check upon a mechanistic and materialistic conception of power.[13]

Born in Italy, where, in the sixteenth century, it moderated the frenzy of power (*das Pathos der Herrschaft*, said J. Burckhardt), the policy of balance spread everywhere from the moment when the French and Spanish interventions faced Europe with the Italian problem. In France's long struggle, beginning in the sixteenth century, with the House of Austria, English diplomacy found its inspiration in the idea of the balance of power. Confirmed by the Treaties of Westphalia, this policy was explicitly inscribed in the Treaty of Utrecht between England and Spain (1713). If it could not alone pretend to establish a moral order, it did at least provide a precept of prudence for the individualist policies of sovereign States.

The beginnings of modern positive international law are generally traced to the establishment of the great national States and more precisely to the Peace of Westphalia. This opinion is accurate if the law is regarded solely from the point of view of its subject, that is to say as a discipline applicable only to equal sovereign entities in simple juxtaposition. It leads to error when the political system with which it was bound up from that point of time—a system born of a mere transformation in the distribution of power—is presented as a natural or even necessary thing, or when we overlook the anarchic

---

of a system characterized by "the neighborhood of a large number of States too unequal to escape mutual fear, but equal enough to resist one another."

13 As a condition of stability in a system made up of autonomous forces, balance is a universal phenomenon, necessary in all political organization. We are here concerned only with its historical manifestations in international relations since the sixteenth century.

ferments implicit in the new atomistic and mechanistic conception of power.

Section II

The Doctrines

This immense political transformation, the slow growth of centuries, proceeded *pari passu* with a profound intellectual change. There is no epoch in which the reciprocal action of material forces and moral ideas is more visible. The social conception of a universal order that subordinates all power to divine ends is gradually replaced by a lay and human ideal of power, while a vision of institutions gives way to the regime of contractual agreements between juxtaposed political units.

Otto von Gierke showed that as early as the thirteenth century medieval political thought had been influenced by the concept of the State, inherited from antiquity, that contained the germ destined to destroy the medieval order. This new outlook supported the claim of the kings to be emancipated from imperial tutelage, and it gathered strength in the long conflict between the Papacy and the Empire.[14]

It would be a mistake to conclude that sovereignty so early claimed independence of law. Medieval thought was too thoroughly impregnated with the pre-eminence of natural law over any human institution to dispute the principle of the subordination of civil power to an objective order or, more particularly, its duty to respect in man the inalienable rights that he derives from his eternal purpose. It was only in the fifteenth century that the ancient and wholly political idea of the State, regarded as an abstract and dominating entity, began to separate itself from the moral ideas that guarded human liberties against the omnipotence of power. Between liberties and power there would henceforth be a tension, at times admitted and at times concealed, which, bearing on the very center of the modern conception of the State, would provide matter for every controversy in the domain of public law. From that point on,

[14] Precisely at the moment when the prestige of the monarchy was on the rise in France the legists found, in certain theses propounded by the Popes on the independence of the temporal kingdoms in their mutual relations, arguments that were to be useful in constructing the doctrine of royal absolutism. Cf. Hrabar in *Revue de Droit International* (Paris), 1936; vol. 18, p. 375. The famous formula *superiorem non recognoscentes*, used for the first time, it seems, by Pope Innocent III in the decretal *Per Venerabilem*, took on a classic quality in the writings of the legists of the Crown.

two divergent currents of thought are discernible. One is authoritarian, tending to subordinate everything to the "immanent ends" of the State in search of power. The other takes its inspiration from natural law—a natural law with the imprint of the Renaissance upon it and with a tone more philosophic than religious, but still, despite certain deformations, the defender of moral values against the abuses of power. These competing currents of thought were destined to have a direct influence on international law. Political writers, philosophers, and jurists set themselves zealously to the task of defining and systematizing the consequences of the new distribution of power.[15]

§ 1. THE PURELY POLITICAL CONCEPTIONS OF POWER

Certain theories make politics an autonomous category. Politics obeys its own laws; for its ends, being solely those of power, dictate the means to be employed. That is the conception implicit in Machiavelli's empirical formulas. As for morals, politics takes precedence, either because the reason of State, or in other words public safety, is the supreme end, or because "men, being more or less generally evil, turn to the good only when they are forced to it."[16] If therefore we would speak of morals, we shall say that they need power, not that they can pretend to direct power. One way or another the notion of fact, of the "actual truth," precedes that of law: *factum valet*. Later, Hobbes would say, "Therefore before the names of Just and Unjust can have place, there must be some coercive Power. . . ."[17] Everything being subordinated to State interest, law can be regarded only as the expression of the State's will, that is to say as a command calculated to maintain or augment its power: *jus est quod jussum est*. Hence legal rules have no binding force when they are of a nature to injure the Prince or the State.

From the moral point of view, Machiavelli's ideas raise only one question, though a fundamental one, namely that of his absolute

15 "The thought of the later Middle Ages," says van Vollenhoven, "as manifested in acts, moved towards the creation of institutions. Modern historical thought, on the other hand, is that of a political system. Later medieval thought recognized a common law binding states as it bound individuals. The thought informing modern political history rejects a reign of law fettering the liberty of sovereign States." *Le Droit de Paix*, 1932, p. 71.

16 *The Prince*, chap. XXIII. Cf. Renaudet, *Machiavel*, 1942, p. 10: "Machiavelli and Guicciardini reduce politics to the art of winning, cultivating, and organizing power, independently alike of the pagan ethic and of Christianity."

17 *Leviathan*, chap. XV.

separation of politics and morals. For the rest, it is from the political point of view that we must judge the work of a man of whom it has been justly said that "the political idea is his whole ideal" (Bluntschli). That is the origin of all the narrownesses that strike his modern readers. The Christian idea of man as the end of the State is absent from his work. In his eyes the State is an end in itself; everything bows to its preservation and greatness.[18] This authoritarian inspiration of public safety is especially emphasized in the constant subordination of moral considerations, such as the good will or the hatred of peoples, to the necessities of power.[19] Whether it is a question of conquests, of the conduct of war, of the treatment of conquered populations, or of respect for the given word, the sole motive for moderation or even humanity will be political expediency and their sole measure the calculation of forces.

Pure politics speaks only for its time, for its maxims are the dictates of opportunism. This is how what is called Machiavelli's realism must be appraised.[20] The *homo politicus* begotten by his mathematical mind seems to us now a very artificial creature. The Florentine secretary lived at a time when public opinion hardly counted among the forces that might oppose the enterprises of power. The day would come when his imitators would learn to capture this new force in order to make the State itself the principle of all morals and all law.[21]

Machiavelli's pessimism on the subject of human nature—a pessimism found in all champions of absolute power—was connected with a psychological tendency, which, as we shall see, plays a leading role in the formation of political oppositions. This is the tendency towards anxiety and fear, progenitor of hatred at home and abroad. The Italian tyrants, says J. Burckhardt, lived an uneasy and ac-

18 Thomas B. Macaulay, *Essays*, on Machiavelli: "The good of the body, distinct from the good of the members, and sometimes hardly compatible with the good of the members, seems to be the object which he proposes to himself. Of all political fallacies, this has perhaps had the widest and the most mischievous operation."

19 "It is as useful for the Prince to persevere in the good, when this is not inconvenient, as to know how to abandon it when circumstances demand," *The Prince*, chap. XVIII.

20 "There is such an abyss between the way men live and the way they ought to live that anyone who holds for real and true that which doubtless ought to be but unhappily is not courts inevitable ruin." *ibid.*, chap. XV.

21 On the destiny of this work, in which "the corrosive strength of thought and style went infinitely beyond the object of the moment," see Jean-Jacques Chevallier, *Les Grandes Oeuvres Politiques*, pp. 33-37.

cursed life, in an atmosphere saturated with treason, under the constant obsession of violent enterprises. The Prince to whom Machiavelli addressed his counsels was, moreover, the "new prince" whose power, obtained by force or ruse, was still insecure, and who had neither the support that the "natural prince" finds in the affection of his subjects, nor that antiquity of government that effaces memories and discourages occasions for change.[22] With everything to fear, he will make himself feared rather than loved, avoiding the imprudence of making himself hated.[23] There is hardly a chapter of *The Prince* where the intensity of the political motive is not connected in one way or another with this fundamental tendency.

§ 2. PHILOSOPHIC AND JURISTIC THEORIES OF POWER

The theories of both philosophers and jurists develop in a way to accommodate the new fact of the distribution of power among independent political entities. Two modes of thought confront one another, their differences more and more sharply defined as the new order consolidates itself. One mode, faithful to the essential inspiration of the Middle Ages, derives from natural-law doctrine a moral and finalist or functional conception of power. The other places at the service of modern absolutism two abstract notions already familiar in medieval political philosophy, the notion of a state of nature anterior to political society and the assimilation of corporate entities to the individual.[24]

To the State's tendency to omnipotence the medieval tradition of natural law had opposed a spiritual and ethical doctrine of power. According to this doctrine, the State, though sovereign, that is to say independent of all secular authority, is not absolute. Unlimited power is in itself nothing more than a phenomenon of greater force; it does not confer the authority which alone gives moral title to obedience. There is no authority save that which, in the sight of God, finds in the consent of the people[25] and in the public welfare at once the basis and the limit of its power. Thus, though entrusted to the Prince, sovereignty cannot isolate itself from the people and pursue independent ends not in harmony with the common good. Even in the absolutist theories the idea of a contract by which the people had definitively submitted itself to the sovereign (*translatio*

22 *The Prince*, chap. II.
23 *ibid.*, chap. XVII.
24 O. von Gierke, *Les Théories Politiques du Moyen Age*, pp. 168 seq., 254 seq.
25 *Popolo faciente et Deo inspirante.*

imperii) reserved to the community the right to insist that the Prince exactly fulfill the duties of his office. On the other hand, the natural-law theories firmly maintained the capital idea of inalienable rights possessed by man in virtue of his superterrestrial ends and inviolable by the State. This is a conception of power which, both in the foundation assigned to it and in the limits imposed upon it, tends to subject it to law. Threatened from the fifteenth century by the ancient notion of sovereignty, this conception would from the very threat take clearer cognizance of its aspirations and appropriate role. It had developed in the Middle Ages in the complex of organic and universalist ideas, such as the Christian community and the universal monarchy. It would henceforth be based upon the at once reasonable and social nature of man.

Thus above the States dedicated to their political and contingent task, the spiritual action of the Church upheld a common ideal which, through the doctrines of natural law, became the foundation of an international law among Christian States. The great school of Spanish jurist-theologians combined with a realistic view of the requirements of the new political order the desire to establish upon a moral and legal basis the relations between independent and equal States. In this spirit it fought against any survival of the idea of a universal monarchy and introduced, alongside a *jus gentium*, common to all men, a *jus inter gentes* applicable to the relations of States as such.[26] The difficulty was to reconcile the Christian conception of the unity of the human race with the historical fact of the distribution of power among sovereign States. It was accentuated by the spread of the Aristotelian conception, accepted by Saint Thomas Aquinas, that saw in the State a perfect community and the highest form of human society.

Francisco had cut the Gordian knot by declaring that particular sovereignty is void of authority when it encroaches on what belongs to the universal community.[27] This community remains the fundamental fact, and against it the division of humanity into nations cannot prevail, for the nations are still united, without distinction of race or religion, by the natural bond of brotherhood.

[26] C. Barcia Trelles, *Francisco de Vitoria et l'Ecole moderne du Droit international, Rec. A.D.I.*, vol. 17 (1927); J. Kosters, *Les Fondements du Droit des Gens*, Bibliotheca Visseriana, vol. IV, pp. 34-35; Edwin D. Dickinson, *The Equality of States*, p. 37.

[27] *Relectiones*, De Indis et de Jure Belli, 1532, Carnegie edn. Introduction by Ernest Nys.

The thinking of Francisco Suarez already shows more nuances. Writing at a time when modern political ideas and manners are finally implanted, he is visibly more conscious of the obstacles with which the division of mankind into independent States confronts any universalist conception. He sees clearly the political unity of the State but seeks, like his illustrious predecessor, to bring it under the higher unity of the human race. Thus every State, republic or kingdom, however complete in itself, is yet a member of the grand whole constituted by the human race. But this ethical factor, drawn directly from the organic conceptions of the Middle Ages, is not the sole foundation of the law of nations. It is combined with a realistic principle, the common utility. "As experience proves, no State can ever be so self-sufficient as to require no reciprocal support, no association, no mutual relations for advantage or need."[28] The *jus inter gentes* is the law that governs States in this kind of relationship and society. This addition of the utilitarian to the ethical principle was to be highly significant for the future theories of international law. It promoted a fusion which, later, sustained the fatal illusion of a natural harmony of interests counterbalancing the anarchic individualism of sovereignties.

Grotius, too, recognized States as subjects of the law of peace and of war. His ideas on the international community and the relations between it and the States are not always very precise. On the other hand he shows a clear tendency to accord a beneficent priority to the idea of justice enlightened by right reason over the notion of common utility.

For all their distinguishing nuances, these doctrines had a common element—a moral concept that refused to accept the greatness of the State as the sole end of public life. To the omnipotence of power this concept opposed the moral limitations deduced from the higher good of humanity or from the independent ends and inalienable rights of man. From this point of view the long struggles of the sixteenth and seventeenth centuries for liberty of conscience were particularly significant; they bore witness to the vitality of the rights-of-man tradition in spite of territorial exclusiveness (*Cujus regio illius religio*) and the persecutions inspired by reason of State.

Towards the end of the sixteenth century, the disorders arising

[28] Suarez, *Tractatus de Legibus*, vol. II, chap. XIX. This duality, not absolute but merely relative in Suarez, is the origin of the distinction between natural law, which imposes itself logically on the reason, and a positive law of nations derived from human consent.

out of the religious struggles nearly everywhere encouraged the return to absolutist regimes. The need for security and the tendency to fear were the foundations of the doctrines of Hobbes and Spinoza. Fear and the instinct of self-preservation, says Hobbes, induced men to give up by an alleged contract their state of natural liberty, in which everyman's will to power made for the war of all against all, and to submit without reserve or limitation to the absolute power of the State. Between nations the "law of nature" persists; because they are independent, force dominates everything.

Hobbes' idea can lead only to the denial of international law.[29] The secret of his influence on political thought lies not in any new developments that he brought to the concept of the state of nature and the social contract, but in his observation of man's proclivities and his penetrating analysis of the motives of human conduct. In this psychological aspect his work is related to Machiavelli's.

It is again the theme of fear that Spinoza elaborates in the passage devoted to the law of nations in his *Treatise on Politics*.[30] Every being has as much right as he has power. Brought together by their consciousness of weakness, and by reason, individuals have found refuge in social life. States, on the other hand, are free from these subjections because they are self-sufficient. Powerful enough to fend off every danger, they are inaccessible to fear. In their state of nature, says the author, they need consider only their own interest; the only law that governs them is the public safety. No one could have been more mistaken about the enormous inequalities of strength among States—inequalities that destine some to be the prey of others—or could have ignored more completely in the international order the dictates of that reason that Spinoza places at the foundation of relations between the State and individuals. Nothing could bear more eloquent testimony to the hold already won upon minds by the idea of State in international relations than

[29] *Leviathan*, chap. XIII, *in fine*. Cf. H. Lauterpacht, "Spinoza and International Law," *B.Y.B.I.L.*, 1927, p. 95. On the relations between Hobbes' doctrine and international law see Edwin D. Dickinson, *op.cit.*, pp. 69 seq.; J. L. Brierly, *Le Fondement du Caractère Obligatoire du Droit International, Rec. A.D.I.*, vol. 23 (1928), pp. 494, 505-507. On the common element of absolutism revealed by a comparison between Hobbes' City and the modern totalitarian State, see J. Vialatoux, *La Cité de Hobbes, Théorie de l'Etat Totalitaire*, 1935; on the doctrinal differences, see René Capitant, *Hobbes et l'Etat Totalitaire*, Archives de Philosophie du Droit, 1936, p. 46.

[30] *Tractatus theologico-politicus*. Cf. H. Lauterpacht, *op.cit.*, and P. Vinogradoff, *op.cit.*, vol. I, p. 48; Krabbe, *L'Idée moderne de l'Etat, Rec. A.D.I.*, vol. 13 (1926), p. 553.

this passive submission to facts in one of the boldest philosophic geniuses of modern times.

§ 3. MODERN SOVEREIGNTY, ITS CHARACTER AND CONSEQUENCES

From these long political struggles, from these divergent ideas, from these conflicting aspirations, was born the modern political-legal theory of sovereignty as it was formulated by Jean Bodin. For Bodin the State's welfare demands unity of power. Sovereignty therefore becomes something more than mere superiority; it is at once the greatest force and the supreme authority within defined territorial limits. It cannot be perfect unless it is absolute and indivisible, that is to say free of any subordination without and of any division within.

This doctrine is far from being what it has sometimes been called, a merely political theory of power. For Bodin, faithful on this point to the medieval tradition, the sovereign is bound not only by divine law, but by natural law as well, which also proceeds from God. If he is the source of law, he is himself subject to justice, which is the end of law. But of his duties he owes account only to God; they provide no basis for opposition to his will on the part of his subjects.[31]

Having borrowed from the universal monarchy which they had dethroned the idea of the divine origin of power, the sovereigns must, at least in theory, regard each other as equals. Here again they were constrained to respect justice, for they could not, says Bodin, "break the bounds set by the laws of nature established by God in his own image." The monarch was therefore bound to observe treaties with strangers, for, being guarantor of contracts between his subjects, "he must *a fortiori* be just in his own deeds."[32] However, adds Richelieu, "God alone can be his judge. Therefore kings sin only against Him to whom alone belongs cognizance of their acts."

But between doctrine and facts there is a great and ever-widening gulf. In a society moving constantly further away from the religious ideal of the Middle Ages, the political element of sovereignty expanded into unlimited power. Despite what was often the highest moral inspiration, these doctrines helped in various ways to build

[31] A. Esmein, *Eléments de Droit constitutionel français et comparé*, pp. 378-379; A. Gardot, *Jean Bodin, Rec. A.D.I.*, vol. 50 (1934), passim, especially pp. 580 seq.

[32] J. Bodin, *Six Livres de la République*, book I, chap. IX, pp. 150 seq.

the State up into a dominating entity and little by little to undermine the social concept of a community of peoples.

Thus, in the modern perspective of international relations and under the pressure of facts more than of theories, the new distribution of power developed and revealed its full consequences. Born of a claim for equality and a will for emancipation from a common supremacy, modern sovereignties rest historically upon a negative idea. Hence their exclusiveness and their deeply individualist tendencies. While the State seeks to attract to itself the whole of public life, sovereignty at the same time claims recognition as the supreme force and asserts its independence of any law. The State has its own morality, which gradually imposes itself on political thought, displacing the medieval idea of human community. The natural-law tradition retains its vitality in theory, but becomes more and more remote from governmental practice, for which "everything in the end comes down to power."[33] The day came when this political inspiration captured even legal doctrine.

Formally equality is the rule in the mutual relations of sovereignties, and logically this equality demands mutual respect.[34] But logical argument can set no limit to ambitions guided by reason of State. A purely theoretical consequence of a new distribution of forces, equality held no moral principle strong enough to check the appetite for domination, even when, become a "right of equality," it was elevated by the philosophers of the law-of-nature school (Wolff, Vattel) to the rank of essential attribute of the State. Obeying only the power impulse, sovereigns found in the unlimited right of war the means of harmonizing their ambitions with respect for legal forms. Thus they persisted in living in contradiction with the order of coordination which they invoked.[35]

The law that from this time on grew up between the new political structures was of a sort to confirm their recent independence and answered to their image of their powers. Doctrine assigned to it as basis the so-called fundamental rights of States and contract. These two explanations, far from being mutually exclusive, were complementary. Both were essentially individualistic.

[33] Bielfeld, cited by A. Sorel, *L'Europe et la Révolution Française*, vol. I, p. 26.

[34] Cf. G. Gidel, *Droits et Devoirs des Nations*, *Rec. A.D.I.*, vol. 10 (1925), p. 593.

[35] What doctrine would later be pleased to describe as a state of coordination was usually nothing more than a mere juxtaposition.

The fundamental rights of State (self-preservation, independence, equality, respect, and international commerce) were presented in doctrine as the residuum of a state of nature or complete liberty supposed to have existed among human groups before their entry upon political life. Having their foundation in the idea of a natural equality, they are attached to the personality of the State as individual rights are attached to the human person. This assimilation, already to be found in Cicero and Saint Augustine, had at first a beneficent influence. Thanks to it, it seemed possible to subject States to the rule of law. But pushed to an extreme and vitiated by the absolutist notion of sovereignty, it ended by turning to the profit of the political organization the concept of "innate," "inherent," or "natural" rights, which natural-law doctrine had claimed for man by reason of his personal and superterrestrial ends.[36] The natural tendency of power to unlimitedness and the influence of Roman law soon made of these fundamental rights of State subjective rights, inalienable and equally absolute, on the basis of which each could threaten its neighbor, with no superior principle to decide between rival claims.[37] Born with modern States, the theory of fundamental rights betrays its origin; it is the direct reflection of their struggles for independence and "a product of the pure gospel of individualism applied in the international domain."[38]

The medieval concept of a Christian community set limits to the recourse to war—limits that the doctrines of Saint Augustine and Saint Thomas Aquinas had tried precisely to define. The theory of just war had set the problem of war's legality on the moral plane of the conscientious duties of sovereigns responsible before God for their acts. It had proved disappointing in the face of facts, for it could provide none of the indispensable external criteria for legal construction.

From the beginning of the modern era, the wholly political theory of the relations between sovereigns tended to confirm the

[36] Cf. Hrabar, in *Archives de Philosophie du Droit* (1932), no. 3-4, pp. 432-433; G. Gidel, *Droits et Devoirs des Nations, Théorie Classique des Droits fondamentaux des Etats, Rec. A.D.I.*, vol. 10 (1925), pp. 593-594; J. L. Brierly, *Le Fondement de la Force obligatoire du Droit international, Rec. A.D.I.*, vol. 23 (1928), pp. 472-476; J. Haesaert, *Les prétendus principes généraux de la politique international et du droit des gens*, Bulletin de la Classe des lettres et des sciences morales et politiques de l'Académie royale de Belgique, 1950, p. 354.

[37] G. Gidel, *op.cit.*, p. 541, describing also the propitious influence originally exerted by egalitarian ideas.

[38] J. L. Brierly, *Rec. A.D.I.*, *op.cit.*, p. 474.

absolute right of war. The men of law succumbed to the eternal temptation of the jurist; they sacrificed the substance to the form. They introduced into the law of nations the distinction between legal and licit wars. A war unjust in its causes may nevertheless be licit if it is carried on by a sovereign prince and preceded by a declaration of war. Competence and form—law would thenceforth ask nothing more. It would recognize the equal position of both parties as belligerents. In fact everything would from this time on bow to sovereign power; "the dogma of unlimited sovereignty killed the theory of just war."[39]

§ 4. FIRST POSITIVIST DOCTRINES

"The union of reason and custom," says Westlake, "has been the great desideratum of international law from the peace of Westphalia to our day."[40] Despite oscillations, which at times indicate a singular uncertainty of thought, most of the writers visibly tried to keep a just balance between reason and will as factors in the development of law. But in their minds the meaning of these two constitutive elements, and consequently the relation between them, kept changing. On the whole the evolution favored the voluntarist and formal conception of law, thus opening the way for contemporary positivist doctrines.

The absolutist conception of power tends to make law exclusively the word of him who has the right to command others. Law is law simply because the sovereign decrees it. "Right ceases to mean, as in the Middle Ages, a particular aspect of universal justice; it comes to mean that which emanates from a single centre in the body politic and by its predominating unity gives strength and decisiveness to the striking power of the community."[41]

The high thought of Leibnitz rebels against these wanderings of the voluntarist conception from which spring all later attempts to detach law from its objective basis. Right, he declares, is anterior to law, and he was bold enough to write: "Das Recht ist nicht Recht weil Gott es gewollt hat, sondern weil Gott gerecht ist."[42]

[39] N. Politis, *La Neutralité et la Paix*, p. 19.

[40] *Etudes sur les Principes du Droit international*, tr. Ernest Nys, 1895, p. 71. The same idea is expressed even by authors of a positivist bent, such as Richard Zouche, who speak of international law as a law "accepted among most nations by customs in harmony with reason."

[41] Harold J. Laski, *Grammar of Politics*, 5th edn., 1948, p. 45.

[42] Cited by O. von Gierke, *Théories politiques du Moyen Age*, p. 231 and note.

Of the prevailing political theories, legal theorists kept only the idea of a state of nature between nations;[43] from it they would deduce the equality and independence of States along with the whole individualistic theory of fundamental rights. With the exception of Christian Wolff, they would dispute, in the name of State sovereignty, the idea of an institutional pact or social contract as basis of a community of nations. Vattel particularly would come out against the *civitas maxima gentium* preached by his predecessor.[44]

However, doctrinal development for the most part exhibited great prudence. Attentive as he was to the practice of States, the great Dutch jurisconsult, Cornelius van Bynkershoek, stated in particularly happy terms the proper relation between reason and positive law: "In the law of nations," he wrote, "reason is sovereign. . . ." But if, though reason is always in harmony with itself, it seems to us possible for both parties to invoke it, as so often happens, then recourse must be had to usage accepted as more or less constant to decide what the law is. Though he relies on the practical judgment of statesmen to assess the authority of treaties in the formation of law, he admits in the final analysis that "this is subject to the condition that reason is on their side."[45]

The tendency to dissociate the law of nations from the law of nature and to regard it as entirely positive is but rarely found in authors before the nineteenth century. Neither Samuel Rachel nor G. F. Martens can be ranked with the champions of positivism in the modern sense of the term. These authors never presented positive international law as a closed and self-sufficient system. Their thought was much closer to the opinions held today by the apostles of a reformulated natural law than to those which were basic to the classical positivism of the nineteenth century. J. Moser alone, in the

43 Montesquieu observes that men are free in their individual relations because they live under civil laws, but that princes, who in their mutual relations do not live under such laws, are governed by force; "Hence it follows that the treaties that they have imposed by force are as obligatory as those entered into voluntarily. A prince who is always forcing or being forced cannot complain of a treaty imposed on him by violence. That would be like complaining of his natural state. . . ." *De l'Esprit des Lois*, book xxvi, chap. xx.

44 E. de Vattel, Preface, p. xvii. It is often forgotten that the social contract expresses fundamentally the necessity, in the ethical sense, of living together and the duties which that entails. Cf. G. del Vecchio, *Justice, Droit, Etat*, p. 375.

45 *Quaestionum Juris Publici Libri Duo*, Ad Lectorem. This idea that customary positive law must conform to reason had already been argued in England by Richard Zouche, here following his predecessor A. Gentile. It had been propounded in Germany by J. W. Textor.

eighteenth century, made himself the protagonist of an international law wholly detached from natural law.[46]

Voluntarist positivism attained its full rigor and its narrowness only in the course of the nineteenth century when the movement of nationalities had multiplied tenfold the power and exclusiveness of sovereign States. For a time the unitary conception of the State was prominent enough to dominate international legal relations. Doctrine not only made the State sole subject of all norms, but regarded the will of the State as their exclusive source. This was an idea calculated to endow legal technique with a high degree of security, all external relations being focused at one point of imputation—a condition eminently favorable to the precise definition of obligations and to the organization of responsibilities. But voluntarist positivism achieved this strong systematization around the State only by sacrificing the idea of an objective order to a purely formal conception of international law. It excluded from law the higher considerations of reason, justice, and common utility which are its necessary foundation.

[46] Cf. A. Verdross, "J. J. Mosers Programm einer Völkerrechtswissenschaft der Erfahrung," in *Zeitschrift für öffentliches Recht*, 1922, p. 96.

CHAPTER II. THE CONSOLIDATION OF THE STATE

GROWING PREDOMINANCE OF THE POLITICAL SINCE THE TREATIES OF WESTPHALIA

IN the European order established by the Treaties of Westphalia, the new distribution of power developed all its individualist consequences. Between States equally imbued with their sovereign prerogatives, competition became the law of international relations. This was the more virulent as the princes felt more assured of the means of action provided by the growing centralization of their power; the more nearly continuous as it was fed by the overthrow of alliances and the displacement of forces caused by the appearance of new Powers on the scene; the less orderly as, forgetful of all solidarity, even that of monarchs, it sacrificed more and more to the passion of aggrandizement and to immediate and at times contradictory interests. A long-range policy can accommodate itself to moderation and respect for the given word. Even in the eighteenth century, the classic epoch of balance, Europe knew hardly any but short-run policies subject to constant alarms occasioned by the displacement of forces.

What made these political mores dangerous was the growing cohesion of peoples and the consolidation of State power. Territorial unification was being achieved or pursued; national consciousness was finding itself amid regional particularisms; administrative centralization was accentuated; economic protectionism, direct in France, indirect in England, and tariff wars were already closely associated with the development of military establishments and with belligerent enterprises. All the vital forces, stimulated by mercantilism, rallied to the service of monarchy, pending the day when they would be absorbed in that vague and formidable personality, all the more powerful because it is less personal, the modern nation.

At the same time the idea of reason of State took on new scope. Machiavelli had placed it frankly on the exclusively political plane. From the eighteenth century on, it assumed a moral tincture thanks to the broadening notion of public utility, which shifted from the interest of the prince to that of the State. The State was to reap an enormous advantage from this enlargement, since any concept of utility tends to rise to the level of a moral principle when it moves from the advantage of an individual or privileged group to that of a larger collectivity. This adaptation of the reason of State to the mores of the period is clearly exemplified in Frederick the Great, most modern sovereign of his time. For him, the good of the State is the absolute good; the service of the State the supreme law of the prince and his subjects. Reason of State thenceforth had its morality, founded on the vital interests of the most strongly organized human grouping. So understood, it could without scandal or contradiction serve the policy of those who ruled.

The secret of the power of the modern State, and consequently of the predominance of the political in international relations, lies in this growing capacity of the political organization to rally about itself the moral aspirations of men, to develop *group morals*, at the cost of *morals*. "Loyalty to the group comes to be regarded as a cardinal virtue of the individual, and may require him to condone behavior by the group person which he would condemn in himself."[1]

The anarchic concept of unlimited sovereignty found its strongest support in this pseudo ethic, which is no less effective in begetting unconscious perversions of the moral sense than in unloosing popular emotions. Promoting nationalism, as it later did, it would complete the process of making the State an absolute center, and its greatness the supreme end, of human activities.

Section I

The Balance and Liberal Ideas

Until the last years of the nineteenth century, the principle of balance more or less adequately served the essential purpose assigned to it by British policy, in which it found its most constant support. Having checkmated the successive claims of the House of Austria and of Louis XIV to hegemony, it raised the coalition of Europe against imperial France. It could not set up a true order. Powerless to impose the *status quo*, it showed itself equally unable to secure, by the purely mechanistic idea from which it springs, peaceful change in the relations of States. Only "moderation in force,"[2] by infusing it with a moral element, could have raised it to the level of a principle of public law protecting the interests of

[1] E. H. Carr, *The Twenty Years' Crisis*, p. 202.

[2] A. Sorel, *L'Europe et la Révolution Française*, vol. I, p. 280.

all. For the balance is like all concepts that rely solely upon force: not necessarily false, they are always inadequate, since force is good or bad according to the use made of it. The Powers invoking it appealed only to the purely material element of a "ratio between the reciprocal forces of resistance and of aggression at the disposal of the various political bodies";[3] they hardly found in it a principle to moderate their ambitions.

Such a conception makes the use of force a matter of expediency and flair rather than of moderation and wisdom. It is more an inciter to vigilance and suspicion than a promoter of collaboration and confidence. Based essentially on a calculation of opposing forces, it must make allowances for the chance of error invariably accompanying such calculations. It thus drives each Power to create for itself a margin of security and, with this in view, to expand its means of action beyond actual need.

The ambitions of princes are served by the anxieties of their peoples: fear is the secret spring of the system; war, even preventive war, its instrument. "A new disease has spread over Europe," wrote Montesquieu, "it has laid hold on our princes and makes them keep up an unreasonable number of troops. It has its paroxysms and becomes inevitably contagious, for as soon as a State adds to its troops, the others at once increase theirs, so that nothing is gained but common ruin. Each monarch keeps on foot as many armies as he could have if his people were in danger of extermination; and this state of effort of all against all is called peace."[4]

In the eighteenth century the entry of Prussia and Russia upon the scene had multiplied the antagonisms that the balance of power must control, at the same time increasing the number of States powerful enough to change it. The pursuit of a balance always more elusive in the growing complexity of affairs took on its own movement, not so freely regulated by governments. In this incessant weighing of forces, governments are drawn into the wake of the most powerful or most ambitious and carried one after another beyond their original objectives. Thus while the mechanics of the system went awry, its immorality became even more pronounced.

[3] The King's instructions to Talleyrand, cited in Charles Dupuis, *Le Ministère de Talleyrand en 1814*, vol. II, p. 348.

[4] Montesquieu, *L'Esprit des Lois*, book XIII, chap. 17. Voltaire's judgment was the same. On the balance of power he writes: "Then ambition is contained by ambition, then dogs of equal strength show their teeth and rend each other only when they have prey to dispute."

Soon, to redress the balance, compensations would be needed: the weak would be the victims; the exact division of their territories would often be considered a regular application of the system and the masterwork of diplomacy. The balance, as practiced in the eighteenth century, was neither security for peaceful possession nor guarantee of law.

Its action was nevertheless at intervals undeniably useful, sometimes in raising a coalition of threatened interests against an attempt at hegemony, sometimes in stimulating a spirit of moderation at moments of doubt or extreme weariness. Europe compelled Louis XIV to respect the balance. The relative abasement of France, the fear that she might finally be the dupe of a "co-partnership system," operating thenceforth in favor of her rivals, induced Vergennes, then Mirabeau and Talleyrand, to adopt policies of moderation.[5]

The French Revolution, as it began, proclaimed its will to peace. But, at the same time, it introduced into international relations a new idea of the State, subversive of the established order, namely the idea of the nation's sovereignty. Rationalist in inspiration, the Revolution deduced the concept of the nation from the idea of liberty and was led on to dispute the legality of any authority that did not proceed from the people. Universalist in action, it would extend "fraternity and succor to all peoples bent on recovering their liberty" (decree of November 19, 1792).[6] The Constituante had inherited from the weakened monarchy a program for preserving peace; the Convention inaugurated revolutionary interventionism. Slow at first in grasping the profound meaning and universal character of the event, Europe set up the coalition of sovereigns against the Revolution.

War is not long obedient to a policy of principles. France, false to its nationalistic ideology, soon justified its annexationist designs by reasons of pure convenience;[7] she defeated the coalition only by

5 A. Sorel, *op.cit.*, vol. I, pp. 310-319. A note sent by Vergennes to Vienna (September 1, 1783) denounced the fatal emulation promoted by the policy of compensations that had its origin in the fear of displacements of power; see Ernest Lavisse, *Histoire de France*, vol. 9, part 1, p. 119. On the humanitarian formulas expressing the spirit of moderation of politicians of the period, see Mirkine-Guetzevitch, *L'Influence de la Révolution Française sur la Developpement du Droit international dans l'Europe orientale*, *Rec. A.D.I.*, vol. 22 (1928), p. 307.

6 A. Mathiez, *La Révolution française*, vol. 2, p. 164.

7 See in Johannet, *Le Principe des Nationalités*, p. 114, Merlin of Douai's

exploiting the selfish ambitions of the kings; she won peace only by treaties of compensation and division, contrary to the spirit of the Revolution. Europe, for its part, only gradually awoke to the common danger. Even the threat of the Napoleonic domination found it long divided. The system of balance once more displayed the weakness due to the individualism of sovereignties. Years were to pass before, under England's leadership, the coalition would be imbued with a conception of the balance truly inspired by the general interest.

The "spirit of moderation" had a momentary triumph at the Congress of Vienna. Experience and general weariness enlightened the sovereigns and their advisers on the dangers that they had run in the excesses of an individualist policy that limited its horizon to the immediate interest. They had gained a respect for stability and a taste for moderation. The authoritarian rationalism of Metternich met the opportunistic realism of Talleyrand to introduce a minimum of order into the direction of European affairs. The balance sought by Metternich would be based upon the principle that "political bodies can no more exist independently than the individuals who make up society." The "society of States" is an essential part of the modern world, and the recognition of their common interests will guarantee the existence of all.[8] The balance thus incorporated a moral principle whose vitalizing influence would raise it for a moment above itself. Talleyrand emphasized this progress by contrasting with the old conception of an "artificial and precarious equilibrium" that of a balance that could last only so long as some great States were animated by the saving grace of moderation and justice.[9]

Thus, after an enterprise of universal domination, Europe felt the need to define the moral basis of the policy of balance. Despite their inadequacies, the Holy Alliance and the Concert of Europe tried to institutionalize the old notion of balance and give it new life by importing into it rational and moral elements.[10] There never was a

---

declaration: "The French Republic can and must either keep by title of conquest or acquire by treaty countries useful to it, without consulting the inhabitants."

8 Constantin de Grunwald, *La Vie de Metternich*, p. 202.

9 Instructions of the King of France to his Embassy at the Congress of Vienna, in Charles Dupuis, *op.cit.*, vol. II, pp. 333 seq., and, by the same author, *Le Droit des Gens et les Rapports des grandes Puissances avec les autres Etats*, pp. 59 seq.

10 Cf. Hans J. Morgenthau, *Politics among Nations*, p. 161.

time when the balance seemed more capable of safeguarding common interests. A European directorate, a union of sovereign courts the more real and lasting in that it sought no isolated interest and no merely momentary combination,[11] was charged with maintaining it.

While experience of the anarchy of sovereignties stimulated the search for the bases of an international organization, in this new climate the first outlines were being drawn of an international law foreign to the strictly political interest of States, inspired by the principles of civilization and by the needs of commercial relations between the peoples. The Declaration of the Powers on February 8, 1815 condemned the slave trade in the name of humanity and morals; the Final Act of the Congress of Vienna, June 9, 1815, embodies the charter of international river law. Thus an attenuation, even momentary, of the spirit of political competition between the great Powers created conditions favorable to the establishment of an international law directly inspired by human interest.

The wisdom of the negotiators at Vienna was the wisdom of old men. The one merit of their political views was moderation. Passionately desiring stability, they were blind to the need for change. The meaning of the events and the power of the ideas launched by the French Revolution escaped them. The famous "system," product of classical reason, left out of account both popular aspirations to political liberty and the new demands of social evolution. Metternich saw clearly when he sought in the establishment of a directory a method calculated to vitalize the principle of balance and to develop in the great Powers the sense of common interest and a readiness for the concessions indispensable to any collective action. One error of the system was that it raised to the level of a doctrine conceptions which cannot be entirely removed from the domain of compromise and expedients, that it tried to make of the balance of power among States a force independent of their internal evolution, above all that it based on "legitimacy" a policy of narrow conservatism. Its other weakness was its failure to integrate the secondary States in the system. The inability of the victors to create an organic bond between the directorate and the small States was a major lacuna in the system and one of the chief causes of its collapse.[12]

11 Protocol of Aix-la-Chapelle, November 15, 1818.

12 C. K. Webster, *The Foreign Policy of Castlereagh*, vol. 2, pp. 57-58. It was because they had not been integrated in a real international organization that

Two new forces were soon at work: nationalism and the industrial and capitalist revolution. They fundamentally altered the conditions governing the exercise of power and carried the power of the State to heights previously unknown. In the dual form of nationalistic and of economic imperialism, they multiplied international antagonisms. They destroyed the old edifice of sovereignties juxtaposed in a mechanical balance of forces, and they dragged Europe and the world into gigantic conflagrations that brought final condemnation of the modern system of the distribution of power among peoples.

Behind these vast movements can be seen the elements of a liberal ideology that took final form at the beginning of the eighteenth century, propagated by the growing force of public opinion and the belief in a natural harmony of interests. Though rationalist, this ideology paradoxically enough sought justification for the social disciplines, not in a higher moral law imposed on men, but in a mysterious correspondence supposed to exist between these disciplines and the egoistic proclivities of human nature. The philosophy of enlightenment, seeking to provide men with "reasons for voluntarily attaching themselves to society, to make of the social bond a rational bond willed as such,"[13] claimed to teach them the secrets of this natural harmony. Aiming to integrate particular interests in the general interest, it proposed to make a reasoned and scientific perception of social solidarities the principle of morals and of happiness.

The mistake in this doctrine was to subordinate the moral question, which is an absolute, to the social, which is relative.[14] So understood, the notion of the just is reduced to that of social utility as conceived by the rulers; morals is confounded with politics. The dangerous consequences of this inversion of concepts did not immediately make themselves felt. So long as the struggle continued against princely absolutism, the political philosophy of the period

---

certain secondary States, especially those of the Balkans, never ceased providing objects of competition among the great Powers. Their instability contributed directly to the gradual deterioration and ultimate collapse of the European balance.

[13] E. Bréhier, *Histoire de la Philosophie*, vol. II, p. 763.

[14] F. Brunetière, "L'Erreur du XVIII Siècle," *Revue des Deux Mondes*, 1902, vol. x, pp. 634 seq.: "The eternal relations of things are debased or rather inverted when the moral question is subordinated to the social" (p. 646).

hardly differed in its conclusions from the natural-law traditions that fostered the human ends of power. If people no longer accepted the State as an order of things dictated by Providence or founded on prescription and were beginning to "reason about it," they proposed to prescribe its duties to the individual and to discuss the best means of guaranteeing him full use of his natural liberties. The Declaration of the Rights of Man is faithful to this liberal inspiration when it proclaims that the "end of every political association is to safeguard the natural and imprescriptible rights of man." This object of political society, intimately bound to the very essence of civilization, assigns a moral limit to power. Political liberalism reinforces this with organic limitations implemented in the structure of the State and finding expression in the theory of checks and balances and the separation of powers.[15]

The doctrinal error implicit in the predominance of the social and utilitarian over the moral point of view was to bear its fruits when the philosophers undertook to build, upon the hypotheses of a state of nature and a social contract, the democratic theory of popular sovereignty. Because it seemed to them established by the freely consented concessions of individuals in its favor, popular sovereignty was regarded by them as an unlimited power. Thus the device of the "general will" led from individual liberty to the limitlessness of power. No one saw more clearly than Benjamin Constant the perils of this ideology: "When it is established that the sovereignty of the people is unlimited, this amounts to creating and turning loose in human society a magnitude of power too great in itself and an evil in whatever hands it be placed." Men err, he remarks, when they blame the forms of government: "The fault lies in the degree of power and not in its depositaries . . . there are weights too heavy for the hands of men."[16]

[15] The spread of these new modes of thought is attested by contemporaries: "It is observed," wrote the Marquis d'Argenson in his *Journal*, "that never before were the words nation and State on people's lips as they are today. The two words were never heard under Louis XIV, and the very idea scarcely existed. People were never so informed as they are today of the rights of the nation and of liberty. Even in my own case, though I have always studied and meditated upon the materials relating to these subjects, conscience and conviction pointed in a direction altogether different from today's." Cited by Johannet, *op.cit.*, p. 89.

[16] Jurieu had already written: "The people is the only power whose acts need not be right to be valid." Rousseau was merely following him when he declared: "The people is sole sovereign; it cannot be wrong; the general will is always right."

Pushed to the extreme, the principle of popular sovereignty ended by destroying the idea of individual liberty in which it had its historical origin. In the nineteenth century it promoted the excesses of statism and nationalism; later it prepared the way for totalitarian despotism.

It was still utilitarian morals that informed the encyclopedists' optimistic and largely utopian view of international relations.[17] With Bentham, the rationalist concept of common utility took precise form in the search for the greatest good of the greatest number. It was thought that if the peoples, and individual men, could be made to understand the laws that govern their natural solidarity, then the free competition of selfish interests would result in general harmony. Baron Holbach pointed out that because of their very inequalities peoples, like individuals, are mutually dependent: "The nature of a social and rational being imposes upon every people the same duties as upon every man. . . . Experience and reason teach the rules that result from these duties and, brought together, they form a universal code which should govern all the nations of the world without distinction, but which is unfortunately ignored, despised, arbitrarily interpreted by most princes, who decide how peoples act."[18] Because it is largely an intellectual construction, this political philosophy, which could inspire doctrines, remained powerless to convert its generous universalist aspirations into fact. In the international order the abstract concept of natural harmony could not prevail over the belligerent drive of nationalities.

As early as the second half of the eighteenth century, the ideas that sustain internal sovereignty begin to shape views of international relations: the conception of power in the State was already profoundly influencing the coordination of powers among States. That is a law that has not altered since the historical consolidation

[17] This optimism was not shared by all minds. The study of history and of positive law led Montesquieu to conclusions close enough to those of Hobbes. Men have liberty only because they submit to civil law; not being governed by such law, princes are not free and constraint governs their mutual relations. In Rousseau, a generally pessimistic view of international relations did not prevent a search for the causes of the evil. Rousseau with remarkable intuition discerned these in the faulty distribution of power between juxtaposed sovereignties, in "that partial and imperfect association that produces tyranny and war" and for which he apparently desired to substitute a federal organization.

[18] Cf. G. Gidel, *Droits et Devoirs des Nations, Théorie Classique des Droits fondamentaux des Etats, Rec. A.D.I.*, vol. 10 (1925), pp. 556, 558-559.

of States as sovereign and independent entities. It explains why international law cannot dispense with a general theory of the State. Rationalist philosophy had derived national sovereignty from individual liberty; from national sovereignty the French Revolution would deduce the principle of nationalities. Since the nation precedes the State and is the true titulary of sovereignty, its right of free determination is not exhausted by the choice of rulers in the internal order; it includes the right in the external order to change the territorial configuration of States in order to enable peoples to escape from a power which, being no longer sustained by their consent, is nothing more than a hated domination. The principle of nationalities, in its original form of nationality of election or choice, was a direct product of the rationalist philosophy of the eighteenth century—child of the generous spirit of that philosophy, which saw nature and humanity behind the State, but also of its ignorance of history and inability to grasp the real laws of collective life.

To proclaim that sovereignty resides in the nation was merely to transfer the powers of the prince to the people, that is to a collectivity clearly defined by its historical relation to a specific territory, merely to recognize "that nation and State are identical in the sense that the latter can only be the personification of the former."[19] But when the Revolution took it upon itself to affirm the right of nationalities to form States, it dissociated the historical and legal State from the nation. It set over against the State an emotional and vague but singularly dynamic conception that was as refractory to analysis into its constituent elements as it was unsubmissive to law in its power of expansion. The nationalistic ideology, soon abandoned in the arena of political realities by the Convention, brought small profit to France. It contributed indeed to her gradual decline in the nineteenth century and at the same time to the destruction of the European balance. From a general point of view, it profoundly altered not only the forces operating in international relations, but the very nature of those relations. Far from helping to stabilize relations, it brought into them the blind force of the masses, the excitability that exposes the masses to "impulses in logical garb" (Ortega y Gasset), and the passions that deliver them into the hands of anyone who knows how to exploit for power purposes their combativeness towards all that is foreign.

Animated by confidence in life and the aspiration to progress, the

[19] Carré de Malberg, *Théorie Générale de l'Etat*, vol. I, p. 13.

intellectualist optimism of the eighteenth century believed in the infallibility of human reason in defining the rules of the social order. It elevated "the perfectibility of man and society to the rank of a central dogma."[20] Its utilitarian morals came from the rationalist conception of the supremacy of intelligence over men's behavior. As for method, it remained, except for Montesquieu, abstract and antihistorical. Reason was held to be independent of experience. The reformers threw off history as a shackle on the human spirit in its march towards progress.

This ideology largely inspired the democratic liberalism of the nineteenth century. Transplanted to the international domain in the twentieth century, it opened a glorious but short career for liberalism by lending the promoters of the League of Nations its essential postulates: confidence in the universal virtue of rational criteria as correctives of the anarchy of international relations, plus belief in the natural rightness of public opinion and in its all-powerful influence on the course of events.

Section II

Changes in the System of Balance

The nineteenth century was the era of nationalities. It was also, subsequently, the century of nationalism, that is to say of the aggressive tendency to approach and resolve every question from the point of view of the political oppositions produced by the consciousness of national differences. By its sentimental hold on men, by the power that it conferred on the State, by the food it supplied for international antagonism, the national idea gave these political oppositions a scope and intensity unprecedented in history. It gave rise to doctrines which, though sometimes opposite in their points of departure, always in the end ensured the triumph of statism. It began in a movement of political liberation and territorial regrouping; having reached its goal, it joined forces with the State and multiplied its power. It did not do this without a change of essence. Arrayed against oppression it had appealed to liberty; associated with power, it sacrificed liberty to the "historic vocation" of the nation. The ethno-historical theory of nationality hatched a nationalistic determinism that built up the nation into a mystical and extra-personal entity. The State, charged with ensuring its continuity, tended to become an organism of domination.

20 Huisinga, *Le Déclin du Moyen Age*, p. 46.

The system of balance had been able to come to terms with the nationality movement; it gradually deteriorated, especially after 1880, under the drive of political and economic nationalism. At the end of the century it gave way in Europe to two vast alliances whose composition and hostile aims from then on assumed a formidable fixity; these presaged the great conflagrations to come.

Certain factors still retarded this development. The fundamental movement of expansion which in this period characterized the world economy was served by the free circulation of goods and capital, by the facilities offered to emigration, by the existence of numerous still-unoccupied lands, and by vast reserves of raw materials. At the same time, liberal ideas still dammed up the interventionist, centralizing, and warlike tendencies of the national State. But soon nothing would stop the State in its march towards expanded activities and increased powers.

§ 1. NATIONALITIES AND NATIONALISMS

Metternich had tried to anchor the repose of Europe in "security of possession." The new order rested at once on the principle of legitimacy and on the historical conception of territorial sovereignty. Conservative as it was, the "system" was designed less for the pure and simple preservation of an impossible *status quo* than for setting up a just balance in the changes that must come. But Metternich intended to permit these changes only on condition that they resulted from careful deliberation in the European directorate. He would not allow them as surrenders to the obscure forces set loose by the spirit of the Revolution. The great protagonist of balance foresaw that a doctrine demanding the exact and constant control of political forces by the rulers would go ill with the irrational dynamism of the masses.

Despite repression in most countries, the national movements that sprang from the July Revolution showed how impossible it was to cling any longer to a conception of balance based upon the ideas that had guided the Congress of Vienna. Detached from this doctrinal foundation, the practice of balance returned to the political opportunism which was its habitual climate. But thenceforth nationalistic aspirations were a force with which it had to reckon. An idea of which Mazzini was to be the apostle was already in process of formation, namely that the regrouping of nationalities in new political settings would stabilize international relations.[21] It took

[21] Clearer-sighted in the face of disaster than he was thereafter, Renan de-

final form when, in 1848, the principle of nationalities headed the program of democracy. Lamartine's manifesto was the ideological preface, still on the whole prudent, to the adventurous policy by which Napoleon III would try to remake the map of Europe through active intervention on behalf of nationalities. Italian unity and German unity were achieved at the cost of France. Victim of a development which she had hoped to direct, she witnessed, powerless, a complete disintegration of the European equilibrium.

The national idea aims at various objectives which, according to the historical circumstances, according to the genius and traditions of each people, may affect profoundly its direction and potentialities. The direction that it takes depends essentially upon the shape it assumes in men's minds, and the thoughts and images associated with it.[22]

During the first half of the nineteenth century, the nationalist movement was guided chiefly by the individualist and liberal ideas of the preceding century and of the French Revolution in its early stage. That was the classic period of the movement. Its doctrine was the rationalist or elective theory of nationality. The nationalistic ideal here affected the form of a struggle against oppression; in the garb of the plebiscite it presented itself as a principle of legitimation providing a legal justification for the territorial changes called for by the increasing convergence of nation and State.[23]

But an ideology so closely linked with political practice is always in danger of abandoning liberty in order to justify the enterprises

---

nounced this illusion in 1870: "The principle of independent nationalities is not one, as some think, to deliver the human race from the scourge of war; on the contrary, I have always feared that the principle of nationalities, replacing the mild and paternal symbol of legitimacy, might debase the struggles of the peoples into racial extermination and might throw out of the law of nations those temperaments, those civilities that were possible in the small political and dynastic wars of earlier times." *La Guerre entre la France et L'Allemagne, Oeuvres Complètes*, vol. I, p. 434. No less striking is the idea expressed as early as 1862 by Lord Acton: "Nationality does not aim either at liberty or prosperity, both of which it sacrifices to the imperative necessity of making the nation the mould and measure of the State. Its course will be marked with material as well as moral ruin." Cited by E. H. Carr, *Nationalism and After*, 1945.

[22] G. Jellinek, *L'Etat moderne et son Droit*, part I: "Introduction a l'Etude de l'Etat," tr. G. Fardis, p. 205.

[23] The doctrine was preached in its most radical form by Gioberti; who regarded the political division into States as the arbitrary work of man, while national union seemed to him to be dictated by the immutable law of nature.

of power. In Germany, from the beginning of the nineteenth century, the national idea took on an authoritarian character; its aspiration to political organization, so imperiously felt in the Napoleonic wars, was so urgent there that it merged at once in the State. In this fusion it developed in close harmony with the Hegelian concept of the State as at once the synthesis of moral life and an autonomous and irreducible center of power, and with the historical determinism that makes of the nation a quasi-mystical entity directed by obscure but ineluctable forces in the accomplishment of its destiny.

Fichte and Hegel closely associated an absolute moral ideal with their conception of the nation and State. Fichte had placed this in the unorganized national collectivity. Hegel makes the State the most perfect manifestation of Mind; he looks upon it clearly as an extra-personal entity whose historical vocation can be accomplished only through governmental absolutism.[24] Nothing did more to ensure the predominance of the political in the nineteenth and twentieth centuries than the dangerous conception that makes the historically given State a transcendent entity incarnating the spirit of a people in its evolution through the ages. In vain the French conception of nationality opposed the dynamism of the Hegelian idea with the elective principle and the plebiscite; neither of these did more than disguise the defeats of the Second Empire's foreign policy.

These views were succeeded by the ethnic conception of nationality. A conjectural and haughty science, fundamentally alien to the great humanist currents with their spirit of tolerance and measure, and menially associated with the political enterprises of the day, set itself to discovering in the remotest past of humanity the titles of the peoples to nationality. This "human paleontology,"[25] fanatically building upon the primitive and obscure instincts of races the foundations of doubtful nationalities, played a large part not only in the destruction of Europe's political balance but in the retrogression of civilization.

§ 2. NATIONALISM AND DEMOCRACY

Democracy is a bridle on the exaltation of national sentiments only insofar as it does not surrender to statism. Rare were the

[24] E. Bréhier, *Histoire de la Philosophie*, vol. II, p. 769.

[25] Emile Bourgeois, *Manuel historique de Politique étrangère*, 11th edn., 1948, vol. III, p. 182.

countries in which it avoided this reef. The guarantees of liberty seem less necessary against an impersonal power; democracy, says Tocqueville, "dematerializes despotism." That is what preserves its seduction even when it has ceased to be liberal.[26]

Propagating in the masses the illusion that they are governed only by themselves, democracy not only has expanded the activities of the State, but has sometimes put at the State's service a combative opinion ill informed of the conditions of international life. It is well known how disappointed in the event were the hopes that the pacifist movement had placed in democracy. Opinion itself is only a social fact, in large part a resultant of the moral and material forces, historical and contemporary, that act upon the State.

Marxian socialism long mistook the importance of nationalism. It undervalued its hold upon the mind of the working classes, who, as their lot improved, rallied to national conformity. "The socialization of the nation has as its natural corollary the nationalization of socialism."[27] This explains the weaknesses of the socialism which in its Workers' International bore the hopes of pacifism: it was divided against itself, split between its will to conquer the State for the proletariat and its aspiration to achieve on the basis of class interest a union of the working classes that would transcend frontiers. Its materialist inspiration had led it greatly to exaggerate the pacifying influence of certain new conditions in international life, such as the growing economic interdependence of the peoples and the development in the means of communication. In those countries, still much the most numerous, where liberal traditions and the sense of personal responsibility had no deep roots, the historical determinism of socialism, its naïve belief in a constant rise in the level of mass consciousness, disposed minds to a passive acceptance of the decisions of power. Hence it was powerless to prevent the explosions of a nationalism which, since the beginning of the twentieth century, has found its most dangerous fuel in the exploitation of popular passions.

§ 3. THE DECLINE OF LIBERAL IDEAS

Up to the first world war, liberalism held its essential positions in the internal political order: the functional conception of the role

26 H. Kelsen, *La Démocratie*, 1932, p. 11: "The personification of the State is a veil that hides the fact, insupportable to democratic sensibilities, of a domination of man over man."

27 E. H. Carr, *Nationalism and After*, 1945, p. 20.

of power; guarantees of the rights of man and citizen; distinct but coordinate authorities so balanced as to leave place for "those peaceful resistances that safeguard public liberty."[28]

While political liberalism learned from the experience of power, economic liberalism continued to cling to illusions about a natural harmony of interest. Noninterventionist, free-trade, and in certain quarters pacifist, it was the credo of an epoch of easy prosperity that could foresee neither the excesses of unbridled competition nor the dangerous dependence that the concentration of enterprises and the development of capitalism would create between the interests of industrial production and those of the State.

In international relations, free trade was only an "episode."[29] The United States, and later Germany, built their industrial power behind tariff walls. As early as 1841 the precursor of economic nationalism, Frederic List, reproached *liberal* orthodoxy with making economics a matter at once individual and cosmopolitan, forgetting that humanity is divided into nations and that it is from the organization of national power that individuals draw most of their productive strength. In fact the growing concentration of business, and the vast capital investments that it demanded, had the effect from the end of the nineteenth century of binding the national interest more and more firmly to industrial prosperity and the widening of markets. This involved a change of economic structure that vastly expanded the role of the State. Within, it multiplied the interventions of public power to keep up exports or to meet the henceforth national risk of industrial crises. Outside, it led the industrialized States to secure the control of regions producing raw materials and to lend governmental support to the great companies and the banks in the conquest of new markets.

With the decline of liberal ideas the checks upon the development of centralizing statism gave way one after another. While imperialist drives gained power outside, in certain countries totalitarian aspirations penetrated the internal order.

§ 4. END OF THE CONCERT OF EUROPE

The nineteenth century, which spread the sparks of world conflagrations, was on the whole an era of relative stability. The Napoleonic wars had wakened in the great Powers a sense of collective

[28] Esmein, *Eléments de Droit constitutionnel français et comparé*, p. 314.
[29] W. Sombart, *L'Apogée du Capitalisme*, p. 182.

European interest. If the authoritarian Directorate dreamt by Metternich speedily disappeared, the Concert of the Powers, taking over its succession, was responsible for safeguarding the general peace by maintaining the territorial balance. The Concert fulfilled this mission insofar as the common interest of Europe guided the enterprises of the great Powers. In many circumstances it was inadequate or powerless in action; but it must be admitted that in some grave crises the method of permanent consultation advocated by Castlereagh averted the danger of a European war by facilitating compromise settlements. In a word, its efforts were effective so long as it did not collide with a will to change in one or more of the great Powers so fixed that it would not shun the test of force to attain the national objectives. The Concert was charged with maintaining the balance as a principle but in fact had to depend upon the attachment of the Powers to a given historical balance. It was the manifestation and symbol of balance more than its security or guardian.[30] The successive enterprises of Prussia and Germany, the Eastern question and the Balkan crises, and finally the rivalry for colonies broadened the scope of competition, accelerated the rhythm of change, whetted ambitions and mistrust, sanctioned the philosophies of violence, and finally destroyed, in the first years of the twentieth century, that minimum community spirit which is indispensable to any international collaboration.

In 1870, Germany's victories had assured her a preponderant position on the continent. They would not, however, have finally compromised the practice of European balance if the annexation of Alsace and Lorraine had not begotten the fear of revenge in the conqueror. This was to push Bismarck along the dangerous path of alliances. The Austro-German Alliance of 1879, extended three years later by the Treaty of Triple Alliance, left France completely isolated until her agreements with Russia (1892-1894) restored her sense of security. Great Britain long remained reserved, Bismarck's prudence in the handling of alliances having won for Germany the sympathy of British statesmen. They observed her predominance but, believing her satisfied because satiated, thought they saw in

[30] Quite as much as the individualism of national interests, the conviction of inevitable change prevented the European Concert from transforming itself into a regular mechanism of guarantee. Those who participated in its operations wished to use it only as a system enabling them to invoke their moral obligations to justify their interventions, without admitting legal obligations that would have subjected them to decisions contrary to their immediate interests.

the grouping over which she presided a factor of stability and peace.[31]

The mutual hostility of the Triple Alliance and the Franco-Russian Alliance inaugurated the era of profound political tensions which were to lead Europe into the war of 1914-1918. Born of Bismarck's policy of isolating France, these two great coalitions gave a cast of dangerous fixity to the policy of the European cabinets. Nothing could be further from the truth than to regard them as a new form of peaceful balance. Despite its inadequacies and its deviations, the traditional balance had a preventive and moderating virtue that sprang essentially from the variety and flexibility of the political combinations calculated to preserve or re-establish the balance of forces. It was a material, even a gross system, but one which, by leaving to all freedom of action against each, brought under one common law the ambitions and abuses of power. Against hegemonies it had arrayed the common instinct of self-preservation; to designs of occasional expansion it had opposed, sometimes with success, the suppleness of a diplomacy, still free in its measures and mistress of its resources, that knew how to use the diversity of interests and even the instability of political relations to uncover points of contact and increase the chances of agreement or at least of localizing conflicts.

Henceforth it was no longer so. Outside of Italy, which kept sufficient liberty of movement, the general policy of the great Powers was determined, from the end of the nineteenth century, by the demands of their alliances.[32] In grave crises their attitudes were fixed in advance. It became more and more difficult for them to deal with questions one by one; at any moment the underlying political tension might sharpen debate into a battle of prestige and power between the two hostile blocs. Deprived of the support of the European Concert, the policy of balance degenerated into a formula for the defense of the *status quo*. When, in the first years of the twentieth century, colonial imperialism projected the trial of strength into remote regions, the political atmosphere became heavy with the rising threat of general conflagration. For a brief moment

[31] Grey of Fallodon, *Mémoires*, French translation, pp. 24-25; Winston Churchill, *La Crise Mondiale* (1911-1915), vol. I, pp. 19-21.

[32] Though they could not break with the system, European statesmen often saw its dangers. In 1907, Isvolsky pronounced himself against general treaties of alliance and in favor of particular agreements for the solution of problems with any Power. Cf. the memoirs of Baron de Taube, *La Politique russe d'avant-guerre et la fin de l'Empire des Tsars*, pp. 135-136.

British policy, by keeping a free hand, held this development in suspense. In 1904, settlement of their colonial rivalries opened the way for England and France to a lasting entente. This, becoming closer with the years, arrayed the whole of Europe in two coalitions and sealed its fate. From then on the positions were taken, there was no longer any force in reserve to impose peace. These years marked the final deterioration of the traditional balance in the sense of a general system for moderating forces. Punctuated by constant alerts, they were nothing more than the tense armed watch of two combat formations.

Section III

Imperialisms and Great Wars

The imperialisms of the end of the nineteenth century display the Nation-States seeking to expand their power in new or unexplored countries. This was a simple fact of growth rather ill named by a word refurbished from antiquity. For it is a long way from the universal domination of Rome to the essentially pluralist conception of power that determined the division of colonies among contemporary nationalisms. They have one essential trait in common, however, namely a social condition in which individual activities are inclined to seek the protection and accept the control of the public power, and in which the State, made guardian of ever greater interests, invested with ever broader functions, seems alone capable of effectively defending against the foreigner the material interests and the political, moral, or cultural ideals of the nation. Imperialisms, whatever their motives, have had for their essential lever the power of the modern State; they are, whatever has been said of them, an essentially political phenomenon.

By 1880, liberal ideas, born of confidence in the natural balance of things and opposing State interventionism, were everywhere in retreat. Along various paths State socialism was advancing, setting up against the immediate interests that shape private activities the permanent interests of the national community, and exalting the State as the only power capable of remedying social inequalities and ensuring moral solidarity among all the classes. The increasing expansion of State activities was no longer merely recognized as a fact bound up with the growing complexity of civilization. It was regarded by some (A. Wagner for example) as a "law of history" perceptible in the "immanent tendencies" of social evolution. For others it became the object of a veritable "mystique" which, especially in Germany, made of the State the very principle of morality and progress. Served by a growing centralization, by a militarism based on conscription and permanent armies, arrogating the role of educator of youth and promoter of the spiritual values of the national culture, the State made itself focus of all thoughts and master of all energies.

Imperialism is the projection of these moral attitudes and of these forces into international relations. Nations that had known constant growth in a long period of exceptional prosperity found themselves ready for the mobilization of all their resources by the State with a view to expansion beyond the boundaries of the metropolis. The enormous drive of their industries shaped the policy of the great Powers. Battle was joined over raw materials and the new outlets called for by a production that had been stimulated to excess by the overrapid growth of population and by the plethora of capital. The struggle was all the more bitter because the competitors now knew that the existing distribution of colonies was final. Governments encouraged exports and gave protection to the great industrial syndicates and steamship companies. Their diplomacy assisted enterprising businessmen in capturing foreign markets and winning concessions for public works or mining in new countries. More or less fictitious "occupations," recognition of "spheres of influence," disguised protectorates, financial controls, were the product of these interventions and manifestations of mounting national competition.

The State's participation in economic and colonial competition bore its usual fruit: its power, beginning as mere means, became an end in itself; the political interest gradually occupied the foreground as the general tension of international relations rose. "In a word, what has finally dominated the colonial effort, taking priority over even economic interest, is political interest. Mere countinghouses, groups of emigrants, zones of influence, points of support have acquired a more political character from day to day. Now it is a question of national greatness and of defending national interests of every sort by occupying convenient regions or spots of the globe. That is what the words empire and imperialism mean."[33]

[33] Henri Berr, Foreword to G. Hardy's work *La Politique coloniale et le partage de la Terre*, pp. xiv-xv. Cf. G. Schwarzenberger, "The Rule of Law and the Disintegration of the International Society," *A.J.I.L.*, 1939, p. 69: "Similarly, the principle that the flag follows trade or even stimulates com-

Bound up with the problems of foreign policy raised by imperialist expansion was the demographic problem of the State. Since the beginning of the nineteenth century, the unprecedented increase in the population of Europe produced a constant heightening of pressure which only manifested its full consequences in the following century. This prodigious growth was made possible by the industrialization and internationalization of the economy. These, however, could not eliminate the formidable political problems raised by the accumulation of vast proletarian masses now bearing with all their weight on the policy of governments, and unconsciously working by their narrow nationalism and their docility to the appeal of agitators to destroy the very conditions of free movement, reciprocity, order, and peace which in the previous century had made their peaceful coexistence possible.[34]

What characterized the conflict of imperialisms, particularly the long and stubborn rivalry which from the accession of William II until 1914 set British imperialism against Germany's *Weltpolitik*, was the absence of clearly stated and precisely circumscribed claims. A diffuse struggle in several dimensions carried on in the triple economic, maritime, and colonial domain, it had no object other than a general displacement of power, and no real cause other than, on the one side, the will to hold the advance made, and on the other the feeling that there was an unjust disproportion between the positions established and the changes that had taken place in the ratio of interests and power.

In the last years of the nineteenth century, statesmen of real enlightenment foresaw a profound and definitive change in international relations and had a presentiment of general conflagration.[35]

At that moment old and new imperialisms, having collided at the four corners of the earth, turned back towards their center in Europe. The great alliances completed their consolidation; the armaments race took on a headlong pace. In 1898 Czar Nicholas II tried in vain to placate the fates with a proposal to stop the race for arms. He mistook the deep causes of political tension. Arma-

---

mercial expansion was bound to lead to additional friction and to a race between the Powers anxious to preserve the balance of acquisitions in the 'Black Continent,' or of spheres of interest and influence all over the world."

[34] W. Röpke, *La Communanté internationale*, 1947, pp. 123 seq. "Modern mass civilization became economically possible thanks to principles which in the last analysis are not adequate to its spirit" (p. 130).

[35] Winston Churchill, *La Crise Mondiale*, vol. I, chap. II.

ments are but the instrument that the Powers forge, some to hold, the others to change, the ratio of the forces that are the foundation of political supremacy; they are symptoms and aggravations of the disease, never its true cause. This truth became apparent when, a few years later, England and Germany undertook to adjust their programs of naval building; the technical *pourparlers* proceeding under the menace of general and growing political tension could lead only to an impasse.

CHAPTER III. INTERNATIONAL LAW FROM THE CONGRESS OF VIENNA TO THE FIRST WORLD WAR, 1815-1914

Section I

General Character of International Law during This Period

FOLLOWING the wars of the Empire, the ratio and disposition of forces in Europe for some time promoted a stabilization of which the European Concert and the policy of balance were the essential instruments.

The practice of balance implied a certain equality in the distribution of forces implementing policies that were at once diverse in object and circumscribed in operation. It offered to diplomacy the almost infinite resources of a system of relations founded on the plurality of independent States: multiple auxiliary weights available for alternate adjustments; supple combinations to neutralize forces, moderate claims, or localize conflicts.

This development was assisted by the structure of the liberal State, based as this was on the separation of the sovereign functions belonging to politics from the individual activities belonging to economics. By the end of the century, this state of affairs had been altered from top to bottom by the consolidation of threatening coalitions, and by the expansion and concentration of State power.

International law reflected the phases of this evolution. Undeniable progress was made in various branches during the quiet period which the nineteenth century owed to the concerted action of the Powers. The law found its inspiration here: it bore the marks of continuity, while the liberal conception of the State provided criteria by which to define and circumscribe international obligations and responsibilities. The law's weaknesses became apparent as, with the deterioration of the system, grave political tensions brought it rudely face to face with problems with which only a very advanced type of international organization could have coped, the problems of peaceful change and of security. At The Hague the timidity of governments would bar the road to the political organization of international relations. Imbued as it was with sovereign individualism, the law would fail in the constitutional task called for by new times. Speedily overtaken by events, it would prove powerless to change their course.

§ 1. THE DEVELOPMENT OF TREATY LAW

The notable development of international treaty law, beginning with the Congress of Vienna, was one of the characteristic traits of this period. Perfectly adapted to the individualist structure of international relations, the treaty is the instrument of legal development among States which, though ready to collaborate, refuse to be bound by anything but a special exercise of their will.

Among the treaties of a juristic nature there were some which, while they served the high policy of the great Powers, nonetheless established legal situations and rules of law. Others, though not devoid of political significance, were designed chiefly to promote common economic or cultural interests. Others, again, were dedicated to the protection of the individual and had an essentially humanitarian scope.

In the first group we may cite the Declaration of the Powers, dated November 20, 1815, on the perpetual neutrality of Switzerland; the Acts of the London Conference establishing permanent neutrality for Belgium (1831); the Declaration of Paris on maritime law (1856); the Declaration of the Berlin Conference (1885) on the conditions of occupation on the African coasts and the neutrality of territories included in the treaty basin of the Congo; and the series of conventions establishing regulations for the Turkish Straits, the Black Sea (1841, 1856, 1871, 1878), and the Baltic Sounds (1857), and setting up regimes for the Panama (1850, 1901) and Suez (1888) Canals.

Among multilateral treaties devoted primarily to international commercial interests may be listed the Final Act of Vienna (1815) on the navigation of international rivers, still the fundamental charter of international river law; the navigation acts which refined and extended the Vienna principles for application to the Rhine (1831, 1868), the Elbe (1821), the Scheldt (1839), the Danube (1856, 1878, 1883); the clauses of the General Act of the Berlin Conference on navigation of the Congo (1885); and finally the very numerous international "union" conventions concluded in the second half of the century to implement the common interests of States in various spheres. These last contributed to what has somewhat optimistically been called international administrative law.

In the class of multilateral treaties dedicated to the protection of the human person, we must mention, out of many, the clauses of the Treaties of Vienna (1815) providing for abolition of the slave trade, and the similar provisions of the Brussels Anti-Slavery Conference (July 2, 1890), together with the Geneva Convention of 1864 on the treatment of the sick and wounded in time of war.

All this regulation has proved remarkably viable, the result of its exact correspondence with the needs and possibilities of the time. It has been no less notable for its effective observation, contrasting happily with the frailty of so many stillborn international acts in our time.

§ 2. GEOGRAPHIC EXTENSION OF INTERNATIONAL RELATIONS. THE "GOLDEN AGE" OF SECONDARY STATES

Held within limits traced by the underlying accord of the Concert and the balance, the rivalries of the great Powers and the policy of counterweights promoted a certain legal equality among States. This manifested itself in the entry of new States into what is called the international community and in the protection generally given in this period to the interests of small States.

The Treaty of Paris (1856) declared the Porte "admitted to the benefits of the public law and the Concert of Europe." The signatory Powers thus bound themselves severally to respect the independence and territorial integrity of the Ottoman Empire. They agreed upon a common guarantee of this undertaking and consequently declared that they would regard any act at variance with it as "a question of general interest." The policy of the "open door," primarily a product of the combined political and commercial rivalry of the Powers, hastened the entry of China and Japan into international relations.

The action of the Concert of Powers, and that momentary neutralization of their strengths which is the essential object of the practice of balance, account for the favor in which permanent neutralities were held in this period and for the respect that surrounded them. The long security that they brought to certain States sometimes obscured their inevitably political origin.

As for the so-called equality of States, by the nineteenth century a distinction was being made between equality before the law and equal participation in deliberations where the general interests of Europe or the world were at stake. Neither the Concert of Powers nor their policy of balance would accommodate such participation. In fact the equality of States bowed to direction by the great Powers whenever these set out to impose their views in order to reach agreement among themselves or to ensure peace. True, in various circumstances they admitted secondary States to their discussions, but this deference is to be explained less by any recognition of equality than by the stabilization of political relations between the great Powers. The epoch of the great law-making treaties, those that have really counted in history, was also that of an organization of international relations which, though doubtless rudimentary, was effective.[1]

The secondary States profited little by the decline of the European Concert. With its disappearance, even their equality before the law, long protected by the Concert's moderating action, was exposed to all the risks of great political tensions.

§ 3. CONSOLIDATION AND PROGRESS OF THE LAW OF NEUTRALITY

The rarity of armed conflicts and their localization favored free exercise of each State's right to remain neutral and the consolidation and observance of the rules of neutrality. The entry on the political scene of a new great Power, the United States, which was determined to guard its independence from the danger of complications arising out of Europe's wars, gave a decisive drive to this movement.

The principle of the inviolability of neutral territory, and the neutral State's corresponding obligation to prevent belligerent use of its territory, acquired at this time a precision and firmness that they had long lacked in earlier centuries. But it was in regard to freedom of trade, particularly in maritime war, that the liberal spirit of the age stimulated greatest progress in international law. Moreover, this resulted less from a clearly defined legal conception of the rights and duties of neutrality than from successive compromises between the opposed interests of belligerents and neutrals. Some of these compromises produced rules that for a considerable time were effectively applied. Others amounted to merely artificial solutions that did not survive the test of facts.

1 On this point, as on others, the atmosphere of The Hague Conferences bred some illusions. But it must be observed that the application there of the principle of equality, especially when it came to voting, was the subject, in the public opinion of the great countries, of criticism that already raised the question of equitable representation for States in international organization. Cf. Hicks, "The Equality of States and the Hague Conferences," *A.J.I.L.*, 1908, p. 530; Edwin D. Dickinson, *The Equality of States*, chap. VIII; J. Goebel, *The Equality of States*, 1923; Herbert Weinschel, "The Doctrine of the Equality of States, and Its Recent Modifications," *A.J.I.L.*, 1951, p. 417.

It was again the tradition of the liberal State, supported by concomitant development in the technique of international law, henceforth regarded as an exclusively inter-State law, that made possible the famous Rules of Washington, 1871, on the responsibility of the neutral State. Two distinctions are fundamental to this responsibility—the distinction between acts of the neutral government and acts of its nationals; and the distinction between individual activities that a neutral government is bound to prevent in virtue of its duty of "due diligence" and individual activities for which it assumes no responsibility. The same idea is at the root of the principle that a neutral government cannot be held responsible for deliveries to belligerents of arms, munitions, or war materials made as a private speculation by its nationals. It is also the source of the conception that the carriage of contraband, so long as this is the work of individuals having no official character, is not a delict under international law. Individuals here must take the risks of a "venture" which, because it is purely private, cannot entail State responsibility.

§ 4. ARBITRATION AND THE ORGANIZATION OF PEACE

Faced with the essentially political dilemma of peaceful change or war, the Powers refused to accept either arbitration without the traditional reservations of sovereignty or institutional limitations on the right of war. The Hague Conferences made a pretence of referring to legal settlement problems that could be disposed of only by political decisions. But, left at the Conference door, "politics held the key."[2] Despite brilliant appearances that deceived the epoch, international law suffered from this shifting of political problems to the legal plane.

Hopes in the development of compulsory arbitration were disappointed by the very comprehensible refusal of the great Powers "to chain politics to an unchanging law that would have judges in its service to perpetuate it, but no legislators standing over it to make amendments."[3] Such was the underlying cause of the resistance of States to any multilateral treaty of compulsory arbitration, and of their refusal to give up, even in particular or bilateral conventions, reservations touching independence, vital interests, or national honor. The Hague Conferences certainly cannot be denied the

[2] Charles Dupuis, *Le Droit des Gens et les Rapports des grandes Puissances avec les autres Etats*, pp. 358-359.

[3] *ibid.*, p. 360.

merit of having surrounded arbitration with an atmosphere favorable to judicial settlement; but it must be admitted that, in the narrow confines to which it was restricted by the hostility of the Powers to the very principle of a serious arbitral obligation, international justice had no chance to contribute to the maintenance of peace.

Still more disappointing were the results of The Hague Conferences in the matter of preventing or stopping war. Holding war to be a legitimate way of settling international disputes, the negotiators devoted all their efforts to "humanizing" it. They embarked on the vain enterprise of regulating what is the anarchic phenomenon par excellence by prescribing laws for the use of forces which, once loosed, know no law but success. The Powers had forsworn viewing the problem in its true light, which was political; they thus closed the only effective approach, which even then was no longer inter-State but institutional.

Section II

The Doctrines
Their Lacunae and Their Arbitrary Limitations

The dominant doctrine, as the nineteenth century ended and the twentieth began, was positivism. Two principal modes of thought were current, corresponding to two different views of the basis of obligation and the ends of power. While G. Jellinek and his disciples identified the objective foundations of law with the ends of the State, the great majority of positivists, more responsive to the demands of their method, professed a thesis that denied the relevance to law of any norm superior to those willed by the State and formally expressed in positive international law.

§ 1. THE DOCTRINE OF THE STATE'S AUTOLIMITATION

This theory, represented most authoritatively by Jellinek, does not make the will of States the ultimate foundation of the law. Will here creates norms only because it proceeds from legal conviction, that is to say from a deliberate adherence to common ideas of justice and social necessity. Jellinek understood that a law so imperfectly developed as international law could not in any case be separated from a superior objective order and made a purely formal autonomous system. In the complexity and even contradictions of his doctrine there is an effort to embrace the legal order in its total reality.[4]

But, caught between the search for a higher objective order and respect for sovereignties, Jellinek finally surrendered to the latter. Sovereignty, he says, implies the absence of any subordinations other than those created by the State's capacity to bind itself. This autolimitation, it is true, does not amount to mere moral subjectivism, for it is dictated by the common legal conviction and has nothing arbitrary about it. Nevertheless, Jellinek's theory must be rejected. The autolimitation of power is a valid explanation only in a social environment already profoundly responsive to the fundamental demands of life in common.[5] It is insufficient for the international environment, where solidarities are still so weakly felt. The contradiction becomes clear when Jellinek, still asserting the existence of an objective order informing the State will, rejects as contrary to sovereignty any obligation that does not spring from the State's free volition. He falls back into voluntarism, not in deference to the formal requirements of his system, but from respect for the principle of the political distribution of power among nations. His error is especially serious, since it places the State's moral and legal duty at the center of the political organism. Thus Jellinek subordinates such duty to the exigencies of the State itself, for the State remains sole judge of its political needs. It is not surprising that from these beginnings the author reaches and declares the conclusion that international law is, after all, nothing more than an anarchic law.[6]

German writers after Jellinek show even more clearly the purely political tendency to "sublimate"[7] the ideal and ends of the State. Personifying the highest moral and cultural values of the nation, the State bears sole responsibility for them, owing account to no one on earth. Notwithstanding the ideal that it professes and the reservations with which it surrounds itself, this haughty doctrine

[4] The criticisms aimed at Jellinek sometimes lose sight of the hierarchic relation that the author established between the legal and for him merely formal and secondary basis of international law and its ethico-social basis, which in his thought was its ultimate foundation. Cf. Hold-Ferneck, *Lehrbuch des Völkerrechts*, vol. I, p. 186; J. Spiropoulos, *Théorie générale du Droit international*, pp. 46-50.

[5] Autolimitation has an important place in the internal legal order. See especially M. Hauriou, *Précis de Droit constitutionnel*, 1929.

[6] *Allgemeine Staatslehre*, 2nd edn., p. 368.

[7] G. Scelle, *Précis du Droit des Gens*, vol. I, p. 35.

of the relations between sovereignty and law ends by attributing to the political organization a transcendency of purpose that subordinates human interests to the greatness of the nation.[8]

§ 2. VOLUNTARIST POSITIVISM

The weakening of natural-law doctrines in the nineteenth century proceeded *pari passu* with the predominance of political factors in international relations. As States, under nationalist pressure, more openly pursued policies of power, the idea of a law based on the moral needs of human nature, a "necessary" law, was in unbroken retreat in the minds of internationalists. Positivist thought substituted for the search for the principle the search for the criterion, and found this in effectiveness. The characteristic of such thought was an attitude, not of negation, but of scientific indifference touching the existence of an objective order superior to the law established by human will. Legal positivism does not dispute—is indeed, from a philosophic point of view, often ready to admit—the reality of such an order. It simply denies that it has any legal relevance.

It is a fact, however, that this current of ideas was only truly built into a system with the aid of philosophic positivism, particularly the sociological positivism of Auguste Comte and his disciples. The ambition to make a science of law went a long way, it seems, to account for the singularly detached if not negative attitude adopted by the positivists in regard to the ethical and social bases of international law. True to the essence of positivist thought, which tends to discard any data not verifiable in experience, the doctrine attributed the obligatory character of legal norms, not to their conformity with superior considerations of reason, but solely to the circumstance that they find their expression in a tangible external fact: *their recognition and effective observation* by States. This was the legal phenomenalism that led most authors to reduce all international law to international practice. It was largely due to the very small part that individual consciences played in the formation and application of the rules of that law.

The original weakness of voluntarist positivism was due to the habit, encountered so frequently in jurists, of considering law only from the point of view of its formal procedures of elaboration. The doctrine was concerned solely with the manifestations of State

[8] As early as 1902, O. von Gierke drew attention to these trends in German thought and observed that they threatened "the very idea of law by making utility the criterion of its content, and force the essence of its operation."

wills, it regarded as legally pertinent only the last phase in the process by which norms are formed, and it deliberately excluded from its horizons the ethical, political, and social factors that are the foundation and ultimate explanation of law. Thus it came to strengthen, usually with no political afterthought, an intransigent conception of sovereignty at the very moment when vast upheavals called for radical revision.[9]

But the authors rarely preserved this attitude of moral indifference. Ethical considerations reappear in most of them in the form of captious arguments that seek to legitimize the accomplished fact, identifying it with law.

The fundamental position of positivism, excluding as it did from international law everything that could not be traced to agreements of State wills, impressed a markedly static character upon this law. By reducing the formative factors of the law to such agreements, which would logically have to be renewed for every amendment of the law in force, voluntarist positivism singularly accentuated the propensity of international law to immobility. It incontestably lessened the productivity of the sources. This static posture of positivist doctrine corresponded to the general spirit of the age that saw its birth. Being a period of calm and prosperity, the nineteenth century placed a large premium on stability at the cost of aspirations to change.[10]

As a reaction against a deformed and sterile law of nature, the positivist theories had the indisputable merit of offering a clear and generally true picture of international relations in the period of relative political stabilization that characterized the nineteenth century. Their irremissible weakness was their moral indifference to the human ends of power and their passive acceptance of the individualism of sovereignties. Cutting norms off from their deepest roots for the sole purpose of integrating them in a scientific but purely formal system, they constantly desiccated and impoverished them. This explains the discredit into which these theories fell.

[9] This agnostic mode of thought led particularly to the view that any war regularly declared is lawful. Positivism preferred to recognize the right of war as a sovereign prerogative rather than appeal to moral criteria that would have implied abandonment of its method.

[10] Voluntarist posivitism was thus in the international order what the exegetic school was in the internal order. It corresponded to a "period of pause" marked by a "tendency to repose" that showed itself in blind worship of the rule, love of form, and the coagulation of all effort in stereotyped canons. H. De Page, *Traité de Droit civil,* vol. I, p. 15.

CHAPTER IV
BETWEEN THE TWO WORLD WARS
1919-1939

"I cannot recall any time when the gap between the kind of words which statesmen used and what was actually happening in many countries was so great as it is now." WINSTON CHURCHILL (1932).

AFTER the first world war all hopes of international law focused upon the international organization that President Wilson had promoted. Concern for the maintenance of peace and international security gave birth to a new ideology which, despite all too certain weaknesses, had the great merit of throwing light upon the basic requirements for permanent collaboration between States and the correlative need to limit national sovereignty. In this respect the creation of the League of Nations was a decisive step in the orientation of political thought and in the development of international law.

Section I

The League of Nations; Its Optimistic Ideology. The Search for Security; the Defeats

Set up after the first world war, the League of Nations had taken as its essential purpose the safeguarding of peace. Its failure, which was resounding, was due to reasons whose complexity has been as badly misunderstood by its adversaries as by its partisans. The new organization's chances of success depended on the one hand upon the peace settlement, that is to say the political order inaugurated in 1919 by the Allied and Associated Powers; and on the other, upon the readiness of the States members to subordinate particular or national objectives to collective ends.

World peace is not organized in the abstract.[1] International organization, whenever or in whatever conditions it is established, is born in a given political climate. After a prolonged and general war,

[1] Cf. M. Bourquin, *Vers une nouvelle Société des Nations*, p. 122.

this climate is largely fixed by the hegemony that temporarily belongs to the winner. Whether appended to or separate from the peace treaty, the covenant intended to be the instrument of general pacification runs head on, when it comes to application, into the political tensions sooner or later engendered by the peace settlement. The Treaties of 1919 were perhaps less hard than many others torn from the loser. They had the misfortune of never being upheld by a great directing force, powerful enough to impose a measure of stability, foreseeing enough to permit necessary adjustments when the time came. The resistances that they provoked, the violations of which they were the object, the divisions among the Allied and Associated Powers called forth by their application not only compromised the political settlement of 1919, but also brought the League of Nations face to face with problems that neither its ideological principles nor its organization prepared it to resolve.

By its whole ideology, the Covenant tended to set the League apart from European political contingencies that awoke neither interest nor sympathy in President Wilson. Hence its abstract posture; hence also its optimistic assumptions, a curious throwback in the international order to the liberal philosophy of the eighteenth century.[2] Like that philosophy, the Covenant was imbued with the idea of a natural harmony based upon the equal interest of all peoples in the preservation of peace. Like so many liberal ideas, this is not false, but it can be verified only in the long term, and in any event lacks the power to dominate human motives. It has never deterred from warlike enterprise anyone who believed himself the stronger and so master of the hour. There is no people that does not prefer peace, if peace can keep for it what it has or give it what it covets. Peace or war depends on the price that nations are willing to pay at any given moment, some to hold their positions, the others to improve them.

The Wilsonian principle of national self-determination contributed even less to the stabilization of Europe and the world than did the nineteenth-century principle of nationalities. When they

[2] See, on this subject, E. H. Carr, *The Twenty Years' Crisis* (1919-1939). It is an exaggeration, however, to accuse the authors of the Covenant of proceeding on a purely theoretical plane. Many of its clauses, particularly those on the settlement of disputes and maintenance of peace, exhibit a very accurate sense of political realities. It was only later that a tendency to "perfectionism," stimulated especially by the abuse of logical reasoning, begot a legalistic passion for new formulas that degenerated into "pactomania" and a rigidity that collided head on with active political forces.

increased the number of political units, the negotiators of the Treaties of 1919 did not pay enough attention to the possibility of integrating them in a lasting political and economic order. The new States, badly built, and much exposed to external pressures, were too weak to support an independent life, and sometimes too conscious of their recent sovereignty to reckon with realities. Their fragility whetted ambitions and appetites for revenge; their anxious efforts kept up the general agitation. Any political creation not backed by adequate strength stimulates in other countries the will to change, a will to power that is naturally refractory to order and law.[3] More illusory still was the hope that the authors of the Covenant had placed in the judgment and pacifying influence of opinion. The liberal philosophy of the eighteenth century had relied upon "enlightened" opinion, that of philosophers and scholars; the power attributed to it was that of reason. The democracy of the nineteenth century substituted for enlightened opinion that inferior form of human thought that is dubbed public opinion; it gave little attention to raising this to a sense of its new responsibilities. Save in a very few countries, public opinion has shown itself unequal to exercising any useful function in external relations. Incapable of seizing the complexity of international problems, or fashioned by the holders of power, it lives in this context on ready-made formulas, a captive of fictions or half-truths. ". . . the whole conception of the League of Nations," wrote E. H. Carr, "was from the first closely bound up with the twin belief that public opinion was bound to prevail and that public opinion was the voice of reason."[4] The myth of a public opinion in the service of peace was

[3] As early as 1893, the anonymous author of an article in the *Revue des Deux Mondes*, "Les transformations de la diplomatie," wrote, "We are just reaching the critical age when the sentiment of nationality after drawing peoples together tends to divide and consequently to weaken them," and, addressing himself to nationalities impatient to throw off certain yokes: "Have you calculated the consequences of your smallness of stature in the contest of peoples? What will replace the rampart that cramps but shelters you? Do you know what money, armaments, diplomacy it takes to defend a territory?" And further on: "A people that will not make sacrifices to the interest of the State does not merit the name of nation; it vegetates in eternal childhood."

[4] *op.cit.*, p. 45. Henri de Jouvenel wrote in 1928: "There are times when one wonders if appearances are not more important than realities in international relations. This would not be impossible in a period when more and more people are occupied with things to which they give less and less time. Opinion takes precedence over knowledge. A sort of cheap truth is established with no care for the truth that costs long years of study and meditation." *Journal de Genève*, March 27, 1928.

still at the center of the Genevese ideology when totalitarian regimes took command of the impulses of the masses and called them to combat.

Nevertheless, neither the ideological weaknesses of the Covenant nor the inadequacy of its constitutional organization would doubtless have prevented the League from making some progress in international security if the abstention of the United States had not, from its first steps, annulled its possibilities of action. Doomed to failure was the subsequent effort to do by purely legal means what only the concerted action of the Powers could have accomplished. The British Government in 1925 met the abstract and universalist logic of the Geneva Protocol with the cold language of facts: "As all the world is aware, the League of Nations, in its present shape, is not the League designed by the framers of the Covenant. They no doubt contemplated, and, as far as they could, provided against, the difficulties that might arise from the non-inclusion of a certain number of States within the circle of League membership. But they never supposed that among these States would be found so many of the most powerful nations in the world, least of all did they foresee that one of them would be the United States of America."[5] From this observation the British Government drew the conclusion: so amputated, the League could doubtless deal satisfactorily with minor disputes; it was not equipped to prevent powerful States from engaging in wars that spring from deep-seated and general tensions.

The successive stages in the discussion of the security problem vividly displayed the two tendencies in constant alternation at Geneva. The Protocol of 1924, of which a great jurist (V. Scialoja) could say that it sinned by "an excess of legal perfection," was the typical example of a construction in which pure Cartesian logic conflicted with reality. Inspired by more realistic views, but limited to a regional sphere of operation, the Locarno Treaties sought security along the traditional paths of agreement between great Powers and the European balance. They were the fruit of a happy and passing conjuncture, the tentative resultant of a momentary balance of forces in a given region. They were concluded at the exact psychological moment when France's fear of Germany was practically equal to Germany's fear of France, and when Germany,

[5] Balfour Memorandum, 1925, H.M.'s Stationery Office, Cmd. 2368, p. 4. Cf. A. Zimmern, *The League of Nations and the Rule of Law* (1918-1935), pp. 304-305.

temporarily abandoning the hope of changing her western frontiers, declared herself ready to confirm and guarantee them. It has been correctly remarked that they could not have been concluded either two years earlier or five years later.[6]

With the economic crisis of 1929, Japan's aggression against China under the eyes of a powerless League of Nations, and Hitler's accession to power in Germany, political tensions became menacing. From that time on the prospect of a new world war never ceased weighing on deliberations at Geneva. It was easy to see what would become of the plan to reduce armaments in this atmosphere. The truth is that the governments, knowing the irremediable weakness of the international organization, had long before this stopped approaching the problem in the cooperative spirit called for by Article 8 of the Covenant. It was a true paradox to assemble at Geneva, with a view to limiting the military strength of their respective countries, the representatives of States that already regarded each other openly with the deepest mistrust and that now thought only of taking the measure of their antagonists. Without deceiving anyone, every effort was strained to give a technical appearance to a problem which was and will always remain essentially political.

In 1933 the radical change in the ratio of forces and the growing discredit of the Geneva procedures opened the way for the Italian proposal of a Four-Power Pact. By this time indeed it seemed proved that nothing useful could be done without a system of regular consultation between great Powers, in other words a return to the policy of the European Concert. The Italian Government's proposal, however, was too openly directed to the revision of the Peace Treaties and expressed too clearly the expansionist aims of the totalitarian Powers not to arouse the more or less clearly declared opposition of Great Britain and France. It was nonetheless indicative of the movement of ideas. Under the cover of western

[6] E. H. Carr, *op.cit.*, p. 136. Yet it is well to remember the reflections of a strategically placed German witness, Ernst von Weizsäcker (*Memoirs*, tr. J. Andrews, 1951, p. 59): "The Locarno Treaty was, I thought, a formal piece of self-deception on both sides. I did not indeed suspect that there was any evil intention in the minds of those who signed the Treaty, but I feel that they lacked any real support in the public opinion of their respective countries. It was overlooked at that time that the sentiments which a treaty of this kind expresses must first be engendered in the public mind, or must at any rate exist when the treaty is signed, if it is to have any permanence. With the Locarno Treaty this was not so, as was soon to emerge."

regionalism and within the framework of the League of Nations, it sought to inaugurate a directorate of four great Powers which would substitute for the impotent egalitarianism of a universal assembly the authoritarian drive of a policy which proclaimed at once respect for contractual obligations and the necessity of adapting the treaties to the changes that had taken place in the ratio of interests and forces.

The defeat of sanctions against Italy was the *coup de grâce* for the League of Nations. On October 7 and 10, 1935, the representatives of more than fifty nations in the Council and Assembly had declared Italy in violation of the Covenant and recommended a conference of States belonging to the League to coordinate the sanctions to be imposed under Article 16. By July 1936, economic and financial sanctions had proved powerless to change the course of events in Ethiopia, and the delegates of these same States with one exception pronounced themselves in favor of abandoning the attempt. The statements made on this occasion sharply emphasized the cause of this defeat. Against a great Power, effective economic and financial sanctions might have degenerated into military action. But "from the outset there was a tacit or explicit agreement to avoid military sanctions or economic sanctions the effects of which would ultimately have merged into military sanctions."[7] In other words, none of the States that had voted for sanctions were "prepared to commit their people to war for a cause which does not vitally concern their immediate national interests."[8] This was the reality. In admitting it, the Assembly of the League of Nations implicitly recognized the predominance of national individualisms over the imperatives of collective security.

Truncated in membership by the successive withdrawals of Japan, Germany, and Italy, discredited in action by the resounding defeat of the sanctions experiment, the League of Nations ceased to be regarded as a center of international cooperation in a universal cause.

[7] Statement by M. Motta, delegate of Switzerland, Records of the Sixteenth Ordinary Session of the Assembly, 21st Plenary Meeting, July 2, 1936, pp. 42-43.

[8] Statement by Mr. Bruce, delegate of Australia (*ibid.*, p. 39), and in a similar sense those by Mr. Anthony Eden and other delegates.

Section II

The Underlying Causes of the Failure of the League of Nations

Apart from these immediate causes, there were underlying reasons for the failure of the League of Nations. The twenty years that separated the peace of 1919 from the beginning of World War II were stamped with the seal of political insecurity, economic chaos, and, above all, moral instability.

Following the gigantic conflict of 1914-1918, Europe was exhausted and needed repose. She was caught in a frenzy of nationalisms. The nascent international organization called for a great directing force bringing to the service of peace a policy of moderation. The efforts of its promoters were checked from the beginning by the division of the victors of 1919, and later by the ideologies propagated by the totalitarian governments. The first world war had implanted in the peoples anxiety about the morrow and a certain propensity to violence. "This hallucinating fear of unlimited and irremediable future disasters kept democracy in a state of anxiety, took away its self-confidence, made it timid and so inclined to be led away into violence and dictatorship."[9]

In troubled times, popular anxiety engenders ideologies that increase their sway the more completely they fuse morals and power in the hearts of the people,[10] and the more deeply they implant in the masses the conviction of the justice of their claims and the drunken sense of power. The State provided a focus for these mass impulses, obscure and chaotic as they usually were. Drawing strength from the Hegelian fountain, the claims of the unsatisfied peoples exalted the Nation-State as universal ethical will and invoked the vital law of change. Directed to concrete achievements, they spread with great rapidity. Their diffusion brought about the most dangerous concentration of political power ever seen. As for the "satisfied" Powers, they could set up on their side only the liberal and abstract concept of the common interest of the peoples in the preservation of peace. Their policy, aimed as it was at stabilizing a state of things of which they were the beneficiaries, was bound to be identified with the defense of the *status quo*. This kind of pacifism, sans inspiration or radiance, had no influence on the course of events.

[9] R. B. Mowat, *L'Esprit international*, April 1, 1934, pp. 248-249.

[10] L. Sturzo, *Politique et Morale, Cahiers de la Nouvelle Journée*, no. 40, p. 16.

In the years following the great crisis of 1929, planned economy, product of nationalism and State socialism, became the tool of a policy of power which in certain countries openly subordinated prosperity to the political and extra-personal ends of the State. There everything was sacrificed to efficient governmental action.[11] In times of economic contraction, authoritarian discipline becomes the refuge for mass anxiety. Where the sense of liberty—meaning here the individual's readiness to defend personality against abuses of power—has no deep roots, the phases of contraction coincide with the apparition of mythical images of power.[12]

The inauguration in Europe of totalitarian regimes marked the return to a primitive type of political and social organization. As the frightening development proceeded, it invoked familiar themes: the blood myth, the myth of encirclement, the myth of living space —obsidional images all making the group interest an absolute moral good and the authority of the "leader" an unlimited power.

The totalitarian governments set the methods of a pseudo-democracy to work for a pseudo-ethic. While, in consciences, a perverted mysticism concealed the collective appetite for domination under the guise of individual renunciation, military expansion became the very principle of public life and its most powerful stimulant to action. By internal discipline and external tension, the totalitarian State raised the political phenomenon to its highest power.

The short history of the League of Nations was that of a triumph of historical nationalisms over a noble but abstract and remote ideal of international cooperation. Its promoters, too confident of the power of reason, had underestimated the sentimental forces that nourish the "sacred egoism" of the Nation-State. Rare were the countries where democracy brought the support of an enlightened opinion to the League of Nations.[13]

[11] E. H. Carr, *Nationalism and After*, p. 23: "Planned economy is a Janus with a nationalist as well as a socialist face; if its doctrine seems socialist, its pedigree is unimpeachably nationalist." Cf. W. Rappard, *Le Nationalisme économique et la Société des Nations*, *Rec. A.D.I.*, vol. 61 (1937), Introduction.

[12] V. Larock, *La Pensée mythique*, 1945, pp. 64 seq. "Where the gregarious urge masters the idea of individual autonomy, of free and peaceful intellectual and moral development for persons and communities, it is inevitable that the clan spirit should resume its rights, that authority within the State should tighten into the harshest restraints, and that the passionate will to power should join combat with everything outside that stands in the way of its supremacy."

[13] Lord Baldwin: "The weakness of democracy is a certain proneness to short views, hastily formed and vigorously asserted on an inadequate basis of

Collective security, common interest of all nations in the maintenance of an indivisible peace, outlawry of war—none of these high objectives could touch off that instantaneous rational illumination of public opinion, or, better, that swift onrush of sentiments that could have penetrated the depths, enlarged horizons, and convinced men of the new necessities of international life. It became clear that the maintenance of peace, as a general and human problem, awakens very few men to knowledge of the sacrifices necessary for its defense and organization. It seems that peace only becomes precious to the masses when invasion threatens. Then it is too late; blinded by their passions, they let themselves be sucked into war. It is only too obvious that law between 1920 and 1939 was too far ahead of facts.

Despite these weaknesses, it remains true that the League of Nations marked a decisive step in world organization. It had first of all the incomparable merit of lifting the problem of organizing peace from the domain of speculation and placing it at the center of governmental interest, of making the preservation of peace a common and public object of the policy of governments. In this sense the Covenant corresponded precisely with the needs of the epoch that witnessed its birth. When it declared that "Any war or threat of war, whether immediately affecting any of the members of the League or not, is . . . a matter of concern to the whole League" (Art. 11), it stated a principle which the growing universality of the risks of war is implanting in the mind of humanity.

Section III

The Gropings of Doctrine

From our point of view here, which is the relations of law and power, the evolution of doctrine between the two world wars bears the imprint of the contradictory aspirations of the period. The general works, whether treatises or manuals, for the most part follow the traditional lines of thought. With the classical conception of the individualism of sovereignties they combine the descriptive methods of legal positivism. There is a sharp contrast between the passages, usually brief, devoted to the "new law" issuing from the

reflection and knowledge." Quoted by N. Henderson, *Failure of a Mission, Berlin* (1937-1939), p. 65.

League of Nations and strongly infused with an ideal of international cooperation, and the ritualistic exposition of the rules of positive law sanctioned by the practice of States. Persistent attachment to legal formalism, and the absence of constructive effort to reduce disparate or heterogeneous notions to some unity, bear witness to intimate hesitations and contradictions of thought.

An effort at innovation was made by authors who, realizing the need to "rethink" international law and to subject it henceforth to work in depth, devoted special studies to the revision of its fundamental data. Their common weakness was excessive confidence in the virtue of abstract reasoning. The attack that they mounted on the absolute conception of sovereignty was conducted with more brilliance than discernment; it often displayed the utopian or antihistorical spirit that is apt to be widespread in periods of political or social upheaval.[14] The fact was overlooked that, like all legal theories, that of national sovereignty is in the last analysis only the projection of certain realities into the domain of doctrinal constructions.[15]

Amid these gropings and these unsuccessful sorties certain authors of the interwar period nevertheless gave evidence that they accurately appreciated the inadequacies of the voluntarist positivism of the preceding period. Some had the merit of breaking with formal methods, all too often sterile, and of seeking to re-establish contact between the realm of norms and that of moral and social realities.[16]

In the final result the doctrinal effort bore fruit. To be convinced of that it is only necessary to compare the boldness of thought, a little confused in its exuberance though it has sometimes been, evidenced by the writings of the last thirty years, with the narrow, stereotyped views of most nineteenth-century authors. By its frontal approach the discussion of fundamental problems prepared minds

14 This is a good example of scientific autosuggestion: "A change in jurisprudence is interpreted as a change in the law." U. Campagnolo, *Nations et Droit*, p. 145.

15 J. L. Brierly, "International Law: Some Conditions of Its Progress," in the review *International Affairs*, 1946, p. 353: "Unfortunately theories of sovereignty are only formulas which academically-minded people have invented from time to time in order to explain certain facts about the way in which States behave."

16 For example, Max Huber's well-known monograph *Die Soziologischen Grundlagen des Völkerrechts*, and the course given at the Academy of International Law, The Hague, by D. Schindler, *Contribution à l'étude des facteurs sociologiques et psychologiques du Droit international*, *Rec. A.D.I.*, vol. 46 (1933).

for a total revision of ideas, replacing the legal atmosphere of the last century with fresh air.

For this work of doctrinal renovation, many internationalists sought inspiration in two general theories of law which, after the war of 1914-1918, had their hour of fame: the sociological positivism of Leon Duguit and Hans Kelsen's pure science of law. Certain similarities have been observed in the thought of these two authors. Duguit himself emphasized the affinity. Their work is related in certain common objectivist tendencies. Both very rightly tried and found wanting the voluntarist conceptions of the basis of the law. But there the resemblance ceases. Duguit's realism, a little short of the mark as it is, is as the poles removed from Kelsen's transcendental logic; his sociological bent, always closely though often unconsciously associated with the idea of purpose, is the reverse of the relativism of the leader of the Vienna school. Duguit accepted neither the total separation between the world of facts and the world of norms, between the *Sein* and the *Sollen*, so much emphasized by Kelsen, nor the dangerous identification of law and State. Between the two doctrines there are less real connections than false analogies; the spirits that animate them are entirely different.[17]

Duguit exerted an incontestable influence on the doctrine of international law immediately after the first world war and in the earliest years of the League of Nations. This was due less, however, to his demonstration of an objective law, which is inadequate and in certain respects contradictory, than to the punishment he administered to the notion of sovereignty as the law-creating power. "His great concern was to eliminate power as the source of law."[18] His distinction between normative and constructive rules, corresponding to F. Geny's between the given and the construct, is correct in its principle if not in its scope, which he often and obviously made too absolute.[19]

Being profoundly liberal, Duguit thought he could base the rule

[17] G. Davy, *Le Problème de l'obligation chez Duguit et chez Kelsen*, Archives de Philosophie du Droit et de Sociologie juridique, 1933, pp. 7 seq.

[18] M. Hauriou, *Précis de Droit constitutionnel*, 1929, p. 12. "The essential thing," wrote Duguit, "is to understand and to assert with tireless energy that there is a rule of law superior to the public authority limiting it and imposing duties upon it." *Traité de Droit constitutionnel*, vol. III, p. 548.

[19] Certainly the role of the State in law making is reduced too far if it is conceived as limiting itself to recognizing and equipping technically a law already complete in that "mass consciousness" to which Duguit decidedly sacrificed too much.

of law upon men's direct perception of social necessities. According to him, the State would merely implement this rule. It is itself subject to it, being itself only means and not end. The decisions of rulers are binding not because they express a legally competent will but because they accord with the social imperatives springing from the sense of solidarity and of justice.

Duguit's mistake was to push to an extreme ideas generally sound in their foundations and, still more, to take too easily as given any object of his conviction or hope. It is easily understood that, as a "positivist," he should not have inquired into the metaphysical or transcendental considerations which the philosopher of law finds at the foundation of authority and the power to command. It is not so obvious why, as a "realist," he so far ignored the psychological factors that group men around the State and in their consciences transmute subjection into a duty. The sovereignty and personality of the State, denied by Duguit, are ideas that cannot be explained by mere technical necessities such as the need to ensure the continuity of power and the concentration of responsibilities. Whether one likes it or not, they are historically in the eyes of men the expression and symbol of the supreme values of the nation, those to which the individual believes himself bound to sacrifice his own interests and even his life. These are matters are of emotion and passion which speculation tends to neglect, but whose depth and power the least political shock reveals.

As for the political consequences of his thesis, Duguit was certainly not aware of them. Opposing the notion of subject of right and, more generally, of any subjective right at all, he did not realize the terrible danger to which his theory of objective law, based solely on a social solidarity interpreted in fact by the holders of power, can expose individual liberties.

It easily leads to sacrificing human ends and values to the State, that is to say to politics. To reverse the liberal direction of Duguit's objectivist system, it is only necessary to substitute for the concepts "duties of solidarity" and "social ends" those of "civic duties" and "State or national ends." Experience has proved how easy it is to slip from one to the other. As everyone knows, one of the characteristic traits of totalitarian legislation was to eliminate the category of subjective public rights, which is an essentially liberal concept.[20]

20 This danger, already clearly perceived by R. Saleilles in 1910 (*De la personnalité juridique*, pp. 545-557), was later emphasized by Prélot, "La

The literature of international law between the two wars felt the influence of some of Duguit's unrealistic views. Its utopian character and its deceptions spring partly from this source.

Hans Kelsen's neopositivism is of all contemporary doctrines the most deliberately and most completely isolated from social realities. For the author "any content whatever can be law," for the positivity of norms depends solely on their quality of being logically reducible to one fundamental (and moreover hypothetical) norm (*Grundnorm*), regarded as the ultimate source of the legal order. So understood, law can be analyzed as a formal technical order, with no intrusion of substantive elements not already molded into forms.[21] It is reduced to the ordering of competences, to the schematic arrangement of powers and attributions; it is stripped of the teleological direction which nevertheless, as Kelsen admits, has never ceased dominating it. The ultimate source of *reine Rechtslehre* is to be found in philosophic relativism.[22]

The pure theory of law, as presented by its founder in those of his works that are most truly characteristic of his school, is the most significant manifestation of a certain contemporary tendency to limit arbitrarily, on pretext of science or unity of method, the subject matter of law, narrowing or distorting legal reality. Kelsen justly emphasized the inability of voluntarist positivism to explain the compulsory character of law; but his own relativism brings him up against the same obstacle. It leads him, again, to admit the perfect indifference, from the point of view of legal science, of the choice between the primacy of municipal and the primacy of international law. This is logical, moreover; for if the validity of positive law depends solely upon a choice of two initial hypotheses equally acceptable in law, it would be impossible to make the existence of supra-State rules convincing to anyone who adopts the exclusive validity of municipal law as his fundamental hypothesis.[23]

Théorie de l'Etat dans le Droit fasciste," *Mélanges Carré de Malberg*, p. 465, and by R. Bonnard, *Le Droit et l'Etat dans la Doctrine nationale-socialiste*, pp. 264 seq.

21 M. Hauriou, *op.cit.*, Preface, p. viii.

22 In his later thought Kelsen seems to have abandoned some of the dogmatic rigidity of his earlier writings: *Allgemeine Staatslehre*, 1925; *Reine Rechtslehre*, 1934; *Les Rapports de Système entre le Droit interne et le Droit international public*, *Rec. A.D.I.*, vol. 14 (1926). Some attenuations are to be found in his recent works: *General Theory of Law and State*, 1945; *Principles of International Law*, 1952.

23 The validity of the fundamental norm, upon which that of all subordinate

There is no branch of law that lends itself less easily than international law to this reduction to a system of the mere imperatives of abstract logic. The dangers of schematic conceptualism are never more apparent than when it is applied to relations where particular situations are far more important than general situations and where, consequently, general norms are still far from occupying the place that belongs to them in the internal order.[24]

Kelsen has seen clearly that the theory of international law oscillates between an individualist conception of the State and a universalist conception of humanity, between the subjectivism of State primacy and the objectivism of the primacy of the international order.[25] He was not mistaken in considering the traditional notion of sovereignty incompatible with a true international legal order. But his purely formal image of the legal order led him to an identification of the State with norms—an identification at once unreal and mortally dangerous for his objectivist view of law. It is by no means as complexes of norms that States are seen to enter into relations with one another and to acquire rights and assume responsibilities. The State is a social reality whose elements and activities cannot be brought within the confines of so transcendental a view. Graver still in its consequences is the distortion which this "panstatist legal monism"[26] imposes upon law. Consubstantial with law, the State cannot violate it. Regarded from this point of view, the elimination of the State-law dualism, sought by Kelsen for the sake of systematic unity, is immediately seen to lead to the exclusion of all resistance to laws dictated by the State in conformity with the normative order of which it is the supreme personification. This consequence is entirely irreconcilable with the doctrine's objectivist point of departure.[27]

---

norms depends, is in Kelsen's thought an assumption; but he does not escape the necessity of explaining the choice. This ultimate justification is according to him to be found in the title conferred by mere historical priority. "The ultimate hypothesis of positivism is the norm authorizing the historically first legislator. The whole function of this basic norm is to confer law-creating power on the act of the first legislator and on all the other acts based on the first act." *General Theory of Law and State, op.cit.*, p. 116.

24 See infra, Book III, Chap. I, "A Problem of Method."

25 *Les Rapports de Système, op.cit.*, p. 325.

26 G. Davy, *op.cit.*, p. 19.

27 Cf. François Guisan, "La Science juridique pure: Roguin et Kelsen," in *Zeitschrift für Schweizerischesrecht*, 1940, p. 229; G. Leibholz, *Les Tendances actuelles de la Doctrine du Droit public en Allemagne*, Archives de Philosophie du Droit, 1931, p. 212. It is understandable that this normativist and formal

By his purely normativist method, Kelsen proposed "to exclude absolutely and vigorously any intrusion of the political point of view.[28] This was an impossible undertaking in a domain where the State (the unit of power), and consequently politics in its individualism and fluidity, still operate with clearly preponderant effect. His mistake lay in trying to apply abstract logical procedures to the fundamental problems of international law, which for the most part are situated on the borders of law. Such procedures are at most usable in certain very developed disciplines where legal thought can deploy the resources of a tried technique and of a really autonomous method. The abuse of intellectual constructs led the author to that "extreme and, so to speak, dizzy" height so well described by Fr. Gény, where "the idea, completely detached from its object, finds its own realization and lives a life of its own deprived of all contact with the living reality. At this point, abstraction can play nothing more than the role of a tool operating in a vacuum."[29]

---

interpretation has seduced certain minds that have claimed to reduce the problem of the basis of law to one of authority or choice of rulers. In their eyes, that is law that is propounded as such by authority, the procedure of issuing norms alone being a concrete and observable fact.

[28] *Les Rapports de Système, op.cit.*, p. 248.

[29] *Science et Technique en Droit privé positif*, vol. I, p. 133.

BOOK II

GENERAL RELATIONS OF POWER AND LAW IN INTERNATIONAL RELATIONS

"The greatest disorder of the mind is to believe things because one wants them to be so and not because one has seen that they are so." J. B. BOSSUET.

ENTRENCHED in its formal positions, doctrine long evaded direct confrontation of international law with politics. At times it simply ignored the political, at others it attempted to eliminate it by artifically bringing even its most elementary data under legal criteria. The defects of such methods became increasingly marked as the profound upheavals in the life of the peoples forced the man of law to grasp realities more firmly. Law has everything to gain from dispelling by degrees "the dangerous mystery surrounding the antithesis of the political and the legal."[1] One segment of contemporary doctrine must be given credit for a new diligence in direct observation, a broader view of the factors of every sort that govern changes in international relations, and a better appreciation of the resistances offered by the present distribution of power to legal regulation.

[1] Jean Ray, *Des conflits entre les principes abstraits et stipulations conventionnelles*, *Rec. A.D.I.*, vol. 48 (1934), p. 637.

CHAPTER I. THE POLITICAL FACT: ITS CRITERION

POLITICAL DISPUTES. POLITICAL TENSIONS: THEIR VARIOUS FORMS

FROM a neutral and purely formal point of view, politics may be defined as the pursuit of the common good, understood as that which in a community should ensure the good of each in the good of the collectivity. In spite of its abstraction, this notion occupies an important place in the management of social relations. The less advanced the positive organization of these relations, the more essential that place is. By the twofold idea of order and justice that it embodies, by the free criticism that it invites, and by the achievements that it stimulates, the notion of the common good sets before the human spirit aims which, for all their shifting and changing, nevertheless mark the stages in the pursuit of an ideal. From this point of view, every attempt at organization of international relations is an offshoot of the notion of the common good.[1]

It is another matter when, abandoning the formal point of view for that of concrete achievements, we look for the elements of common welfare in the contingent versions of it presented by political institutions. When we are concerned with powers, we pass from the order of ends to that of means, from the ideal plane to the plane of historical experience, where all is relative. From this point of view, we find that the search for the common good has nowhere so small a place as in international relations. This state of affairs is intimately related to the present distribution of power among States that are sovereign and simply juxtaposed. It will endure so long as the ideas of order and justice have not been embodied in a supranational organization adequate to the notion of a common good in terms of ends transcending the Nation-State. But it should be borne in mind that the common good is an accepted and not a decreed good, and that it will become a living reality only when "man has ceased to regard the State as the highest form of social organization."[2]

[1] For further discussion see: G. Burdeau, *Traité de Science politique*, vol. I, pp. 57 seq.; J. Dabin, *La Philosophie de l'ordre juridique positif*, pp. 153 seq.; J. Delos, "La fin propre de la politique; le bien commun temporel," *Semaine Sociale de France*, 1938, pp. 215 seq.

[2] G. Burdeau, *op.cit.*, p. 208.

We shall see that this very weak perception of common good prevents us from speaking of an international community as something already established. It prevents us especially from assimilating resort to force in the present regime of self-help to the legal sanction, monopoly of power in the internal order. We minimize the separation between them, and fail to get beneath the surface of things, if we see in self-help only the consequence of a lower degree of centralization in international society, particularly in those of its organs that are charged with coercive action.[3] The difference goes far deeper. There is no sanction properly speaking except where solidarities generally and firmly felt lend to the use of force the impersonal character of constraint in the service of law.[4]

Section I

The Criterion of the Political

A more or less random competition is today the normal relation between States. This is the fundamental political fact, historical result of the individualist distribution of power among national entities. An egocentric image of international relations, and the aspiration to preserve and to increase the power of the State relative to that of its competitors, are its natural fruits.[5]

Taking a political position is always an expression of the priority that a government assigns to certain interests of State. It is the resultant of all the forces which, at a given moment, weigh upon decision. In this connection it is impossible to isolate economic interests from major political decisions and treat them separately by what are traditionally called businessmen's methods. Economic solidarities exercise a pacifying influence in international relations only so far as political conflicts remain limited; they are powerless to disarm political antagonisms that are already consolidated.[6]

[3] See for example Hans Kelsen, *Principles of International Law*, 1952, pp. 15-16, 22.

[4] Cf. infra, Chap. II.

[5] The sociologists are right in seeing in peace between peoples "a state of sufficient contention of hostile forces rather than any generalized amity." E. Dupréel, *Sociologie générale*, p. 147.

[6] Bertrand Russell, *Power*, p. 123: "It has been customary to accept economic power without analysis, and this has led, in modern times, to an undue emphasis upon economics, as opposed to war and propaganda, in the causal interpretation of history." When the Hitler regime had shorn the League of Nations of its last chances of political action, it was thought possible to open

The specifically political quality is to be seen in the particularly close relation that rulers assert from time to time between the State and certain goods or values that they hold indispensable to its security or greatness. Object or matter provides no firm criterion in this context; much more suggestive, and the only useful guide from the legal point of view, is the external behavior of the interested States. "The notion of the political is not necessarily inherent in certain specific objects, as it is not necessarily absent from other specific objects"; having no fixed content, determinable a priori, it constitutes rather "a quality, a tone, that may belong to any object, that is attached preferably to certain objects but not necessarily to any. . . . One question, considered political today, may not have that character tomorrow, while another, unimportant in itself, may suddenly become a political question of the first magnitude."[7]

If it is so, it is primarily because the political is here in the highest degree the expression of vital and moving forces and because there is no possibility of locking up in a definition what is only tendency to constant change. There is clearly no question that can be classed a priori in a category labelled political, and it is equally impossible to list others in a category labelled apolitical. At the most it can be observed in fact that certain matters or questions generally have a political character at a given time, while others become political only exceptionally.

In international relations, dominated as they are by competition, the political reaction is externally marked by a special insistence in the governmental action designed to obtain satisfaction of a demand. From the outside, this insistence may appear out of all proportion to the actual importance of the stake; for it is the peculiar quality of the political reaction to be dependent on the connection that rulers see at any given moment between certain goods or in-

new paths for it by proposing that it seek in economic internationalism a mitigation of political tensions. Since then, similar proposals have been advanced whenever political antagonism has become so sharp as to leave them no chance of success; Kenneth E. Boulding, *The Economics of Peace*, 1946, p. 237.

7 H. Morgenthau, *La Notion du politique et la théorie des différends internationaux*, pp. 32-33. For Carl Schmitt (*Der Begriff des Politischen*) the State, expressing the political unity of the nation, is characterized by the power to decide unitarily between friends and enemies. His antithesis "friend-enemy," the essence of political opposition, is set up on a metaphysical and purely formal plane. The author's method endows political opposition with a rigid quality that is quite out of keeping with the fluidity of the political phenomenon observed in the reality of international life.

terests and the development of State power. Political thought turns towards action and, consequently, towards the future. The calculation of chances and of the ratio of opposing forces in their future development has an important place in it. It embraces all factors, even those that are merely potential or hypothetical, that might weaken or improve the relative position of the State.[8]

The prime necessities of coexistence and reciprocity gradually introduced among States the practice of modus vivendi which, in the normal course of events, coordinate and reconcile their interests sufficiently for them to avoid taking political positions too frequently. These necessities create solidarities that are translated into common value judgments, develop a certain discipline, and promote the formation of legal rules. This legal integration, product of history, is governed by factors of two kinds. It is limited to goods or values which governments have been brought by the exigencies of their mutual relation to regard as objects of collaboration. It makes progress in periods of relative order and calm when precedents can accumulate and practices become fixed; it is impeded when incessant upheavals prevent the necessary stabilizations in social evolution. In troubled times the negotiation of a currently typical convention may reveal factors of imbalance which by their novelty and the absence of recognized criteria bring the discussion back to the political plane.

Interests that governments hold to be intimately connected with the preservation or development of State power must be classified as very generally refractory to legal integration. Treaties that touch these interests—agreements on armaments or conventions bearing upon military or naval policy—spring from momentary convergences of policy and do not survive their passing. This is scarcely-cooled political matter which law only rarely succeeds in jelling.

A policy of prestige, whether it aims at preserving the *status quo* or has imperialist aims, widens the circle of political interests. It assumes a haughty and forbidding posture, designed to give an impression of strength. The amplitude of the goals that the State adopts and of the means that the concentration of its internal powers provides, together with the support found in the nationalism of the masses, imposes increasingly broad and numerous objectives

[8] The opposition between political and legal thought is not here on the level of the basic idea that guides them. The idea of law, as the image of a social order regarded as desirable, also turns towards the future. It is the rule of positive law, expressing a temporary stabilization, that conflicts with political dynamism.

on "high policy." The hypertrophy of power makes its reasoned use difficult for the statesman.[9]

Political interest, being by definition that of which the State seeks to retain discretionary judgment, escapes any conventional regulation that would restrain this power. This feature of the political is especially notable in those clauses of collective conventions that make provision for amendment. Technical conventions easily permit amendment by qualified majority determined by votes weighted according to the relative importance of interests and contributions. Political conventions, which by their nature exclude such weighting, retain the unanimity rule.

Section II

Political Disputes

While political interest may have the most indefinite objects and reveal itself by the most varied attitudes, political disputes imply a conflict circumscribed in object, characterized by opposing claims and by the disposition of the adversaries to insist upon personal settlement.[10] This disposition is particularly marked in questions of high policy, where the stake consists of essential interests of the State regarded as a unit of power. We are here in the political domain par excellence, where, owing to their fundamental individualism, questions are kept within the circle of discretionary appraisal and evade the regulatory function of law.

It was in the attempts, vain as they were, to classify international disputes according to their justiciability that the political criterion was for a long time most carefully studied. Before the war of 1914-1918, international-law doctrine, close enough on this point to international realities, was agreed in regarding disputes of major importance as not arbitrable or justiciable. The authors who had gone most deeply into the difficulty found precise expression for their thought in the observation that this class must include all those disputes whose settlement "might seriously affect the future possibilities of State power.[11] Others remarked that questions of

[9] On the accuracy of calculation demanded by reason of State in its classic period, see Friedrich Meinecke, *Die Idee der Staatsräson*, 1929, pp. 510 seq.

[10] Cf. G. Morelli, *Estinzione e Soluzione di Controversie internazionali*, Milan, 1950.

[11] Cf. T. W. Balch, "Différends juridiques et politiques," *Revue Général de Droit international public*, 1914, p. 181; Westlake, *International Law*, vol. I, pp. 300 seq., pp. 350 seq.

high policy are by reason of their character not reducible to rational analysis and in any case scarcely susceptible of formulation in legal terms.[12] Though summary, these pointers, confirmed as they were by the arbitral practice of the period, might have led to the gradual determination of the inner nature of the political in its whole complex social reality. The somewhat superficial movement towards rapid extension of arbitral and judicial settlement, beginning immediately after the League of Nations was established, deflected doctrine from this realistic observation and led it into paths that seemed to promise more immediate results.

This explains how legal and political disputes came to be represented as belonging to two entirely distinct categories, the applicability of the rules of positive international law forming the line of demarcation. Such a criterion satisfies the requirements of judicial settlement, the question of justiciability being decided by setting over against one another the rules of international law and the terms of a claim. Any claim supposed to relate only to acquired rights, to relations belonging exclusively to the past, would thus be regarded as adapted to judicial requirements. Such legal optics do not reach the political problem. "The notion of what is political and what is legal do not form an antithetical pair."[13] The same dispute may appear clearly legal to the man of law considering it solely from the point of view of the applicability of norms, and definitely political in the eyes of a government which, though not disputing this legal view, nevertheless refuses to surrender its personal protection of the interests involved.

These two points of view which, though not mutually exclusive, are in practice the starting point for opposite conclusions, were clearly brought out in a memorandum addressed in 1928 by the British Government to the Committee on Arbitration and Security of the Preparatory Commission on Disarmament: "It is because it is so generally felt that there are some questions—justiciable in their nature—which no country could safely submit to arbitration that it has been usual to make reservations limiting the extent of the obligation to arbitrate. These limitations may vary in form, but their existence indicates the consciousness on the part of Govern-

[12] A. W. Heffter, *Das europäische Völkerrecht der Gegenwart*, ed. Heinrich Geffcken, 1888, p. 231; Friedrich von Martens, *Völkerrecht*, ed. C. Bergbohm, vol. II, p. 466.

[13] H. Morgenthau, *op.cit.*; and the remarks of Antonio de Luna, *Annuaire de l'Institut de Droit international*, 44 (1952), vol. I, p. 328.

ments that there is a point beyond which they cannot count on their peoples giving effect to the obligations of the treaty. That there are limits beyond which a State cannot go in accepting binding obligations to arbitrate justiciable questions in all cases is recognized in Article 13 of the Covenant of the League of Nations. By that provision the members of the League accept *in principle* but not definitely the obligation to arbitrate justiciable disputes. The framers of the Covenant realised that it was not feasible to embody in the Covenant a definite and comprehensive obligation to arbitrate all justiciable disputes."[14]

These are observations that must be kept in mind if one is to get a correct view of those arbitration treaties that contain particularly long lists of disputes declared justiciable. Any list of this kind is to be explained by general political relations that make it highly improbable that disputes of real gravity will arise between the parties. Inclined as they were to give priority to legal settlements, the authors of the Covenant understood perfectly that, when peace is at stake, recourse to diplomatic methods which permit direct consideration of the relevant interests in their total reality may be preferable to judicial procedures. Doctrine went astray when, inspired it seems by the Locarno definition of legal disputes, it tried to provide a legal basis for what it has sometimes called "the rational conception of the political dispute." The notion of the political covers in international relations realities as yet uncontrolled not only by law but even by reason; its fluid and capricious character defies all attempts at classification.

There is yet another aspect of the political that confirms this way of looking at things. The most serious and most deeply felt grievances do not result in a real political conflict except when the party seeking redress occupies a place in the hierarchy of forces that enables him to exact it by his own means. The relative importance that States attach to their claims is thus not the sole criterion of political conflicts, nor by any means the sole measure of the danger that such conflicts constitute to peace.[15] This inequality raises the whole problem, which is primarily political, of the place of intimida-

[14] League of Nations, Official Journal, May 1928, p. 696.

[15] "Unredressed wrongs do not endanger social stability merely because they are profound or because the complaint is just: the question depends rather on the strategic position and number of the victims. Thus a small country may have to accommodate itself to conditions for which there is no moral justification." C. A. W. Manning, "Les éléments de la sécurité collective," in the work *La Sécurité collective*, published under the direction of M. Bourquin, 1936, p. 231.

tion in the settlement of international disputes. The problem has an important bearing on international procedures for the maintenance of peace. Any condition which makes the use of these procedures dependent on a certain degree of intensity in the threat to the peace is necessarily connected with the measures of reciprocal intimidation that the adversaries take or might take.[16] It may be that such measures are a priori closed to one adversary by reason of a decisive inequality of strength, or that the condition required may push him into artificial aggravation of the dispute by a particularly intransigent or insulting attitude or by incitement to violence. In practice it has been rightly concluded that the condition involves an examination of each case as it arises. If the parties must be allowed to choose the moment when the gravity of the disputes justifies in their eyes reference to the Security Council, the latter must be permitted to make its own estimate of this gravity and to guide its action accordingly.[17]

Section III

Political Tensions and Their Various Forms

Political tension is an antagonism which is still limited in the means of action employed, but which has already gone beyond any circumscribed or well-defined object. At this degree of intensity, the notion of object, which is inherent in that of dispute and essential for any reasoned discussion, recedes into the background. The statement of definite claims is succeeded by the much more clearly political disposition to take advantage of circumstances and make capital of old grievances and faults or weaknesses of the adversary in order to broaden the debate and change the ratio of power. That is why tensions are dangerous to peace: the antagonism that they imply and develop is more to be feared as it is less susceptible of rational analysis, less reducible to a criterion of justice or reason. Defying rational expression, they assume a passionate quality that makes them refractory to pacific settlement.[18]

[16] Cf. Arts. 12 and 15 of the Covenant of the League of Nations: "dispute likely to lead to a rupture"; Arts. 33, 34, and 37 of the United Nations Charter: "dispute, the continuance of which is likely to endanger the maintenance of international peace and security."

[17] On this point see the reply of the Committee of Jurists set up after the Corfu incident (1923).

[18] Cf. H. Morgenthau, *Politics among Nations*, pp. 343 seq. The United Nations Charter (Arts. 34 seq.) speaks of a "situation qui pourrait entraîner un

These characteristic elements of political tension have been well brought out by a German diplomat: "The strange thing about this crisis of August, 1939 was that the object in dispute between Germany and Poland was not clearly defined, and could not therefore be expressed as a concrete demand. It was part of Hitler's nature to avoid putting things in a concrete form; to him differences of opinion were questions of power and tests of one's nerves and strength."[19]

The man of law is naturally liable to misunderstand the character of political tensions and the conflicts to which they give rise. He is inclined to see in them only "the object of litigation," to cast in the terms of legal dialectic what is in the highest degree refractory to reasoning, to reduce to order what is essentially unbridled dynamism, in a word to depoliticize what is undiluted politics. The difficulty here is not only, as had been too often repeated, inadequate machinery for changing the law, or gaps in the legal system. This is a sphere into which, a priori, law rarely penetrates. Law can enter only where there are elements assimilable to it, that is to say facts or demands which, by reason of their regularity and a minimum correspondence with a given social order, can be subjected to reasoned analysis, classified under some known category, subsumed under an objective value judgment that in turn can serve as the basis for applying established norms.[20]

The most serious tensions are obviously those where the stake is a new distribution of elements constituting the relative power of States, such as territory, colonies, naval bases, raw materials. Here reason vainly searches for a criterion, coming to a dead stop before

désaccord entre nations ou engendrer un différend." The English text, more expressive, reads: "any situation which might lead to international friction or give rise to a dispute." The word "situation" describes a state of things which might give rise either to political tension, or to a dispute, depending on whether the conflict that may result from it has or has not a definite object.

19 Ernst von Weizsäcker, *Memoirs*, English translation by John Andrews, London, 1951, p. 202.

20 This initial obstacle to the legal appreciation of conflict arising from such tensions was well described by a former ambassador of the United States in London, Walter H. Page: "Now the philosophical pacifists have never quite seen the war in this aspect (i.e. as a robber's raid). They regard it as a dispute about something, about trade, about more seaboard, about this or that, whereas it is only a robber's adventure. . . . Now confusing this character of the war with some sort of rational dispute about something, the pacifists try in every way to stop it, so that the "issue" may be reasoned out, debated, discussed, negotiated. . . ." Burton J. Hendrick, *Life and Letters of Walter H. Page*, part II, p. 337.

the historical individuality of the State, which is nowhere more insistent on inviolability than in connection with the existing distribution of power. Reason may have been pushed to the bold height of a genuinely social conception of international relations, as it was by the sincerest promoters of the League of Nations; it is still paralyzed by the absence of objective rules of justice or reason strong enough to control the individualism of States.

The obstacle is again in evidence, though in lesser degree, when a legitimizing principle is brought forward, one which, like the principle of nationalities, is widely recognized but has not yet attained the degree of precision and authority that alone can make it the starting point for clear-cut conclusions. A good example is President Wilson's attempt to provide an objective basis for the reshuffling of territories demanded by the aspirations of peoples or by changes in political relations. President Wilson had originally regarded these peaceful redistributions, a counterpart of the guarantee of territorial integrity inscribed in Article 10 of the Covenant of the League of Nations, as governed by the principle of free national self-determination. As is well known, he subsequently shrank from the grave consequences of a League guarantee conditioned by so vague an idea and finally abandoned any concrete proposal of this kind. His attempt foundered on the individualist structure of international relations and the impossibility of reducing to common criteria of appraisal the extraordinarily complex historical factors that governed the division of human collectivities into territorial compartments.

All that international law has been able to do up to the present is to fix with some precision the conditions of establishing sovereignty in a given territory. Vague in its statement as in its applications, and dangerous in its anarchic consequences, the right of national self-determination cannot prevent such establishment. The result is that a territorial status brought about in one of the ways recognized by international law, by treaty for example, belongs to the reserved domain (Art. 2, para. 7, of the United Nations Charter).[21]

[21] A. A. H. Struycken, "La Société des Nations et l'intégrité territoriale," in *Bibliotheca Visseriana*, vol. I, p. 94: "It was impossible to close the eyes to the truth, clearly revealed by history in all ages, that the political division of the peoples and the fixing of their frontiers on the surface of the globe are the product of a more or less uninterrupted process of change, peaceful or violent, under the pressure of centripetal or centrifugal forces, the true nature of which is so complicated that it is to this day hardly understood." And on p.

Though it is true that in the present state of our knowledge tensions are more or less proof against reasoning, it may be that better acquaintance with the social factors of all sorts that enter into them would open up new perspectives. Especially promising would be an entirely unprejudiced study of a large number of historical cases embracing all the data that have contributed to the formation, recrudescence, or relaxation of given tensions.

From the political point of view, tensions show variable degrees of intensity. They also present different historical forms the analysis of which (a morphology of tensions) has only recently been attempted, but might contribute richly to our knowledge of political conflict. For this purpose political tensions may be divided into balanced tensions and hegemonial tensions. These categories differ in the distribution of forces in play and the extent of their field of operation.

The nineteenth century had known political tensions which the system of the European balance, defined by the common needs of the Concert of the Powers, was intended to moderate. If they were not always contained, but at times degenerated into wars, they still seem benign in comparison with the hegemonial tensions that made their appearance in the twentieth century. Alternating adjustments, with multiple and various points of support, left sufficient room for limited competition and for a time barred the way to the vast coalitions whose growing fixity and tenseness was to lead to world conflagrations. In the heyday of the balance, Canning liked to emphasize the variety and suppleness of its resources: "Thus, while the balance of power continued in principle the same, the means of adjusting it became more varied and enlarged. They became enlarged, in proportion to the increased number of considerable states—in proportion, I may say, to the number of weights which might be shifted into the one or the other scale."[22]

This was a mechanistic view, limited to diplomatic combinations; it took no account of the factor which sooner or later destroys the balance, namely the inequalities in the internal evolution of peoples, some of whom advance while others fall back. Political tensions are no longer in balance when these changes in depth incite some States

98: "Is it possible to state the objective moral principles, or does the sense of law common to humanity contain rules, that can lead to solving the many-sided problem of the justice and necessity of territorial readjustment among States?"

[22] December 12, 1826, *The Speeches of the Rt. Hon. George Canning*, vol. VI, London, 1828, p. 110.

to count only on force and set them on the path of separate alliances and the race for armaments. The diplomacy of balance then gives way to that of coalitions. In 1893 the ambitions and the clumsinesses of Germany drove Russia, long hesitant, to substitute for the still supple formulas of the Franco-Russian entente of 1891 the rigid clauses of a military convention.[23] A growing competition, henceforth without counterweights, broke the last curbs; to balanced tensions succeeded hegemonial tensions (between bloc and bloc).

In such a climate the movement is usually irreversible. Limited agreements may bring a passing relaxation; they cannot dispel the underlying tension. In spite of the Franco-German agreement of November 4, 1911, which brought to an end the difficult negotiations over Morocco, the political tension between the two countries retained all its sharpness.

By reason of the stakes, and the concentration of internal powers that it brings with it, hegemonial tension represents the highest degree of political antagonism. It is characterized by the ubiquity of its manifestations, by the diversity of the motives to which it appeals and of the means that it brings into action, and by a tendency to consolidation and organization according to its own peculiar demands.

Hegemonial tension—dubbed "cold war" by a generation obsessed by the idea of wars—is no longer a species of competition; its stake is domination. In its military aspect it takes the form of "a race for bases, allies, raw materials";[24] it has neuralgic points along what has been called "the international frontier" where the main opposing forces are in direct contact.[25] In full diplomatic peace, and long before the proclamation of the Continental blockade, the France of the Consulate waged against England an economic war to the death, with the "coastal system" as frontiers.[26] Today on the periphery of the two hostile worlds, from the Baltic to the China Seas, the cold war multiplies the zones of friction or sensitivity, with calculated pressures heightened or relaxed according to circumstances and aimed less at winning a premature decision than at testing resistances and asserting the prestige of presence.

In its ideological aspect, hegemonial tension takes the form today

[23] Boris Nolde, *L'Alliance franco-russe; les origines du système diplomatique d'avant-guerre*, 1936, pp. 577-692.

[24] R. Aron, *Les Guerres en chaîne*, p. 212.

[25] H. Duncan Hall, *Mandates, Dependencies and Trusteeship.*

[26] Cf. Bertrand de Jouvenel, *Napoléon et l'économie dirigée, le blocus continental*, 1942.

of an enterprise of subversion that has found its reply in a crusading program. The mobilization of minds and psychological warfare support the military effort. This tension calls for a strong centralization of power and finds sustenance at the sources of collective psychoses. It produces generalized anxiety, creator of distorting myths. It promotes moral justifications that confusedly associate with national objectives the imperatives of an ideological credo. The themes of provocation, encirclement, self-defense, the obsession of diminishing open space and markets and of inequality in the rhythm of increasing strength, all conspire to ensure the conformity of minds and stimulate their combativeness.

Given the present balance of forces, every hegemonial enterprise is based on long-term expectations and must count with time. The more alive both sides are to the risk of total war, the greater is the tendency for cold war to establish itself, to develop certain practices, and to obey certain conventions. These practices and conventions rest upon a tacit mutual recognition of a certain ratio of forces; they are shaped by this ratio, and they permit all pressures except such as would put an end to coexistence by creating the irremediable. These practices are well illustrated in the wars "by proxy," which involve indirect and carefully graduated participation in insurrections or civil wars. Such participation may extend from the provision of arms and munitions to the provision of contingents, from economic aid, military instruction, and equipment to promises of open intervention in case the course of events should threaten to crush the undeclared ally or extend hostilities to a zone considered vital.

If prolonged, political tensions, especially hegemonial tensions, confirm a fundamental observation of sociology: any lasting antagonism produces a measure of similarity in the opponents. "While the characters of aggressor and defender intermingle and merge, the opposing forces tend to balance each other and they take the same forms in order more completely to meet and neutralize each other."[27] Methods become similar: the psychological war preached by Secretary of State John Foster Dulles answers the Soviet Government's propaganda of subversion.

Hegemonial tensions, when really active, stimulate change in the political structure of the "in-between" countries. The fates of these transformations vary. Some have been consolidated to the point

[27] E. Dupréel, *Sociologie générale*, p. 151.

of becoming a common denominator in the policy of balance, while others have disappeared with the tension that produced them. Embodying an idea of Richelieu and the United Provinces, that the Belgian provinces should be made a buffer State, the Barrier Treaties were designed to make of them "a dike, a rampart, and a barrier" against the hegemony of France. The creation of the unitary Kingdom of the Low Countries sprang from the same idea, and Belgium, independent but neutralized, was its last embodiment. In Napoleonic Europe, Metternich and Talleyrand dreamt of peaceful coexistence in a shared continent, while the Emperor raised against England and Russia the ephemeral structures of his new kingdoms and the Confederation of the Rhine. In our day the struggle between East and West for world hegemony draws Europe along a similar road; the United States of America's patronage of "European communities" is the reply to the establishment of the satellite States.

By their nature, hegemonial tensions are the most difficult to reduce or eliminate. Diplomacy perhaps never suffered a more conclusive proof of this than in the disappointing proceedings when the representatives of the four great Powers met in Paris (at the Palais Rose) in the spring of 1951. The agenda called for a study of the causes of international tension in Europe and of means by which a real and lasting improvement might be brought about in the relations of the United States, the U.S.S.R., the United Kingdom, and France. In vain the delegates tried to separate the questions before them, to order and circumscribe the subject of their discussions. The implacable logic of their positions constantly brought them back to the fundamental issues of general policy, as these were shaped by the ratio of forces. The breakdown of these *pourparlers* on the question of including the North Atlantic Treaty in the agenda emphasized the real nature of the obstacle: no understanding was possible on the renunciation of a military agreement that was manifestly the result and not the cause of the existing tension.

The explanation of this setback is simple. In periods of high tension, each adversary tries to establish positions of strength, which, as time goes on, assume growing importance in his general policy. Any proposal which in aim or effect would threaten an adversary's positions of strength inevitably arouses his deepest distrust.

The same reason explains the failure of attempts to reduce armaments. It is to fight against the evidence to persist in trying to solve on the plane of military technique a problem which should be approached only by way of a preliminary relaxation in political relations. The same observation holds for international conventions designed to prohibit the spreading of false news or of charges of a sort likely to incite to war: like material armaments, psychological campaigns are a symptom much more than a cause of the disease.[28]

Political tensions may be interrelated in ways that vary according to the level on which they develop. The object of a tension may be confined to the interests of the Powers directly involved; it is then an independent tension. On the other hand, a tension may be interwoven in the complex of a wider tension that dominates it. In this case the reactions which it evokes are often affected by the dominant tension. This is particularly true when the dominant tension brings into play conflicting interests of great Powers. In the Russo-Turkish tensions over the regime in the Straits, the policy of the great Powers has had a decisive part.

It also happens that a generalized political tension between States, especially between great Powers, may momentarily invest an apparently limited stake with exaggerated importance, making it a center of fixation. The Free City of Danzig played this role in Germany's program for revising the frontiers laid down by the Treaty of Versailles. The same was true of the Free Territory of Trieste after the second world war, so long as this held its political significance in the East-West conflict. Such oppositions remain in a high degree political. The delimitation of their object is no more than apparent: the stake has the importance of a symbol and sets off a battle of prestige. These secondary and symbolic tensions frequently accompany hegemonial tensions; they are apt to multiply in zones where the rival policies most openly confront each other. Such tensions generally exclude recourse to public procedures. Experience with them tends at present to turn statesmen against such recourse. The unhappy experience of the Formosa debate in the Security Council (February 1955), the satisfactory results finally

[28] Though impossible between States separated by high tensions, such agreements have sometimes marked an at least temporary or apparent *détente* in international relations. This was the case with the agreements concluded in the interwar period between the U.S.S.R. and various States, and between Germany and Poland and Germany and Austria. Cf., on the international plane, the Convention on the Use of Radio, concluded at Geneva on September 23, 1936; and, on the rather discouraging prospects of a convention governing information or prohibiting the spreading of rumors likely to incite to war, Julius Stone, *Legal Controls of International Conflict*, pp. 318-323.

obtained in the problem of Trieste by traditional diplomatic methods, and Sir Anthony Eden's advocacy of those methods, may well mark a return to more discreet procedures better calculated to spare the susceptibilities of the parties.

The bearing of political tensions on the preservation of peace and on international law has for fifty years been too manifest to call for elaboration. They engender a noxious climate in which States, in mutual imitation, tend to reduce everything to political calculation. Repeated and often premeditated betrayals of the given word, aggressions or threats directed at the external independence of States, subversion of their internal organization, enslavement of human values under the authoritarian discipline of the State—all this, which is only too familiar, is the end result of growing tensions in which hypertrophied powers labor for mutual destruction.

These enterprises of strength, however, are only one aspect of things. Less conspicuous but no less evil is the paralyzing and deforming action of prolonged political tensions on the reasoned development of law. They produce a general insecurity which is in the highest degree prejudicial to the establishment of regular practices and to continuity in the application of law. They impede the development of general conventions by reducing the number of participants or multiplying reservations incompatible with their object; they promote unilateral denunciation. They restrict commercial channels to the point of strangulation, subjecting them to the artificial directives of economic nationalism. Even international organization itself deteriorates profoundly in spirit through the substitution of political objectives for goals of general interest. The risk is particularly great for international collective action, especially when it happens to coincide with a political tension between great Powers. Even when originally the object of such action was explicitly limited to resistance to aggression, it is liable to deviations imposed by the policy of that great Power that has assumed principal responsibility in the case.

It is true that some hegemonial tensions, while changing political structures, may facilitate transition from the traditional juxtaposition of sovereignties to a confederate or federal organization and thus make possible in the legal domain the progress that may be expected from a reduction of national exclusivisms. Everyone knows the hopes awakened in some quarters by plans for "European communities." These attempts display tendencies that cannot be neglected; but it is much too early to distinguish between the factors of calculated and lasting integration and the wholly political and contingent motives that connect them with the dominant tension.

Political tensions have an especially palpable influence on the settlement of international disputes. The absorption of these disputes in a test of strength covers up and renders unusable elements which, taken by themselves, could be rationally analyzed and formulated in terms of law. This surrounds them with a distorting *ambiance* impermeable to contradiction and gives them overtones of an ungoverned emotion that excludes any peaceful solution, particularly in the form of judicial settlement. In such circumstances governments fear the unforeseeable repercussions of an adverse decision and reject international adjudication.[29]

[29] See below, Book IV, "Politics and Judicial Settlement."

CHAPTER II. IS THERE AN "INTERNATIONAL COMMUNITY"?

BETWEEN the political fact and the law, the philosophers and jurists have always assigned capital importance to a conception of which, to tell the truth, neither group has taken great pains to establish the foundations or define the limits. This conception, more than any other, has led them to hasty conclusions or left them wandering in nebulous speculations. Belief in a community wider and higher than the political units into which men are divided certainly meets a demand of reason. But, though postulated by the law, does this demand correspond to historical reality? Or is it only an aspiration still too ill defined and too limited in its incidence to impose the idea of law and to find embodiment in institutions?

The classical doctrine of the law of nations rests on the postulate of an international society which orders and subordinates sovereignties for the common good of humanity. Such an image, as a social datum, can however be confirmed only by the habitual methods of observing and tabulating experience. Between political organizations historically constructed on foundations of national individualism, on the one side, and on the other an idea of order which presents itself as the ideal synthesis of human solidarities, thought, stimulated by moral aspirations and by a need for unity, can conceive a scale of values arranged in a desirable hierarchy. It cannot from a postulated harmony proceed to the conclusion of a social community. As for taking this as achieved because it would be socially good to have it so, this is a type of argument which, though common in displays of oratory, is nonetheless devoid of scientific value. Of these reasonings, as of all those built upon the primacy of the *Civitas Maxima* or the rationally necessary interdependence of society and law, it may be said that they take as proven precisely what requires proof: namely the existence of a sense of community and the willingness of particular collectivities to keep their conduct in conformity with the higher good of a universal community.

Every society rests at once upon material and upon moral factors. It is the resultant of solidarities active enough to call for an organization of power and sufficiently conscious of a common good to engender the idea of law and the sense of obligation.

Section I

Solidarities and Powers

Do international relations, as they are now, manifest true solidarities? Is power there ordered to the common good and so organized as itself to constitute a "factor of society"?[1]

It is in contact with the world outside that any social group differentiates and becomes conscious of itself; only against the stranger does its solidarity fully assert itself. The modern State owes its historical cohesion and strong individualization to external pressures and the sentiments of loyalty to the national collectivity that they have generated and stimulated. Its strong relief and its unique density are due to its character as framework of security and instrument of power. National solidarities have triumphed over internal tensions, even the most deep-rooted, such as those between class and class.

The international community has no such decisive factor of social cohesion. It has no substitute for it save the infinitely less powerful appeal to sacrifice, to a common supranational good. And this, a perception which is the source of all progress, is hardly accessible to the immense majority of men. Nothing makes the contrast sharper than a comparison of the reactions provoked in the two orders when their essential interests are at stake.

In the State it is the vital interests, the most highly political, that evoke the supreme solidarities. The opposite is the case in the international community. There one observes minor solidarities of an economic or technical order, for example; but the nearer one approaches vital questions, such as the preservation of peace and prevention of war, the less influence the community has on its members. Solidarities diminish as the perils threatening them grow. The solidarities that then assert themselves turn back towards their traditional home, the nation. On the rational plane, men do not deny the existence of supranational values; in the sphere of action they rarely obey any but national imperatives.

Neither the group mentality nor the actual structure of international relations permits any other state of affairs. Compare in this connection constraint in the international domain with coercion inside the state. The latter is accepted as an impersonal emanation of law in an order of subordination. In the order of juxtaposition,

[1] M. Hauriou, *Précis de Droit constitutionnel*, 1929, p. 15.

which is that of international relations, international collective action is not really depoliticized; at the least it still appears to be that of a majority against a minority and therefore liable to be deflected towards particular ends.[2] It will be so as long as the idea of a common supranational good has not implanted in human consciences a new sense of the human solidarities and of the discipline that they demand.

This state of things explains the strange paradox of international law in the matter of effectiveness. It is a law whose stronger parts, assured of regular observation in the practice of States, relate to questions that have no bearing upon truly vital problems, and whose weaker parts, consisting merely of formal prescriptions, concern the use of armed force and the choice of peace or war between peoples.[3] An optimistic philosophy long masked this profound weakness of international law. Just as the philosophers of the eighteenth century had dreamt of basing the social harmonies upon a reasoned coordination of human egoisms, nineteenth-century doctrine tried to place international law on the double foundation of the natural interdependence of national interests and a synthesis of sovereignties in an ideal community. To these flattering images the system of balance lent the frail support of an entirely materialist conception of power. Based upon the exclusive calculation of forces, keeping in reserve the *ultima ratio* of war, the system could not engender the solidarities constitutive of an international community.

The theme of natural solidarities lost all its appeal for generations that witnessed not only the two most gigantic conflicts in history, but also the incapacity of men to discern their underlying causes and prevent their return. The abandonment of this fallacious postulate might be a further step on the road of progress. When they give up indulging the illusion of spontaneous harmonies, men are already better prepared to accept the moral law of sacrifice to the common good.

In this bankruptcy of solidarities, power itself has a part, real, sometimes even considerable, but on the nature of which there is much misunderstanding.

[2] Cf. Erich Kaufmann, *Règles générales du droit de la paix*, *Rec. A.D.I.*, vol. 54 (1935), p. 559. A momentary agreement among the great Powers may make the application of sanctions effective. It cannot thereby give them the authority of the legal sanction, an impersonal expression of social solidarities.

[3] Hold-Ferneck, *Lehrbuch des Völkerrechts*, vol. 1, p. 88: "Das Völkerrecht bedeutet Ordnung im Kleinen, die aber stets bedroht ist durch Unordnung im grossen."

In the internal order, power is impersonal. That is why it can be seen as "lawful power," and why the State, in whose name it is exercised, can be regarded as an institution. So understood, power means pre-eminence of the element of authority and competence over the element of force or domination. It is by institutionalizing its power, in setting organic limits for it, that the State establishes the distinction between politics and law—a distinction inconceivable to one who thinks of the State solely as a unit of power.[4] Institutionalized power ceases to be pure coercion in the eyes of men. So long as they accept it as ordered to their common good, they associate it with ideas of social morality and justice; and if they do not always regard the law as just, they hold it just to obey the law.[5] Though this conception of power alone accounts fully for the institutional character of the State, it is by no means uniformly accepted even in the internal order. The appearance of dictatorships and minority governments, and even a rather general return to such regimes, have recently, so to speak, put power on trial. Some denounce it as an evil political entity, dedicated to its own indefinite magnification at the expense of law and the human freedoms. Others take an exclusively materialistic view of it, making brute force the sole prime mover in political relations. These are extreme simplifications, bearing the imprint of an epoch that was dominated by excesses of power.

In the external order the operation of power is determined first of all by its historical distribution among nations. It was to the State that nations assigned by a supreme delegation the external defense of that part of their interests that they held vital, that is to say essential to their independent existence or to their greatness. In this domain the strength and combativeness of national impulses are the mainspring of action; they keep power on the alert and forewarned against the enervation that sometimes weakens institutions in the internal order. The historical cohesion of the nation, largely due to external antagonisms, helps in turn to nourish these

[4] G. Burdeau, *Traité de Science politique*, vol. 1, p. 303: "The State is above all an institution by which the legitimacy of power is ensured."

[5] Even in the internal order, however, as is well known, power loses generality and continuity of action when it has to cope with interest groups whose newness and strength make them refractory to the established order. It then becomes supple and conciliatory, lending itself to procedures of discussion and compromise; it becomes politic in order to discipline forces with which it must reckon. The conflicts of capital and labor, especially when accompanied by strikes that endanger the country's economic life, are examples of such situations.

antagonisms to the detriment of the bonds of community. By projecting them upon the moral plane of loyalties, national cohesion sublimates the propensity and formidable capacity of the modern State to justify as supreme needs of the nation the objectives of a high policy which is too often unrelated to human interests.

This indicates how mistaken regarding the nature of the obstacles to establishing an international community are certain opponents of sovereignty—statesmen who dream of dissolving it quickly in ingenious structures of integration, and jurists who, sacrificing on the altar of international community what they denounce as the "false dogma of sovereignty," believe that they have discovered in the abandonment of a doctrinal conception a decisive advance in the spirit of community. All of this, though it has some truth in it and starts from the best intentions, fails to get to the root of things. If the international community, or more accurately the sense of such a community, finds so little echo in individual consciences, this is less because power obstructs it than because the immense majority of men are still infinitely less accessible to the doubtless real but certainly remote solidarities that it evokes than to the immediate and tangible solidarities that impose themselves upon them in the framework of national life.

The peculiar role of national power in the external action of the State broadens with the conception of this role formed by the regime and the means at its disposal. The conception may become decisive in regimes that impress an authoritarian character upon power. It attains maximum efficacy when absolute ends are adopted as national objectives. Even in democracy, no power is less accessible to the international-community ideal than that which, in the course or at the end of troubled periods, assumes an abstract mission of political or social regeneration.

Historical center of national exclusivism, the State by its mere existence conduces to the intransigent assertion of sovereignty. It is therefore pure illusion to expect from the mere arrangement of inter-State relations the establishment of a community order; this can find a solid foundation only in the development of the true international spirit in men. Thus what concerns us is much less the principle of power than "the position taken by the regime with regard to the very notion of power."[6] What is decisive is the dis-

[6] Jean Rivero, "Introduction à une étude de l'évolution des sociétés fédérales," *Bulletin international des Sciences sociales*, 1952, vol. IV, no. 1, p. 30.

position within the State to keep its action within the limits assigned to it by a functional conception which orders power to human ends instead of dedicating it to its own indefinite extension. Relations between States cannot be isolated from the relations between man and power within the State. There will be no international community so long as the political ends of the State overshadow the human ends of power.[7]

Section II

Morals and the Problem of Obligation

Neither politics nor law will ensure equilibrium and peace in the world without the "moral infrastructure" to which an eminent contemporary jurist, facing the supreme disappointment of his life, dedicated his last book.[8] When all has been said about the rule of law and the obstacles that are placed in its way by the political drive of power, it is to morals that we must return.[9]

It is true that for a long time now the experience of power has taught those who exercise it the useful role that a certain morality should play in it. Infinitely better informed than the theorists on the psychological conditions necessary for their action, they are careful not to make the mere assertion of brute force their active principle. It is by turning the confused moral aspirations of the masses to its profit, and by posing as a moral order, that the State reinforces its power and ensures its stability and duration. There is "a politics of morals" which transforms social constraints into group loyalties based upon moral imperatives.[10]

These connivances of politics and morals are explained by the duality of human nature. Being reluctant to see in brute force the one law of social intercourse, men are prone to transfer their moral aspirations to the group to which they belong, to hypostatize the power which emanates from it, to idealize in it their lusts and their demands. Of the State as ethical power as well as instrument of

[7] See below, Chap. IV, "The Human Ends of Power."

[8] N. Politis, *La morale internationale*, 1942.

[9] M. Hauriou: "The highest forms in which the directing idea of an institution finds subjective expression in it are not properly speaking legal; they are moral or intellectual." *Aux sources du droit*, Cahiers de la Nouvelle Journée, no. 23, p. 117.

[10] Maurice Muller, "Réflexions sur la politique de la morale," *Annales de la Société suisse de Philosophie*, vol. III, 1943, p. 106.

dominion, they expect the rigorous combativity that can get for them what is inaccessible to their individual weakness.[11]

It is in international relations that these deviations of group morals become most apparent. Even when they violate treaties, rulers are careful not to dispute the respect due to the given word; from the written text they appeal to some higher principle, to the right of self-preservation, to inevitable change, to natural law, to the laws of eternal morality. Every political enterprise is clothed in some kind of moral justification, every program of expansion combines with the use of force the formulas of a civilizing ideal. To see in this nothing but calculation or hypocrisy would prove a singular ignorance of the psychology of peoples. The morality that peoples practice in their mutual relations is in large measure the product of their historical partitioning. They are refractory to a higher morality only because their sentiments like their interests continue to gravitate exclusively about the units which are today the Nation-States. These, though theoretically subordinate to the higher unity, are in fact real and almost absolute centers of moral cohesion and material force. The behavior of the peoples depends upon the more or less intimate relationship existing at the time between the protection of certain national interests and the role of the State as a framework of security and instrument of power. "Sacred egoism," the fascist formula, was only the blustering expression of a certain collective morality—that which makes the national good the supreme good and civic duty the absolute duty. The old reason of State dictated the calculated decisions of rulers; the contemporary State morality associates the obscure and emotional impulses of an entire nation with the enterprises of power.[12]

This means that the justification of political decision by invoking the common good calls for serious reservations in the relations of States. The idea of the common good here easily merges with that of State interest. The eternal propensity of rulers to justify their

11 Reinhold Niebuhr: "There is an increasing tendency among modern men to imagine themselves ethical because they have delegated their vices to larger and larger groups." Quoted by E. H. Carr, *The Twenty Years' Crisis* (1919-1939), p. 208; L. Sturzo, *Politique et Morale*, Cahiers de la Nouvelle Journée, no. 40, p. 15.

12 K. Mannheim (*Mensch und Gesellschaft im Zeitalter des Umbaus*, pp. 50-52) shows the immense danger of political immoralism when, no longer a monopoly of government, it spreads, most often unconsciously, through all the strata of society. In the same vein F. Meinecke (*Die Deutsche Katastrophe*) speaks of the "Machiavellianism of the masses," *Massenmachiavelismus*.

will to change by a morality superior to the law in force finds expression in our day in the watchwords of ideological crusades. In this deterioration of values lies the whole problem of the relations between politics and international morals and law. The man of politics can accommodate himself to this suspect alloyage which produces so useful a compromise between interest and duty in the depth of consciences; the man of law must remember the deviations of which it is the source. These are not conspicuous in the ordinary course of international relations, where competition is limited to secondary interests and is governed in accordance with well-known and commonly accepted criteria; but they spring into high relief in the problems connected with the defense of vital State interests. Formidable unknowns weigh upon the decision called for in this defense: there are no common criteria of value, the procedures of peaceful change scarcely exist, ignorant and impassioned opinion takes unforeseeable directions. To these must be added a factor of amorality consisting in the cold calculation of chances and the anonymity of the sacrifices involved. The same man who is moved by the death of a single person reduces anonymous hecatombs to a question of statistics. The law of large numbers, which is precisely that of politics raised to the highest power, subjects the statesman's thought to pressures unknown to private morals.[13]

International collective action itself, moral and legal reaction against the attack upon the law and the peace of the world, bears the marks of these defects and deviations. The sanctions decreed by the League of Nations against Italy were paralyzed by inadequate realization of their League duties on the part of the States members. The action of the United Nations in Korea was essentially American; its conditions and limits were constantly a matter of debate among the Western Powers. It was as easy for the Republican secretary of state, Mr. John Foster Dulles, to speak of it in 1953 in the realistic terms of a policy of strength as to place it with his predecessor on the moral plane of collective resistance to unjust aggression (speech of January 27 of the same year).

What we must understand, and have the courage to say, is that the transition from State to international morality will never take place by way of a mere spatial broadening of the present moral attitudes of men. The historical distribution of power has implanted

[13] "Politics begin where the masses are," said Lenin, "not where there are thousands, but where there are millions, that is where serious politics begin." Quoted by E. H. Carr, *op.cit.*, p. 181.

group morals, which are particular morals, and the relations that spring from them rest neither on the perception of an extranational common good nor on the consciousness of a destiny common to all men.[14]

It has been asked whether certain political and social ideologies are not destined to take the place in the morals of the peoples held hitherto by the national motif. The question deserves examination in connection with the communist ideology. It is a fact that communism constitutes a body of doctrine that offers man a conception of life, that this conception in some aspects reflects the structure of a civilization that tends to become a mass civilization, and that finally communism provides an ideological basis for the organization of power. It is also a fact that the communist ideology now has frontiers that do not coincide with national frontiers and that it is working, sometimes effectively, to break down the historical unity of certain countries. But the facts do not justify regarding its influence as sufficiently predominant to make the Nation-State henceforth merely a center of subordinate allegiance. Favorable or hostile reactions to the communist ideology have nowhere been independent of national reactions. These latter are manifest in the two great Powers which in Europe and in Asia have made themselves the protagonists of communism, the Soviet Union and China. It may be doubted, moreover, whether communist ideology without their political and military intervention would have spread as it has in other countries. On the other hand the connection of the ideology with Soviet imperialism is certainly what aroused national resistance and stimulated rearmament, especially in Yugoslavia and Western Europe. At any rate, though more powerful and more combative, the communist ideology up to the present has a place in the international sphere analogous to that of former political ideologies: it does not replace; it intensifies national reactions.

More profound and more general in its influence upon international morals, as upon morals as a whole, is the increasing trend towards the depersonalization of the human being that an invading technology and the levelling of intellectual and moral values in a mass civilization bring in their train. The crisis of the elites is one of the most disquieting manifestations of this trend, for only the elites have a profound sense of individual liberty, that active liberty

[14] G. Burdeau, *op.cit.*, vol. I, p. 195. Cf. H. Bergson, *Les deux sources de la Morale et de la Religion*, p. 288; A. Dandieu, *Y a-t-il un seuil entre Cité et Humanité?* Archives de philosophie du droit, 1933, p. 204.

which implies the critical faculty and which exercises itself in discussion. Only they can have any idea of the constantly more complex moving forces of that international life which so few men personally live, and can bring into them a spirit of measure and tolerance. It has been justly observed that "so long as the elite was the directing force in modern States, nationalism could never become excessive."[15] The future of international morals depends upon the survival of personal values in a mass civilization.[16]

The basis of the obligatory character of international law is a theme that in all times has had a large place in the literature of the subject. The problem that it raises is not simply one of abstract reason; internal changes and the evolution of international relations unceasingly transform its elements.

Owing to the historical distribution of power among equal and merely juxtaposed States, the problem of obligation in the international order gravitates about the notion of sovereignty. Now, with sovereignty we enter a domain where subjective conceptions are inextricably mingled with contingent historical facts. Sovereignty is itself the product and image of this fusion. Because sovereignty in its existing structure is at once a political and a legal concept it offers no solution of the problem of obligation. The contrary has been asserted only by those who subsume the principle of power under the idea of command. In this view, law is what is established as such by authority. Obligation is justified solely by its formal source, by the stamp of authority—*jus est quod jussum est.*[17]

The mind is not satisfied with this authoritarian explanation which makes the governed unreasoningly accept the act of power. Such acts belong to the normative order only by the legitimizing title of satisfying the moral and social needs of men.

Many theories fail to recognize this specific character of law, a normative discipline which has for its object the ordering of the conduct of men by assigning duties to them. This is true of the sociological theories that represent the rule of law as a notion of experience: legal norms are those rules that are supported by

15 R. B. Mowat, *La Crise des Elites*; *l'Esprit international*, 1934, p. 246.

16 E. H. Carr, *The Soviet Impact on the Western World*, p. 103: "The contemporary problem of individualism in a mass civilization has no precedent anywhere in history."

17 See, among others, Decencière-Ferrandière, "Considérations sur le droit international dans ses rapports avec le droit de l'Etat," *Revue générale de droit international public*, 1933, p. 67.

enough force to ensure their regular observance in a given group. In the world of facts or phenomena, regularity, a matter of observation, permits the formulation of laws which are laws of causality. Such regularity is never of itself decisive in the normative sciences. It is of course a condition of obligation, in the sense that obligation assumes that the debtor has the very general possibility of fulfillment; it is not the foundation of obligation, which is governed by laws proper to it—the laws of final cause.[18]

The same inadequacy is apparent in the work of the positivist or neopositivist theorists who, though conscious of the necessity of founding international law on a norm independent of the will of States, make this norm merely a scientific hypothesis or the basic assumption of a system, or, again, a postulate which, though demonstrable from other points of view, it would be irrelevant to international law to demonstrate.[19] Products of abstract logic, these views vary from one author to another. The dichotomy which they propose to maintain sacrifices any justification of the obligatory character of the law to systematic unity.

The problem of obligation in international law is part of the problem of obligation in general and this in turn is a moral problem. The distinction between ethical and legal categories, reasonable in itself and in many ways necessary, must not be pushed to the point of completely separating law from the primary moral notions to which all the normative disciplines are attached as to a common stem. Between States as within the State, law belongs to morals insofar as the idea of the just, which forms its specific content, is inseparable from the idea of the good, which is a moral idea. What, then, in the international sphere, is the order of facts, interests, ideas, or sentiments that can provide the moral substratum of obligation? Merely to invoke the idea of an international community, as the habit is, is immediately to move into a vicious circle, for it is to postulate in men, shut in their national compartments, something that they still largely lack, namely the community spirit, the deliberate adherence to supranational values. No society has any legal foundation unless men believe in its necessity. The

18 This error appears again in certain positivist authors like A. Cavaglieri and K. Strupp, who, after making the norm *pacta sunt servanda* the basis of the obligatory character of international law, then present it as part of customary law. Care must also be taken to avoid the inverse exaggeration that separates the normative point of view, proper to law, from the explicative, which is that of sociology and politics.

19 See above, Book I, pp. 51 seq., pp. 65 seq.

ultimate explanation of society as of law is found beyond society, in individual consciences.[20]

The obligatory character of international law is not to be explained without a general theory of power in its relations with the social order. State systems, traditionally dominated as they are by the drive towards their particular political ends, feel nothing but repulsion for merger in larger social solidarities.[21] The intermittent contacts that they maintain in zones of minor interests, under the constant threat of a resort to violence that may put their very existence in question, cannot be regarded as manifestations of true community.

The international community is a potential order in the minds of men; it does not correspond to an effectively established order. It falls short of a legal community in that it lacks legal control of the use of force, which essentially implies three things: general adherence to the distinction between the legal and illegal use of force,[22] establishment of a system of peaceful change, and organized collective repression of aggression. The human ends of power alone, as we shall see, can provide a moral basis for its action. It is by a return to man, by linking the conception of the State, organization and means, to the person who is its end, that we can find, on the plane of an impersonal but not extra-personal common good, the sole moral and legal justification of the obligatory character of international law.[23]

The idea of an international community belongs to those great intuitions, to those "civilizing ideas"[24] which, though slow in their action and subject to eclipses, are nevertheless positive forces that generate political and social change. The most intransigent realist cannot deny their reality or their strength, for it is observation itself that establishes the refusal of man's active nature to consider

[20] H. Bergson, *Les deux sources de la Morale et de la Religion*, p. 102: "The error would be to believe that moral pressure and aspiration find their final explanation in social life regarded as a mere fact. It is said that society exists and by that very fact necessarily exercises a constraint on its members and that this constraint is obligation. But first, in order that society may exist, the individual must bring to it a whole group of innate tendencies; society, then, is not self-explanatory."

[21] G. Scelle, *Précis de droit des gens*, 1932, vol. I, p. 34.

[22] "The most elementary distinction that any legal system may be expected to make," rightly observes J. L. Brierly, *The Rule of Law in International Society*, Acta Scandinavica juris gentium, Nordisk Tidskrift, 1936, p. 15.

[23] See below, Chap. IV, "The Human Ends of Power."

[24] M. Hauriou, *Précis de Droit constitutionnel*, pp. 62-63.

itself subject to ineluctable laws and the unwillingness of his moral nature to regard as invariably just what is effectively imposed in fact. All moral judgment involves elements that transcend the results of experience; all human activity postulates some ideal the pursuit of which is the sole alternative to passive contemplation.

CHAPTER III. SOVEREIGNTY AND INTERNATIONAL ORGANIZATION

"The world is a comedy for the man who thinks, a tragedy for the man who feels." OLD SPANISH PROVERB.

Section I

Sovereignty in the External Order

IT IS generally recognized today that the successive legal conceptions of sovereignty are reflections of historical changes in political power both in its internal organization and in its external relations. What doctrine is still unwilling to admit is the persistence in the reality of international life of a conception of sovereignty which in some respects contradicts the doctrinal conception. Doubtless the contrasts have been exaggerated. The politician does not usually mistake the limits imposed on State action by the existence of other States. In the ordinary course of things he accepts the duties and burdens which these limits imply. But the fact remains that over against the law the State holds in reserve the plea of sovereignty. A unit of power, it balks at being a mere subject of law. It proposes not only to define for itself those of its interests that it holds vital but also to defend them with all the means at its disposal, including that of armed force, the use of which in the external order is the negation of the common law of coexistence.

In this political perspective, sovereignty shares the concrete and eminently contingent character of all political conceptions. In fact there is often little relation between the measures that it dictates to Powers of the first magnitude, animated by vast ambitions, and the attitude that small States take in wholly similar circumstances. Of course, considerations of prudence, the desire for an economic superiority that finds in a peaceful climate its best chance of development, or the wish not to interrupt a sequence of political events that is proceeding to their advantage, may moderate the claims of the great. When moderate in substance, these claims readily take legal form. But adjustments of this sort, counselled by convenience, do not alter the political character of sovereignty. At times dangerous for peace, when a stubborn will to change meets an equally resolute will to preserve the *status quo*, at times critical for law, when a superior force has only a feeble resistance to reckon with, sovereignty unveils and takes command—the sovereignty fixed in political thought by the secular distribution of power among nations and immensely reinforced by an unprecedented concentration of powers in the modern State.[1] It then reveals the advanced positions that it has never abandoned since States took their stand on the negative idea of equality and, determined to be independent, declared themselves supreme.[2]

No legal construction must mask this political face of sovereignty. Law can progress only if it does not deceive itself as to the realities that it seeks to order.

The legal image of power is of course never a mere reflection of the forces that constitute and animate it. This image always tends to give power a direction that may deviate more or less from that in which it is carried by its natural make-up and its spontaneous impulses. It is normal, even necessary, that there should be some difference between the largely individualist and unordered practice of external sovereignty and the conception that international law forms of it for purposes of common interest.[3] But this difference must not become so great that the law loses contact with life and thereby ceases to play its ordering role.

International-law doctrine has long tried to come to terms with sovereignty. It has attempted to domesticate sovereignty, to bend it towards a conception of its prerogatives that could submit to the imperatives of law. The vague and equivocal terms "limited" and "relative" sovereignty are indicative of these efforts. The first world war demonstrated their inadequacy, but the establishment of the League of Nations seemed to bring them closer to reality. To many jurists the League, despite the absence of the two great Powers destined from then on for a world role, looked at the time like a federation or confederation which by its vocation to universality might become coextensive with the community of the law of na-

[1] W. Röpke, *La Communauté internationale*, p. 88: "The problem today is not whether we must have sovereign States; it lies rather in the fact that with the growing trend of men to nationalization, Statism, and politicization, sovereignty attains a degree that threatens to break the last barriers and give it a total character."

[2] G. Gidel, *Droits et Devoirs des Nations*, *Rec. A.D.I.*, vol. 10 (1925), pp. 598 seq.

[3] D. Schindler, *Rec. A.D.I.*, vol. 46 (1933), p. 241.

tions. The vision of a legally organized society was in their minds linked with that of an institutionalized order within which power loses its subjective attributes and takes on a functional aspect. So understood it ceased to be sovereign and became a *competence*, that is to say an "objective power fixed by a legal system superior to the subjects of law."[4]

It will readily be conceded that this purely legal image of international relations is the one most satisfactory to the man of law. Because it is an order in force, law objects to a view of State prerogatives that makes them anything other than objective powers adapted to common social ends. Now, thirty years later, it must be recognized that the theory which reduces the rights of States to competences assigned and portioned by international law was too far ahead of the facts, and that the organic and highly juristic conception from which it springs is still very largely nothing more than an intellectual construct.

The theory is moreover disaffirmed by the data of history as well as the general conviction of States. As D. Anzilotti so justly observed, "international law is superior to the State in the sense that it sets a legal limit to the State's power, but not in the sense that this power is a delegation of international law. This last thesis, besides not being logically necessary, has against it not only historical experience, but also, and most importantly, the conviction of the States. To States, nothing is more repugnant than the idea of exercising a power conceded to them by the international order."[5]

Inspired by an excessively abstract and schematic view of international relations, the theory of the attribution of competences reflects the antihistorical mentality that characterized much of the doctrine prevailing between the world wars. Historically and logically, international law presupposes the State. Itself born of the plural system of States pre-established on a territorial basis, modern international law did not attribute to the State what the authors call its territorial competence: it could only accept the consequences

[4] G. Scelle, *Précis de Droit des Gens*, vol. I, p. 80.

[5] *Cours de droit international*, tr. Gidel, p. 51. Some theorists overlook the fact that even in the internal legal order, which is so much further developed, governments reserve to themselves a discretionary power in regard to certain questions—a power especially visible in constitutional and administrative law, which is more directly associated with the political interests of the State. This is the case in France with questions to which the theory of "acts of government" applies. The principle has been disputed; but there is no denying the persistence of the practice.

of this competence as one of the factual data of the exercise of political power.

The relation of sovereignty to law really depends on the degree in which the political power has been historically integrated in the legal order. The further this integration goes, the more does sovereignty, losing its character of domination, become legal authority.

Within national frontiers the State power has a historically acquired and more or less natural plenitude. Its political elements are there so far integrated in the law that the terms sovereignty and exclusive jurisdiction appear interchangeable. It will be observed, however, that this full integration has turned to the advantage of State individualism, international law here sanctioning the results of the historical walling off of nations within their frontiers. In the present state of international relations, it is premature to see in the idea of attribution of competences a general principle coordinating State powers and activities with a view to common social ends.

Whether we like it or not, sovereignty as forged by centuries of history belongs to politics as well as to law. Neither the articles of the Covenant nor those of the Charter brought any appreciable change in the discretionary power that States propose to keep over those interests which they hold vital, and experience shows that these interests still find shelter from the interference of international organs in the idea of "exclusive jurisdiction" or "domestic jurisdiction." There is always some risk in too quickly matching a legal theory to diplomatic instruments deeply involved in political relations; only actual use for a considerable period of time fixes their lasting significance and effective scope. There should then be no surprise at a fact observed by M. Charles Rousseau, "that no author has yet presented a general theory of competences in international law."[6]

The idea of attribution of competences has no basis except in relation to a federal order. Competence is then the attribute of organs devoted to the common purposes of an institutionalized group. The authors who have given the most study to federation, like M. Georges Scelle, have clearly seen the support that federal organization, based on free association, provides for a wholly legal view of the rights of the State. Whatever hope may be attached to the future of federalism, it is premature to place existing international relations on that plane and to regard as a bundle of legal

[6] *Droit international public*, 1953, no. 247, note 1.

competences the group of prerogatives and claims that are today embraced in the notion of sovereignty. The vices of a system are not remedied by abstract conceptions that denature the forces animating it; doctrinal anticipations cannot triumph over the age-old propensity of nations to make the State the guardian of their supreme interests. The possibilities of law here depend entirely upon the progress of international organization, and this in turn upon the evolution of man's spirit.

Section II

Law and Politics in International Organization

Ill suited to the historical structure of international relations, law proposes to assert itself in international organization. How does its action there combine with that of politics?

Thirty years' experience has demonstrated that any international charter calls for the particularly close collaboration of the politician and the lawyer. The reason is evident. From the moment when States no longer confine themselves to the occasional coordination of their interests and activities, but propose to establish a new order of international relations by subjecting these to organic and permanent regulation, the gap diminishes between "substance," formerly reserved for political decision, and "formulation," the particular task of the jurist. The business being one of entirely new construction, not merely of arranging or interpreting elements already legally integrated, the two approaches, political and legal, while remaining distinct, combine in the manipulation of ways and means. In this context the mission of the constitution-building jurist is as the poles removed from that of the jurist-codifier. Structure and composition of organs, fixing their attributes, distribution of competences, rules for collective decision-making, all these fundamental questions can be clearly conceived, expressed, or discussed only in terms of law. Their novelty and their technical character force the statesman, often ill informed on the constitutional aspects of international organization, to make constant appeal to the jurist.[7]

But the drafting of an international charter is, or should always

7 The reef in this legal orientation is in the facilities that it offers for formal planning. The draft plan of a European political community is an example of this architecture born of the speculative spirit. The minutiae of federal technique in it contrast singularly with the continuing uncertainty about the competence and attributes of the supranational authorities.

be, only the last stage in an enterprise which, to be adapted to life, demands at once a just appreciation and a new balancing of all the forces, political, cultural, economic, and social, that shape the structure of international relations. Associated in a common task, politician and jurist owe it to each other to get a clear perception of its object, without losing sight of the particular demands of their respective disciplines.

By its object, any organization of international relations tends to change more or less profoundly the conditions of exercise or even the principle of the distribution of political power among nations. For a long time, jurists regarded the federative phenomenon, which in a broad sense moves from a union of States to properly federal integration, merely as a succession of episodes consisting in a few State organizations given a particular structure as a result of international conventions or of their own constitution.[8] A descriptive analysis established the distinctive criteria of their constitution and classed them in categories corresponding to particular subjective characteristics. In varying degrees these States represented a particular order within the general legal order.

This perspective has been overreached by the magnitude and novelty of the problems raised by the present enterprises in organization on a world scale, as compared with the very partial experiments that history offers. Its inadequacy is especially apparent when we consider the aims of international organization and the principles that govern it. These are no less than the establishment of a pacific order by way of law.

This teleological and normative aspect of international organization defines the jurist's mission and distinguishes it from that of the sociologist as from that of the politician. Exempt from responsibility for errors that the complexity of the factual data and the uncertainty of the processes of investigation render almost inevitable for the statesman, he cannot escape the duty to penetrate the spirit of the enterprise to which he brings active cooperation or moral support, and to separate what is justified by the sincere desire for a better international distribution of power from what, under the mantle of ethics or law, is inspired by particular political aims. His role in this context cannot be that of the old Crown legist entrusted with the defense of his prince's interests. He must also put himself

[8] Georges Scelle has rendered the service of showing the fundamental unity of the federative phenomenon; see his *Précis de Droit des Gens*, vol. I, pp. 187-287. Cf. G. Burdeau, *Traité de Science politique*, vol. II, pp. 391 seq.

on guard against the idiosyncrasies to which his mind is naturally exposed; the prejudice of uniformity that inclines him to the abuse of generalization, and the tendency to sacrifice too much to form, thus isolating regulation from its social context.

In international organization all dogmatism must be resolutely banished. The short history of experiments in organization is strewn with the errors and defects for which dogmatism is responsible. At the head of the list must be placed those springing from the prejudice which, in reaction against a unitary sovereignty all too often in default, sees progress in any redistribution of power whatever. In this order of ideas there are neither valid precedents nor established principles. The thesis, for example, of the continual and irreversible integration of political units in always vaster collectivities is an intellectual construction which obstructs objective study and which is belied by historical facts.[9] The transformations of power, in particular its evolution towards federal forms, obey laws whose complexity tempts analysis but up to the present prevents any general conclusion.

But it is in the organization of international security that the errors of judgment and perspective have accumulated. The League of Nations tried to implement an abstract, almost metaphysical conception of security. This rested upon the idea of the equal interest of States in the maintenance of peace. A purely legal organization of security sprang from this image of an indivisible peace. When growing political tensions revealed its inadequacies, the States members returned to the practice of limited agreements and of alliances, disguising these in formulas general enough to be adapted to the League ideology.[10] The abstract and universal conception of international security is adapted to the impersonal perspectives of law; it contradicts political realities. It has been justly observed that the legal schema which in the time of the

[9] J. Rivero, "Introduction à une étude des sociétés fédérales," *Bulletin international des Sciences sociales*, 1952, vol. IV, no. 1. It is not even certain that one is justified in describing our epoch as that of the territorial super-Powers. The drive of nationalisms is today partitioning Asia into smaller political units as in the nineteenth century it fragmented the States of Europe; cf. J. Gottmann, *La politique des Etats et leur géographie*, p. 76. The phenomena of political structure must not be confused with the concentration of power.

[10] The compatibility of particular (regional) understandings with a universal security system is less a problem of law than of the efficacy of this system. The controversies to which it gives rise are identical with those that arose formerly in the internal federal order, in Switzerland notably on the occasion of the Sonderbund (1843-1848).

League of Nations served as foundation for the organization of that body implies for the associated Powers two conditions of fact in the absence of which it can be nothing but pure theory. One is such a fragmentation of material forces as would, while leaving it possible to carry on a sufficiently independent policy, permit regroupment against any aggressor whatever; the other, a sufficient political homogeneity to escape a priori obstacles to majority rule.[11]

To appreciate the work of San Francisco from the point of view of international security, we must distinguish its strictly political from its institutional aspect. Politically, it seemed more urgent in 1945 to preserve for the immediate future the peaceful relations between the great Powers than to organize the peace on an institutional plane. The postulate of unity of action among the great, unreal in itself, had its origin in the political desire to affirm an understanding which was already threatened but which everybody agreed was indispensable. The structure of the international organization was largely determined by this necessity.

To organize peace is essentially to establish an order of political relations that will preserve a measure of agreement among those who by virtue of their strength are in a position at once to guarantee and to disturb peace. To achieve this result and to make a reality of the directing role of the permanent members of the Security Council there would have had to be a minimum political settlement to establish a climate of confidence. A pretense was made of relying upon the institutions and the soothing qualities of an organization depending on international cooperation. The Charter was drawn up in an atmosphere of suspicion and unreality.[12] A few months were enough to reveal the impasse. A fundamental political tension cannot be appeased by inviting the antagonists to enact constitutional norms for their future relations.

Compared with this capital error, which from the very first doomed the United Nations to impotence, the disadvantages of the connection between the League of Nations and the Peace Treaties of 1919 now look trifling.

The abuse of abstract constructions is also responsible for errors about the significance of the voting rules, especially in the Security Council. When they are not, as they are in the Charter, the result

[11] René de Lacharrière, *L'action des Nations Unies pour la sécurité et pour la paix*, *Politique Etrangère*, 1953, pp. 317 seq.

[12] The phraseology that paints the San Francisco Conference in the colors of a "great hope" belongs to the literature of imagination.

of false political calculation, the statutory rules on this subject are up to a certain point a useful measure of the community spirit invested in a corporate organization by its founders. But no voting formula in itself has any decisive influence; its results always depend on the spirit of the participants, on their more or less sincere intention to adapt their decisions to the ends of the institution or, on the contrary, to individual ends. In this context there is no substitute for an established sense of social solidarity; it is useless, often even dangerous, to anticipate its natural development by procedural reforms. There has been a great deal too much discussion in general terms of voting procedures, and too little study of the motives that shape them.

Experience shows that the rule of unanimity must hold wherever there is not a high enough degree of solidarity in an area of vital or major interests to permit exceptions without arousing in States particularly liable to find themselves in the minority a spirit of mistrust that sets them a priori against any concession to general interest. This is especially true of relations between great Powers touching questions that involve their political responsibilities for the preservation of peace. Already under the Covenant of the League of Nations, the Permanent Court of International Justice made this observation, in regard to the voting procedure in the Council: ". . . it is hardly conceivable that resolutions on questions affecting the peace of the world could be adopted against the will of those amongst the Members of the Council who, although in a minority, would, by reason of their political position, have to bear the larger share of the responsibilities and consequences ensuing therefrom."[18]

In the Security Council, which was highly institutionalized by unprecedented powers of decision, the so-called Yalta formula, reproduced in Article 27 of the Charter, was designed at once to protect the great Powers against each other and to protect them as a group against majority votes. The permanent members' right of veto was the *sine qua non* of the Charter. It might be said that the principle was inscribed in international reality even before it was sanctioned by a text. Criticism errs when it treats the veto as the decisive factor in the paralysis that has overtaken the Security Council. With or without the veto, no decision of real political

[18] Advisory Opinion No. 12, Art. 3, para. 2, of the Treaty of Lausanne (frontier between Turkey and Iraq), p. 29. Cf. Wellington Koo, Jr., *Voting Procedures in International Political Organizations*, 1947, pp. 122-123.

importance, and especially no measure of coercion, could have been taken either directly against a great Power or even, in the present divided condition of the world, against a State protected by a great Power. In all this the veto is only an instrument; the real cause lies in the state of basic political relations among the great Powers.

The veto is open to criticism from two points of view: for the scope given it in the Charter and for the inevitable deviations in its use in a milieu so politically divided. The very omission in the Charter of any precise limitations on the right of veto revealed a general absence of solidarity. Its extension by the "chain-of-events" theory, and with the insubstantial exception of purely preliminary investigation and discussion, to the pacific settlement of disputes revealed the will of one of the great Powers to keep political control of litigious situations.

The statutory reservation of a veto for the strongest is itself an incitement to abuse the power so conferred. Entrenched in his privileged position, one who has the weapon is likely to use it. He will certainly do so when the discussion brings his individual political aims into open conflict with views shared by the other States. It is a fact that the veto has not only impeded the growth of a spirit of compromise and collaboration in the United Nations; its mechanical use has prevented political ideas from maturing there.

There was a different spirit in the working of the unanimity rule at Geneva. Thanks to a better political climate, there existed in the League that underlying and fundamental unity of views which, transcending momentary divergencies, affirms fidelity to the institution and the will to avoid jeopardizing its existence.[14] Because unanimity was law for all the members without distinction, the rule inclined each one to seek a common alignment by reciprocal concessions. In the present climate the veto has too often assisted a single Power in its effort to compel the others to take positions that it preferred.

Certain uses of the veto, hardly foreseen at San Francisco, have exposed its insidious aspects. Great Powers can use it to cover a satellite, to consolidate a sphere of influence and make it a "hunting preserve." They may even try to use it to support one of those "wars by proxy" beyond their frontiers which, spreading into an

[14] As has been justly noted, the heterogeneity of international institutions and the degradation in their spirit are manifested in the growing tendency to politicize them by substituting the principle of representation by States for selection based upon personal qualities.

especially sensitive contact zone, carry with them the constant threat of general conflagration.

It is an exaggeration to say that the effort in the Charter to institutionalize the Security Council by giving a compulsory character to its decisions touching the preservation of peace has been "destroyed" by the operation of the veto, which was the counterpart of that character and the price paid for it. The truth is that this authoritarian centralization never had any solid political foundation. All that can be said is that, in the present divided state of the world, the practice of the veto has emphasized the unreality of the Charter's security system by bringing into the light of day two essential facts: coercive action is possible only against a secondary State, and such a State may escape if its foreign policy is sufficiently in line with that of a great Power to win the protection of the veto. Thus it becomes perfectly clear that the present possibilities of the international organization of security stop at the precise point where the danger begins.[15]

A deserving effort was made by the Interim Commission of the General Assembly to limit the use of the veto. The proposals in its report of April 14, 1949 were opposed by the Soviet delegation. Put in political terms by the Yalta agreement, the problem of the veto remains basically political.

The impotence of the Security Council would no doubt have continued without provoking any reaction other than renewed criticism of Soviet obstruction if the invasion of South Korea had not necessitated coercive action. Made possible in the first instance by the absence from the Council of the Soviet delegation, coercive action was from August 1950 on impeded by the veto.[16]

On November 3, 1950 the General Assembly adopted a resolution justly described as historical, less doubtless for the increased efficacy

[15] J. L. Brierly, *The Law of Nations*, 4th edn., 1949, p. 106: "But it seems probable that the result of insisting that only a body that had power to make binding decisions could act effectively has been to give us a body that can neither decide nor act." There is no reason to regard as a precedent in the other direction the collective action called for in the resolution ("invitation") of June 25 and 27, 1950 against North Korea. There were very special circumstances connected with the absence of the Soviet delegation that made this resolution possible.

[16] There have been various opinions on the effect of a permanent member's absence from Security Council proceedings. Cf. Georges Day, *Le droit de veto dans l'Organization des Nations Unies*, 1952, pp. 127 seq.; Pierre-F. Brugière, *La règle de l'unanimité des Membres permanents au Conseil de Sécurité; droit de veto*, 1952, p. 141; A. J. P. Tammes, *Hoofdstukken van Internationale Organisatie*, pp. 117 seq.

that it brought to collective security than for the displacement of the center of gravity that it entailed in the system established by the Charter. While reaffirming the primary responsibility of the Security Council for the maintenance of peace and international security, the resolution provided that in all cases contemplated in Chapter VII of the Charter where, because unanimity had not proved possible among the permanent members, the Council failed to discharge this responsibility, the General Assembly should at once examine the question with a view to making appropriate recommendations concerning the collective measures to be taken, including if necessary the use of armed force.

It is entirely useless to seek any basis for this resolution in the texts, which all require or assume the unanimous agreement of the permanent members of the Council in the matter of sanctions. The problem was not one of an accidental defect in the organ, but of a failure brought about by the very operation of the rules governing its proceedings; and the question was whether, failing the not exclusive but certainly primary and specific responsibility of the Council, the clearly accessory responsibility of the General Assembly could up to a certain point replace it. It was necessary either to abdicate the essential role of the United Nations or, by an appeal to the higher demands of the Organization, to recognize the General Assembly's power to recommend what the Security Council was unable to command. The United Nations in 1950 chose this second solution, holding that the life and purpose of an institution established for permanent ends must not be compromised by the weakness of one of its organs.[17]

Considered in its consequences for the general operation of the United Nations, the innovation does not justify unmixed satisfaction. One cannot with impunity so bluntly enlarge the role of an organism which, for purposes of discussion and recommendation only, has been endowed with a competence limited solely by the very general aims of the United Nations. To the attractions of the platform is added the sense of irresponsibility. Under cover of factitious majorities, various States exercise an influence in the General Assembly out of proportion to their place in the world. This has at

[17] Hans Kelsen resigns himself to the same position touching not only the resolution of November 3, 1950, but other expedients invented to compensate for the Security Council's impotence. Cf. his *The Law of the United Nations*, p. 912. On the many difficulties of interpretation presented by the General Assembly's resolution, see Julius Stone, *Legal Controls of International Conflict*, pp. 266-281.

times perverted the entire mechanism. Recently aggravated by the establishment and recognition of artificial State units, this state of affairs has brought to the forefront of attention the fundamental problem of something more rational than equal representation by States.

The Security Council's resolutions of June 25-27 and July 27, 1950 launched the United Nations upon the first experiment in armed coercion in the service of collective security. This experiment calls for certain reflections.

Whatever opinion one may hold on the general character—political or legal—of the measures contemplated by the Charter in the event of threat to the peace, breach of the peace, or act of aggression,[18] it was the legal version that prevailed in the Korean affair. The United Nations denounced the attacks launched by the North Koreans along the 38th Parallel as an act of aggression against a State created with its assistance, thus clearly opting for the notion of coercion-sanction. Experience, however, showed that in a deeply divided world it is difficult to preserve the character of legal sanction for such an enterprise, especially when it is prolonged. Three principal factors influenced it from beginning to end, introducing a highly political coefficient.

The most important of these factors was certainly the underlying East-West tension. Carried out in an internationally dangerous zone, along a world-strategic frontier, the intervention of the United Nations constantly ran the risk of degenerating into a vast conflagration. Typical example of the armed conflict "by proxy," the Korean affair took the form on the diplomatic plane of a struggle waged by the Soviet Union to exploit to the full against the United States the fears aroused in the other States members of the United Nations by the prospect of broadening conflict, and thus to break the united front formed by the resolutions of June 1950. The structure of the Organization had little to do with this distortion of a procedure which is theoretically the highest manifestation of international solidarity. The absence of the Russian veto in the initial proceedings could not prevent the sanctions from heightening the political tension between the two Powers that compete for world hegemony.

The two other factors are complementary to the first. The great inequality in military participation in the coercive action was bound in the long run to deepen the rift between the point of view of the

[18] In the system of the Charter the question is much debated; see Hans Kelsen, *op.cit.*, pp. 732 seq.

United States, which was more and more dominated by the demands of the high command, and that of the other Powers, particularly the United Kingdom and France. The Truman-Attlee meeting (December 4-7, 1950) succeeded in preserving at an especially critical moment the unity of views which had been shaken by the crossing of the 38th Parallel and the advance towards the Manchurian border. In these transactions, which bore most directly upon the peace of the world, the role of the United Nations was singularly inconspicuous: everything went on as if the Organization's sole function was to follow passively the development of an enterprise in which it had taken the initiative and for which it remained responsible. The facts demonstrated that coercive action in which a great Power takes so preponderant a part comes very largely into the hands of that Power. Though international in its original abstract form, it begins to lose this character when political and military factors come to determine the concrete conditions of execution.

No less instructive were Asia's continental reactions to the use of coercion. There is no doubt that from the beginning the memory of foreign interventions and colonial occupations went some way to determine the reserved and, everything considered, moderating attitude of several Asiatic countries towards an expedition under the command of the United States with the aid of contingents furnished almost exclusively by great Powers foreign to Asia. Any future coercive action must take account of such sentiments, which can only grow stronger as new nationalisms waken to consciousness of a continental solidarity.

The Korean experience already appears as nothing more than a phase of the vast political tension which in the Far East sets the Communist against the Western Powers, especially the United States of America. In the form, now a matter of style, of a treaty of self-defense against aggression, combined here with a pact for consultation in case of threatened subversion, the South-East Asia Treaty (S.A.C.D.T.) reflects the common fears of the contracting Powers as well as the reservations felt by several of them regarding certain of its provisions.

Section III

The Treaty and the Institutional Organization of Security

The maintenance of peace is the international Organization's reason for existence. In what was, after the League of Nations, an ungrateful recommencement perhaps already doomed to a second failure, we must distinguish permanent ends from contingent and secondary aspects. The United Nations today symbolizes, more than it represents, humanity's hope for peace. If in the existing distribution of power, peace or war continues to depend essentially on the relations between the great Powers, it must nevertheless be admitted that the Organization offers a propitious meeting-place for those who seek pacification. That is enough to justify its existence; it is too little to warrant any expectation of security.

The organization of security since the League of Nations is characterized by two general traits. It takes the form of international conventions which all aim at an institutional arrangement of the relations between States. It is universalist in its essential conception, but leaves a large place for particular agreements between States members, thus revealing, under the appearance of institutionalization, the political reality of independent sovereignties.

§ 1. CONVENTIONS AND INSTITUTIONS IN INTERNATIONAL ORGANIZATION

There is very general agreement that progress in international law is linked from now on with progress in international organization. But experience shows what misunderstanding there still is as to the present possibilities of organization and as to the procedures for bringing it about. To organize international relations is essentially to try to arrange them on another plane and in accordance with other principles than the juxtaposition of sovereignties; it is to create, as part of a new distribution of power, new political and economic structures. From the legal point of view it is also to move from the individualist and voluntarist conception of law by agreement to the organic conception of institution. This transition must be made by treaty, traditional instrument for the expression of sovereign wills.

The frequent inadaptation of the instrument of agreement to realities in treaties of international organization is explained by errors as to the degree of social integration attained by the collectivities for which the instrument is designed. Into the mold of conventional undertakings are poured matters that have never been subjected to such regulation. This is done under political pressure and without adequate preparation or reflection. An overformal notion of the treaty-contract inclines men in government to look upon the development of international relations too exclusively as an exchange of consents, and to forget that a treaty creates institutions only on condition that these find their "point of balance with the external world,"[19] which implies that when facts press upon them they are sustained by a sufficiently enlightened opinion of their needs.

The propensity to anticipation by convention naturally increases at times of political tension or economic recession. Such anticipation throws the field open to ideology and the systematizing spirit. Statesmen and parliamentarians are inclined to formal planning, to a certain dogmatism that at times makes them attribute exclusive validity to constructions suggested to them by a priori reasoning. There is the treaty; it projects its textual light upon confused aspirations and lends them an appearance of reality. To sign and to ratify become the primary objective. There is all too much evidence nowadays of the dangerous facilities that the treaty offers to hasty and superficial enterprises.

The European Defense Community was the most perfect example of this vicious use of international conventions. From a limited sector of the economy, coal and steel, supranational organization was projected into the military domain without regard for the order of magnitude of the interests involved. Nor was any greater attention paid to the fact that the coal and steel community was based upon positive solidarities, whereas the plan for a Defense Community owed its existence wholly to French fears of a rearmed Germany. The ratification in France of so eminently political a treaty immediately became the issue of political conflict. Against a background of apathetic because ill-informed public opinion, the Government used the issue as a means of pleasing some and bringing pressure upon others. Failure is the natural end of such enterprises. Instead of staking the federal idea on a purely institutional and formal plan, it would have been better to implement it little by little in areas which would not at once demand either ideological unity or the serious concessions of sovereignty called for in the military and political domain.

For the man of law, these unwelcome ventures are highly instructive. The treaty is the most powerful instrument of change in international relations; to abuse it is to risk losing its moral authority and to jeopardize what is most fundamental in the international

[19] M. Hauriou, *Principes de Droit Public*, p. 131.

order, faith in the given word. The spirit that accounts for this rapid accumulation of international instruments is antihistorical and inclined to attribute creative virtue to mere expressions of intent. Nothing is gained by doing violence to facts. A few years have been enough to reduce the United Nations to a conventional regime of precarious coexistence, excluding all true institutionalization, and to retreat from the ideal of an organized community back to the most primitive organization of security: alliances and particular agreements.[20]

§ 2. TREATIES OF SELF-DEFENSE AND REGIONAL SECURITY AGREEMENTS

The easily foreseeable weaknesses of the Security Council, combined with the determination of the Latin American Republics to preserve the pan-American principle of continental security affirmed by the Act of Chapultepec, prevented the San Francisco Conference from approving in its extreme form the universalist conception of security organization. The Council assumes "primary," not exclusive, responsibility for security. Self-defense, "an inherent right" which "nothing in the present Charter shall impair" (Art. 51), compensates for the deficiencies of collective security.

As in all primitive societies, self-defense has a place in the international order that is at once essential and ill defined. Undisputed in principle, its organization by treaty and its exercise in concrete cases almost always runs into contradictions, owing either to opposing political views or to the uncertainties surrounding the conditions of fact that justify its use.[21] It must even be admitted that there will always be, if not a contradiction, at least a degree of tension between the universalist conception of security, which, precisely because of its abstraction, is not pointed at anyone, and a treaty of military defense having, in the grouping that it involves and the eventualities that it evokes, a clearly individualized political character.

The San Francisco Conference introduced the provisions regarding self-defense into the Charter in close connection with the recognition of regional agreements and agencies mentioned in Chapter VIII therein. But the Charter also recognizes self-defense as an

[20] Cf. Julius Stone, *Legal Controls of International Conflict*, pp. 246, 264-265, 275, 281.

[21] E. Giraud, *La Théorie de la Légitime Défense*, *Rec. A.D.I.*, vol. 49 (1935); H. Saba, *Les Accords Régionaux dans la Charte de l'ONU*, *Rec. A.D.I.*, vol. 80 (1952); Julius Stone, *Legal Controls of International Conflict*, pp. 243 seq.

"inherent right" and, consequently, one that has an autonomous existence, independent of any regional arrangement or agency. A treaty of collective defense may therefore have a regional or nonregional base. In the latter case, which is that of the North Atlantic Treaty, the treaty has no connection with the Charter other than that specified in Article 51.[22] In particular, it escapes the rule applicable to regional arrangements which prohibits any enforcement action without the authorization of the Security Council (Art. 53).

The North Atlantic Treaty was concluded in exercise of the liberty which the Charter leaves to the States members of the United Nations. It does not become part of the Charter or integrated with it; "it is marginal to the Charter"[23] and, to speak bluntly, helps to fill the large vacuum left by the present impotence of the collective security system. Legally, it cannot be held contrary to the Charter. Politically, it is indisputable that such treaties, which, whether we like it or not, end by hardening antagonisms, harmonize ill with its spirit.

Further, it must be admitted, any control that the political organs of the United Nations might be called upon to exercise, under Article 51 of the Charter, over enforcement measures taken by the signatory States of the North Atlantic Treaty in the event of armed aggression, would be quite illusory. Looked at in the light of reality, the reservation of the Security Council's powers is here merely nominal. The complete impotence of the Charter's mechanism makes it necessary to observe and legitimize the existence of defense communities which, on a regional or nonregional basis, become definitely "separate from the universal federation of collective security as that was planned within the framework of the United Nations."[24]

Thus, however we look at the problem of security, we are driven to the same conclusion. When carried to a certain degree of tension, great-Power antagonisms militate against any objective organization of security. Confronting a politically and militarily unified

[22] F. J. Krezdorn, *Les Nations Unies et les Accords Régionaux*, University of Geneva thesis, 1954, p. 121.

[23] J. Nisot, *Le Traité de l'Atlantique Nord et la Charte des Nations Unies*, *Revue de Droit International et de Droit Comparé*, 1951.

[24] See the observations by P. Guggenheim, *Universalisme et Régionalisme Européen en Droit International*, in *Cahiers de Bruges*, 1954, pp. 9-10; F. J. Krezdorn, *Les Nations Unies et les Accords Régionaux*, pp. 144-145; R. O. Yakemtchouk, *La Légitime Défense et l'Article 51 de la Charte des Nations Unies*, Annales de Droit et de Sciences Politiques de l'Université de Louvain, 1954, p. 80.

bloc, the North Atlantic Treaty marks the return to the practice of alliances; it is the image of a world deeply divided.

Insofar as they are not purely and simply treaties of collective self-defense, regional arrangements (Chap. VIII of the Charter) differ considerably in their historical origins, their content, and their spirit. That explains the obscurity of the subject and the impossibility of expounding it in general terms. Each arrangement has its special problems; each may cover a military alliance. The balance that the Charter theoretically sought to establish between the universalism of the United Nations and regional arrangements should not make us ignore the pressure to which the latter are subjected by the growth of political tensions that now transcend all frontiers. The consequence for the preservation of peace and international security is to make the efficacy of these arrangements dependent on the way they fit into the political action of the great Powers. This is what essentially determines their ability to settle "local disputes" (Art. 52, para. 2, of the Charter) and the exact nature of the links which they retain with the Security Council in their function as devices complementary and subsidiary to the United Nations. It is self-deception to regard the regional arrangements as a way of remedying the serious deficiencies in collective security caused by the bad relations among the great Powers. Clearly what we are in reality witnessing is less a conflict between a universalist and a regional conception of security than the entirely contingent and rather precarious ability of certain groupings to maintain within their spheres of interest and with the aid of one or more great Powers a measure of stability in harmony with their common aspirations. This general perspective, together with the more particular principle of nonintervention in internal affairs, helps towards understanding the attitude of abstention adopted by the Security Council, with the support of the United States and despite serious reservations on the part of other permanent members, in regard to the events in Guatemala in May and June of 1954.

CHAPTER IV. THE HUMAN ENDS OF POWER

"Men recover from all diseases except self-abdication. Individualities once destroyed by the State are not regained; for the State never gives back the liberties it swallows." J. E. RENAN.

Section I

The Tendencies to Depersonalization and the Defense of Human Values

WHEN the notion of the common good is no longer harnessed to human ends, there sets in a deterioration in the ends of power. Diverted from its mission, which is to serve men and not to enslave them, it adopts extra-personal objectives that lead it into excess and sometimes tyranny.

Respect for the human person, "end of every public establishment" (E. J. Sieyès), was the foundation of nineteenth-century constitutions. Inspired by the American and French declarations of the rights of man, they surrounded power with counterweights (separation of powers, delimitation of competences, judicial control) that rendered public liberties inviolable even by the legislator. Moral convictions ensured the efficacy of organic restrictions: inherited from the Christian tradition of natural law, they affirmed the existence of certain inalienable rights of man that were not reducible to political values. This liberal conception did not "array the individual against the State, but set him up face to face with it."[1] Watchful for excesses of power, these liberties, as Royer-Collard puts it, constitute "resistances" to such excesses.

For thirty years a profound crisis, moral and spiritual, has brought with it "an unheard-of displacement of weight from the individual to the State."[2] To attribute this dangerous slipping to the characteristic action of power is an error that leads, moreover, to discounting the evil. As we have seen, the way for such a movement

[1] Léon Blum, *L'Etat moderne; Encyclopédie française*, chap. IV.

[2] W. Röpke, *Civitas Humana*, p. 173. Cf. Max Huber, *Gesellschaft und Humanität*, vol. III, p. 49.

was prepared long ago by the development of a special ethic that makes national loyalties the supreme duty of man. The movement has been strengthened by popular psychoses inseparable from contemporary commotions: fear, and the crushing obsession of a future full of threats, have driven men to sacrifice to the search for a largely illusory security not merely the rights of liberty, but even the taste for it.[3] But depersonalization has a deeper cause: in large measure it results from the transformation of economic activities, from the State's need to coordinate them, and from the phenomena of concentration that call for the State's interventions. It grows with the inertia of opinion, which cannot grasp the complexities of the directed or planned economy and is still less capable of discerning "the immeasurable potentialities for evil, inherent in the state in this age of science and organization.[4]

It is clear that the chief beneficiary of this technological depersonalization is today the State in its political action. Any planning enterprise, because it calls for apportionings and long-term choices, demands above all energetic political direction that is able to make its own conception of social justice prevail among the masses.

Personalism, in its original purity, was the revolt of conscience against the excesses of totalitarian regimes. Calling the State back to the duties of its human mission, personalism urges upon it a functional and moderating conception of its powers. Its objectives are compatible with the present evolution of economies except in the writings of those who clothe it in the outworn forms of a liberal individualism based upon natural harmony of interests. Man has his social as well as his individual ends, and there can be no question of denying the State that legitimate measure of control called for by a sharpened sense of social justice, technological developments, and the urgency of certain nonremunerative undertakings. In the international as in the national order, the only way open is the *via media* which endeavors to reconcile the amount of organization

[3] B. de Jouvenel, *Le Pouvoir*, p. 520: "The essential psychological characteristic of our epoch is the predominance of fear over self-confidence."

[4] Sir Hartley Shawcross, British solicitor-general, at the Nuremberg Trials, Introductory Statement, *Trial of the Major War Criminals before the International Military Tribunal*, vol. III, p. 105. Cf. G. Bernanos, *Lettre aux Anglais*, 1941: "If you are not careful, what the dictators wished to do in a few years will be done in fifty or a hundred, but the result will be the same; the State will have conquered everything, seduced everything, absorbed everything; you will have escaped the totalitarian demigods only to fall back gently into the lime of anonymous dictatorship. The State will have decisively taken your welfare in charge, and only death will deliver you from its enormous solicitude."

without which there is only disorder and the respect of human values without which there is only slavery.[5]

Section II

Human Ends, Basis of the International Order

Nothing better demonstrates the profound influence of human values in the establishment of an international order than the closer and closer bond that history has forged in their behalf between the prescriptions of international law and the exercise of the State's sovereignty over its own nationals. For a long time the contacts between the internal and external orders in this context remained intermittent and confused. The treaties by which States bound themselves to treat their own nationals in a certain way appear only as isolated phenomena inspired first by political interest and later by considerations of humanity. The series of particular agreements inaugurated in 1660 by the Treaty of Oliva after a century and a half of religious commotions bore this aspect. In these, States receiving cessions of territory guaranteed to the ceding States the continuance and protection of the religion existing in the ceded territories. This protection, granted first to individuals, was gradually extended to minority groups, to religious minorities first and afterwards ethnic or national minorities. While this protection was becoming collective, it was also being institutionalized by the stipulation of permanent guarantees for minorities which were then confirmed by internal constitutional laws.

The same broadening occurred in the moral and legal basis of the humanitarian interventions of the nineteenth century. In 1827 the joint intervention of France, England, and Russia on behalf of the Greek insurgents was still justified primarily by nothing more than material damages to nationals of the intervening Powers and to these Powers themselves. The "sentiment of humanity and interest in the repose of Europe" figured only in the second rank of reasons invoked. But in 1902 on the occasion of the persecutions of the Jews in Rumania, the United States, though not a signatory of the articles of the Treaty of Berlin protecting the Balkan minorities, put the problem in its true light. If, said Secretary of State Hay, the United States was not entitled to invoke the clauses of the Treaty, it "must

[5] On the depersonalization of modern man, cf. the Christmas message of H. H. Pope Pius XII, December 24, 1952.

insist upon the principles therein set forth, because these are principles of law and eternal justice."

Thus from that moment the practice of humanitarian intervention began to emphasize the idea today embodied in the United Nations Charter (Art. 2, para. 7). In exceptional cases respect for the internal order gave way to the universal demands of humanity and peace. And it is very significant that it was through the protection of human rights that this principle, which limits internal political power, made its way into international law. It was still necessary, with a view to preserving its twofold moral and legal value, to define its contours and entrust its application to an impartial authority, and, with a view to its effectiveness, to surround it with permanent and precise guarantees. This was done in the minorities treaties of 1919. In addition to having the clauses, politically the most important, guaranteeing the rights of allogeneous groups, they ensured all the inhabitants, and so man as such, the right to life, to liberty, and to freedom of conscience.

But it was after the second world war that an immense and sudden enlargement of the problem threw new and revealing light upon the bond between the rights of man and the creation of an international order founded on law. Inspired by a perverted morality, the totalitarian ideologies had made it their task to sublimate loyalties that enslave the human person to the power ideal of the Nation-State. The opposite of that "rule of law" which in the countries of liberal tradition protects man from the arbitrary use of power, national-socialist law eliminated from the constitutional texts all mention of the fundamental rights of man. The totalitarian experience at the same time revealed the constant threat to peace implicit in the existence, especially in the great Powers, of regimes dedicated to the exploitation of nationalist passions by a single party, master of power. The totalitarian State does not only make of its opponents, that is to say virtually all its citizens, minorities of a new type, political minorities exposed to power persecution. By the implacable grip of power on the individual and the unexampled psychological tensions that it creates between people and people, this State represents a type of political phenomenon carried to the highest degree of intensity. Aggressiveness is its principle of action and its rule of life; it is born enemy to international organization and peace.

But this characteristically political form of State oppression is neither the most widespread nor perhaps the most dangerous. More insidious and more universal is the menace implicit in certain aspects of contemporary social organization by reason of the almost indefinite extension of State intervention. Since the danger here lies at the very heart of the State, it is vain to expect a regeneration of the international order from mere technical arrangement of relations between political entities which themselves strive for constant extension of their power. Regeneration depends upon psychological factors, and these are necessarily human.[6] The crisis in international relations is a crisis of the spirit and structure of contemporary society; it can be resolved only in respect for human values. The moderating conception of power represented by the personalist doctrine is the one common denominator of the internal and the international order. The key to the problem lies in men's idea of power, in the relations that a regime establishes between the person and the State, in those spiritual and institutional checks and balances which in the truly democratic countries resist extra-personal conceptions of the common good. There is no foundation for the international order if the internal order does not provide it.

This was the deeper meaning of the second world war. The lesson was unhappily to be lost in the vain discussions about the Universal Declaration of and draft conventions on human rights.[7]

In the sphere of international law, however, this assertion of the fundamental role of human values needs to be properly understood. It does not imply the rejection of current technical conceptions, those notably concerning the distinction between international and municipal law. Any technique, insofar as its object is the application and the practical utility of rules, is necessarily associated with the contingent structure of the powers that ensure the effective application and sanctioning of the law. The distinction between the two orders has therefore only a relative significance; it is bound up with the existing forms of distribution of power among nations. But care must be taken not to confuse technical conceptions with values and thus to disfigure the latter. The whole recent evolution of international law tends to reject the much too sharp separation that dualistic systematization had established between the international and internal orders.

[6] Cf. the Preamble of the Convention establishing Unesco: ". . . that since wars begin in the minds of men, it is in the minds of men that the defences of peace must be constructed."

[7] It is very clearly brought out, on the other hand, in the resolutions adopted on August 9, 1947 by the Institute of International Law in its Lausanne session. *Annuaire de l'Institut*, 1947, p. 258.

Neither does the personalist conception imply present adherence to doctrines that make the individual a direct subject of international law. That is an entirely contingent question. It depends on the degree of effectiveness that might one day accrue to the action of the individual isolated from that of the State, and that is a point on which there should not be too many illusions.

What the personalist conception asserts is the supremacy of human interest in the order of values; the necessity that States should make human interest the focus of their collaboration, seeking in it a more concrete and directly accessible principle of obligation than the general idea of justice, but one no less imperative in its civilizing virtue and universal significance.[8]

The rights of man, so frequently mentioned in the United Nations Charter, have a place there which is at once eminent and ill defined —eminent and in full conformity with the postulates of a personalist philosophy in the rank assigned to them by the text; ill defined, however, because between solemn affirmation and effective observance rises the exception of the reserved domain, aggravated in its effects by the form given it in Article 2, paragraph 7, of the Charter. In fact there are profound differences of opinion about the few really essential legal problems raised by the Charter provisions regarding the rights of man, and these will undoubtedly remain unsolved for a long time yet.

The confusion surrounding the whole problem of human rights today is an example of the distortions that impatient radicalism and ulterior political motives may force upon an idea which is profoundly just in itself but which could be brought into application only with much wisdom and circumspection. The authors of the Charter saw in respect for the rights of man the "matrix of the whole ideological structure of the new organization."[9] This is plain from the Preamble, where the order of the texts displays the sequence of ideas. The clause that proclaims the faith of the United Nations "in fundamental human rights, in the dignity and worth

[8] Positive international law is moving towards wider recognition of the interests of the individual, even in so definitely inter-State an institution as diplomatic protection (see below). It may be thought that this trend will find its logical complement and sanction one day in easier access for the individual to international procedures. But though no doctrinal (dualistic) prejudice should close our eyes to these new developments, the grave objections to them from the point of view of the internal and external political order of States must be noticed.

[9] André Salomon, *Le Préambule de la Charte, base idéologique de l'O.N.U.*, pp. 78-79.

of the human person" was quite deliberately inserted between that in which the peoples of the United Nations declare themselves "determined to save succeeding generations from the scourge of war," and the paragraph asserting their resolution "to establish conditions under which justice and respect for the obligations arising from treaties and other sources of international law can be maintained." This was how the eminent place of the rights of man was fixed in the order of values. From the political point of view they stand forth as one of the guarantees of peace; from the legal, as a condition closely linked with respect for international law.[10]

The Charter envisaged human rights as a source of moral inspiration and a principle of collective action for the organs of the United Nations. That is why in a series of articles it assigns to the United Nations the functions of promoting the ideal of such rights and stimulating respect for them. But the Charter nowhere defined the rights of man. Leaving them undetermined in object and scope it could not have intended imposing upon States members the legal obligation to grant or guarantee them to their nationals by internal legislation.[11] The discretion left to the States members by reason of this inorganic situation may suffer two limitations. One, legal in character, would result from an international obligation, whether of customary origin like that concerning the most fundamental rights (life, liberty, and freedom of conscience), or arising

[10] After the second world war Marshal Smuts expressed the common feeling of the delegates to the San Francisco Conference when he declared his wish to have the Preamble recall the common faith of the peoples allied in the long struggle against the totalitarian governments: "This war," he said, "has not been an ordinary war of the old type. It has been a war of ideologies, of conflicting philosophies of life and conflicting faiths. . . . We have fought for justice and decency and for the fundamental freedoms and rights of men, which are basic to all human advancement and progress and peace." United Nations Conference on International Organization, Documents, vol. 1, p. 425.

[11] The duty prescribed for States members in Article 56 is only "to take joint and separate action in cooperation with the Organization. . . ." Cf. Manley O. Hudson in *A.J.I.L.*, 1948, p. 105; Hans Kelsen, *The Law of the United Nations*, p. 29; Lawrence Preuss, *Article 2, Paragraph 7 of the Charter of the United Nations, Rec. A.D.I.*, 1949, vol. 74, pp. 686 seq. This interpretation, which is the most generally accepted, is confirmed by the purely moral force attributed to the Universal Declaration of Human Rights (1948) by the authors of this complement to the Charter. *Contra*, H. Lauterpacht, *International Law and Human Rights*, pp. 145 seq. The reaction in the United States to a judgment of the California District Court of Appeal (April 24, 1950, Fujii case) is well known. This decision recognized a "self-executing" character in Articles 55 and 56 of the Charter; cf. Paul De Visscher, *Les tendances internationales des constitutions modernes, Rec. A.D.I.*, 1952, pp. 560-562.

from an international convention. The other is connected with the political mission of the United Nations to maintain peace and in some ways recalls one of the justifications of humanitarian intervention. Flagrant and systematic violation of the fundamental human rights may become so serious as to endanger peace and to justify measures of coercion provided for in Chapter VII of the Charter. This exception to respect for the reserved domain embodies the directing idea of the Charter. A regime founded on oppression is by the unlimited scope of its powers a threat to peace in the external sphere as it is to liberty within the country. If in this matter Article 2, paragraph 7, of the Charter is not as precise as could be desired, the explanation must be sought in the historical circumstances surrounding the conclusion of the Charter; relations with the Soviet Union did not permit raising in all its amplitude the vast problem implicit in the existence of totalitarian regimes.

Charged with the promotion of respect for rights left completely vague by the absence of any definition, the United Nations logically set about the task of defining them. It brought to this task a somewhat excessive zeal. The Universal Declaration of Human Rights, a document with merely moral force, is a catalogue of rights which no State today would recognize in their totality. It put side by side rights that are essential and others that are not, and still others that it was frankly utopian to proclaim. While appealing to common aspirations, it in fact embodies two opposing conceptions of man's relation with power. In one conception, Christian and Western, the whole value of human rights, designated for this reason fundamental or inalienable, lies in the fact that they can be pleaded against the State. In the other, man exists only insofar as he is integrated in a totalitarian order that entails his depersonalization. The whole efficacy of the proclamation of human rights depends upon the spirit of the regime and the resources that it offers for the defense of the individual against the omnipotence of power.

Though the draft conventions on human rights now in process of gestation give evidence of a little more conservatism, the whole enterprise still bears the imprint of an impatient levelling spirit, inclined to seek in the abstraction of formulas the solution of problems conditioned by historical, psychological, economic, and social factors of extreme complexity. The method of universal conventions does not seem most appropriate to the nature of such a task. There is an enormous difference between the atmosphere of assemblies which enthusiastically adopt texts on human rights and that of national parliaments called upon to provide for their application through municipal law.[12]

In its sixth session the General Assembly of the United Nations decided to include in the draft conventions on human rights an article declaring the right of self-determination for all peoples. It would seem difficult more completely to confuse values and to wander farther from the spirit in which the defense of human rights was contemplated. The Charter placed these rights in relations between the individual and internal public authority; it conceives of them as moral and legal limitations on the political action of the rulers. The right of national self-determination mentioned in Article 1, paragraph 2, and Article 55 of the Charter is a notion that belongs to an absolutely different order of ideas. The aspiration to independent political existence directly concerns the mutual relations of States; in combination with other factors it provides political decision with a principle for the distribution of human groups in separate political units. In its present total lack of precision, it in no way represents a principle of law. Applied without discernment, self-determination would lead to anarchy.[13] The United Nations has rightly set itself to examining the very numerous criteria by which the limits of self-determination may be better fixed. The examination has brought out the complexity of the problem and has unfortunately also revealed the unreasoned positions taken in certain quarters in response to nationalist passions. Emancipation by the United Nations surely calls for a different spirit from that recently manifested in those quarters.[14]

[12] Apart from treaty regulation, governments hold their relations with their nationals to be essentially within their domestic jurisdiction. In the present stage of international law, the only exception admitted is in the case mentioned in Article 2, paragraph 7, *in fine,* when oppression constitutes a threat to peace. The coming into force of the European Convention on Human Rights has not changed this situation.

[13] If, as a principle of political action, the right of national self-determination is in harmony with the spirit of Chapters XI and XII of the Charter, it is significant that, in those chapters that deal with non-self-governing territories and the international system of trusteeship, the drafters avoided this expression, which is obviously too vague for a text of legal import. The cautious wording of Article 76b speaks only of the "progressive development" of the inhabitants of the trust territories "towards self-government or independence as may be appropriate to the particular circumstances of each territory and its peoples and the freely expressed wishes of the peoples concerned. . . ." On the Soviet origin of the mention of national self-determination, see Fernand van Langenhove, "Aspects récents du principe des nationalités," *Revue générale belge,* November-December, 1952.

[14] The General Assembly, having assumed the power to determine the prin-

It is the fate of any idea of a highly spiritual character to be exposed to some distortion when it is introduced into a new environment. What the defense of human rights is suffering at this moment justifies neither pessimism nor surrender. The bond that is being established beyond any shadow of doubt between the rights of man on the one hand, and the maintenance of peace and respect for law on the other, constitutes the first assertion by the international Organization of a great moral and civilizing principle. A teleological and functional conception of power here joins hands with Christian doctrine, making human values—the only values that can command universal acceptance—the ultimate point of convergence of peace and law. We must neither count upon its immediate efficacy, nor reject the hopes that it awakens.

ciples upon which a territory is to be classified as one "whose peoples have not yet attained a full measure of self-government" (Art. 73 of the Charter), recommended, by resolution of November 27, 1953, a list of factors that might serve as guide for this purpose. Their number and extraordinary complexity are such that they certainly cannot give legal meaning to the vague phraseology of Article 73.

BOOK III

CONVERGENCES AND TENSIONS OF LAW AND POWER IN POSITIVE INTERNATIONAL LAW

"It is not by speculating on the abstract relations of ideal nations that men will bring more order and justice into the relations of States; it is by looking at the facts in their reality and seeking, without illusion, without passion, and without surrender, the laws that govern them." FUNCK-BRENTANO AND A. SOREL, *Précis du Droit des Gens*, p. 496.

CHAPTER I

SOCIAL FACTORS AND POLITICAL FACTORS IN THE DEVELOPMENT OF INTERNATIONAL LAW

IT MAY seem banal, but it is necessary to recall that positive international law is the law which is effectively applied in the relations of States by reason of the obligatory character that they recognize in it. The basis and the measure of application are to be found in the adaptation of norms to the demands of order and justice in international relations. This adaptation results in the concrete dispositions of positive law only through certain processes or modes of expression which constitute what are conventionally known as the formal sources of international law: treaty and custom.

The formal sources are not the ultimate bases of rules; but they make them manifest by certifying their origin, and effective by endowing them, through appropriate technical processes, with that degree of practicability[1] without which law is powerless to fulfill its social function.

Every rule of positive international law thus presents two essential aspects for critical examination on different planes: the degree in which its content corresponds to social needs, and the accuracy of its formal expression compared with the practice of States.

The rule of international law retains its full force in application only insofar as it satisfies this double requirement. This is a fact of experience particularly well illustrated in treaty regulation. A normative (law-making) treaty the content of which is too far in advance of development in international relations is stillborn, just as a treaty that ceases to be exactly observed in the practice of governments is no longer valid in its formal expression.

Any study of the action of power on international law therefore demands knowledge of all the social realities that determine this action as well as knowledge of the processes of formal elaboration by which it takes effect.

[1] Cf. J. Dabin, *La Technique de l'élaboration du Droit positif*, 1935, pp. 19 seq.

Section I

A Problem of Method

For many authors the problems approached here do not exist. In their eyes the formulation of a rule by a formal process appropriate to the international order is the sole criterion of its validity. The social fact, material of the law, is thought to have found adequate expression in the process of formal elaboration; any later verification of this adequacy is regarded as outside the law and devoid of legal relevance. This view is common to all the jurists who, from too exclusive a concern for the independence of their discipline or for purity of method, enter the blind alleys of sterile formalism where logic alone animates the systematized relations between abstract norms.

True, some degree of formalism is inherent in all legal regulation. By the precepts that it imposes, by its peculiar technical character aimed at simplification, certainty, and security, legal regulation inevitably preserves a gap between its norms and the spontaneous activities of society.[2] But there is no absolute value in formal methods, and the use to be made of them varies from one discipline and one moment to another.

Formalism is of a pair with the generality of law—a generality only fully attained where well-known social data, uniform and regular enough in their occurrence, are firmly integrated in the rule of law. Civil law is impregnated with formalism. Its rules are made for an undetermined number of subjects with identical attributes and have an impersonal or objective character. For them the condition of all recourse to formal methods is realized, namely the predominance of typical or general over particular situations. Law in its technical aspect here acquires a marked autonomy over against facts; but this autonomy lasts only so long as the underlying social data are not again in question.

As we know, the international environment presents an entirely different character. Nowhere is there less reason to be content with the convenient presumption of valid enactment and to ignore the social content of regulation. Individualization is here much more pronounced, consideration of the personal interest of the State playing an infinitely greater part than the interest of the individual

[2] F. Russo, *Réalité juridique et réalité sociale*, p. 132: "Law is first of all and above all social life in its most logical and universal aspect."

plays in the internal order.[3] These profound differences, springing from the peculiar ethnic and historical individuality of nations, the inequalities of their physical make-up and economic resources, the small number of States compared with individuals, the eminently political character of their peculiar ends, and the irregularity and comparative rarity of their mutual relations, lead here to the predominance of particular over general situations. One consequence, often remarked, is that in international relations particular norms, limited to a small number of subjects, often only two, are much more numerous than general norms.[4]

This observation must not lead to error as to the importance of general rules in the development of law. Less involved in the political action of power, general rules always have an authority and, as it were, a density out of proportion to their number. The concepts and categories used in particular law are borrowed from general law. The latter moreover retains an important complementary and interpretative function.[5]

The role of formalism varies not only with the degree of generality of social relations, but quite as much with their relative stability. It is a fact of current observation that, in periods of crisis and especially of violent commotion, municipal law itself always loses something of its continuity; the rapid succession of statutes, the abandonment of the principle of nonretroactivity, and the tendency to legislative individualization to cope with particular or unforeseen situations, all attest not only the more direct grip of power but the instability of social relations. Such instability, exceptional in the internal order, is the more or less general condition of the international order, dominated and constantly troubled as this is by the factor of force. This is a terrain of fluctuation and contingency, naturally refractory to that formal "setting-apart" which only social regularities make possible and which is the characteristic mark of the rule of law in the fullness of its development. This tendency to

[3] Max Huber, *Vermischte Schriften*, vol. III, p. 208. J. L. Brierly, *The Outlook for International Law*, p. 40: "In contrast with a national society, the two most prominent characteristics of the international society are the fewness of its members and their heterogeneity."

[4] D. Anzilotti, *Cours de droit international*, p. 46; J. L. Brierly, *op.cit.*, p. 45: "The legal purist may object that such an outlook means the continued presence of a strong political element in the international legal system, but the admixture is made inevitable by the nature of the entities with which the system has to deal."

[5] Cf. Erich Kaufmann, *Règles du droit de la paix*, *Rec. A.D.I.*, vol. 54 (1935), p. 489.

instability borders on confusion and disorder in periods of generalized high political tension such as ours. It strips international relations of the regularities necessary to the development and continuity of law. It impedes the consolidation of practices and their evolution into customary rules. Inversely, it precipitates the conclusion of international conventions of political content to the point where this degenerates into pactomania. The ratification of even the most solemn treaties depends at times upon considerations of sheer opportunism and loses much of its meaning in the public mind.

The general propensity to formalism in nineteenth-century doctrine is easily explained. First there was the exceptional stability of international relations—mark of the epoch and safeguarded by a degree of balance in the forces at play. This fixed the climate in which the voluntarist doctrines were able without excessive unreality to attain their degree of abstraction from the living matter of international law and reduce this law in its entirety to a systematization of formal sources. They lost credit when the violent commotions of the twentieth century shattered their tranquil assurance and revealed the yawning gap between the norm bearing the official stamp and the needs of a society in full transformation.

But there is another and more fundamental explanation of nineteenth-century formalism. In its deepest meaning the international law of the period was the expression of a community of thought and moral attitudes, the Christian heritage of the peoples of European civilization. In its application to large spheres of common or parallel interests, this law showed a basic homogeneity lending some color of justification to the doctrine that made the formal elaboration of norms the exclusive test of their validity. This homogeneity vanished in the years following the first world war. The spread of new political ideologies and the sudden entry of peoples of highly diverse civilizations into international relations drastically reduced the common ethical basis of international law. At the same time the extension and growing intensity of these relations themselves uncovered new and unsuspected problems arising out of particular geographic or demographic situations, the transfer to the State of activities previously left to private initiative, and the new demands for the international protection of human rights.

Apart from the legal validity of the formal process by which law is developed, the very social validity of the present structure and distribution of power among States is today in question for the lawyer as well as the sociologist. Thus, simultaneously with the diversification and individualization of legal data, we have the problem of international organization, that is to say, at bottom, the problem of limiting sovereignties in the higher interest of the human collectivity. Now such a problem cannot be approached by formal paths, because a new structural arrangement of international relations presumes deliberate adherence to a hierarchy of values adapted to the pursuit of a common goal. Associated in this creative effort, the jurist is confronted with a task very different from one that was limited to the definition and coordination of established rules. And because, in spite of still stubborn resistances, the idea of organization has for thirty years been making its way in men's minds, workers in the field of international law are gradually abandoning the traditional formalism of their methods to scrutinize the basis and content of the legal rule and set it in the whole complex of social realities.

The present structure of international relations still more sharply contradicts the thesis that represents international law as an order at once universal and logically closed, embracing all relations of international interest. This is the thesis of the so-called formal completeness of international law. There are in international relations many matters which, however desirable their regulation may seem in the common interest, remain outside international law either by the deliberate will of States to reserve discretionary judgment on them, or because the States find it impossible to agree on the terms of regulation. In this domain, extra-legal factors of all sorts continue to exert an inhibiting influence not only on the regulatory action of power but on public opinion as well.[6]

The obsession of unity is found again in the "double-function" theory developed with rare talent by M. Georges Scelle.[7] Unity here postulates a final synthesis of the action of power and the require-

[6] It matters little that for the sake of a doctrinal conception this state of things is regarded as the result of willed omissions in the legal order. Those who champion the thesis of the completeness of law often lose sight of the fact that even in the internal legal system the circle of interests calling for legal regulation and the circle of the positive law do not wholly coincide. The gap between them, which is particularly striking in the conflicts of capital and labor, exists wherever power is at grips with social forces that it has not yet wholly succeeded in ordering. Cf. Julius Stone, *Legal Controls of International Conflict*, pp. 152-164.

[7] *Précis de droit des gens*, passim; *Théorie et pratique de la fonction exécutive en droit international*, *Rec. A.D.I.*, vol. 55 (1936); *Manuel élémentaire de droit international public*; *Rapport à l'Institut de droit international sur la révision dans les conventions générales*, *Annuaire de l'Institut de droit international*, 1948.

ments of the international order, and the theory is to the effect that international society even now possesses, though in a precarious and very imperfect degree, the organs necessary to its legislative, executive, and judicial functions. The executive function in particular—the most important in the existing stage of international relations—is represented as being fulfilled by the national governments acting as *negotiorum gestores* for the international collectivity; witness the directive action of the great Powers, especially in the great historical settlements.

In this presentation the generally accurate description of facts must be distinguished from the legal version of the same. Whatever importance may be attributed to power, effectiveness, the accomplished fact, and, in a word, to force in the existing process of developing international law, the jurist cannot agree to regard the activities cited, where particular and contingent political interests play so large a part, as the performance of constitutional functions. It is one thing to admit the role of power in international relations; it is quite another to integrate it, in its present form, in an institutional and at best problematic image of international relations.

The completeness of international law is an ideal and a potentiality, like the aspiration to international community in which it originates. Scientific objectivity forbids accepting it as an accomplished reality. Doctrine does better service to the progress of law when it points out the sometimes openly antisocial consequences of the present distribution of power than when it gives rein to a sort of "legal totalitarianism" which masks behind a façade of unreal architecture the present disorder of international relations.

The temptation to formalism, and the proneness to generalization by abstract concepts and to premature systematization, represent one of the most serious dangers to which international-law doctrine is still exposed. It escapes only by constant return to respect for facts and by exact observation of the concrete and very special conditions which in the international domain contribute to forming the legal rule and govern its applications. Of course the legal rule never embraces social reality in all its fullness and complexity. Attempting to do so, law would risk compromising its proper ends as well as overshooting its possibilities. If abstraction carried to an extreme degenerates into unreality, individualization pushed to excess leads to the destruction of the rule. International justice especially must maintain a proper relationship between social data and the rules designed to govern them.

Much has been written on all this. It may be judged, however, that the discussions of method will remain inconclusive so long as both sides limit themselves to the necessarily vague glimpses suggested by the general relations of law and sociology. Only by penetrating to the core of the subject by a critical study of the rules of law in their positive organization can one hope to grasp either their correspondence with social needs or their inadequacy, recognizing here the strong and living parts that ask only appropriate technical development, there the weak elements doomed to growing inefficacy. A complex task, which only the jurist can undertake, but which he can carry through only if he brings to it knowledge of the deficiencies of his own discipline, an exact sense of the real, and a solid experience of international relations.

Section II

The General Action of Power in the Formation of Rules of International Law

The relations between power and law have at all times been the subject of the most serious inexactitudes and misunderstandings. They must not be presented, following the recent tendency, in the terms of a conceptual antinomy which is neither supported by reason nor confirmed by the observation of facts. Law finds its objective expression and its sanction only in the support of power; power remains precarious if it collides too openly with law. So long as the potential tension between them does not exceed certain limits, concern for an order to be preserved may hold the political action of power within the orbit of law. The necessity of the order is thus the point of coincidence where politics and justice may meet and complete each other.[8] The fact that in the international order the tensions are more frequent and the limits more easily crossed does not change the fundamental relation. The general assent which certain rules of that order enjoy is largely due to the action of power.

The predominance of power in this domain, a predominance to which we shall have frequent occasion to refer, has in itself nothing

[8] G. Leibholz, "Le but du Droit," *Annuaire de l'Institut international de philosophie du droit*, vol. III, p. 86.

of the arbitrary. It is explained first by the position of the State at the center of international relations and by the strong concentration that the conduct of foreign affairs demands. It has deeper reasons in the fact that the great majority of men have only the faintest perception of a conscious social goal in this order of interests, and in the resulting atony of public opinion. Having their source in governmental practices inaccessible to the immense majority of men, the rules of international law bear for the most part no clearly perceptible relation to the necessarily very summary ideas that opinion forms of international relations.

This does not justify the conclusion that the action of power on law is without social direction and inapplicable to ends other than such as are purely political or national. Outside the sphere of "vital interests," in which reason of State is still largely sovereign, the demands of coexistence awaken a consciousness of certain social values which shapes and sustains a teleological and functional conception of power. (See above, Book II.) It remains true, however, that in the international domain, much more than elsewhere, not only the technical formulation of legal rules but also the decision as to their matter and content belongs to the State, which is to say to the rulers. The action of power is thus necessarily decisive in what is called the legal policy or the real or sociological technique of international law.[9]

§ 1. THE GENERAL ACTION OF POWER ON COLLECTIVE OR MULTILATERAL TREATIES

The extent of conventional regulation with a legal content is now the most tangible outward manifestation of the action of power in the international legal order. Of course the effective contribution made to law by the pacts, treaties, and conventions of all sorts is far from being proportionate to their number or scope, and it is hardly an error to describe their accumulation and their frailty as the mark of discontinuity in the law and of the insecurity caused by the predominance of political factors. But that is only one aspect of things. This regulation, though too often given to improvisation and in many ways utopian and plethoric, is nevertheless an index of an anxious search for order and, up to a certain point, of a sense of the growing dependence of political action on law.

Collective or multilateral treaties, which are much the most im-

[9] Cf. J. Dabin, *La technique de l'élaboration du droit positif*, p. 40; H. De Page, *De l'interprétation des lois*, vol. II, pp. 74-80.

portant in the formation of legal rules, may be divided, from the point of view of the action of power, into two very distinct categories.

Some, born of agreement among a limited number of States, nevertheless set up a politico-legal statute which extends its effects to States not parties to the original act. History shows that the production of such statutes, like the stability of the objective legal situations which they bring about, is a function of the general political relations of the great Powers. They are produced at times when these Powers are sufficiently in agreement to play a leading part in the settlement of questions which they regard as of general interest; they degenerate and lose their efficacy when the political balance of which they form an element is disturbed.

The most characteristic examples of objective legal situations have to do with special arrangements for certain States. For the most part they date back to the nineteenth century, the golden age of the European Concert's directive action. The perpetual neutrality of Switzerland became a legal status of general interest and a principle of "the public law of Europe" by a Declaration of the great Powers on November 20, 1815.[10] But the practice of Swiss neutrality was affected by changes occurring on the borders of the country, particularly by the unification of its two great neighbors, Germany and Italy, in accordance with the principle of nationalities. More threatened, neutrality became more watchful and more strict.[11]

Even more explicitly than the perpetual neutrality of Switzerland, that of Belgium was justified by the Powers as founded upon the general interests of Europe, and for this reason was regarded by them as binding upon all nations. They had expressed this constituent role very clearly in the Protocol of February 19, 1831 when they declared: "Each nation has its particular right; but Europe also has its right, conferred by the social order." Guaranteed by the

10 See the Declaration of February 13, 1920 by the Council of the League of Nations: "The Council . . . recognizes that Switzerland is in a unique situation, based on a tradition of several centuries which has been explicitly incorporated in the Law of Nations." *League of Nations Official Journal*, March 1920, p. 57.

11 W. Martin, *Histoire de la Suisse*, p. 284: "Neutrality, as we conceived it on the eve of the last war (1914-1918), does not date from 1516 or even from 1815; it dates from 1860." This orientation has since become more sharply defined; practiced as a freely chosen maxim of State, neutrality induced Switzerland to adopt attitudes that went beyond the obligations of neutrality. Cf. D. Schindler, "La neutralité suisse de 1920 à 1938," *Revue de droit international et de législation comparée*, 1938, p. 444.

Powers, the permanent neutrality of Belgium long appeared as a legal status indissolubly linked with the primordial needs of the balance of Europe, binding for this reason not only upon those who had enacted it but upon all States equally. That was its strength, but also its weakness. Undoubtedly time had consolidated it; but it remained dependent on the political system that had given it birth. The profound changes that broke up this system at the beginning of the twentieth century at the same time weakened the foundations of Belgian neutrality.

More precarious, by reason of their still closer ties with high policy, were the arrangements that imposed a special military status upon certain zones. The dominant issue in the regime of the Bosporus and Dardanelles has always been one of naval policy—namely, whether or not they shall be open to the warships of foreign powers. This regime showed some stability only so long as the principle of closure, supported by the Porte, coincided with the political interests of the great Powers. The principle, successively confirmed, with some exceptions in favor of the Sultan, by the Treaties of 1814, 1856, 1871, and 1878, was sometimes described as founded upon the collective interests of Europe. Since the war of 1914-1918, the incoherence of the political relations of the great Powers has been reflected in the successive revisions of the Straits statute (Treaty of Sèvres, 1920; Treaty of Lausanne, 1923; Convention of Montreux, 1936). As M. Georges Scelle observes, "it is hardly law, for such regulations, in constant flux, are entirely ineffective as soon as the balance of forces to which they correspond begins to waver."[12] The attitude adopted by the Government of the U.S.S.R. in its notes to the Turkish Government concerning the revision of the Montreux Convention (August 8 and September 26, 1946), and the participation of the United States in the negotiations touching this revision, though based on the Potsdam Agreements (1945), at bottom signify nothing more than that these Powers are taking new political positions in the eternal rivalry of which the Straits are the stake.[13]

A report drawn up in 1920 by the Commission of jurists appointed by the Council of the League of Nations to define the regime of demilitarization imposed on the Aaland Islands by the Convention and Treaty of Paris, March 30, 1856, threw new light on the specific character of these objective legal situations. It recalled the practice

[12] G. Scelle, *Manuel élémentaire de Droit international public*, p. 342.

[13] By a note of May 30, 1953, the Soviet Government declared that it had reconsidered its opinion on the Straits regime.

of the Powers in the nineteenth century when they sought "to establish true objective law, true political status, the effects of which extend beyond the circle of contracting parties." Such a regime represents "a positive settlement of European interests" which cannot be reduced to "mere individual and subjective political obligations."[14]

Politically, it is nonetheless true that all agreements concluded with the direct object of striking a military or naval balance in a region where powerful political antagonisms confront each other are threatened by the instability of the momentary balance of forces which they reflect. This frailty reaches its maximum when the regime is decreed for one of those positions or bases, such as straits or great maritime canals, that, because of the communications they command and the strategic and commercial importance of their control, are the constant stake of rival policies of the great Powers. More constantly than space, certain positions are arenas of political competition.[15]

Unlike the statutes enacted by the European Concert, which certainly had some permanence and contributed their share to the regularization of international relations, those established since the first world war have known no stability. On the contrary, most of them have become the object of the most dangerous political tensions. One need only cite the demilitarization of the left bank of the Rhine, the regime for the Free City of Danzig, and, coming closer to ourselves, the Free Territory of Trieste (Annex VI of the Treaty of Peace with Italy, 1947).

In many of these treaties setting up international statutes, political, geographic, and economic factors conspire to particularize the regime. This has happened even to the regime of international rivers. (See below, Chap. II.) For certain straits and for canals of great international interest, this process has been pushed to its last stage, that of complete individualization.

The vast majority of treaties have no other aim than to secure for the parties a temporary adjustment of their own interests. These highly individualized contractual balances offer little for use in the

[14] Cf. J. O. Söderhjelm, *Démilitarisation et neutralisation des îles d'Aland en 1856 et 1921*, Helsingfors, 1928; Fernand De Visscher, "La Question des îles d'Aland," *Revue de droit international et de législation comparée*, 1921, pp. 260 seq.

[15] J. Gottmann, *La politique des Etats et leur géographie*, 1951, p. 81.

development of law. An exception must be made for particular or bilateral treaties concluded with the same object and repeating identical provisions. This is the case with treaties of extradition, which are usually bilateral, but which contain typical provisions so commonly reproduced that they have become clauses of style. Their repetition proves that they express principles and not simply individual and contingent considerations. For this reason they may develop into a sort of customary law on the questions with which they deal. It remains true, nevertheless, that the general preference for the merely bilateral form denotes the political interest that States attach to the matter of extradition and their will to retain a character of particularity in its regulation.

Much more interesting for the development of law are the collective treaties of normative content (law-making treaties) concluded for the specific purpose of defining the legal rule and affirming its authority. These are the treaties that embody what is conventionally called, despite the confusions to which this expression has always lent itself, the codification of international law.

Thirty years of defeated efforts have made evident what the rare experiments in codification in the nineteenth century had already demonstrated, namely that any enterprise of this nature requires at once a sufficient moral and legal community and the active assistance of power. Far from benefiting from the strong community impulse that the national concentrations of the nineteenth century brought to the codification of municipal law, the codification of international law, by its direct appeal to the explicit agreement of States, elicits the full measure of their natural individualism. The risk is limited when the enterprise is one of a small number of States, near enough in civilization and tradition to constitute a legal community; it grows into a definite menace to the development of international law as the undertaking extends to a more numerous and less homogeneous aggregation.

It has been equally well demonstrated that no venture in codification can succeed without the active support of governments practically interested in its success. Codification is never a mere "declaration" (restatement) of rules said to be already in existence: it always aims to replace divergent views and practices with some unity in the interpretation and application of law. It is thus on the object and content of rules that it calls for agreement among governments, on the practices which they propose to maintain and on those which, out of regard for the views of others, they consent to rectify or abandon.[16] That is a task very different from that of the jurist exclusively concerned with formal technique; it is first of all a political task which governments will not take up or support unless they are led to do so by a practical and tangible interest.[17]

The Declaration of Paris, April 16, 1856, which indisputably was part of positive international law until a relatively recent date, was a good example of codification brought about by the concordant action of governments and sustained by a corresponding development in international relations. It had its origin in the need of Great Britain and France, at war with Russia, to adjust their traditional practice in the matter of maritime prizes. The British Government had renounced for the duration of the war the right to capture enemy goods on neutral ships, while the French Government renounced that of capturing neutral goods on enemy ships, with the exception in both cases of contraband of war. These two renunciations were confirmed in the Treaty of Paris. The seven signatory Powers there asserted their intention to make of the four rules constituting the Declaration "fixed principles" of international relations. Great Britain obtained in addition the consent of the other contracting Powers to the abolition of privateering. Privateering had been a source of anxiety to her during the war, and the United States at that time still supported the principle.[18] A work of

16 E. Root, in *Revue de droit international et de législation comparée*, 1911, pp. 445-447, and in *A.J.I.L.*, vol. 5, p. 579; Charles De Visscher, *La codification du droit international, Rec. A.D.I.*, vol. 6 (1925), pp. 381-384. Cf. the excellent pages by J. L. Brierly, "The Future of Codification" in *B.Y.B.I.L.*, 1931. Also Sir Cecil Hurst, "A Plea for the Codification of International Law on New Lines," *The Grotius Society, Transactions for the Year 1946*, vol. 32, p. 135: "No matter how well the preparatory work for the Conference in the way of the scientific investigation and determination of the existing rules is done, the moment the Government Delegates assemble and decide to conclude a Convention to render the rules so defined binding on States, their efforts are directed to laying down the law as it ought to be and not as it is."

17 E. Root, in *Revue de droit international et de législation comparée*, 1911, p. 448, and in *A.J.I.L.*, vol. 5, pp. 579-580. In the latter he says:

". . . Governments are practical organizations dealing with actual conditions, continually pressed by immediate difficulties, and the men engaged in them ordinarily have but little time and strength to devote to questions which for practical purposes, so far as they themselves are concerned, seem academic because they have not yet arisen or may possibly never arise.

"Every foreign office is fully occupied with questions that it must decide, and, as a rule, foreign offices will not concern themselves with any other question unless they are moved by some special impulse of external pressure or by the promptings of exceptionally far-sighted policy."

18 H. W. Malkin, "The Inner History of the Declaration of Paris," *B.Y.B.I.L.*, 1927, p. 1; V. M. S. Crichton, "The Pre-War Theory of Neutrality," *B.Y.B.I.L.*, 1928, pp. 101 seq.

compromise, product of a happy conjuncture in politics, the Declaration of Paris also expressed the liberal ideas of the time. These were eminently in favor of commercial freedom for neutrals by reason of the demarcation that such freedom implied between war, an enterprise of State, and trade, an individual matter.

A less favorable political conjuncture defeated the naval Declaration of London, February 26, 1909. Despite its title and the statement contained in its preamble, this Declaration was anything but an expression of generally recognized principles of international law. Product of ingenious compromises which were sometimes also rather artificial, it was largely a work of legislation which propitious circumstances might have consolidated, but which was fated to collapse in the rapid deterioration of international relations. On December 12, 1911 the Naval Prize Bill was thrown out by the House of Lords, and as a sequel to this vote the Declaration remained unratified by any of the Powers that had participated in drafting it.

The gradual codification of international law on which work was begun in 1924 under the auspices of the League of Nations was profoundly different in its abstract and academic spirit. The experience showed that the somewhat vague and remote interest of the States in a better statement of international law could not compensate for the absence of a firm will on the part of the governments and of the conviction that the task to be done was one of immediate usefulness.[19] The check that the enterprise suffered, at the 1930 Conference, though in many respects disappointing, has its useful lessons.

It has shown first of all that governments cannot be asked to define their views on the rules of international law without baring the political interests which the rules hold in balance and thus running the risk that these interests may be called in question.[20] In the always somewhat factitious setting of diplomatic conferences for the codification of international law, differences that cannot be brought out in open confrontation on their proper terrain, which is political,

[19] H. A. Smith, *Transactions of the Grotius Society*, vol. 16 (1930), p. 96: "It (the League) can supply the machinery, but it cannot supply the motive power."

[20] See on this subject the sound observations of Arnold Raestad, in *Revue de Droit international* (Paris), 1931, vol. VII, p. 109: "It is scarcely possible, save by abstraction, to regard these rules as purely legal, that is to say put once and for all in a class above political conflict. The political oppositions enter again with all their weight, the interests with all their force, the moment we begin to formulate and improve or modernize the rules of law."

are concealed under tendentious statements of the law in force. The arguments that these provoke give currency among the delegates to the fatal notion that the obligatory force of the rules under discussion depends in the last analysis on nothing more than the decisions of the governments which they represent. Thus there is danger of weakening and unsettling the law which codification was to clarify and consolidate.[21] This risk is increased by the search for compromises that will win unanimity and that expose progressive States to the danger of aligning their positions with those of more conservative or less advanced States.[22]

These negative observations happily do not exhaust the lessons to be drawn from the codification undertaken by the League of Nations. With the passage of time it has become clear that on many points the differences were due less to the desire of certain governments to resume their freedom of action at the expense of the law than to fundamental disagreements over still-unclarified aspects of the problems attacked. In this context the 1930 Conference was rich in its instruction. In the three subjects on the agenda (nationality, territorial waters, international responsibility of States), the preparatory work and the discussions revealed particular situations of fact and of law which make it necessary either to reconsider the basis of certain rules too uncritically taken as established, or to limit their field of application or qualify the terms in which they are expressed.[23] This recall to some of the realities of international regulation and to the necessity of more exact individualization or particularization of the law has helped to introduce a less abstract or schematic style in statements of doctrine. It has brought the law back to international life in its diversity and growing complexity.

Today the chance of codification of international law on a universal scale is nil. The gap between the conceptions of law which

21 See the Resolution adopted at Lausanne by the Institute of International Law, *Annuaire de l'Institut*, 1947, pp. 261-262.

22 Following the miscarriage of the 1930 Conference at The Hague, some delegations in the Assembly of the League of Nations understood the lesson. A resolution proposed by Great Britain, France, Germany, Italy, and Greece declared without equivocation "that it was not for the League or for Conferences convened by it to define the rules that are binding on States as part of customary international law." On some improvements in method, see Sir Cecil Hurst, *op.cit.*; R. Y. Jennings, "The Progressive Development of International Law and its Codification," *B.Y.B.I.L.*, 1947, p. 301; Paul De Visscher, "Considérations sur la technique de la Codification du droit international," *Rapport en vue de la Session de Prague de l'International Law Association*, 1947.

23 The General Conference on Communications and Transit (Barcelona, 1921) had already pointed the way to similar conclusions.

confront each other in the General Assembly of the United Nations, even on the most fundamental points, has become so wide that any further enterprise of this order must be regarded as a danger to the progress of international law.[24]

§ 2. THE GENERAL ACTION OF POWER ON CUSTOM

The voluntarist doctrine sees in international custom the product of a tacit agreement of wills among States. This plainly fictitious construction proceeds from a fallacious view of the action of power on the formation of customary law. Instead of looking at a practice in the stages of the historical process of its development, this school reconstructs it ex post facto and projects it, completely formed, on the plane of contractual notions. Nothing is more calculated to miss a true perspective on the growth of custom.[25] In international relations more than elsewhere, the fact precedes its classification. Precedents, which are often conscious derogations from the law in force, or which at least are almost always autonomous and uncoordinated acts, do not win the general adherence that makes custom until they take on the appearance of a coherent practice containing the elements of an order that is morally and socially acceptable because it is sustained by sufficient forces and is adapted to generally felt needs.[26] This is because order remains the primordial need of international relations, but also because if order postulates power, power can ensure its own continuance only by winning a measure of moral assent.

From the assimilation of custom to tacit convention, which in our judgment is quite fictitious, must be distinguished the requirement of *opinio juris sive necessitatis*, regarded here as reflecting the attitude of power in relation to a given practice. In its judgment of November 20, 1950, in the case of the right of asylum (Colombia-Peru)—a judgment which fixes its jurisprudence on this subject—

[24] Cf. H. Lauterpacht, "Codification and Development of International Law," *A.J.I.L.*, 1955, pp. 38-39.

[25] It is true, however, as M. Sörensen observes (*Les Sources du Droit international*, p. 85), that in order to prove the existence of a custom the interpreter follows a train of reasoning which "infers from the concrete behavior of the subjects of law an abstract rule the content of which conforms with that behavior."

[26] G. Scelle, *Précis de Droit des Gens*, vol. II, p. 307, and, by the same author, "Essais sur les sources formelles du droit international," *Mélanges Gény*, vol. III, p. 421. Jean Ray: "There are in custom forces quite other than mere respect for a tacit consent; there is especially respect for an established order. . . ." *Rec. A.D.I.*, vol. 48 (1934), p. 697.

the International Court of Justice clearly asserted the necessity of this psychological element in custom.[27] In rejecting the contrary thesis, defended by certain authors attached to a more formal conception, especially the champions of the pure theory of law,[28] the Court is much closer to the realities of international life. Governments attach importance to distinguishing between custom, by which they hold themselves bound, and the mere practices often dictated by consideration of expediency and therefore devoid of definite legal meaning. The fact that this is often a political interest is no reason for denying its significance.[29]

Every international custom is the work of power. It proceeds from practices to which the individual remains a stranger, hardly even perceiving the links that connect them with the social interests they are intended to serve. There is no customary law that individuals take so little a part in forming as international custom.

The slow growth of international custom has been compared to the gradual formation of a road across vacant land. To begin with, the tracks are many and uncertain, scarcely visible on the ground. Then most users, for some reason of common utility, follow the same line; a single path becomes clear, which in turn gives place to a road henceforth recognized as the only regular way, though it is impossible to say at what precise moment the latter change took place.[30]

This is an exact comparison that may be completed by the observation that follows. Among the users are always some who mark the soil more deeply with their footprints than others, either because of their weight, which is to say their power in this world, or because their interests bring them more frequently this way. Thus it happens that the great Powers, after imprinting a definite direction upon a usage, make themselves its guarantors and defenders.

27 For the Court a usage, though constant and uniform, does not become a custom unless the alleged rule has been applied as a right belonging to the States granting asylum and respected by the territorial States as a duty incumbent on them. Reports of Judgments, 1950, p. 277. This view is moreover fully supported by Article 38 of the Statute of the Court, which recognizes the existence of a custom only if the practice which is its content has been "accepted as law."

28 See Guggenheim, *Traité de droit international public*, p. 47.

29 The case referred to the Court shows that proving the existence of the psychological element of custom does not present the insurmountable difficulties sometimes alleged. It may perfectly well be inferred from the external qualities of the precedents invoked, especially from their coherence or discordance.

30 Pitt Cobbett, *Leading Cases on International Law*, 5th edn., vol. I, p. 5.

Their role, which was always decisive in the formation of customary international law, is to confer upon usages that degree of effectiveness without which the legal conviction, condition of general assent, would find no sufficient basis in social reality. Many customs owe their origin wholly to decisions or acts of great Powers which by their repetition or sequence, and above all by the idea of order that finally grows out of them, have little by little lost their personal, contingent, in a word political character and taken on that of a custom in process of formation. The strong impulse given by the United States, from the end of the eighteenth century on, to the development of the law of neutrality may be cited as an example.

Clearly, without conflicting, the legal perspective, which is one of legitimation, and the political perspective, which is one of historical facts, remain distinct. The jurist, seeking a principle of legitimation, justifies established custom ex post facto by its concordance with the requirements of order; the historian uncovers the play of political forces that determined its formation. The two points of view are not mutually exclusive. International custom is one of the most important manifestations of the joint action of force and law.[31]

The very large part taken by power relations in the formation of customs being conceded, it nevertheless remains true that a custom becomes compulsory only from the moment when the practice which is its material substratum is generally accepted "as law" (Art. 38 of the Statute of the International Court of Justice). This psychological factor implies a moral judgment which, relying on criteria of reason, justice, and common utility, separates what in a given practice appears to be dictated by a certain conformity with the general interest and with principle from what appears to be due solely to accidental circumstances or individual motives. In fact decided opposition to a practice by a large number of States, the contingent character of the precedents that make it up, and especially any tendency to confirm momentary inequalities of force

[31] Though regularity of observance is the essential criterion in the formation of custom, it must nevertheless be admitted that the mental process by which the human mind associates the idea of obligation with the social fact of regularity is an uncertain one. Any conception of order brings into play a vast complex, at once psychological and social, the elements of which cannot be specified a priori. Hence the impossibility of foreseeing the detailed facts to be taken into account or even the direction in which these facts will move at the end of the development to take the form of "precedents" constitutive of custom. This observation accounts for the difficulty, often noticed, of indicating in general terms at what moment a custom must be considered formed and, inversely, at what moment it falls into desuetude.

among States, in a word an adventitious character and individualist motivation, generally prevent the transformation of even widespread usage into custom having the force of law.[32]

The role of power in setting the precedents upon which international custom is based has two aspects. Precedents involve a positive act on one side, and some degree of passivity on the other.[33] It has been asked whether this degree of passivity may be inferred from repeated abstentions or prolonged silence on the part of the generality of States. This problem—which is of an entirely different order from the part played by abstention in the acquisition or loss of subjective rights (prescription)—is still debated. We must first of all put aside the fairly numerous cases in which abstention cannot reasonably be interpreted as anything but assent. Such is the case of certain "negative" practices that so closely touch territorial sovereignty that they cannot be regarded otherwise than as a positive taking of position.[34]

Moreover, it seems necessary to distinguish the part that abstention could play in the historical formation of customary international law from that which we can attribute to it now. The place and the legal relevance of passivity in the formation of international custom were certainly important at a time when the law, being still very uncertain, showed a special plasticity; the failure to react then easily led to the consolidation of a custom. It is different when legal relations multiply and their content and contours have become more clearly defined. When law is thus better defined, it appears more difficult to attribute a probative character to mere abstentions. The view here expressed is confirmed by the attitude of governments. This shows a very marked tendency to claim free choice of the position to be taken in relation to the acts of other States, but gives no justification for the view that abstention, which is often in fact dictated by opportunistic considerations, has the legal effect of assent.

32 The practice of pacific blockade as a form of reprisal is an example. It has remained a mode of political pressure, and the attempt to give it a legal construction proceeds from doctrinal views resisted by many States.

33 Express opposition prevents the creation of a precedent. The attitude of States regarding the conditions governing the formation of precedents is a question entirely distinct from the contractual view of the basis of custom taken by the voluntarist theory.

34 M. Sörensen (*op.cit.*, pp. 98-101) cites as an example the custom authorizing innocent passage of foreign warships in territorial waters. To the same effect may be cited the exemption of certain categories of vessels from capture; the "Paquete Habana," U.S. Supreme Court (1900).

This explains the conservative position taken by the Permanent Court of International Justice in the *Lotus* case. The Court was there called upon to judge the role of abstention in a situation characterized by a conflict of jurisdiction in which both sides invoked clearly defined legal principles. While implicitly admitting that abstention may constitute an element of custom, the Court attributed this character to it only if it has been shown that the motive of abstention was consciousness of a duty.[35] The same consideration explains the continuing doctrinal hesitations on this subject, especially the refusal to attribute probative character to abstention in so-called matters of "discretionary jurisdiction," where State prerogatives stand on a particularly firm legal foundation.[36]

It is well known that acts of municipal law may contribute to the formation of practices which are the material of international custom. This is true of laws, decrees, orders or ordinances, and judicial decisions handed down in matters which fall either principally or in certain aspects under international law. Such internal acts are relevant in that they are to be taken into consideration when the number and importance of parallel instances justify regarding them as a line of conduct adopted by States in the belief that it is in conformity with international law. In this decentralizing role the movement of municipal law is simply complementary to inter-State activities. It is nevertheless a generalizing instrument of international law on its customary side; it merely makes this customary law concrete, adding the coefficient of particularism inherent in the coexistence of sovereign and independent States.

The tendency to differentiation becomes more marked when the internal legislation, while respecting the principle of a custom, makes a definitely individualized adaptation of it owing to exceptional conditions of fact. The judgment rendered by the International Court of Justice on the Royal Norwegian decree of 1935 in

35 Publications of the Permanent Court of International Justice, series A, no. 10, p. 28. See in this connection J. L. Brierly, who observes that it is not easy to deduce from the practice followed by a State in a matter of jurisdiction the principle on which the practice is based, "since we cannot safely argue from the fact that it assumes jurisdiction only in certain cases that it regards those cases as the only ones in which the assumption of jurisdiction would be legitimate." *Criminal Competence of States*, Committee of Experts for the Progressive Codification of International Law, Publications of the League of Nations, 1926, vol. 7, p. 2.

36 See on this point Georges Scelle, *Précis de Droit des Gens*, vol. II, p. 309: "In this case mere abstentions do not seem probatory; positive acts would be necessary to establish the custom."

the Fisheries case (Great Britain–Norway, December 18, 1951) provides an example.

A wider field for this differentiation of custom by the internal power is offered by the "reserved domain." Here the process may run the whole gamut. Sometimes, and still in conformity with the law, it takes the form of free decision by the State in an order of interests where the State retains discretionary judgment. A case in point is the choice by each State of the criteria for acquiring its nationality (*jus soli* or *jus sanguinis*) subject to the customary rule that prohibits the grant of nationality in the absence of any recognized bond of attachment. Sometimes, on the other hand, the internal law, departing from the principle of a custom, embarks upon a course of international illegality. Thus, though every State freely organizes its courts, a law imposing discriminatory conditions on access to them by aliens would be contrary to customary international law.

Finally, special conditions common to several States may induce them to enact laws which by their concordance and constant application produce regional or local customs. The legal community thus created is limited to the mutual relations of the participating States.[37]

There is general agreement that it is in customary international law that we must look for the general or common law of nations. This explains its obligatory character for States that have not participated in its formation as well as the subjection of new States to the whole body of existing customary norms. But we must avoid exaggeration. There are particular customs, and it is observable that the sedimentation of international practices forms strata of unequal importance. If there are basic elements in the customary rule which, owing to their exact correspondence with the common needs of the great majority of States, call for general application, there are others, of a secondary character, which can only be applied with differentiations adapting them to particular situations. The malleability of custom here enables it spontaneously to achieve the individualization of the rule which must elsewhere be the deliberate work of an international convention.

In other cases this individualization will be effected by international case-law. Asked to pronounce upon the validity of the straight

[37] It was upon a practice common to the riparian States of the Baltic that the Danish and Swedish Governments based their protests (1951-1952) against the Soviet Government's extension of its territorial waters to twelve miles.

base-lines adopted by the Norwegian Government to delimit its territorial waters along part of its coast, the International Court of Justice recognized that a coast so much and so deeply indented could not be subject purely and simply to the customary low-water-mark rule. For this exceptional case, the Court held that the only truly fundamental principle was that of a necessary connection between the marginal sea and the configuration of the coast, and it relied especially upon the degree of intimacy between certain stretches of sea and the earth formations that separate or surround them. It rejected the more refined technical formulas invoked, though in many regards insufficiently established, by the British Government, as ill adapted to a littoral which because of its exceptional conformation called for a different method.[38] The case clearly showed that an international custom of which the elements and contours have not been adequately analyzed and grasped may be made up of elements of unequal density or value, some deeply rooted in the general practice of States, others neither so firmly implanted nor so universally diffused.

The tendency towards some individualization of the rules of international law as they were understood in the last century thus does not spare the rules of custom. This tendency is due to a more exact knowledge of the concrete conditions of application. It is inseparable from a certain refinement of the law, and from its more regular and more frequent application—an application therefore more differentiated and better adapted to the diversity of factual situations. Hence there is no reason for seeing here a threat to the existence or unity of customary international law; these retouches do not reach the foundations but only the constructional or technical features. It is only in its essential components that an international custom escapes these individualizing influences and remains the expression of the common or general law.

International case-law has done more than the Codification Conference of 1930 to clarify the new factors which, sometimes without the governments being precisely aware of what is happening, affect the evolution of customary law. The exercise of the judicial function

[38] J. L. Brierly: "Uniformity is good only when it is convenient, that is to say when it simplifies the task in hand; it is bad when it results from an artificial assimilation of dissimilar cases. . . . The nature of international society does not merely make it difficult to develop rules of international law of general application, it sometimes makes them undesirable." *Rec. A.D.I.*, vol. 58 (1936), pp. 17-18.

reveals the growing complexity of international relations, the unsuspected diversity and importance of intermediate or even strictly individual situations, and the reasons that prevent applying without nuances or distinctions a customary rule that has become too absolute in its traditional expression.[39] This refinement of customary law by international judgments is of very special interest at a time of general instability and uncertainty.

What gives international custom its special value and its superiority over conventional institutions, in spite of the inherent imprecision of its expression, is the fact that, developing by spontaneous practice, it reflects a deeply felt community of law. Hence the density and stability of its rules. The contractual origin of rules laid down in multilateral (law-making) treaties remains for them a cause of weakness. Insofar as the treaty has no foundation in custom, this origin exposes its rules to the difficulties of interpretation and the risks of nullity that attach to all regulation based upon manifestations of will.

The profound divergence on this subject between Soviet doctrine and that of the Western countries is striking evidence of the absence of any community of law. Except in a few matters, the Soviet jurists are disposed to regard customary international law as a body of ideas and practices imposed on weak nations by capitalist imperialism. Against this form of oppression the reaffirmation of sovereignty appears to them the only effective safeguard, and the treaty, free expression of wills liberated from an antisocial past, the true foundation of international relations.[40] This conception was the basis of the resolutely negative attitude of the Soviet delegation to the San Francisco Conference towards any proposal to insert in the Charter a text along the lines of Article 19 of the Covenant concerning the revision of international treaties.

In less extreme form and in a different spirit, positions are beginning to be taken favorable to a critical examination of customary rules which are most directly affected by especially important political or social changes, such as the extension of State powers, developments in the institutions of property, the international protection of human rights, the growth of international organiza-

[39] See on this point the judicious observations of L. Cavaré, *Le Droit international public positif*, vol. I, p. 218.

[40] On the entirely subordinate role of custom, Soviet doctrine is unanimous. See, among others, S. Krylov, *Les notions principales du Droit des Gens; la doctrine soviétique du Droit international*, *Rec. A.D.I.*, vol. 70 (1947), pp. 441-442.

tion, or the retrogression in the law of neutrality. We shall cite many examples further on.

It is easy to recognize the causes which, in a time such as ours, limit the development of customary law and obstruct its adaptation to particular situations and to new needs. One of the causes draws immediate attention: that is the extreme instability of international relations. Malleable as it is, custom can neither establish itself, nor evolve and so remain a source of living law, when, owing to the rapidity with which they follow each other or to their equivocal or contradictory character, State activities cease to crystallize into "a general practice accepted as law." Acceleration of history, and above all diminishing homogeneity in the moral and legal ideas that have long governed the formation of law—such, in their essential elements, are the causes that today curtail the development of customary international law.

If we seek an over-all view of the general conditions governing the present development of international law in its relations with power, we find this development responding to certain dominant influences which, very briefly and subject to corrections suggested by inevitable intervening factors, may be summarized as follows:

1. Heavy reinforcement of the deliberate action of power, supported by all the moral and material forces at the disposal of the modern State, such as profound and often exclusive national motivation and the constant expansion of the sphere of action by the growing control of public authority over private interests and activities.

2. Sudden and unprecedented expansion in international relations, both as to the human communities that participate and as to the interests involved—an expansion which, by its additions to the bulk of relations, and by the complications and the instability to which it gives rise, diminishes the homogeneity of the traditional communities of law on the one hand and, on the other, emphasizes the extreme slowness and the defects of the old processes by which law developed.

3. Better knowledge and more refined appraisal of the data of all sorts that govern the action of power—a knowledge and appraisal that widen the horizons of doctrine, reveal to it unsuspected complexities and qualifications, and induce it to abandon excessive formalism and generalization out of respect for a social reality more clearly perceived and more courageously accepted.

Section III

Political Doctrines—The Soviet Conception of International Law

It is not a rare thing for States or groups of States, seeking either to consolidate ill-defined or disputed legal claims, or to ensure their independence, their security, or their special interests in certain regions of the world, to formulate their views or announce their line of conduct in a declaration cast in more or less solemn doctrinal terms. Authors are inclined to deny that such declarations have any legal effect in the international order. History shows, however, that the positions so taken, though political in their motives and in their unilateral character, have had an influence, sometimes considerable, on the formation and application of international law.[41]

The leading and on the whole beneficent part played in the development of international law by the doctrine of balance professed and sustained by the Concert of Europe in the nineteenth century is well known. Extension of conventional international law, regular observation of treaties, fairly general respect for the independence and rights of small States, growing precision in the law of neutrality, such were some fruits of the nineteenth-century practice of balance. A political principle, the balance helped powerfully in the development of international law, by assuring it for a time of that tempered climate which is indispensable for the effective observance and lasting progress of law.

Already in the eighteenth century the manifesto by Catherine II (February 27, 1780), basis of the League of Neutrals or First Armed Neutrality, offers an example of political doctrine destined to amend international law. Though at the time a purely political act, Great Britain having refused to change her maritime practices, the manifesto expressed a new consciousness of neutral interests and already contained the substance of the rules which were to be laid down in the Declaration of Paris, 1856.

Of incomparably greater significance, the Monroe Doctrine is

[41] These doctrines with their historically established effects upon law are not to be confused with the "constants" or mere regularities of the foreign policy of certain Powers. For example, Great Britain's assertion of "special or vital interests in certain regions of the world" (British note to the United States, May 19, 1928) is not to be placed on the same plane with the Monroe Doctrine. Though politically very important, these "constants" usually have no definite legal sense.

inseparable from the general policy of the United States. It is a highly political doctrine—in its basic principle, which is national security; in its program, long founded on the unilaterally interpreted principle of nonintervention in the American continent; in its interpretation and application, which remained at the complete discretion of the United States, to the exclusion alike of any joint action and of any international control.[42] The United States, which formulated it under its sole authority, proposes to keep its interpretation and application exclusively in its own hands.

Such a doctrine necessarily evolves according to the relative power of the State which makes it its rule of conduct and with the extent of the responsibilities which the growth of that power entails. As the United States has risen from the rank of guardian of the Western Hemisphere to that of first Power, the security idea on which the Monroe Doctrine is based has detached itself from its continental setting and entered that of world politics.

The great majority of States have of course acknowledged the Monroe Doctrine, in particular by recognizing that the participation of the United States in various international conventions did not oblige that country to abandon its traditional policy in questions of purely American interest.[43] Mere acquiescence in a policy, this recognition of the Monroe Doctrine by the other States has changed neither its character nor its methods. It is nonetheless true that the Doctrine, followed with tenacity and sustained with all the resources of a great Power, has had a profound though often indirect influence on the application of certain rules of international law to the American continents.

Thus for example the principle of noncolonization has been amplified to the point of prohibiting any transfer of territory, even by genuine consent, to a non-American Power—a prohibition probably justified from the political point of view but certainly unknown to the common law of nations.[44] Thus, also, moving from actual defense to preventive protection, the Washington government has sometimes opposed not only attempts at colonization by a non-American government but even the cession of certain points or zones to private companies, proclaiming, moreover, the special

[42] Charles Evans Hughes, "Observations on the Monroe Doctrine," *A.J.I.L.*, 1923, pp. 615-616. Cf. Charles Cheney Hyde, *International Law*, 2nd edn., vol. I, pp. 301-302.

[43] Cf. Art. 21 of the Covenant of the League of Nations.

[44] Hackworth, *Digest*, vol. V, pp. 440, 457-460.

interest of the United States in those zones on the ground that they are particularly important for its communications or security.[45]

But it is especially in the matter of intervention as a mode of coercive action, and in inter-American relations, that the interpretation of the Monroe Doctrine by the Washington government has given rise to differences on important principles of international law. Unlike the Latin Republics of the New World, which are resolutely hostile to all individual intervention, the United States has made a distinction between political and nonpolitical interventions, the latter, commonly called "interpositions," being regarded by it as admissible even in the form of armed intervention when it held them justified by their cause (diplomatic protection of nationals and cases of denial of justice) and not of a kind to lead to permanent occupation or political control.

This distinction, which tended to regulate rather than proscribe intervention, met with determined opposition from a large number of delegations from Latin America at the Pan-American Conference (1928) in Havana—an opposition directed less against any risk of European intervention, by this time hardly serious, than against that of "interpositions" by the United States.[46] These differences had profound repercussions on the development of the law: they crystallized opposed views on the closely related problems of the treatment of aliens and of international responsibility (exhaustion of local remedies and denial of justice). The state of mind so produced contributed substantially to the double failure of the Conference of Paris in 1929 (the treatment of aliens) and the Hague Conference in 1930 (codification of international law).[47]

At the Buenos Aires Conference in 1936, the United States signed the additional Protocol on nonintervention prohibiting any direct or indirect intervention in the internal or external affairs of the

[45] *ibid.*, pp. 437-438 (Magdalena Bay incident).

[46] J. M. Yépès, *Philosophie du pan-americanisme et Organisation de la Paix*, 1945, pp. 275 seq., and, by the same author, *Les problèmes fondamentaux du Droit des Gens en Amérique*, *Rec. A.D.I.*, vol. 47 (1934), pp. 73-80; C. Barcia Trelles, *Rec. A.D.I.*, vol. 32 (1930), p. 571.

[47] On the different trends in the matter of intervention, see *Dictionnaire diplomatique*, verbo *Intervention*, articles by J. G. Guerrero and Charles Evans Hughes. Under the Charter an armed intervention would have to be considered "inconsistent with the Purposes of the United Nations" even though its object were merely to protect the nationals of the intervening State and not to attack the territorial integrity or political independence of another State; cf. Art. 2, para. 4, of the Charter.

contracting parties "on any pretext whatever."[48] The Bogota Charter, April 30, 1948, affirmed this principle.

In the Drago doctrine, a legal thesis, which was to be given at least partial recognition at the Second Peace Conference, was grafted upon a political thesis, namely that which prohibited any European Power from using force to secure repayment or the service of contractual debts claimed from a country by a foreign government as due to its nationals. Drago logically invoked the original statement of the Monroe Doctrine which absolutely condemned any sort of intervention. The thesis had not, however, the unreserved support of the United States, for the internal disorders of certain Latin Republics and its own interest as a potentially creditor Power had led that country to distinguish between lawful and unlawful interventions. The Second Hague Peace Conference (convention on limiting the use of force for the recovery of contractual debts, 1907) accepted the idea that a State should not be gravely disturbed in its public life or driven to ruin by a foreign armed intervention to enforce repayment of contractual debts. But it had to make an exception in favor of such intervention if the debtor State refused to arbitrate, prevented the conclusion of a *compromis*, or refused to carry out an award. Thus a political doctrine which was too unilateral was remedied by a legally acceptable compromise.

The Tobar and Wilson doctrines that made the recognition of new governments conditional upon the constitutional legitimacy of their establishment sprang from a political ideology in which concern for the free consent of the governed mingled with a particular view concerning the stability of international relations. Their application was limited to the countries of the American continents. The political aspects of Wilsonian practice, which were hardly consistent with the principle of nonintervention, led to its speedy abandonment.[49]

The Calvo doctrine is another example of a thesis which, though political in its original motives, nevertheless had at least an indirect influence upon the practice of international law. The doctrine owed its inception (1868) to resentment caused by the interventions of European Powers in Argentina, Uruguay, and Mexico. In its original tenor it aimed at excluding all intervention, even of the merely diplomatic variety, by European States seeking to protect the persons, goods, or claims of their nationals, cases of discrimina-

[48] Cf. Charles Cheney Hyde, *International Law*, vol. I, § 83B.
[49] Hackworth, *Digest*, vol. I, pp. 180 seq.

tory measures alone excepted. The Calvo doctrine could be explained, from the political point of view, by the constant risk of interposition to which certain States were exposed because their shortage of capital and technical resources forced them at this time to invite the participation of foreign enterprises. It has been very generally condemned as being incompatible with the sovereign right of States to protect their nationals. Yet it has exerted a real influence through the "Calvo clause" as that appears, with numerous variants, in contracts signed by aliens. The much-debated validity of the clause depends on its bearing on diplomatic protection in case of denial of justice. Recent decisions show a tendency in the arbitrators to recognize its validity if it is interpreted as merely declaratory of the rule of international law requiring exhaustion of local remedies.[50] For this reason these decisions have been criticized by some authors.[51] In reality, they bear witness to the embarrassment of arbiters naturally concerned to reconcile as far as possible traditionally conflicting political views.

Despite their undeniable historical influence on the interpretation and application of international law, most political doctrines are born and develop under the impact of the power relations existing in a given period between States or groups of States. Their future depends upon the forces that sustain and the resistances that oppose them. They are usually either a defensive reflex or an assertion of certain vital or special interests in specified geographic regions. They lose their original shape or disappear with changes in the ratio of interests and of forces. The Monroe Doctrine has continued to evolve to the point of shedding all its isolationist content under the influence of recent events which have made the United States the first world Power and consequently multiplied its need to take positions on all continents. As against an impoverished and enfeebled Europe, the Drago and Calvo doctrines have lost almost all political interest for the countries that championed them.[52]

[50] North American Dredging Co. U.S. v. Mexico; Hackworth, *Digest*, vol. v, pp. 635-654.

[51] A. V. Freeman, *International Responsibility of States for Denial of Justice*, pp. 469-490; Charles Cheney Hyde, *International Law*, vol. I, § 305; K. Lipstein, "The Place of the Calvo Clause in International Law," *B.Y.B.I.L.*, 1945, p. 130.

[52] On American continental notions and the political factors which they reflect, reference may be made to the very suggestive surveys to be found from 1910 on in the works of Alej. Alvarez: *Le Droit international américain*, 1910, and *Codification du droit international*, 1912.

THE SOVIET DOCTRINE OF INTERNATIONAL LAW

The doctrines reviewed above occupy after all only a limited place in the general conspectus of international legal relations. Even the States that adhered to them saw in them only the statement of a policy or, at most, an adaptation of the rules of common international law to the ideas or needs of certain regions.

The significance of the Soviet doctrine of international law is quite another matter. This doctrine is based squarely upon a philosophy, Marxism, retouched by Lenin and by Stalin. It is and declares itself utterly alien to the common funds of ideas which gave rise to the international law of bourgeois societies. Between these societies and the Soviet State there can only be a compromise which transitionally governs their unavoidable relations.

The Soviet doctrine borrows from the Marxist interpretation of history its resolutely relativist cast, natural to a movement which proposes to found a new political and legal order upon a new social structure. All law being for it merely an expression of the will of the dominant classes in defense of their power and privileges, international law can be nothing more than a projection into international relations of the ruling social ideas of a given period. Relations between States of totally different social structures can therefore sustain only a very partial and entirely provisional legal integration.[58]

Soviet authors devote their best effort to this critical or destructive part of their doctrine. They are much more reticent when they approach the positive or constructive part of their task. Having pushed relativism to the point of at least theoretically denying any moral absolute, they are visibly embarrassed when they have to define the criteria by which Soviet international law separates norms which, despite their bourgeois origin, it can regard as sufficiently progressive for adoption, from those to which it attributes an imperialist character and which it therefore holds inacceptable.

This outlook, natural enough in a movement which, though it plans to win universal ascendency, remains in many respects on the defensive, is singularly conducive to political opportunism.

In the exposition of Soviet doctrines, two theories are most

[58] The ideology of the Soviet jurists has led them recently to give special emphasis to the influence of the particular features of the State's internal structure on international law. They of course interpret this influence in accordance with their general philosophy. This line of thought is clearly marked in Vyshinsky's later writings.

prominent: sovereignty and the equality of peoples. The first is an intransigent assertion of external sovereignty. By its "formal impenetrability" (cf. E. A. Korovin), sovereignty is the rampart of the socialist State and the peoples' democracies against imperialist adventures. The second is an at least provisional insistence upon the equality of States. This justifies supporting throughout the world the cause of liberation for communities which, under various regimes (trust territories, non-self-governing territories), live in dependence on capitalist States.

On the subject of the sources of law, the same care is taken to defend independent doctrinal positions and gradually to establish a new order. International custom is too much impregnated with the traditions of the bourgeois State and, as we have seen, occupies only a subordinate place. It is by treaty, preferably bilateral, that the Soviet State freely defines the relations that its ideology permits it to entertain with States of opposite social structure. Particular regulation, strictly subject to expressed wills, is the modality adapted to the provisional nature of these relations.

Soviet doctrine proudly proclaims its devotion to the principle *pacta sunt servanda*, never failing to cite as proof the opposition of the Soviet delegation at the San Francisco Conference to the proposal that the United Nations should have some competence in the revision of international treaties. But this does not, in the eyes of Soviet jurists, exclude revision made necessary by the kind of change which according to their doctrine calls in question the validity of every legal undertaking. This is the change that takes place when the State adopts a new social structure.

Finally, as the Soviet authors themselves like to emphasize, the absence of legal community is the characteristic of the "relations of emulation, struggle, and cooperation" between the Soviet State and the capitalist States. This explains the Soviet doctrine's distrust of arbitration and judicial settlement and the constant refusal of the Soviet Union to submit to these procedures. It also accounts for the small influence of Soviet ideology in the development of general international law. Except for certain contractual relations such as the conventions concluded on the basis of a State monopoly of foreign trade, the Soviet legal theses, which are strictly adapted to the imperatives of policy, bear in all essentials the negative aspect of sovereign exclusivism.[54]

[54] Cf. S. Krylov, *op.cit.*; E. A. Korovin, "The Second World War and International Law," *A.J.I.L.*, 1946, p. 742, and, by the same author, "Les principles

Section IV

The Application of Positive International Law. Object and Plan of the Following Discussion

The application of the rules of international law, being more concrete in its phenomena and more directly accessible to observation, offers our method a surer field of study than the development of those rules. The field is of course so vast that there can be no question at present of covering the whole of it or exploring all its perspectives. The jurist is not yet in possession of sufficiently abundant and precise data to adopt a program that would survey one after another all the phenomena of international practice and scrutinize, on the borders of law and politics, not only the motives of governments but even the intimate recesses of their attitudes toward international law.

Moreover, such is not our purpose. Working in a field which methodological prejudices have been largely responsible for leaving fallow, we were compelled to make a choice. As our sole object was to open up paths for freer and more extensive investigations, and to illustrate by selected examples views calculated to vitalize the study of positive international law by throwing new light upon it, the choice fell upon the most fundamental institutions. These are the institutions of which practice has sufficiently revealed not only the technical aspects but also the political and social significance. First comes the State itself, basic organism, seat of the only values that can be truly universalized in the bearing upon them of the problems of authority and liberty, of power and respect for human ends (Chap. II). Then come those parts of inter-State relations that form the weft of international life in its most constant and most essential aspects (Chap. III).

One other limit was set to our discussion by the very object of this work, which is not a treatise on international law and which deliberately abstains from describing in the traditional manner the whole body of rules constituting the technical structure of the various institutions in the field. These rules will be considered here only from the point of view of the influence exercised upon them by

de la Souveraineté," *Temps Nouveaux*, October 8, 1947 (no. 41), and "Soviet Treaties and International Law," *A.J.I.L.*, 1928, p. 753; Andrei Y. Vyshinsky, *The Law of the Soviet State*, 1948; T. A. Taracouzio, *The Soviet Union and International Law*, 1935.

the present conditions in international relations and more particularly by the existing distribution of power among nations.

Such a study is rich in instruction for all who are ready to set aside any prejudice of school and to consider in their reality and their flexibility the balances of interests of which the rules of international law are the formal expression.

The manifestations of a profound individualism are still preponderant in this field. This is the case in the international recognition of States and governments, despite the fundamental part of this institution in the establishment of inter-State relations. It is also the case, and in a much higher degree, in the matter of individual resort to armed force and the constant obstacle that the prospect of such recourse presents to any organization of international relations.

In the international treaty and the submission of disputes to judicial settlement, on the contrary, the perception of common interest predominates over individualist aims, making of these two institutions the essential instrument of progress in the international order. Even here it is never strong enough wholly to escape the grip of the political.

Behind these traditional institutions looms the problem, still ill defined in its contours because deeply involved in politics, of peaceful change—a major problem for which the present state of international relations undoubtedly renders any solution impossible, and which marks one of the most costly lacunae in those relations (Chap. IV).

The concrete observation of the way in which positive international law is applied is the surest method of grasping the realities from which it springs and the actual spirit animating it. What is attempted here is not therefore to reconstruct the law from social data too indeterminate to be utilizable, but to rediscover in the compromises of interest of which rules are historically a product at once their explanation and the limits of their validity.

Such a method, which puts us on our guard against preconceived constructions and artificial systematizations, keeps norms in contact with international life. It will help to restore to them, by the patient search for better adaptation to social demands, the minimum of efficacy which is the condition of their authority.

CHAPTER II. THE STATE IN THE INTERNATIONAL ORDER

IN THE orientation of international relations as in the development of the law which should govern them, the role and possibilities of the State remain decisive. Belonging as it does both to the national and to the international order, the State, as Max Huber observes, holds "a key position."[1]

Firmly established in a historical territorial setting, strong in the support of a national sentiment that has constantly grown more intense, the State can nevertheless not maintain itself, even in the internal order, without a minimum of legality. In the national order this minimum guarantees the continued existence of power; in international relations it is the condition of peaceful and ordered coexistence. Even for the basic elements of their internal organization, and in spite of a historical compartmentation that left a deep mark on the spirit of their people, States live in a factual dependence upon one another that calls for regulation by law.

Section I

Creation and Disappearance of States

The historical facts that lead to the formation of new States are "prelegal" data. There is no legal criterion which sufficiently embodies them to provide an undebatable legitimizing principle for the aspiration of a collectivity established on a defined territory to constitute an independent political entity. This is a political aspiration, and it is realized politically by that "organization of power"[2] which in the minds of men is traditionally associated with the concept of the State. The international legal order does not provide foundation for the State; it presupposes the State's existence. Recognizing the appearance on a territory of a political entity showing the characteristics generally attributed to the State, it merely invests it with personality in the law of nations and requires it to fulfill the international duties that correspond to its authority.

This does not at all mean that international law can be indifferent to the aspirations of peoples to form States or to the historical cir-

[1] *Gesellschaft und Humanität*, p. 21.

[2] G. Scelle, *Précis de Droit des Gens*, vol. I, p. 74.

cumstances which result in the creation of States. A sound partitioning of human groups not only contributes to the internal equilibrium of States; it is a condition of the efficacy of international law as of political stability in international relations.[3]

What international law, reduced to its traditional positive norms, is powerless to do, is not necessarily beyond the capacity of an international organization. The Charter proclaims among the purposes of the United Nations the development of "friendly relations among nations based on respect for the principle of equal rights and self-determination of peoples." Such a proclamation is of course not sufficient to introduce into positive international law so vague a notion as the self-determination of peoples,[4] which is certainly more imprecise than the principle of nationalities; but we cannot reject a priori the idea of help in the solution of these problems from a truly enlightened international organization, able to make impartial use of more refined criteria than the purely material one of the effective exercise of power, upon which now depends recognition that a new State-entity exists. The possibility of such control, which would in fact apply mainly in the case of groups without common historical past or clearly defined national personality, would depend on the ability of the organization to "depoliticize" by means of objective criteria a problem of which the data are almost all in the highest degree political. To demonstrate this political character, it is only necessary to recall the following among these data: the definition of the groups, now subject to the authority of another State, whose degree of development qualifies them for liberation; the recognition of legitimate means of satisfying this aspiration (secession, revolt); and the duties of third States in relation to their claims. These political data, so imprudently brought forward in the tumultuous atmosphere of the United Nations, could not be distinguished too sharply from the protection of human rights with which they have been so arbitrarily associated.

It happens that States may owe their existence to external political action running counter to those requirements of the effective exercise of power upon which the future of any political entity depends. Diplomatic history, ancient and recent, offers examples of States artificially created, either during a war and to influence

[3] Cf. the introductory part of Art. 55 of the Charter.

[4] On the lack of precision in the drafting of Article 1, paragraph 2, of the Charter, see H. Kelsen, *The Law of the United Nations*, pp. 51-52.

its course, or during a period of high political tension and to secure positions of advantage or useful assistance in "cold war."

This distorting action of politics assumes various forms. In 1918 the artifice known as "recognizing a nation" enabled the French and British Governments to give their political support to mere missions or "national councils" set up abroad. These were classified as "*de facto* independent organizations" representing collectivities which in reality were in the enemy's power. This initiative, which had for its admitted object the encouragement of these organizations in their struggle against the German occupation, led in 1920 and 1921 to the Supreme Council's *de jure* recognition as States of some of these collectivities, notably Lithuania, Estonia, and Latvia.[5]

The history of the last thirty years shows how heavily future international relations may be weighed upon by measures of this sort, taken to promote a unilateral and immediate political interest and without adequate consideration of the permanent geographic, ethnic, or economic factors upon which the fate of a State depends. The fictitious entities established in this way nourish the antagonisms to which they owe their existence. In this respect they differ sharply from the rather contemptuously named "buffer States" created in the nineteenth century to balance political pressures and, by the same token, dedicated to a pacific function. Because they are often established along major lines of political tension, their defense calls for agreements of military assistance and territorial guarantee which, though phrased in language borrowed from international organization, are hardly to be distinguished from the traditional alliances. No less serious and legally more relevant is the reproach of unreality levelled at these artificial creations. Notwithstanding the texts by which they are bound, the Powers that created them continue to have doubts about the solidity of their work. When, in contact with facts, it shows signs of wear, their promises fade out; in the presence of imminent danger the guarantees prove illusory. The Baltic States disappeared in 1940, without a move made to save them. Of them it could be said that their fate was inscribed from the beginning on the political map.

Certain recent creations of Asiatic or Arab States proceed largely from similar calculations, which are related to the manipulation of votes in the United Nations. They offer no better assurance of stability or duration.

[5] On the recognitions accorded under such conditions, see Hackworth, *Digest*, vol. I, pp. 199-202 for the Department of State's objections.

With these adventurous and unsound specimens of unilateral political action, nineteenth-century diplomatic history can to its great advantage contrast the considered decisions by which the Concert of Powers, acting in the general interests of Europe, now created a totally new State, now lent some collectivity in the last stage of its struggle for independence the political support of recognition. By their stability, several of these new entities became factors of balance and peace. This was because the spirit of moderation which was a condition of their agreement generally inspired the Powers in their political creations.

International law, being devoted above all to order and security, has always been more interested in facts that threaten the existence of States or bring about their dissolution than in those which account for their birth. But since it is subject to the rule of effectivity, it has never pushed to an extreme its protest against the violent destruction of a State organization. Subjugation, *debellatio*, retains its place among the ways in which States cease to exist. This does not mean that a State disappears by the mere fact that it is no longer able to keep up the struggle with means of its own, even though its territory is entirely occupied by the enemy. The effectiveness of the conquest may be offset, so long as the struggle goes on, by the effectiveness of resistance by third States. Without going so far as to say that the disappearance of the State remains in suspense so long as it has not been positively acknowledged by the generality of States, we must admit that it is not legally an accomplished fact until the day when attempts at restoration cease to enlist effective help.

This view of things, based in traditional international relations on the principle of effectivity, would be still more justified in collective action against aggression by the international Organization. That such action is still far from being an absolute guarantee of survival for the threatened State is a fact demonstrated by Italy's conquest of Ethiopia. The attitudes taken by the States members of the League of Nations on this occasion left few illusions on this subject. In particular, the distinctions that they tried to make between the effect of their *de facto* recognition of the annexation and those of a *de jure* recognition were entirely out of harmony with the principle of collective nonrecognition of situations brought about by force. No one can doubt that the qualifications attached to most of these *de facto* recognitions would shortly have given way to recognition *de jure* if the second world war had not reopened the whole question. It was to the result of that war and not at all to the principle of collective nonrecognition of illegal situations, solemnly proclaimed by the League of Nations on March 11, 1932, that Ethiopia owed the restoration of its independence.[6]

Connected with the disappearance of the State is the problem of the extinction or transmission to another State—"succession" in a current but inexact terminology—of the inter-State rights and obligations of the entity that has ceased to exist.[7]

In treaty relations there is no doubt about the principle: failing agreement to the contrary, treaties come to an end with the personality of the contracting State.[8] The principle is applied without qualification to treaty relations so strictly personal that their transmission is inconceivable. This is the case with relations arising out of treaties of a political character, such as treaties of alliance or those that stipulate an economic or tariff policy on the part of the defunct State which could not be binding on another State, as for example treaties of commerce or navigation. On the opposite side, there is a marked tendency to recognize the transmission of relations based upon a political statute established in a matter of general interest by the great Powers,[9] and of obligations formulated in a law-making treaty, insofar at least as this appears to be declarative rather than constitutive of legal rules. These exceptions are significant in the contrast that they show between the frailty of agreements of merely individual interest, dependent as these are upon transitory political relations, and the relative stability of conventions dictated by concern for order or respect for law. The ideas recently expressed by competent authors in favor of the transmission of obligations assumed in multilateral treaties merit attention. The reproach that they level at the contrary thesis, which is generally accepted in doctrine, that it relies too exclusively on the

[6] Cf. Charles Rousseau, "Le Conflit italo-éthiopien," *Revue générale de Droit international public*, 1938, pp. 83 seq.

[7] On the question of the vested rights of individuals, see below, Sec. II.

[8] On international practice, see Guggenheim, *Traité*, pp. 459-478; Arnold McNair, *The Law of Treaties*, pp. 389 seq.; M. Udina, *La succession des Etats quant aux obligations internationales autres que les dettes publiques*, *Rec. A.D.I.*, vol. 44 (1933). The question is not properly put as one of the transmission of treaties as such. Transmissibility depends on the intrinsic nature of the legal relations set up and not on the type of treaty which gives rise to them.

[9] See for instance the Protocol of January 20, 1831 drawn up by the London Conference on Belgium's share in the European duties of the defunct Kingdom of the Low Countries, and the Report of the Commission of Jurists (1920) on the status of the Aaland Islands as a matter "of European public law."

contractual nature of treaties as instruments of the particular interests of the signatory States, is well founded. No less cogent is the argument that the growing part played by multilateral treaties in the development of international law should count in favor of the transmission rather than disappearance of obligations. But the analogy of the necessary acceptance by a new State of the duties imposed by customary law cannot be held decisive in this context. The customary process is in itself a guarantee of the complete integration of law in the social order. This certainly cannot be said of multilateral treaties, which in troubled times such as ours succeed and intersect each other at a rate that leaves no room for the consolidating action of time.[10]

International practice, still ill defined, is inclined to recognize the principle of transmission in the case of legal relations which, by reason of their connection with the territory of the defunct State, take on an objective character in which some authors discern a notion related to that of "real rights" or "servitudes." Examples are the transmission to a State acquiring territory of the defunct State's obligations arising out of the delimitation of its territory; the transmission of obligations, to be carried out in a given territory (localization), that have permanent economic interest for other States.[11] This is an important implementation of the idea of continuity in the application of law.

The disappearance of States is too often linked with war to permit ignoring the practice in peace treaties. The Treaties of Saint-Germain (Arts. 234 seq.) and Trianon (Arts. 261 seq.) on the one hand listed multilateral treaties, conventions, and agreements "of an economic or technical character" concluded by the former Austro-Hungarian monarchy, which they declared alone applicable to Austria and to Hungary respectively; and on the other hand reserved for each of the Allied and Associated Powers the right to notify these States of the bilateral conventions of every sort of which they would demand execution.

The very marked political character of such arrangements contrasts with the purely legal and uniformly recognized rule of non-transmission for obligations *ex delicto* incumbent on the defunct

[10] Cf. the excellent study by C. Wilfred Jenks, "State Succession in Respect of Law-Making Treaties," *B.Y.B.I.L.*, 1952, p. 105.

[11] H. Rolin, *Principes de Droit international public*, *Rec. A.D.I.*, vol. 77 (1950), p. 339; M. Udina, *op.cit.*, p. 717. For the opposite view see A. Cavaglieri, *Règles générales du droit de la paix*, *Rec. A.D.I.*, vol. 26 (1929), p. 375.

State under the heading of international responsibility. This rule indeed springs wholly from the legal principle of the personal character of fault and has been repeatedly confirmed in the awards made by claims commissions.[12]

Section II

Man and the State in Positive International Law

In the international as in the internal order, human values are the reason behind the legal rule. Based upon moral conceptions which are the very essence of civilization, they impose themselves upon the State, whose mission is to ensure their protection and their free development. There is no context in which power has a more definitely functional character. We have emphasized elsewhere the intimate and indissoluble connection between this moderating view of internal power and the effectiveness of international law.[13] Frederic de Martens had already remarked the historical concordance between the development of positive international law and the respect shown the individual within the State.

The nineteenth century, a period of calm and of liberalism, was generally favorable to the protection of human rights. Prohibition of the slave trade in the Final Act of the Congress of Vienna (February 8, 1815), renewed in the Congresses of Aix-la-Chapelle (1818) and Verona (1822); repression of slavery and of the slave trade and protection of native peoples in the Acts of the Berlin (1885) and Brussels (1890) Conferences; humanitarian interventions, sometimes individual, sometimes collective, by the great Powers to put a stop to the persecution of their own nationals by certain States—interventions which, notwithstanding their sometimes political aims, helped to implant the idea of limitations upon sovereignty imposed by respect for man:[13a] affirmation, especially in

12 The Brown case, *American and British Claims Arbitration Tribunals*, 1923; cf. Sir Cecil Hurst, "State Succession in Matters of Tort," *B.Y.B.I.L.*, 1924, p. 163.

13 "An effective legal order among States is inseparable from respect for the human person in the internal order of each State." Resolution of the Institute of International Law, Lausanne session, *1947*.

13a It was moral considerations that justified the practice of humanitarian intervention, a practice that classic international law held irreconcilable with sovereignty. Sir W. Vernon Harcourt emphasized this opposition of views: "Intervention is a question rather of policy than of law. It is above and beyond the domain of law, and when wisely and equitably handled by those who have

favor of minorities, of freedom of conscience and religious toleration as a condition of recognition of new States or States with new territory; such were some characteristic manifestations of a current of ideas that linked international-law observance with respect for human personality in the internal order.

Unhappily this liberal tradition, nourished by most varied and at times incoherent ideologies, and associated with contingent political forms or debatable economic theories, never had the strong moral and spiritual foundations that alone would have enabled it to limit the authoritarian action of the centralizing State. As for international law, its doctrinal deficiencies were still more serious. Dominated by the dualistic separation of the internal and international orders, it affected to take no interest in man, regarded indeed as a mere object of international relations, except insofar as his treatment abroad might influence relations between States. Thus it found itself powerless when the great commotions of the twentieth century shook the very moral and social foundations of the protection of man's rights and everywhere diminished his security in foreign lands.

Nationalism, in the service of the State, gradually put a political imprint upon human values. Totalitarianism, which is its brutal but logical end-result, looks upon man only from the State's point of view. Nowhere is the decline of law more marked than in its growing impotence to protect man against the abuses of power.

Contemporary laws on the acquisition and loss of nationality testify to the State's tendency to lay hold on individuals when it finds them politically useful, and to leave them without any protection when it does not. The abandonment of treaty systems for the protection of minorities, and the degrading practices of population-transfers and mass expulsions, demonstrate the retrogression in respect for the fundamental rights of man at the very moment when the international Organization complacently and theoretically proclaims them. The decline of individual rights is no less notable in the protection of acquired rights, particularly in relation to respect for property. The insecurity of these rights denotes not only a weakening of the idea of law, but instability in international relations.

the power to give effect to it, may be the higher policy of justice and humanity." *Historicus*: Letters on Some Questions of International Law, 1863, p. 14.

§ 1. LAWS OF NATIONALITY. DENATIONALIZATIONS. EXPULSION

The leading role of the nationality principle in the constitution and transformation of States since the nineteenth century could not fail sooner or later to bring about the classification of statutes relating to the nationality of individuals as part of public law. Indeed the principles governing the distribution and allegiance of men among political entities may be regarded as directly affecting the political organization, the independent life, and the very substance, of the State. It is nevertheless significant that it was during and after the first world war that doctrine began to emphasize the political character of the notion of nationality and that the subsumption under public law of the rules relating to its acquisition and loss, despite their inclusion in the Civil Code, was solemnly declared in French legal decisions.[14]

An institution of public law in the internal order, nationality in the international order is a matter which not only belongs to the sovereignty of each State, but which at least in principle is "essentially within the domestic jurisdiction" (Art. 2, para. 7, of the Charter of the United Nations) or "solely within the domestic jurisdiction" (Art. 15, para. 8, of the Covenant of the League of Nations).[15] It is nonetheless true that the distribution of men, like the distribution of land, among States is a problem of indisputable international interest, and that, though common international law has until now hardly set any general limits to the power of States to legislate on this matter, there are certain boundaries, at least in the attribution of nationality, which a State cannot cross without exposing itself to diplomatic protests.[16]

[14] *Cass. fr., Chambres réunies*, February 2, 1921.

[15] That is why the title of nationality of origin is always a title of authority, act of the public power. Cf. the argument of A. de Lapradelle before the Permanent Court of International Justice in the matter of the nationality decrees; H. Batiffol, *Traité élémentaire de Droit international privé*, 1949, pp. 68 seq. It is admitted that treaty obligations may limit the State's liberty to decide as it will and may transfer the question from the reserved domain to the domain of international regulation.

[16] Cf. J. Basdevant, *Rec. A.D.I.*, vol. 58 (1936), p. 609. A message of the Swiss Federal Council dated November 9, 1920 (cited by Alex N. Makarov, *Allgemeine Lehre des Staatsangehörigkeitsrechts*, 1947, p. 72, note) expressly declares that the principle of good faith is the only limitation imposed by the law of nations on the sovereign power of the State to legislate in this matter. Cf. Harvard Law School, *Draft Convention on Nationality*, p. 26: "It may be difficult to precise the limitations which exist in International Law upon the power of a State to confer its nationality. Yet it is obvious that some limita-

It is the antinomy of these two views that gives rise to nationality conflicts. This antinomy is clear even in the text of the Convention adopted on April 9, 1930 by the Conference for the Codification of International Law. This text, while declaring in its preamble that "it is in the general interest of the international community that all its members should recognize that every person should have a nationality and should have one nationality only," nevertheless recognized that "It is for each State to determine under its own law who are its nationals."

The conflicts that may arise from this state of the law were dealt with in this same Convention. It lays down the rule (Art. 1) that a law enacted by one State is not binding on other States unless it is in accord "with international conventions, international custom and the principles of law generally recognized with regard to nationality"; but the Convention did not suggest the criteria of regulation. Regulation would demand a preliminary agreement on the natural bonds which, attaching the individual to a political entity, would determine the competence of each State in regard to nationality. The existence of such bonds generally recognized by civilized nations was asserted by some of the governments that participated in the 1930 Conference;[17] but no firm agreement on them could be reached.

In fact every State has its nationality policy, expressed in relatively stable form in its domestic legislation. The determining factors vary from country to country. The factor which is most influential and certainly most clearly discernible in its bearing on nationality of origin is the demographic one considered in its relation to movements of population. This has an important part in the choice between *jus sanguinis* and *jus soli*. The first criterion favors the countries of emigration which for various reasons (repatriation

---

tions do exist." This uncertainty of the law increases the danger of the international tensions created by these problems; cf. P. Louis-Lucas, *Rec. A.D.I.*, vol. 64 (1938), p. 14, and H. Lessing, *Das Recht der Staatsangehörigkeit*, Bibliotheca Visseriana, vol. XII, pp. 172 seq. In its judgment of April 6, 1955 (the Nottebohm case, Lichtenstein v. Guatemala), the International Court of Justice considered the international aspect of naturalization in its relation to diplomatic protection. The decision confirms what has been said in the text on the necessity of a bond of attachment to justify the attribution of nationality, and on the absence of general agreement regarding the criteria of international law on the subject.

17 See particularly the written replies of the United States and of the Netherlands. Publications of the League of Nations, Conference on Codification, vol. I, "Nationality," pp. 16, 18, 145.

of savings, possible return of the emigrant, economic penetration, cultural diffusion) seek to hold their nationals in the bonds of a prolonged allegiance. The second, which permits rapid assimilation of the descendants of newcomers, is alone acceptable for countries of immigration.[18]

It is vain to discuss from an ideal point of view the intrinsic merits of these criteria or the legitimacy of the various ways of combining them in positive systems of law if we overlook the political interests of the State that enacts them. These here in fact often take precedence over the interests of the individual and the family. This was admitted by the Codification Conference of 1930 when it recognized "the impossibility of reconciling now, by setting up rules which would be in the nature of a compromise, the vital interests of emigration and immigration States."[19] Facts like these must be admitted before we judge the laws that result from them.[20]

The close connection between the currents of migration and the law of nationality was strikingly illustrated in the nineteenth century by the shift within a few years from the principle of perpetual allegiance to the opposite doctrine of the right of expatriation. Stripped of the doctrinal trappings in which it was somewhat artificially clothed ex post facto, the right of expatriation appears as the direct result of the policy inaugurated by the United States in view of the great streams of migration which were beginning to flow in 1840. Until then faithful to the principle of perpetual allegiance, the United States repudiated it at the same time as it disputed the right of the European States to forbid the emigration of their nationals. The joint resolution of Congress in 1868, "Whereas the right of expatriation is a natural and inherent right of all people," was less the expression of a particularly lofty conception

18 The various aspects of the problem are well brought out in the notable observations of A. de Lapradelle reproduced in *L'Annuaire de l'Institut de Droit international,* 1950, vol. I, p. 503. These same demographic reasons very generally lead States of emigration to apply the national law to the status of persons, while States of immigration deal with this under the law of the domicile and often even go so far as to "subordinate, in the matter of personal status and capacity, not only nationality to domicile, but domicile, and with it personal status as a whole, to territorial residence." *loc.cit.*

19 *Acts of the Conference for Codification of International Law,* vol. 1, *Plenary Meetings,* p. 69.

20 Various solutions have been proposed to reconcile these naturally opposed interests, particularly by limiting the principle of filiation in favor of the country of immigration and continuous residence. Harvard Law School, *Draft Convention on Nationality,* Art. 4, p. 30.

of individual liberty than the statement of a policy of assimilation made necessary by the growing tempo of migration.[21] On this point the issue of this conflict of interests was highly beneficial. The individual's right to expatriate himself and to acquire a new nationality, already proclaimed in the French Constitution of September 3, 1791, received, thanks to the United States, a political impetus; from that time on it left its mark on all legal systems and was gradually recognized as inherent in the human person. Declared in 1868 in the Bancroft Treaties, and confirmed by judicial decisions, the principle took rank in doctrine among "the general principles of law recognized by civilized nations."[22] It must be observed, however, that the matter is still subject to fluctuations. Between the two world wars several systems of law made the loss of nationality by naturalization following prolonged residence abroad conditional either on the express consent of the government of the country of origin or even on the completion of military service in that country. Similar provisions, inspired by highly political considerations, are to be found in recent laws of several Eastern European countries. By parallel but inverse reasoning it must be held contrary to law to impose collective and compulsory nationality on aliens by reason either of their acquisition of immovable property or of their residence in the country. Such measures, inspired by a radical policy of assimilation, and adopted in some South American legal systems, have been condemned by international tribunals.

While internal laws reflect the regular and slow movement of policy in regard to nationality, certain acts and facts in international life emphasize its sharp oscillations and dangerous tensions. Among these manifestations denationalization unhappily today has first place. By this we are to understand, not the individual withdrawal of nationality, of the sort that the most liberal States have decreed in times of crisis, but the mass forfeiture that cuts groups of individuals off from the national collectivity, not for treason to their country, but for their want of attachment to a governmental regime.[23]

21 Elihu Root, "The Right of Expatriation," speech delivered in the United States Senate on December 19, 1911 (*Congressional Record—Senate*, December 19, 1911, p. 483), reprinted in *La Politique extérieure des Etats-Unis et le Droit international*, pp. 161-170.

22 Cf. Alex N. Makarov, *op.cit.*, pp. 77 seq.; Tor Hugo Wistrand, *La diplomatie et les conflits de nationalités*, pp. 97 seq.

23 On the eminently political character of denationalization laws, see H. Lessing, *op.cit.*, vol. XII.

Inaugurated by the U.S.S.R. in 1921 and sanctioned one after the other by the laws of the other totalitarian States, this practice has made statelessness, previously regarded as an accident and an anomaly, the condition of millions of human beings. Of course the Hague Codification Conference unanimously declared the desire "that States should, in the exercise of their power of regulating questions of nationality, make every effort to reduce so far as possible cases of statelessness" (Final Act, p. 14), but it took care not to pronounce upon the legality of denationalizations for political motives. Already great differences were apparent between the States represented, and most of them took shelter behind the plea of sovereignty.[24]

The practice of mass denationalization entails international consequences, the most important of which have to do with the right of expulsion and the right of territorial asylum.

The right of everyone to live somewhere was asserted long ago.[25] This elementary right has been denied in recent times by the combined effect of denationalizations and the indisputable right of every State to expel aliens who by their activities disturb public order and tranquillity. Statelessness in itself cannot be an obstacle a priori to the right of expulsion. If it were, the effect would doubtless only be to make more difficult the admission of denationalized persons into the countries where they seek refuge. On the other hand, no foreign State being legally bound to receive them, the effect of their expulsion has been to create veritable "outlaws," driven out and rejected everywhere, with no possibility of staying even for a limited time in any country.

The present bitterness of ideological conflict prevents any truly adequate remedy for this scandalous state of affairs. That proposed in the Hague Protocol of April 12, 1930, namely to impose upon the denationalizing State the obligation to admit its former nationals, is for reasons of humanity inapplicable to political refugees. It would mean handing them over to their worst enemies. The Institute of International Law, seeking a solution by way of restrictions upon the right of expulsion, laid it down in its Brussels resolution (1936)

[24] Following up its effort to provide more effective guarantees of human rights, the United Nations convened a Conference on the Status of Stateless Persons. The new Convention, signed on September 28, 1954 by sixteen States, gives to stateless persons in general a status analogous to that of refugees under the Convention of 1951.

[25] President Jefferson's message to the Congress of the United States (1801): "Every man has a right to live somewhere on the earth."

that a State "may not expel from its territory a refugee regularly authorized to stay there unless another State is willing to admit him. Short of expulsion, it may take such measures of internal security in regard to the refugee as it deems necessary. In no case may it consign or return a refugee to the territory of the State of which he was a national."[26]

§ 2. MIGRATION

The regulation of migration is a matter which international law in principle leaves to each State; it is a matter of domestic jurisdiction. Yet few social phenomena have so continuous and profound an influence on international relations as the demographic factors and pressures that decide the now liberal, now restrictive, policy of States in the field of migration. Their bearing on the development of public and private international law is not well understood by jurists, who appear more inclined to evade the problem than to undertake the long research that an examination of it would demand.[27] More obvious and better known is the dangerous effect of restrictive immigration practices on international tensions.

In the nineteenth century, free migration was favored by the expanding world economy, by a momentary convergence of the interests of countries of emigration and immigration, and by the predominance of liberal ideas propitious to the free circulation of men and of capital. This freedom of migration was, at the time, a powerful regulator of demographic relations. It helped to relieve the overcrowding of European countries then often tried by the crises of industrial capitalism and of agriculture; and in the New World it made possible the exploitation of unoccupied lands and the development of industries.

At the beginning of the twentieth century, coincidentally with the general tension of political relations, freedom gave way to an era of regulation and restriction. The first world war accelerated the change. Attacked by successive economic and social crises, States thought to meet them by adopting a narrowly nationalist and protectionist policy. France, the greatest country of immigration in

[26] *Annuaire de l'Institut*, 1936, vol. II, p. 299. Cf. J. P. Niboyet, *Traité de Droit international privé français*, vol. II, no. 664 seq. The administrative practice of several States in the matter of refugees is marked by these principles of tolerance and humanity; cf. Felice Morgenstern, in *B.Y.B.I.L.*, 1949, pp. 345 seq.

[27] But see the very suggestive remarks by A. de Lapradelle and J. P. Niboyet in *Annuaire de l'Institut de Droit international*, 1950, vol. I, pp. 503, 523.

Europe, concerned for the protection of her national labor-force, went so far as to permit immigration only within the limits of a strict system of quotas. Italy, country of emigration par excellence, but under an authoritarian regime, undertook to organize emigration as a public service and to keep her emigrants firmly tied to the motherland.[28] The effect of these measures on the rate of migration was the more marked because it coincided in transoceanic emigration with an enormous reduction in the volume of immigration into the countries of the New World and the British Empire. This reduction was due to concern for the defense of the labor market and the standard of living, to changes in the ethnic and social character of immigrants, and finally, after 1929, to the world economic crisis.

These multiplied interventions by the State aggravated the external tensions inseparable from some situations of high demographic pressure by obstructing the international compensation of differences in population pressure and by giving a political character to tension. The resulting dangers of war sprang less from the real state of demographic relations considered objectively and on a world scale, than from the obsidional and aggressive complex that certain types of propaganda in the service of expansionist or warlike ideologies foster in socially unstable masses.[29]

There is no doubt about the right of the State to deny immigrants freedom to settle on its territory, save under treaties governing these matters, and up to now international practice makes no exception to this principle when the right is exercised in discriminatory ways against the nationals of certain States. Immigration, as distinct from access to territory, has economic and social consequences that touch the fundamental interests of the State and must necessarily be left to its discretion in the existing condition of international relations.

On the other hand the problem emphasizes the interdependence of States from the social as well as the political point of view. It

[28] Speech by D. Grandi in the Italian Parliament, March 30, 1927: "Emigration must be regarded as an essentially political phenomenon. The guardianship of the emigrant cannot be divided into material protection and political action; it is entirely political." In 1897 the Institute of International Law admitted no restrictions on freedom to emigrate and immigrate except "within the strict limits of social and political necessities." Then regarded as exceptional, these necessities were the basis for the laws enacted between the two world wars.

[29] Quincy Wright, *A Study of War*, vol. II, chap. XXXI, "Population Changes and War"; W. Röpke, *La Communauté internationale*, pp. 123 seq.

presented itself in a particularly acute form, during the drafting of the Covenant of the League of Nations, as between the United States and the Asiatic countries. While the Japanese delegation to the Peace Conference tried in vain to win recognition for the principle of race equality, President Wilson got inserted in Article 15 of the Covenant the reservation of exclusive jurisdiction which provided protection for the traditional policy of the United States in regard to what were called purely American questions, in particular its complete freedom of action in the matter of immigration. In 1924, American legislation denied admission to the territory of the United States to any alien "ineligible" for American citizenship, meaning aliens other than whites of European origin or blacks of African origin, these alone being eligible, according to Supreme Court decisions, for naturalization. This legislation, which had repercussions throughout the world, aroused deep resentment among Asiatic peoples and particularly in Japan. The Tokyo government's protest, though only weakly supported by positive international law, invoked lofty considerations of international courtesy and cooperation. Complaining of affront to the national dignity, the protest suggested grave consequences in international relations that might follow application of the statute.[80]

The dispute, which at one time took a disquieting turn, awakened an echo in the League of Nations during the discussion of the Geneva Protocol (1924). It was the immigration problem that suggested the Japanese thesis argued by Ambassador Adatci, afterwards President of the Permanent Court of International Justice. This was to the effect that a State could not be presumed an aggressor if, having first submitted a litigious question to the Council or the Assembly, it was subsequently constrained to disregard either a unanimous report by the Council or a judicial or arbitral decision declaring that the dispute arose "out of a matter which by international law is solely within the domestic jurisdiction" of a State. So put, the problem strikingly evoked the individualism of sovereignties and the limits that international law itself sets to the efficacy of the peaceful procedures of settlement.[81]

80 Hackworth, *Digest*, vol. III, p. 761.

81 A great jurist, V. Scialoja, did not hesitate to emphasize on this occasion the urgent necessity of attacking these "ultralegal" questions with a view to dealing with them by treaty. This position will always be preferable to recourse to the notion of abuse of right, which governments reject in such matters. Cf. Jean Ray, *Commentaire du Pacte*, pp. 494 seq. For a Japanese interpretation of the reservation in Article 15, paragraph 8, of the Covenant

Experience, especially in connection with Asiatic immigration into South Africa, convincingly shows that some control of migration is unavoidable. An unconsidered appeal for foreign immigrants may give rise to conflict, if not more serious, at least as sharp as those for which in the longer run prohibitive practices set the stage. But it should be clearly observed that the constant and often contradictory interventions of the State and of labor organizations still complicate the problem. These explain the sharp oscillations in the regulation of immigration in countries where racial hostilities and the xenophobia of trades unions outweigh a sober understanding of economic realities.

Finally the problems of migration, which are clearly of international interest by reason of their general data and their repercussions on demographic conditions, are held today in the reserved domain of the State by the links connecting them not only with the economic conjuncture of the countries of immigration, but with their peculiar psychology and their particular conception of living standards.[32]

§ 3. EXTERNAL ASYLUM AND DIPLOMATIC ASYLUM

The State's right to grant asylum in its territory to aliens fleeing from political, racial, or religious persecution in their country of residence follows from the exclusive character of its territorial jurisdiction. What is called "the right of asylum" is nothing more than the liberty of every State to offer asylum to anyone asking it.[33] Though one may therefore not speak either of a right of the individual to claim the protection of asylum or of a corresponding legal duty of States to grant it, it must nevertheless be observed that the present bitterness of ideological conflict and the scope of the interests brought into play by the mass exodus of hundreds of thousands of individuals have profoundly changed the moral and material data of the problem.[34] It has been noted particularly that as political

---

of the League of Nations, applied to the immigration problem, see Sakutaro Tachi, *La Souveraineté et l'Indépendance de l'Etat et les questions intérieures en Droit international,* 1930, pp. 96 seq.

[32] On treaty practice after the second world war, see M. Sibert, *Traité de droit international public,* vol. I, no. 346.

[33] The constitutional provisions of some countries (France, Italy) that mention a right of asylum have no object other than to define the powers of national authorities in the matter. Cf. Felice Morgenstern, *op.cit.,* pp. 337-338.

[34] Its present importance is emphasized by the texts of several recent constitutions: French Constitution (Preamble); Italian Constitution (Art. 10);

tensions grew in intensity and duration, a great number of persons originally simply displaced from their homeland by events connected with the war, and theoretically free to return, refused to do so because of a regime that they regarded as intolerable and became in fact political refugees.[35] The problem that faced the International Refugee Organization thus became much more one of reclassification or settlement than of repatriation.

These circumstances emphasized the highly humanitarian character of the grant of asylum and also revealed the seriousness of its consequences. Accomplishing a duty of humanity, the State in whose territory the refugees are cannot be bound to impose repatriation when, fully informed on the real situation in their homeland and being neither war criminals nor traitors to their country, they persistently refuse to return. To hand them over to governments which have nothing against them but their want of attachment to the regime would be to betray the principles of tolerance that are the foundation of political asylum. The State granting asylum cannot therefore be held responsible either for the grant of asylum or for the acts of the grantee except in cases where it would be responsible for the acts of any other individual living in its territory.

It is nonetheless true that these vast exoduses raise unprecedented problems for the asylum-granting countries. What in the liberal tradition, which was opposed to all ostracism, was merely the exceptional exercise of a sovereign right, has become for the countries still faithful to that tradition a most burdensome mission of international assistance. It has been called a "humanitarian intervention carried out at home."[36] Asylum so understood touches the immigration and settlement policy of States and has in fact not often been granted except within the limits set by the internal laws on these matters. This transformation, which entails a complete dislocation of the natural balance of State burdens, raises an international problem with which it has been possible to cope only within a framework of international cooperation.

Yugoslav Constitution (Art. 31). The United Nations has attempted to give refugees a minimum of protection. A Convention signed at Geneva on July 25, 1951 grants a minimum status to those who, driven from their country of origin by the fear of persecution, are without diplomatic protection.

35 United Nations Refugees and Stateless Persons, General Assembly, Official Records, Sixth Session, Supplement No. 19.

36 Arnold Raestad, "Rapport sur le Statut des Apatrides et des Réfugiés," *Annuaire de l'Institut de Droit international*, 1936, vol. I, p. 82.

The asylum granted political refugees in the premises of diplomatic missions is an institution that has fallen into desuetude in most countries. It survives in those Latin American States where extreme governmental instability and the violence of political passions have preserved a reason for its existence and multiplied its applications. However, even there, and except for the momentary protection demanded as an imperative duty of humanity, diplomatic asylum has remained what it everywhere was: an institution which in its essential aspects owes more to considerations of expediency, decency, or courtesy than to the principles of law. The arguments which in a recent case attempted to give it a legal basis served only to make this clearer.[37] Even in Latin America the traditional physiognomy of the institution has not been changed either by the number of precedents, which have been too vague or too heterogeneous to establish a custom, or by international conventions, which until recently have found few adherents and which in any case showed in their terms and in their rapid succession more variety of opinion than unity of thought.

Failing relevant treaty provisions, Colombia cited regional custom in support of its claim to classify unilaterally and finally the crime with which the person granted asylum was charged. The International Court of Justice was not convinced that such a custom existed, the Colombian Government having failed to prove that the rule upon which it relied had been established by a constant and uniform usage observed by the States of Latin America or that this usage expressed a legal conviction of the existence of a right in the State granting asylum and of a corresponding duty in the territorial State.

The weakness of the legal position was no less apparent when the treaties, and more particularly their provisions for enforcement, came to be considered. It was Peru this time that invoked the Court's interpretation of the Havana Convention of 1928 in its judgment of November 20, 1950, and demanded surrender of the fugitive. On this point the Court had no hesitation in finding a lacuna or, better, an intentional silence in the Havana Convention. It observed that the text contained no provision on the termination of asylum irregularly granted to political criminals and, further,

[37] Judgment of the International Court of Justice, November 20, 1950, Asylum Case (Colombia-Peru), Reports of Judgments, 1950, pp. 266; Haya de la Torre Case (Colombia-Peru), Judgment of June 13, 1951, Reports of Judgments, 1951, p. 71. Cf. Guggenheim, *Traité*, pp. 505-507.

that the Latin American tradition was opposed to the surrender of a political fugitive. "The silence of the Convention," it said, "implies that it was intended to leave the adjustment of the consequences of this situation to decisions inspired by considerations of convenience or simple political expediency. To infer from this silence that there is an obligation to surrender a person to whom asylum has been irregularly granted would be to disregard both the role of these extra-legal factors in the development of asylum in Latin America, and the spirit of the Havana Convention itself."[38]

Support for diplomatic asylum is linked with the state of political mores. It is for the countries that feel the need of this institution to provide it with a solid legal basis sanctioning its existence and effects. It is by no means impossible—witness memories of the Spanish civil war—that asylum may need to be re-established in parts of the world where nineteenth-century habits of order and tolerance had allowed it to fall into desuetude. Such a rebirth would probably, however, be due less to any concern for the comfort of politicians suffering the vicissitudes of public life than to the higher and truly universal purpose of defending the human person against unjustifiable violence.[39]

§ 4. REPATRIATION OF PRISONERS OF WAR (KOREA, 1952)

A new problem arose in the Korean armistice negotiations. Early in the month of January 1952, the unified command of the United Nations forces proposed to the Sino-Korean delegation that they should proceed to the exchange of prisoners "head for head" on a voluntary basis, that is to say depending upon the individual decision of each prisoner. It was further proposed that prisoners opting against repatriation should be set free on their promise not to take part again in the war in Korea. The proposal was rejected.

The unified command justified its suggestion by the moral impossibility of restoring to the enemy men who openly declared their

[38] Reports of Judgments, 1951, p. 81. On the two judgments rendered by the Court see: P. F. Gonidec, "L'affaire du droit d'asyle," *Revue générale de droit international public*, 1951, p. 547; Laurent Jully, "L'asile diplomatique devant la Cour internationale de Justice," *Friedenswarte*, 1951, p. 20. Cf. Manley O. Hudson, in *A.J.I.L.*, 1951, p. 19, and 1952, p. 8; Alona E. Evans, in *A.J.I.L.*, 1951, p. 755.

[39] The necessity of organizing diplomatic asylum on a treaty basis was at last recognized by the Inter-American Conference at Caracas (1954), where a Convention on the subject was signed and referred to the States members for ratification. Cf. the resolutions of the Institute of International Law, Bath session (1950), *Annuaire*, 1950, vol. II, p. 375.

wish not to be handed over to him. The ideological fanaticisms that characterized this war and the cruelties accompanying it were doubtless responsible for a proposal that sought to rescue certain categories of prisoners from the ill treatment that might have followed their forced repatriation.

The idea was new. International law, customary and conventional, enjoins upon belligerents the reciprocal and unconditional return of prisoners within the shortest possible time after the cessation of hostilities. After the second world war, prisoners, Soviet subjects, were repatriated against their will from Western Germany into the U.S.S.R. The Geneva Convention of 1949 (Art. 118) merely says that prisoners must be freed and repatriated as soon as the active phase of hostilities comes to an end.[40]

Here again we have one of those human problems, made particularly distressing by totalitarian oppression, for which positive international law offers no solution. It matters little that the positions taken by the belligerents in the Korean war may have been decided by contingent considerations. The problem is unhappily one of those that the growing violence of ideological and racial antagonisms may raise again. The question, in a nutshell, is whether constraint, which is forbidden for the retention of prisoners, may be used for their repatriation.

The novelty of the problem is at once plain. Whereas international law formerly sought to give the individual the chance to preserve his original political or religious obedience by protecting him, for example through the treaty option of nationality, against certain consequences of war, the inverse situation presents itself here: the individual invokes his moral self-determination and his physical security to repudiate a cause to which he is supposed to have brought the most rigorous of loyalties, that of military discipline.

From the ethical and humanitarian point of view, solution offers only one difficulty, which is to ensure that men exposed to pressure by their very captivity shall have the opportunity freely to express their will. From the military point of view, the question is how to guarantee the neutralization of prisoners choosing that alternative.[41]

[40] As a precedent the matter raises serious difficulties from the military point of view. On the Panmunjom discussions of the Geneva Convention, see Jaro Mayda, "The Korean Repatriation Problem and International Law," *A.J.I.L.*, 1954, pp. 414-438.

[41] The United Nations should be credited with the clauses in the Panmunjom Convention (June 1953) which, for the first time, declare the principle of

§ 5. THE INTERNATIONAL PROTECTION OF MINORITIES. INTERNATIONAL EXCHANGES AND TRANSFERS OF POPULATIONS

It would be wrong to assign the same importance in the scale of values to the rights of man and to the rights of racial, religious, or linguistic minorities as these were understood and implemented in the Treaties of 1919-1920. The first belong essentially to the moral and legal principles which are largely part of the common fund of Christian civilization; the second, being collective, are still deeply involved in politics.

The problem of the international protection of minorities, as it presented itself in Europe between the two world wars, called for the regulation of concrete data which treaty texts, themselves resting upon a historical tradition, sought at once to clarify and to circumscribe. The minority protected by minority treaties or declarations was a group, historically settled in a given territory, which was traditionally and consciously marked off by certain distinctive features from the mass of the population of the State in which it had been recently incorporated. The distinctive features serving as criteria for international protection were those that appeared to offer at least a relative stability. On this basis the conventional system protected certain minorities of race, language, or religion, but not political or social minorities. It is true that some of these clauses, being stipulated on behalf of all "inhabitants" or "nationals," protected the individual rights of man independently of identification with a minority group; but this was certainly not their specific object. In its truly essential features the international protection of minorities sought to reconcile the traditions and cultural aspirations of certain groups with the unity and consolidation of the State to which a recent transfer of territory had attached them.

It has been said, not without reason, that the system of international protection of minorities broke down because of its purely political orientation.[42] The truth is that it could hardly have been otherwise. The regime was political in essence by reason of the acute problems that it raised not only for the League of Nations, which was responsible for its enforcement, but for the State upon which it had been imposed. That is why the settlement of minori-

respect for the human person in the repatriation of prisoners. These prohibit any use of force to prevent or effect repatriation, and expressly proscribe all violence against their persons or affronts to their dignity.

[42] G. Scelle, *Manuel élémentaire de Droit international*, p. 430.

ties questions was kept, from the beginning and without any cause of reasonable complaint against the organs of the League, "out of the channels of formal jurisdiction, out of the hands of public organs, out of the realm of clear definitions, and in the ambit of unofficial agencies prone to compromise solutions after their own heart."[43]

The regime was doomed finally to succumb to the pressures that piled up against it from inside and from outside. The minorities pushed their cultural claims to establish their character as distinct entities moving towards separatist autonomy; Hitler's propaganda in the service of the German Reich's annexationist policy gave noisy support to minority agitation; while the States with the minorities themselves stiffened under the double threat of internal dissolution and external interference. Such were some of the causes that destroyed the fragile balance on which the system rested.[44]

It is easily understood why the idea of returning to the protection of minorities is greeted today with extreme reserve. Moreover, the massive exoduses of populations following the second world war have diminished the importance of minorities in Europe, and any interest in the problem is shifting towards other continents.[45] But it would be a great mistake to suppose that something equivalent to the system for protecting minorities can be found in the international protection of human rights. There is not *a* problem of minorities; there are minority *problems*, and their individual character keeps them in the political orbit. We may try with more or less success to universalize in some degree the rights of man; it would be useless to dream of constructing a universal system for the international protection of minorities. Every abstract and purely humanitarian plan for such protection breaks against the contingencies of history and politics.

In a world where ideological and racial fanaticism reinforces nationalist passions, there is certainly still every reason for protecting minorities. Unfortunately the need no longer finds that minimum of tolerance and cooperation without which no international regime can succeed.

43 J. Fouques-Duparc, "Le développement de la protection des Minorités," *Revue de Droit international et de Législation comparée*, 1926, p. 515.

44 Charles De Visscher, "Unité d'Etat et revendications minoritaires," *Revue de Droit international et de Législation comparée*, 1930, p. 326.

45 Tennent Harrington Bagley, *General Principles and Problems in the International Protection of Minorities, A Political Study*, Geneva, 1950, chap. VI.

The elimination of minorities, by an exchange conceived as their forced repatriation into their respective "ethnic homelands" or by an international transfer of populations, has been recommended, like a painful but sometimes unavoidable surgical operation, not only by statesmen seeking purely political ends but also by some minds profoundly devoted to individual liberties.[46] The exchange treaties that gave rise to the practice of agreed transfers have this in common with these last, that both involve the moving of certain population groups from one State to another without any complete guarantee that the displacement will be voluntary. In fact, exchanges and transfers are always "directed" operations.[47]

In general, these are practices which in their threat to the fundamental rights of man lend themselves to terrible abuse, and their recent extension calls for unreserved condemnation on principle. But experience shows the need for some distinctions. It is only too true that any mutual tolerance is inconceivable between some populations settled in the same territory but separated by age-old racial or religious hatreds. Coexistence may permanently jeopardize the security and even the life of minority elements. In spite of the miseries that accompanied it and were largely attributable to inexperience, the forced exchange of Greek and Turkish populations under the Convention signed at Lausanne on January 30, 1923 finally had beneficent results. The reason is that here the exchange, unlike the transfer carried out with a view to driving back an alien population, was due less to the political interest of a State than to a concern for human interests and for general peace. Organized in this spirit and under international control, and sustained by adequate financial means, exchange can offer securities, notably those resulting from the existence of a welcoming country where the exchanged populations have some hope of finding sympathy and help. Apart from these exceptional cases and in the absence of such securities, the transfer agreements result in the denial to the minority populations which are their subject that "right to the native soil"[48] that every man can claim. An examination of the conventions concluded in 1939 and the following years shows that transfer was only an element of compromise in high-policy negotia-

46 Nicolas Politis, "Le transfert de populations," in *L'Esprit International*, April 1940.

47 On this see the Report of G. Balladore-Pallieri to the Institute of International Law, Siena session, 1952, *Annuaire*, 1952, vol. II, p. 138.

48 Max Huber, Remarks on the Balladore-Pallieri Report just cited, *ibid.*, p. 165.

tions. This was true of the measures concerted by Germany with Estonia and Latvia respectively for the most complete and swiftest possible evacuation of the German groups settled for centuries in those countries, with a view to transplanting them in the newly annexed parts of Poland—though these measures did not strictly constitute a forced transfer. It was also true of the Convention for the exchange between the Reich and the U.S.S.R. of the German, Ukrainian, and White Russian populations settled in the annexed Polish territories. None of these arrangements had any object but to prevent causes of friction with the Moscow government. As for the agreement concluded in the same year between the Reich and Italy concerning the populations of the South Tyrol, that was designed to tighten the bonds of the Axis. On the threshold of a vast conflict, Germany was seeking to achieve total ethnic homogeneity while at the same time consolidating its diplomatic positions.[49]

§ 6. RESPECT FOR THE PRIVATE RIGHTS OF INDIVIDUALS

The continuity of the law, guarantee of security, is a primordial requirement of the legal order. In time as in space it ensures at least relative stability for established legal situations. A new legal order cannot, without causing profound disturbance in social relations, call in question rights validly acquired before its establishment. This principle, generally respected in periods of calm and of disciplined liberty, is ignored in political crises or social revolutions. Nothing is more indicative of the decay of law and the predominance of political factors than the frequent violation of the principle of nonretroactivity.

Certain ideologies that more or less everywhere sacrifice the individual's subjective rights to a sometimes wholly political conception of general interest propose not merely to lay hold on the future; they also want to make a clean sheet of the past. New social necessities may justify retroactive laws; they do not justify spoliation by a priori denial of equitable compensation. This fundamental distinction, with its brake on legislative action, finds its most important applications today in the international order and in reference to aliens.

[49] Cf. *Les transferts internationaux de populations*, published by the Institut de Statistique et des Etudes économiques (Paris, 1946), where the transfer clauses of twenty-four conventions are studied.

"The principle of respect for vested rights," said the Permanent Court of International Justice, "forms part of generally accepted international law. . . ."[50]

In international relations the question arises principally in two types of case—the transfer of territorial sovereignty that replaces one legal order with another, and new legislation within the same legal order.[51]

International acts, notably the peace treaties concluded after the first world war, show a practice definitely favorable to the survival of rights validly acquired by private persons before a transfer of territorial sovereignty. But, here as elsewhere, the principle of nonretroactivity must be reconciled with the establishment of a new legal order which alone governs the future. The principle of survival of acquired rights means merely that the transfer of territorial sovereignty from one State to another does not entail the extinction of rights acquired under earlier legislation;[52] it leaves the successor State the power to adapt their future treatment to the requirements of its own legal order, subject, in the case of acquired rights of aliens, to the general safeguards of common international law, in particular that of diplomatic protection.[53]

The principle of succession to public debts, while debatable in cases of mere territorial change,[54] is generally recognized by positive international law when the debtor State is completely absorbed. It rests upon respect for the acquired rights of individuals, even though these have no means of direct action against the successor

[50] Judgment No. 7, May 25, 1926, p. 42.

[51] On the principle and its applications prior to the second world war, see G. Kaeckenbeeck, *La protection internationale des droits acquis*, *Rec. A.D.I.*, vol. 59 (1937), p. 321.

[52] This is the principle brought out in the Advisory Opinion of the Permanent Court of International Justice, September 10, 1923, series B, no. 6, p. 36: "Private rights acquired under existing law do not cease on a change of sovereignty." It has had its clearest-cut applications in relation to property. The Court applied the principle with particularly important consequences in its Judgment No. 7, May 25, 1926, on certain German interests in Polish Upper Silesia. Cf. G. Gidel, *L'Arrêt No. 7 de la Cour permanente de Justice internationale*, 1927.

[53] Cf. Annex XIV, No. 9, in the Treaty of Peace with Italy, 1947; see also the resolutions adopted by the Institute of International Law on the Report of M. A. Makarov, Siena session, 1952, *Annuaire*, 1952, vol. II, p. 471, with the Report to the Bath session, 1950, *Annuaire*, 1950, vol. I, p. 208.

[54] See Eugène Borel's award, April 18, 1925, in the Ottoman Public Debt case. *United Nations Reports of International Arbitral Awards*, vol. I, particularly pp. 571 seq.

State. Being aliens, they enjoy the diplomatic protection of the State of which they are nationals.[55]

If the practice of States in these matters is in general harmony with doctrine, that is because the political interests involved in transfers of territorial sovereignty usually coincide with respect for vested rights. From the internal point of view, it is in the well-understood interest of a State receiving such a transfer not to disorganize without grave reason the private-law relations validly set up under the former regime, in order not to alienate the inhabitants of the transferred territory who become its nationals. From the international point of view, it has a manifest interest in respecting the vested rights of persons who, aliens before the transfer or become so in consequence of it (for example by exercising the right of option), are in a situation to invoke the diplomatic protection of third States; as it also has an interest in not arousing opposition in these States to recognition of the territorial change.

This happy conjuncture of interests, emphasized in established treaty practice, is usually absent when the rights of aliens are brought in question not by a transfer of territorial sovereignty, but directly by internal reforms in the political, economic, or social structure of the State. Recent and numerous examples show that the acquired rights of aliens are often threatened or ignored, sometimes even in violation of precise engagements, by laws enacted either to obtain a better social equilibrium by a new distribution of wealth, particularly wealth in land, or to replace a regime of private ownership or exploitation with one of nationalizations excluding private capital, or with one of the numerous forms of mixed economy involving some collaboration between the State and the representatives of private interests.[56]

[55] A contrary thesis was propounded with the support of a definitely political argument by the German Reich in disputing its obligation to assume the federal debt of Austria after Germany's absorption of that country. Cf. Brandt, "Die Regelung der oesterreichischen Bundesschulden," *Zeitschrift für Ausl. Recht und Völkerrecht*, 1939, p. 127; James W. Garner, "Questions of State Succession Raised by the German Annexation of Austria," *A.J.I.L.*, 1938, p. 421; Drost, "Le problème de la succession en matière d'obligations juridiques des Etats," *Revue de Droit international et de Législation comparée*, 1939, p. 700. The distinction between extinction by conquest and extinction by voluntary act is not tenable; it was denied in matters of delict by the Anglo-American Arbitral Tribunal (Agreement of August 18, 1910), Hawaiian Claims, November 10, 1925, *American and British Claims Arbitration, Report of Fred. K. Nielsen*, 1926, pp. 160-161.

[56] On respect for property in the law of nations, see M. Sibert, *Traité de*

One cannot say a priori that these laws are socially unjust in that they necessarily violate essential human rights. They cannot even any longer be represented as so exceptional that all effect in international relations can be denied them.

The reasons that account for nationalizations are various; but in the minds of those who enact such policies they all come down to the higher interest of the collectivity. In some countries, especially those of long-retarded political or social development, a new system of ownership or a new distribution of wealth is closely bound up with political changes which affect not only the internal order of the State but also its international position. Elsewhere nationalization either has been promoted by the extension of State controls imposed by war economy and the connected ideologies, or has been a sequel of certain techniques of production or distribution that involve organizing economic life on a national plane. Whatever the reasons, the rulers alone decide. Nationalization is an internal measure often dictated by reasons that are more political than economic. In principle, its legality is not to be determined by any international criterion.

International practice, as established since the Cannes Conference (1922), is summed up in three words: nonintervention but indemnification. Without claiming the "right to dictate to each other regarding the principles on which they are to regulate their system of ownership, internal economy and government,"[57] not disputing the principle of the right to nationalize, and avoiding any discussion *in concreto* of its motives, the States make adequate indemnification the international obligation, and make refusal to indemnify the basis of a responsibility which is generally delictual, but becomes contractual if nationalization is decreed in violation of an international undertaking. This position represents the present equation balancing the State's liberty to organize as it will and the security of international relations.[58]

Droit international public, 1951, vol. I, pp. 518 seq.; Guggenheim, *Traité*, pp. 334 seq.

57 Resolution adopted by the Supreme Council at Cannes, January 6, 1922, House of Commons Sessional Papers, vol. XXIII, 1922.

58 The final Report of the Mixed United States–Mexico Commission of experts on the expropriation of petroleum deposits in Mexico (April 17, 1942) declared that "Expropriation, and the exercise of the right of eminent domain, under the respective constitutions and laws of Mexico and the United States, are a recognized feature of the sovereignty of all modern states." The Preparatory Committee of the Codification Conference of 1930 had put the question in exact

The object and scope of most nationalization laws entail a series of consequences which seriously offend the principle of respect for the rights of aliens and which sharply distinguish the practice of nationalization from that of expropriation. These consequences present themselves especially in the matter of concessions; they involve the good faith of contracts, the amount of indemnification, and the procedure to be used in recovering damages.

Nationalization strictly so-called, unlike some manifestations of statism, calls in question contracts, especially concession contracts, concluded with aliens. There is an antinomy between the contract, source of individual private rights, and the nationalization which seeks to put an end to all participation of private capital. But the international responsibility of the nationalizing State is brought into play when it nationalizes a foreign enterprise in violation of an obligation freely and precisely assumed by it in an international agreement. This responsibility may also be involved, in connection with an undertaking contained in a contract under municipal law, if there is a denial of justice to the foreign concessionary through default of the ordinary courts or through a refusal to submit the dispute to any arbitral procedure that may have been substituted for internal jurisdiction.

From the political point of view, which is important in this context, we must not, however, overlook the risks necessarily incident to concessions granted to foreign enterprises when these relate to the exploitation of important national resources or are granted for a very long term. The awakening of national sentiment is likely to cast them in the light of intolerable mortgages on public life, wrested from a regime which did not represent opinion.

Recent nationalization laws usually have an indemnification clause, which at times operates in a discriminatory way in some States. But while expropriation, being an individual measure, permits and consequently requires full indemnification, nationalization is a reform of vast scope and hardly ever permits more than partial compensation calculated less by the extent of damage than by the

form (Responsibility of States: bases of discussion, p. 33): ". . . to hold a State to be responsible internationally does not affect the validity under municipal law of the action which it has taken. There is no question of discussing the reasons which it may have for putting an end to a concession or to the performance of a contract; it is merely a question of obliging it to make good the damage which it causes by so doing, in violation, *ex hypothesi*, of the terms of the concession or contract."

capacity and good will of the nationalizing State.[59] The experience of these last years shows that indemnities were sometimes derisory, especially in some countries of Eastern Europe, and that their amount varied greatly according to the character of the political relations that the nationalizing State proposed to maintain with claimant States, or according to the economic or political pressure that these latter could exert upon it.

It is in the procedure of indemnification that the political character of nationalization becomes most evident. The traditional procedure by which in expropriation private persons may individually press their claims before the internal tribunals, with an appeal to diplomatic protection in case of denial of justice, here meets too many obstacles in the difficulty of access to the local courts and the incapacity of the judicial organs to prescribe the only effective ways and means of ensuring a minimum of compensation for foreigners domiciled in other countries. The very abundant treaty practice of recent years has substituted the method of governmental negotiations which turn sometimes on individual compensation, sometimes, and very generally, on a mere global indemnification by lump sum. Though there can be little doubt that the public interests of the States bulk larger than any exact reparation for the damage suffered by individuals, it seems that in the present state of things this is the only practicable legal solution.

It is of course a long way from these practices to respect for acquired rights in a society with an effective legal order. Nationalization offers, both in the internal and in the international order, a striking example of the tensions between politics and law. Between the at times anarchic assertions of reserved domain and the stabilities that law seeks to defend, governmental practice can but compromise.

Section III

Territory in International Relations

§ 1. GENERAL PROBLEMS

1. The Territorial Home of the State. Historically the territorial home of the State is the foundation of the political and legal order born in the sixteenth century and definitively consecrated in Europe

[59] Cf. A. N. Makarov, *Die Nationalisierungsmassnahmen*, in *Um Recht und Gerechtigkeit, Festgabe für Erich Kaufmann*; J. E. S. Fawcett, "Some Foreign Effects of Nationalization of Property," *B.Y.B.I.L.*, 1950, p. 355.

by the Treaties of Westphalia. The essential place that territory holds in the organization of the State and its highly symbolic meaning explain the propensity of authors as well as of State practice to identify the territory with the State, or at least to regard its spatial delimitation as inseparable from that of sovereignty.[60]

Consolidated within the limits of known frontiers, the territorial status of States appears in the international order as an objective situation, valid against all other States, and particularly clear when it rests, as it generally does, upon that form of possession that consists in the continuous and undisputed exercise of State functions. This objective aspect is not less manifest where the title to sovereignty springs from the occupation of land without an owner, since by its nature this title is here established *erga omnes* and not simply as a matter of relations between some States. Max Huber, in his arbitral award on sovereignty over Palmas Island, observes that the characteristic of *terra nullius* is that any State is qualified to exercise State functions there. This is the other face of the objective or absolute character of territorial status.[61]

Fundamental considerations connected with stability and security in international relations lend strength to the legal position of territorial sovereignty. They support its most distinctive characteristic, which is its exclusiveness. The State has the right to exercise sovereignty throughout the length and breadth of its domain and the corresponding duty to abstain from any act of coercion in foreign territory. Thus territory, framework of independence and security in the political order, became in the legal order "the point of departure in settling most questions that concern international relations."[61a]

60 ". . . one of the essential elements of sovereignty is that it is to be exercised within territorial limits, and that, failing proof to the contrary, the territory is coterminous with the sovereignty. . . ." Award of the Permanent Court of Arbitration in the North Atlantic Fisheries Case, Great Britain–United States (September 7, 1910); J. B. Scott, *The Hague Court Reports*, Carnegie Endowment for International Peace, 1916, p. 157.

61 Award of the Permanent Court of Arbitration in the Palmas Island Case, Netherlands–United States, p. 16.

61a Max Huber in the arbitral award already cited. "Now the first and foremost restriction imposed by international law upon a State is that—failing the existence of a permissive rule to the contrary—it may not exercise its power in any form in the territory of another State." Permanent Court of International Justice, "Lotus" Case, Publications of the Court, Series A, Judgment 9, p. 18. Cf. International Court of Justice, Judgment of April 9, 1949, p. 35; P. E. Corbett, *Law and Society in the Relations of States*, p. 91.

Many authors would define State territory as the space in which the State is authorized by international law to exercise the competence necessary for its mission. But this too exclusively legal conception of competence, especially in its application to territory, "has against it the conviction of States, to which nothing is more distasteful than the idea that the power they wield is granted them by the international order."[62] The wholly abstract and as it were unincarnate image that it calls up takes no account of the historical formation of the territory, of the ancestral bond that unites it to the nation, or, above all, of the emotional values which the minds of men find in the possession, delimitation, and integrity of their land. The individualization and unification of the territory within its frontiers were the historical work of power. They were manifestations of the dominion of power before they furnished the State order with the setting for the accomplishment of its functions and the domain of legal validity for its norms.[63] Only such a view as this restores to sovereignty its full human and national significance and gives it the place that belongs to it in international relations.

2. *Territorial Stability.* The firm configuration of its territory furnishes the State with the recognized setting for the exercise of its sovereign powers. The at least relative stability of this territory is a function of the exclusive authority that the State exercises in it and of the coexistence beyond its frontiers of political entities endowed with similar prerogatives.

This stability is above all a factor of security, of the security that peoples feel in the shelter of recognized frontiers—a confidence that has grown in them with the consolidation, in a community of aspirations and memories, of the bonds uniting them to the soil that they occupy. It is this sentiment that explains the extreme sensitiveness of opinion to everything that touches territorial in-

62 D. Anzilotti, *Cours de Droit international,* tr. Gidel, p. 51.

63 Cf. Max Huber in the arbitral award already cited, p. 16: "The development of the national organization of States during the last few centuries and, *as a corollary, the development of international law. . . .*" Political interests common to a certain number of countries may give rise to special regimes (territories under mandate or under trusteeship, for example; see below) which differ more or less essentially from the normal exercise of sovereignty and which only experience can prove stable. It remains true that in the establishment of States the formation of the nation is associated with territorial unification. The exoduses of population that occurred in certain newly established States testify to the constant concern to achieve national unity in a clearly defined territorial framework. Cf. our observations (above, Section 1) on artificial creation of States by political action.

tegrity. Just as any regular operation of territorial delimitation has in it an element of order and peace, so any frontier incident easily degenerates into a serious political conflict.

This was the reality that the authors of Article 10 of the Covenant of the League of Nations had in mind. It was peace, and not an indefensible *status quo*, that they hoped to protect by asserting the principle of respecting and maintaining territorial integrity. It was aggression that they proscribed, without prejudice to the legitimacy of claims and subject always to recourse to procedures of peaceful settlement. This same idea of the possessory protection of territorial sovereignty is the basis of territorial criteria for the definition of aggression, the only ones which, though too automatic, are practically applicable. It is because the State is a territorial organization that violation of its frontiers is inseparable from the idea of aggression against the State itself.[64]

Dismemberment by armed force is the gravest attack upon territorial stability, whether or not it is sanctioned by a treaty the terms of which were dictated by constraint. History shows that the reaction of third States varies greatly according to time and place. An annexation of some importance in a region where the great Powers' lines of strength have established a traditional state of balance may not arouse immediate opposition but is always liable in the long run to produce dangerous political tensions. The annexation of Alsace and part of Lorraine in 1871 appeared to leave the Powers indifferent; but it was one of the causes of the tragedies of the twentieth century. "In the end it will shake Europe to its foundations."[65] It is different when the conquering ambitions of a great Power meet no resistance either because there is less consciousness of a threat to equilibrium, or because the requirements of balance yield to an undisputed hegemony.

There is good reason why authors should recall the pacts and declarations in which international organizations or some States have asserted their intention not to recognize territorial changes brought about by force of arms or without the freely given consent of the populations concerned. But they mistake their significance when they call them "achievements" of positive law. Treaties of cession exacted by armed victory are recognized in international

[64] M. W. Komarnicki, *La définition de l'aggresseur dans le Droit international moderne*, *Rec. A.D.I.*, vol. 75 (1949), pp. 53-55.

[65] J. Chastenet, *L'Enfance de la Troisième* (1870-1879), p. 137.

practice.[66] Effective possession holds a much greater place in the still primitive relations between States than in the internal order.

3. The Notoriety of Territorial Situations. On land, the intimate bond that unites territories organized under a State regime to a political power alert to defend them usually lends notoriety to territorial situations and the activities of State connected with them. Consequently the condition of publicity required in possession *longi temporis* is here almost always so fully satisfied that it can often be presumed.[67] It is not necessarily so in the maritime domain, where some types of State activity tending to create particular rights at the cost of the community of States may at times go on without precise knowledge on the part of interested governments or without placing them under any legal obligation to communicate their views. Precise criteria can hardly be formulated for judging the legal effect of abstention or silence which may in some cases be due to a passing lack of interest. It may be observed, however, that the growing multiplicity of relations among States, the intensity of their competing activities, and the publicity that surrounds them are likely in our time to shorten the period required for consolidation by the passage of time. (See below.)[68]

In the Fisheries case (United Kingdom–Norway) the International Court of Justice held that a system of delimiting the Norwegian fisheries zone, which had enjoyed the general tolerance of other States for more than sixty years, could not have escaped the vigilance of a great maritime Power directly interested in the fisheries regime in those regions. Without going so far as to deduce acquiescence properly so called from its silence, the Court observed that "The notoriety of the facts, the general toleration of the international community, Great Britain's position in the North Sea, her own interest in the question, and her prolonged abstention would

[66] More and more evident in doctrine is the tendency to take a document for a fact, a resolution voted by an organization for a reality. On the duty of non-recognition created by certain international agreements, see below, Chap. III, Sec. I, "International Recognition."

[67] Verykios (*La prescription en Droit international public*, p. 75) goes so far as to criticize the publicity requirement as useless, since clandestine possession is hardly conceivable. On the vigilance implied in this conception, see the arbitral award of January 23, 1933 in the case concerning the Guatemala-Honduras frontiers, *United Nations Reports of International Arbitral Awards*, vol. II, p. 1328.

[68] To avoid useless discussion, the term "consolidation" is preferred to "acquisitive prescription." Cf. D. H. N. Johnson, "Acquisitive Prescription in International Law," *B.Y.B.I.L.*, 1950, p. 332.

in any case warrant Norway's enforcement of her system against the United Kingdom." This is a sane appreciation of the conditions amounting to notoriety, and it is in complete harmony with the requirements of stability in international relations.

4. Consolidation by Historic Titles. The fundamental interest of the stability of territorial situations from the point of view of order and peace explains the place that consolidation by historic titles holds in international law and the suppleness with which the principle is applied. It is for these situations, especially, that arbitral decisions have sanctioned the principle *quieta non movere*, as much out of consideration for the importance of these situations in themselves in the relations of States as for the political gravity of disputes concerning them.[69] This consolidation, which may have practical importance for territories not yet finally organized under a State regime as well as for certain stretches of sea-like bays, is not subject to the conditions specifically required in other modes of acquiring territory. Proven long use, which is its foundation, merely represents a complex of interests and relations which in themselves have the effect of attaching a territory or an expanse of sea to a given State. It is these interests and relations, varying from one case to another, and not the passage of a fixed term, unknown in any event to international law, that are taken into direct account by the judge to decide *in concreto* on the existence or nonexistence of a consolidation by historic titles.

In this respect such consolidation differs from acquisitive prescription properly so called, as also in the fact that it can apply to territories that could not be proved to have belonged formerly to another State.[70] It differs from occupation in that it can be admitted in relation to certain parts of the sea as well as on land. Finally, it is distinguished from international recognition—and this is the point of most practical importance—by the fact that it can be held to be accomplished not only by acquiescence properly so called,

[69] Award of the Permanent Court of Arbitration in the Grisbadarna Case (Norway-Sweden), October 23, 1909: "Whereas . . . it is a settled principle of the law of nations that a state of things which actually exists and has existed for a long time should be changed as little as possible. . . ." J. B. Scott, *The Hague Court Reports*, Carnegie Endowment for International Peace, 1916, p. 130. This consideration had its part in the judgment of the Permanent Court of International Justice in the Eastern Greenland Case (Denmark-Norway).

[70] Acquisitive prescription, on the contrary, has the effect of conferring title only to territory under the sovereignty of another State. Cf. E. Beckett, *Rec. A.D.I.*, vol. 50 (1934), p. 248; D. H. N. Johnson, *op.cit.*, 1950, p. 332.

acquiescence in which the time factor can have no part, but more easily by a sufficiently prolonged absence of opposition either, in the case of land, on the part of States interested in disputing possession or, in maritime waters, on the part of the generality of States.[71]

5. Effective Possession. In the history of territorial acquisitions and mutations, the ratio of strength between States struggling to "reassemble" or to expand their lands has been a preponderant factor. Its historic role in the distribution of territory, and the large part played by constraint in the decisions of the congresses, conferences, or peace treaties that have sanctioned it, cannot be disputed. International law concedes to effective territorial possession consequences that private law would by no means admit in relation to property. A State which has ceased to exercise any authority over a territory cannot, by purely verbal protestations, indefinitely maintain its title against another which for a sufficiently long time has effectively exercised the powers and fulfilled the duties of sovereignty in it. Considerations of stability, order, and peace, analogous to those that justify acquisitive prescription, are here preponderant. The thesis that the consent of a dispossessed State is invariably required to validate a change of sovereignty is in harmony neither with the facts of international practice nor with the still primitive character of international law which in its present stage holds valid territorial changes imposed under constraint upon defeated countries in treaties of peace.[72]

As for territories regarded as still free or ownerless, two factors have had a determining influence in the history of their appropriation: the inequality of their stage of civilization, and concern for political equilibrium. States of advanced civilization that are greedy for colonies have regarded territories inhabited by indigenous populations which were not, from their point of view, organized in State regimes, as not constituting States and therefore open to occupation. On the other hand, out of concern for the political equilibrium and peace, they have gradually adopted various criteria and practices

[71] See M. Bourquin, "Les baies historiques," *Mélanges Sauser-Hall*, pp. 44 seq.

[72] This question has been amply discussed in the now old controversy between the United Kingdom and Persia over sovereignty in the Bahrein Islands. See the documents in H. A. Smith, *Great Britain and the Law of Nations*, vol. II, pp. 62-76. Cf. Sir John Fischer Williams, "Sovereignty, Seisin and the League," *B.Y.B.I.L.*, 1926, pp. 24 seq.; Majid Khadduri, "Iran's Claim to the Sovereignty of Bahrayn," *A.J.I.L.*, 1951, p. 631.

with a view to regulating the acquisition of ownerless territories by occupation or to providing moral or social justification for a state of possession.

Here again effectivity in possession has formed the recognized title of acquisition, serving as the criterion for decision between rival claims by legitimizing exclusive appropriations based upon the fulfillment of the social functions of sovereignty. The criterion has become more clearly defined as ownerless territories have become rarer and the competition for them proportionately keener. The 1885 Berlin Act made it a rule of positive international law for the contracting Powers, applicable to future occupations on the coasts of the African continent. The degree of effectivity required in possession moreover varies greatly according to the particular circumstances of each case. Decision of this question by the judge provides a characteristic example of supple adaptation of a rule of law. International decisions have taken into consideration the circumstances of time and place.[73] It is to be observed, however, that these circumstances have not always been considered for themselves, that is to say for their own independent significance; they have often been taken into account simultaneously with the existence or nonexistence of rival claims to sovereignty. When the Permanent Court of International Justice held that there was no reason to be too exacting in regard to Denmark's acts of sovereignty in an unoccupied or so thinly populated region, it pointed out that no other Power had, up to 1931, date of the case, claimed sovereignty of any part of Greenland.[74] Similarly, the King of Italy's arbitral award in the Clipperton Island case (January 28, 1931) emphasized the fact that the territory was completely uninhabited and accordingly at the absolute and undisputed disposal of the occupying State from the moment when this State made its appearance, and held that the taking of possession should therefore be regarded as accomplished and the occupation as complete from that moment.[75]

[73] Applying this idea of relativity to the continuance of sovereignty acquired by occupation, Max Huber remarked that "The intermittence and discontinuity compatible with the maintenance of the right necessarily differ according as inhabited or uninhabited regions are involved, or regions enclosed within territories in which sovereignty is incontestably displayed or again regions accessible from, for instance, the high seas." Arbitral award in the Palmas Island case, already cited, p. 18.

[74] Publications of the P.C.I.J., series A/B, no. 53, p. 46.

[75] *United Nations Reports of International Arbitral Awards*, vol. 2, p. 1110.

Clearly, subject to the important qualifications reviewed above, modern law recognizes the acquisition of sovereignty by occupation in virtue of a peaceful and sufficiently continuous exercise of State functions. What it seeks on the contrary to interdict is the claim of a State to establish territorial sovereignty on a purely negative basis consisting in the mere exclusion of activities on the part of other States. There is a necessary relation, says Max Huber in his award in the Palmas Island case, between the right to exclude other States from a given territory and the duty to display the activities of a State there, for territorial sovereignty "serves to divide between nations the space upon which human activities are employed, in order to assure them at all points the minimum of protection of which international law is the guardian."[76] This very lofty conception of the social role of territorial sovereignty was carried to its logical conclusion by Huber in the passage of his award where he observes that "an element which is essential for the constitution of sovereignty should not be lacking in its continuation" and that "the growing insistence with which international law, ever since the middle of the 18th century, has demanded that the occupation shall be effective, would be inconceivable, if effectiveness were required only for the act of acquisition and not equally for the maintenance of the right."[77] The eminent arbiter moreover recognized that this extreme consequence can hardly follow in territories already organized in a State regime. There it would, in our opinion, conflict with the primordial requirements of stability. It was in relation to those of ill-defined status that he suggested that a sovereignty acquired by effectivity of appropriation might eventually be lost by a subsequent failure of effectivity in possession, that is to say, in the last analysis, by nonuser.[78]

6. Political Equilibrium and Human Ends in Territorial Status. In our time, when the rarity of unoccupied space sets narrow limits to territorial ambitions and territorial changes are few, it is less the appropriation of territories than the political and legal condition of some of them that holds attention. Diplomatic history shows that

76 *op.cit.*, p. 17. In this respect the spheres of influence maintained by the great Powers were open to criticism. The same objection applies to the "sector theory" as a justification of the claims of certain States in the Antarctic. See G. Smedal, *De l'acquisition de souveraineté sur les terres polaires*, p. 85 seq.; G. Gidel, *Aspects juridiques de la lutte pour l'Antarctique*, p. 43.

77 *op.cit.*, p. 17.

78 Fernand De Visscher, "L'arbitrage de l'île Palmas (Miangas)," *Revue de Droit international et de Législation comparée*, 1929, p. 735.

this condition often has its origin in the rivalries and political tensions of the great Powers and that insofar as it has had any definite legal character it has been a function of balance.

Neutralization of States or of specified territories and some instances of demilitarization and nonfortification were in the nineteenth century characteristic applications of the policy of European balance. They rested on the common will of the great Powers to depoliticize up to a certain point stated zones or regions, imposing on a generally weak or temporarily enfeebled local power a compromise dictated by an aspiration to order and pacification. In Europe most of these arrangements have yielded to the pressure of forces which they were designed to balance, and belong to the past.

In other continents where the problem of political or economic penetration brought great-Power rivalries to grips, the concern for balance brought about the treaty arrangements of "zones of interest" or "of influence."[79] These were questionable expedients if considered solely from the point of view of the exclusive rights that they conferred on their beneficiaries, but justifiable by the concern of these latter to reduce the dangers of their competing ambitions.

Since 1919 these practices have been associated in some regions with a humane and civilizing ideal to produce the systems of mandates and international trusteeship. A balance of mutual disinterestedness took form in the principle of nonannexation which in Africa brought about what has been accurately called "the greatest example in history of peaceful change."[80] Humanitarian ends found their expression in the idea adopted in the Covenant of the League of Nations and resumed in the United Nations Charter of "a sacred trust of civilization" binding upon those States members that have the responsibility of administering territories whose peoples are not yet completely self-governing (Art. 73 of the Charter). In the International Trusteeship System and in the Mandates System this trust is the measure of the rights and duties of the authority responsible for this administration, which thus assumes a very marked legal character.

[79] This search for equilibrium was clear in the old Anglo-Russian Treaty of 1907 delimiting spheres of influence in Persia and guaranteeing for each contracting Power the abstention of the other in the reserved zones. In China the policy of "the open door" or "equal chance" championed by the United States against that of "spheres of interest" was similarly the resultant of a common search for equilibrium.

[80] H. Duncan Hall, *Mandates, Dependencies and Trusteeship*, p. 12.

Not only is the territory here not open to any State's appropriation, it is inseparable from the trust that justifies tutelary authority to such a point that if the trust came to an end this authority would lose all legal foundation. The advisory opinion of July 11, 1950 by the International Court of Justice made clear this consequence of the system.[81]

In this case, where the question was examined much more closely than ever before, it appeared that the notion of sovereignty, which the jurists had for twenty-five years and in the most varied forms persisted in introducing into the institution of mandates, had definitely no place there. This was a typical example of the failure of doctrine to adapt its ideas to a new situation. In fact no international institution has so profoundly changed the traditional relations between power and territory. Interests entirely different from those that had dictated the establishment of historical sovereignties were here the foundation of an institution which is in every respect functional in purpose.[82]

On one important point, this international system has bent under the weight of political tensions that were beginning to be felt when the United Nations Charter was drawn up. Whereas the Covenant of the League of Nations, faithful to the leading idea of depoliticization by demilitarization, prohibited building fortifications or military or naval bases in territories under B and C mandates, and

[81] Advisory Opinion of the I.C.J., International Status of South-West Africa, Reports, 1950, p. 133: "The authority which the Union [of South Africa] Government exercises over the Territory is based on the Mandate. If the Mandate lapsed, as the Union Government contends, the latter's authority would equally have lapsed. To retain the rights derived from the Mandate and to deny the obligations thereunder could not be justified." A minority opinion deduces from this conception the duty of the mandatory State, if not to accept the exact terms of a draft trusteeship agreement, at least to lend itself in good faith to the negotiation of an agreement.

[82] "The Mandate was created, in the interest of the inhabitants of the territory, and of humanity in general, as an international institution with an international object—a sacred trust of civilisation." *ibid.*, p. 132. The experience of the League of Nations showed that in a world where international relations derive their structure and stability from the territorial compartmentation, this absence of sovereignty raised a series of problems in relation to the territories under B and C mandates (problems of status and diplomatic protection of the natives, those connected with the economic and financial consequences of the principle of nonannexation, and those due to the fact that the title of the mandatory Power was in the nature of a *precarium*) for which the Council of the League of Nations tried to find solutions. Cf. D. F. W. van Rees, *Les mandats internationaux*, pp. 19-51.

giving military instruction to the natives "for other than police purposes and the defense of the territory," the United Nations Charter (Arts. 82 and 83) perceptibly departed from this idea when it provided for the designation of strategic areas in a trusteeship agreement. In a resolution of April 2, 1947, the Security Council approved a trusteeship agreement that designated all the Pacific islands formerly under Japanese mandate as strategic areas and assigned the trusteeship in them to the United States.[83]

In highly civilized peoples with a long history, the stability of the State's territories rests on a community of memories, traditions, and sacrifices that associate the integrity and defense of the land with the idea of nation and fatherland. Territory was long a framework for security; it is in this aspect especially that it played a capital role in the establishment of modern States. Many indications suggest that its significance in this regard may diminish by reason not only of the rapid technological developments that rob natural lines and positions of defense of their strategic interest, but also of the growing concentration in certain parts of the globe of that effective political sovereignty which on a world scale decides peace or war.

But it would be risky to infer from these changes that the bonds attaching man to territory are now weakened. Everything points to the conclusion that they will not so soon be affected, for the effects of these developments are not of a sort easily perceived by the masses. It is even curious that our epoch, which is often described as one of great spaces and vast empires, should also be that in which nationalism is more than ever breaking up old political formations, not only in Europe but also in Asia.[84]

As for international law, in every domain it reflects today the tendency of territorial sovereignty to extend its mastery. The international regulation of air navigation on the basis of sovereignty in the subjacent State, the riparian State's claim to a wider zone of territorial sea and its recent claims to the resources of the continental shelf, these are all characteristic manifestations of this tendency. Technological developments here help to accentuate

[83] M. Sibert, *Traité*, vol. I, no. 681: "In reality, discretionary power and military reason will speedily, in order to cope with contingencies, take precedence over all other interests." Cf. G. Vedovato, *Les accords de Tutelle, Rec. A.D.I.*, vol. 76 (1950), p. 626.

[84] J. Gottmann, *La politique des Etats et leur géographie*, pp. 76 seq.

the conflict between historical beliefs and forces that have by no means disarmed and an interdependence that calls for the effacement of sovereignties.

§ 2. PARTICULAR PROBLEMS

1. International River Law. Of all the kinds of territory the international river is the one in which administration is most sensitive to economic and political factors. For twenty years these factors have been largely responsible for weakening the trend that established itself in Europe after the first world war towards maximum uniformity in the regime of navigable waterways of international concern on the basic principle of universally recognized priority for freedom of navigation. In this tendency to universalization there was an overabstract conception that ignored the sometimes profound differences in the economic functions as well as the geographic and hydrographic conditions of the waterways. While in European rivers, which water thickly populated countries and are for the most part naturally navigable, navigation is the primary function, very different factual conditions in the Americas and other continents call for different regimes.[85] These circumstances would be sufficient to explain why, despite periodic attempts at unification, international river law remained very largely a particular law. Less justified are the discriminatory practices induced by the political concern of riparian States to secure, directly or indirectly, monopolies or exclusive privileges.

In Europe it was the joint action of the great Powers that established on certain rivers a regime founded on the principle of freedom of navigation and its corollary, equality of treatment. Interpreting on this point "the principles governing international fluvial law in general" and the position taken by the States signatory to the Treaty of Versailles, the Permanent Court of International Justice saw in the "community of interests of riparian States . . . the basis of a common legal right, the essential features of which are the perfect equality of all riparian States in the use of the whole

[85] On the necessity for some differentiation see: Charles De Visscher, *Le droit international des communications*, pp. 72 seq., 95 seq.; G. Kaeckenbeeck, "International Rivers," Grotius Society Publications; van Eysinga, "Les fleuves et canaux internationaux," *Bibliotheca Visseriana*, vol. II, pp. 124-125; A. W. Quint, *Internationaal Rivierenrecht*; H. A. Smith, *The Economic Use of International Rivers*; G. Sauser-Hall, *L'utilisation industrielle des fleuves internationaux*, *Rec. A.D.I.*, vol. 83 (1953), p. 479.

course of the river and the exclusion of any preferential privilege of any one riparian State in relation to the others."[86]

This ordering action of the great Powers focused upon rivers where their economic and political interests were sufficiently in harmony to call for a common line of conduct. Around the original treaty nucleus there gradually grew up a "public law of Europe" of which subsequent navigation acts were a more or less faithful expression. Being particularly interested in seeing its foreign trade penetrate to the interior of the continent, England exerted in this domain a substantial influence crystallized around a liberal interpretation of the Congress of Vienna texts.[87]

Different ideas prevail, and with good reason, in other continents, especially in the Americas.[88] Freedom of navigation there is simply conceded by the riparians in particular treaties. The preparatory documents and the proceedings of the General Conference on Communications and Transit at Barcelona (1921) showed how impracticable complete uniformity is, and they emphasized particularly the primary interest that attaches to the economic function of the river in determining how it shall be administered. There is therefore no good reason to regard as a priori contrary to the principles or interests of the international community the position taken by non-European States that make freedom of navigation dependent on the consent of the riparians or that subordinate it to other ways of using the river.[89]

With these objective elements are contrasted political attitudes that take effect in discriminatory practices. In the past these sometimes amounted to a complete interdiction of navigation by upper riparian States or to obstructions in the form of special charges

[86] Judgment No. 16 (September 10, 1929), Case on the Territorial Jurisdiction of the Oder Commission, p. 27.

[87] Ruth E. Bacon, "British Policy and the Regulation of European Rivers of International Concern," *B.Y.B.I.L.*, 1929, pp. 158-170. Even in Europe freedom of navigation acquired its priority in the international regime only from the time when the ambiguous text of Article 109 of the Final Act of Vienna was interpreted, in conformity with the British thesis, in the sense of complete equality of treatment in a process of economic development which might not always be constant.

[88] On the diversity of political and economic interests as between England and the United States of America, and the adaptation of doctrinal ideas to these interests in the matter of waterways, see Ruth E. Bacon, "British and American Policy and the Right of Fluvial Navigation," *B.Y.B.I.L.*, 1932, p. 76.

[89] For the practice of the United States in North America and in relation to certain South American rivers, see Charles Cheney Hyde, *International Law*, vol. I, §§ 160-167.

collected for mere transit. In our day they take the more complex form of differential treatment that makes transportation, especially in transit, an item of economic competition between States.[90] A legal monopoly conceding the exclusive right of navigation would be obviously discriminatory. In the Oscar Chinn case the Permanent Court of International Justice did not regard as a discrimination forbidden by the international conventions on river traffic in the waterways of the Belgian Congo the tariff reductions conceded by Belgium to a transportation company controlled by it, for these measures, according to the judgment, had not been taken in consideration of the nationality of the enterprise.[91]

The Treaties of Peace of 1919-1920 on some points exaggerated the trend to internationalization and ran into political resistance from the riparian States. The experience has shown conclusively that administration by international commissions is effective and stable only where, in perfect equality, it wins confident collaboration from the States on the river. Everywhere else, the national susceptibilities of the riparians have finally prevailed over economic or technical considerations that had been invoked in setting up the commission.[92] It was especially the clauses of the Treaties of Peace on the composition of the Commissions that aroused opposition by their unilateral and political character. The reversal in the ratio of forces was bound sooner or later to cause their abrogation. The Powers that dictated these clauses failed to understand that, having set up on four great Central European river systems Commissions in which the introduction of representatives of nonriparian States was an innovation greatly to their advantage, they should have justified this "complete internationalization"[93] as the application of a system of which they were willing to accept the consequences themselves. In fact, not one of them showed any willingness to grant reciprocity. When the German Reich on November 14, 1936 denounced the articles of the Treaty of Versailles on the Interna-

[90] The Barcelona Conference of 1921 undertook to study these questions with more faith in an ideal of economic cooperation than experience of the still profoundly individualist policy of States in this domain.

[91] Publications of the P.C.I.J., series A/B, no. 63, pp. 86-87. See, however, the dissenting opinions, especially that of D. Anzilotti, *ibid.*, p. 112.

[92] The opposition of the river States to the territorial jurisdiction of the commissions was the occasion for two decisions by the P.C.I.J.: the Advisory Opinion of December 8, 1927 on the jurisdiction of the European Commission of the Danube between Galatz and Braila, and the Judgment of September 10, 1929 on the territorial jurisdiction of the Oder Commission.

[93] P.C.I.J. Judgment No. 16, cited above, p. 28.

tional Commissions of the Rhine, the Elbe, the Oder, and the Danube, together with the river statutes enacted in execution of these articles, it relied especially on the unilateral character of this regime.

More than any other, the international regime of the Danube has been marked by political vicissitudes. The development of its law since 1856 has been distinguished at once by the diversity and the instability of the regimes applied in the different sections of the river—a phenomenon wholly due to the preponderance of the political rivalries of which the Danubian basin has always been the stake. Between the two world wars the system administered by the European Commission of the Danube, which amounted to a sort of expropriation of territorial sovereignty in favor of an international organization, met growing opposition from Rumania. In its remarkable technical activities and authoritarian methods, the Commission had long represented the Concert of Europe. The Sinaia Arrangement of August 18, 1938, a result of the weakening of British and French influence, stripped it of its most important prerogatives and transferred them to an autonomous Rumanian service.

The Danubian Convention of August 18, 1948, drawn up by the Conference of Belgrade, came into force over the protests of the Western Powers, who denied that it had any validity. It would be futile to enter into a legal analysis of a convention which was openly a political product. Characterized by the subordination of the international regime to the territorial sovereignty of the riparian States, and especially by the disappearance of the international guarantees of free navigation and equal treatment, its spirit still more than its text marks a retrogression in the development of European river law since the Congress of Vienna. It reflects the complete predominance of Soviet Russia, which is determined to block capitalist influence in a region that it proposes to keep under its exclusive control.

In the reaction against the extreme internationalization of the Versailles Treaty, a large part must be attributed to political tensions and the consequent weakening in the spirit of cooperation, but we should not forget what was legitimate in the reaction or, above all, the danger of uniform reglementations based too exclusively upon abstract ideas. The unity of some problems is only apparent. Beyond the few common essential features lies the diversity of situations that calls for particular treatment.

2. The Delimitation of Coastal Waters. The Continental Shelf. From the point of view of the relations between politics and law, the delimitation of coastal waters is today the major problem of the international law of the sea. The problem always has an international aspect, for the validity of the delimitation as against third States is a question of international law.[94] It has been profoundly affected by new factors. These are due to a more exact knowledge of geographic realities and to recent developments in certain human activities. More precisely, it was these latter that little by little showed reasons for differentiating between various coastal waters and provided criteria for a growing particularization in their regulation. In this domain the reaction against premature systematization was especially sharp. The new orientation touches both the width of territorial waters and the marking of their limits. These developments, following one another over a period of fifty years, all point towards a geographic extension of the right of the coastal State. This "organization in depth" confirms the observation that "if legally the frontier is a line, geographically and politically it is a zone, a band of limitrophe territory"[95] the government of which tends to adapt itself to the physical characteristics of the coast and the human activities that go on there.

The absence of any generally accepted rule on the width of territorial waters accounts for what has been justly called "the chaotic state of their regime." The three-mile measure, as outside limit of jurisdiction, doubtless never acquired universal authority. There could nevertheless be cited in its favor at the beginning of the twentieth century the widest practice, the active support of the principal maritime Powers, and the moderating effect that it had had on the unreasonable claims of coastal States. It was recommended besides by simplicity of application, particularly because it makes it easier to fix the position of a vessel than if a greater width of territorial waters is recognized, the difficulty increasing with the distance from shore.[96] But even before the Codification Conference

94 Judgment of the International Court of Justice in the Fisheries Case (Norway–United Kingdom), Reports of Judgments, 1951, p. 132. There is no foundation for the claim, implicitly condemned by this passage in the Court's judgment, of certain States unilaterally to extend their territorial waters beyond the extreme limits observed by the generality of States and without their consent. The recent claims of Chile, Ecuador, and Peru to extend their sovereignty to a minimum of 200 marine miles from their coasts have been protested.

95 J. Gottmann, *La politique des Etats et leur géographie*, 1952, p. 122.

96 The Hague Codification Conference, Bases of Discussion, vol. II, Territorial Waters, Observations of the British Government, p. 162.

was convened, new claims and divergent practices, all extensive of the coastal State's rights, were making their appearance. Some openly sought to widen the territorial sea under full sovereignty; others moved towards the institution of a contiguous zone on the high sea within which the coastal State would exercise particular rights corresponding to specific interests.

The Codification Conference of 1930 finally shattered the three-mile rule, but without replacing it. Henceforth it represents only the minimum that the riparian State can claim. No agreement could be reached either on a compromise system worked out by the preparatory Committee, or on a treaty limit greater than three miles, or finally on a contiguous zone limited both in space and in the nature of the rights that the riparian State would have in it.[97]

In the background of these legal debates were profound differences of which the unmistakably political character fully explains the respective positions of the governments. This clarification was, when everything is taken into account, the chief benefit of the Conference. There is no doubt that the attachment of the great maritime Powers to the three-mile limit regarded as a maximum is largely explained by the fact that, having no great interest in a legal extension of their own territorial waters owing to the *de facto* superiority that their means of action give them over vast expanses of ocean, they object to establishing the exclusive jurisdiction of other States over parts of the high sea, where, in peace, their ships are subject only to the law of the flag, while in time of war their fleets exercise rights there that would be restricted by any extension of the zone of neutrality. Defense of the principle of freedom of the sea was thus for them a matter of national interest.[98]

National preoccupations, inspired by different interests, equally explain the claims of those States that urge an extension either of territorial waters or of certain kinds of jurisdiction over a supplementary zone. Doubtless some of these, like Norway, had in view at the 1930 Conference only economic interests relating particularly

97 On all this see the masterly work of G. Gidel, *Le Droit international public de la Mer*, vol. III.

98 On these considerations see the significant documents of the Board of Trade and the Admiralty, published in H. A. Smith, *Great Britain and the Law of Nations*, vol. II, pp. 207 seq.

"The greater the maritime power of a State, the more it seeks to limit the extent of the territorial sea. . . . It is not at all surprising that Great Britain, Japan, and the United States in 1930 championed the maximum reduction of the marginal belt." G. Gidel, *Le Droit international public de la Mer*, vol. III, p. 141.

to fisheries which it would have been possible, where there was no well-established historical title, to protect by particular conventions. But no understanding could be reached on claims formulated by other countries in the interest of their naval policies.[99] The exclusion of questions of war and neutrality from the agenda could not dismiss them from the minds of the delegates; "the Conference felt the weight of these problems at least as heavily as if it had directly confronted them."[100]

In fact, fixation of a general limit for peacetime could not have failed to affect the width of the zone closed to belligerent action in time of war, and the zone of maritime neutrality. Now on these points the interests of the States were debatable and their views hesitant and diverse. Whereas some of them, for instance France, claimed a wider extent of territorial waters for application of the rules of maritime neutrality (Hague Convention XIII) than for other interests, other and more numerous States were manifestly inclined to restrict the general limit of their territorial waters in this context with a view to lightening the burdens of the riparian State in protecting its neutrality.[101]

The institution of a contiguous zone, which in many respects would correspond to actual international practice, has met with opposition from several Powers on military grounds, that is to say for highly political reasons. Doubtless the State's right to repulse even on the high sea an already launched or imminent attack upon its territory is well established and quite independent of any such zone. More debatable was the claim to take preventive measures in this zone, the nature of which would be left to each riparian State's judgment of its security needs.[102]

In spite of its defeat, the idea of a contiguous zone, supported by many delegations at the Codification Conference, made some

99 See particularly the statements made in the meeting of April 5, 1930 by the Italian delegate, A. Giannini. Minutes of the Second Commission, p. 142.

100 G. Gidel, *op.cit.*, p. 146.

101 The limits drawn by a government from time to time for the defense of its neutral zone are not decisive in determining the general limits of its marginal belt. See on this subject a letter from the Swedish minister of foreign affairs, Osten Unden, dated October 20, 1951, produced before the International Court of Justice in the argument of the Fisheries case (Great Britain–Norway, Pleadings, Oral Arguments, Documents, vol. IV, p. 503). Cf. the statements made to the Codification Conference by the delegate of Sweden (Minutes of the Second Commission, p. 138).

102 Cf. Jesse S. Reeves, "The Codification of the Law of Territorial Waters," *A.J.I.L.*, 1930, p. 494.

progress after 1930. At the same time the impossibility of strictly maintaining the three-mile limit in the face of political, economic, and social interests that demand its extension became evident. As M. Gidel observed in 1934: "from the moment when a specific width of territorial sea could not be held established by international law as an obligatory rule for all States, the contiguous zone appeared to be the way to adjust the reciprocal concessions that States whose interests favor different widths can make in order to reach an understanding on one and the same width."[103]

Thus put *de lege ferenda,* the problem is one of legislative policy and consequently one for international treaty regulation. It has recently been studied by the International Law Commission. At the end of its seventh session (July 1955), the Commission was able to offer only a very partial solution, which may be summed up as follows: It took note that there is no uniformity in international practice touching the width of the territorial sea, and went on to declare that international law does not authorize extending it beyond twelve miles. But it did not condemn extensions within this maximum.

A study of international practice in marking the base line of territorial waters in bays suggests analogous conclusions. There is no doubt that here again some doctrine has been too zealous in formulating rules so excessively technical that they found no support in the practice of States.

In spite of the rather marked popularity of what has been called the "ten-mile rule," this numerical criterion has not been recognized as universally applicable, and it is not possible to invoke in its support "a general practice accepted as law" (Art. 38 of the Court statute).[104] Nor can this general authority be attributed to certain geographic criteria that have been proposed, to the exclusion of others, to define bays and distinguish them from other indentations of the coast, such as the width of the opening or the ratio between this width and depth of penetration into the land. As was admitted in the arbitral award of 1910 relative to the North Atlantic Fish-

[103] *op.cit.,* vol. III, p. 20.

[104] The I.C.J. merely noted this legal situation when it observed in its judgment of December 18, 1951: "that although the ten-mile rule has been adopted by certain States both in their national law and in their treaties and conventions, and although certain arbitral decisions have applied it as between these States, other States have adopted a different limit. Consequently, the ten-mile rule has not acquired the authority of a general rule of international law." Reports, 1951, p. 131.

eries, the diversity of particular circumstances makes it impossible to apply more or less mechanically a mathematical criterion, or to give sole consideration to the rather vague geographic datum, bay, to the exclusion of other factors that may be equally important. As Maurice Bourquin remarks, if some bays must be legally assimilated to the landed domain of the State, that is "because they are really linked with this domain, because they are of one piece with it, their legal territoriality being merely a recognition of their *de facto* territoriality."[105] The truth is then merely that a geographic peculiarity is here the basis of multiple interests that the coastal State may have in certain stretches of sea by reason of their particularly intimate connection with the land formation about them.[106] The problem of delimiting territorial sovereignty in bays is at present insoluble on the plane of general international law. Authors who, like Professor Schücking, have taken a different position have been guided less by objective observation of the state of the law in force than by a spirit of generalization that pushed them to codify the matter.

The existence of "historical bays" or "historical waters" is the clearest instance of this individualization of the law. Their appropriation has been the result of a peaceful and continuous exercise of sovereignty combined with absence of protest from third States. The antiquity of the established use, the account to be taken, in default of antiquity or in judging of it, of the "vital interest" of the riparian State in the determination of the regime for bays, and the legal value to be attributed to contrary claims—all these involve considerations peculiar to each case, some of which are definitely political.[107]

105 "Les baies historiques," in *Mélanges Sauser-Hall*, pp. 41-42.

106 It was held in the arbitral award of 1910 in the case of the North Atlantic Fisheries that "the geographical character of a bay contains conditions which concern the interests of the territorial sovereign to a more infinite and important extent than do those connected with the open coast. The conditions of national and territorial integrity, of defense, of commerce and of industry are all vitally concerned with the control of the bays penetrating the national coast line. This interest varies, speaking generally, in proportion to the penetration inland of the bay; but as no principle of international law recognizes any specified relation between the concavity of the bay and the requirements for control by the territorial sovereignty. . . ." J. B. Scott, *The Hague Court Reports*, Carnegie Endowment for International Peace, 1916, pp. 183-184.

107 In the North Atlantic Fisheries case the arbitral tribunal, while recognizing that established use may be regarded as a ground for claiming as territorial bays which for this reason may be classified as historical, observes that such claims "should be held valid in the absence of any principle of international

The very special configuration of some coasts puts the problem of choosing base lines in particularly broad terms. When a coast, like that of Norway, is entirely made up of bays, fjords, and indentations of every kind, with islands or islets forming the exterior belt of the land, the base lines cannot follow all the accidents of the littoral. Here, as M. Gidel observes, "the base line ceases to be low-water mark" and some geometric construction must be resorted to.[108] Applicable wherever the configuration of the coast permits, the rule of low-water mark would be only nominally relevant in such a case, for it would be buried under the necessary exceptions. The technically precise criteria proposed by the Government of the United Kingdom before the International Court of Justice in the Fisheries case (1951) to restrict the use of straight base lines to certain situations designated exceptional, or to limit their length, were not sufficiently confirmed by international practice. The Court preferred a more general notion—the natural relations between certain stretches of sea and the land. "It is the land which confers upon the coastal State a right to the waters off its coasts." It is the degree of intimacy between the terrestrial domain and certain parts of the sea looked at in their concrete and particular features that justifies extending the regime of inland waters to them. This criterion, which serves for bays, should, the Court held, be broadly applied all along a coast where the geographic configuration is as peculiar as it is in Norway. Under these conditions the validity of the delimitation decreed in 1935 should not be judged by the minute detail of the sinuosities of the coast: "Such a coast, viewed as a whole, calls for the application of a different method:" that of base lines detached to a reasonable degree from the physical line of the coast.[109] The qualification implicit in these last words is due to the same criterion, the close dependence of the territorial sea on the terrestrial domain. "It follows that while such a State must be allowed the latitude necessary in order to be able to adapt its delimitation to practical needs and local requirements, the drawing of base-lines must not depart to any appreciable extent from the general direction of the coast."[110]

---

law on the subject. . . ." *ibid.*, p. 185. Corresponding to this individualization of the problem are various suggestions made with a view to eliminating or reducing the uncertainties to which it gives rise, such as the creation of an International Office of Waters, establishment of a list of historical bays, and the marking of historical waters on marine charts. Cf. G. Gidel, *op.cit.*, p. 637.

108 *ibid.*, p. 497.

109 Reports of Judgments, 1951, pp. 129, 133.

110 *ibid.*, p. 133.

Such were the reasons that led the Court to regard the system of delimitation ordered by the Norwegian decree of 1935 not as a derogation from common international law, but as an adaptation of the law made necessary by local conditions.

Only an incomplete view can be had of the evolution of the law in connection with these problems unless the conflicts of interest from which they arise are kept in mind. Fishing along the Norwegian coasts, to even greater distances than those fixed in the decree of 1935, had long been considered by the inhabitants their exclusive privilege and had not in fact given rise to any serious international incident. The situation completely changed when at the beginning of the twentieth century British vessels, confronted with the relative exhaustion of their traditional fishing grounds, extended their activities to the especially rich Norwegian coastal fisheries and, strong in the superiority of their equipment, began to offer a competition which was at once a menace to the local industry and a danger to the conservation of certain kinds of fish. It was this competition, the real cause of dispute, that emphasized the interest and complexity of the long-unnoticed problem of selecting base lines. The peculiar geographic configuration of the coast and Norway's historical titles provided the legal case for the scheme of delimitation adopted in the decree; but here as elsewhere it was the use of space by the peoples and the new competitions in this use that gave rise to the problem and shaped the development of the law.[111]

Entirely new are the problems raised by the appropriation and delimitation of the "continental shelf," meaning the bed of the sea and the subsoil near the coast but beyond territorial waters, where the depth is not great enough to make exploitation technically impossible.

International practice has only a few agreements to show, such as that of February 26, 1942 between Great Britain and Venezuela relating to the Gulf of Paria, and a number of unilateral acts, decrees, or proclamations of which the best known is the proclamation of September 28, 1945 by the President of the United States.[112]

111 J. Gottmann, *La Politique des Etats et leur géographie*, p. 69: "In differentiated and organized space, it is organized man that counts."

112 M. W. Mouton, *The Continental Shelf*, 1952, pp. 250 seq.; Edwin Borchard, "Resources of the Continental Shelf," *A.J.I.L.*, 1946, p. 53; J. W. Bingham, "The Continental Shelf and the Marginal Belt," *A.J.I.L.*, 1946, p. 173; Herbert

The legal effect of these unilateral acts is debatable. In any case they are still too few and in many ways too imprecise or divergent to justify the conclusion that there now exists a positive international law on the subject or even so much as a general acquiescence in certain fundamental principles.[113]

Two points are, however, clear. The interested States propose to provide for the exploitation of marine subsoil by exclusive national appropriation, any idea of international exploitation having been discarded as impractical. Further, there is no doubt that the claims formulated are due less to concern for the protection of industries already in operation than to the desire to secure in advance for the coastal States the exclusive development of the submarine wealth close to their shores. No government appears disposed to permit any foreign enterprise to engage in such development without its consent. Exactly as in the case of the surface of the sea, one of the most delicate problems raised by the appropriation of the marine subsoil is that of delimiting it in narrow seas where the submarine extension of land frontiers would bring the sovereignties of the riparian States into direct contact. Particular agreements will here compensate for the absence of applicable general rules.

However that may be, it cannot be admitted that unilateral decisions such as those taken by certain Latin American States (1947-1948) affect the solution of problems that are primarily international, like the width of territorial waters and the exclusive rights—fishing for example—that the riparian States are permitted to exercise there. Nor does the confusion now existing in the delimitation of territorial waters justify recent theories which, under cover of notions as vague as the continental shelf or the unilateral protection of the riches of the sea, aim at what are at times extravagant extensions of sovereignty over the open sea. The continental shelf presents its own peculiar problems which, though they may in some respects bear upon the regime in the marginal belt, call for independent regulation.[114]

W. Briggs, in *A.J.I.L.*, 1951, p. 338; Cecil Hurst, *The Continental Shelf*, Grotius Society Transactions, vol. 35, 1948, p. 153; H. Lauterpacht, "Sovereignty over Submarine Areas," *B.Y.B.I.L.*, 1950, p. 376.

113 See the work of the United Nations International Law Commission and the observations of governments on its proposals (1951-1953), especially the report of J. P. A. François to the fifth session of the Commission.

114 See the important article by Professor G. Scelle: "Plateau continental et droit international," *Revue générale de Droit international public*, 1955, pp. 5-62.

Section IV

The Law of the State and the International Organization. The Reserved Domain. The So-Called Integration Agreements

§ 1. THE STATUS OF THE INTERNATIONAL ORGANIZATION

Independently of their mutual undertakings, which are the object of the United Nations Organization and the reason for its existence, the States members assumed certain obligations to the Organization itself with a view to providing the means for accomplishing its mission. Article 104 of the Charter lays it down that "The Organization shall enjoy in the territory of each of its members such legal capacity as may be necessary for the exercise of its functions and the fulfillment of its purposes." Article 2, paragraph 5, makes it a duty for the States members to give the Organization "every assistance in any action it takes in accordance with the present Charter. . . ."

The legal personality of the League of Nations had been recognized on the basis of certain texts in the Treaties of Peace (1919-1920) and of established practice. But the effect of the limited application of this principle had remained somewhat imprecise. The tragic death of Count Folke Bernadotte, United Nations mediator, who was assassinated at Jerusalem on September 17, 1948 in the performance of his duties, raised the problem of the Organization's status in entirely new and far broader terms, making it part of a system of relations until then strictly reserved to sovereign States, namely international responsibility. The advisory opinion handed down by the International Court of Justice on April 11, 1949[115] is inspired by two ideas: one, the duties of States members to the Organization; the other, the complete independence which the Organization must retain in the fulfillment of its mission.

In case of failure on the part of a State member in its duties to the Organization, resulting in damage to one of the Organization's agents under conditions involving the responsibility of a State, the Court recognized the capacity of the Organization to enter an international claim not only for injury to its own interests, but also for the injury suffered by the victim or his heirs and successors. Further, since the independence of the Organization demands strict respect for the obligation of full assistance to it, its agents must not

[115] Reparation of Injuries Suffered in the Service of the United Nations, Reports, 1949, p. 174.

have to depend for their protection upon any authority other than the United Nations.

The Court, having to cope as it says with "a new situation," did not hesitate to act constructively from two points of view. Rejecting any artificial assimilation between the bond of nationality, traditional title to diplomatic protection, and the administrative relations that are the subject of Article 100 of the Charter, it placed the problem on its true ground, the protection due by reason of office. Going beyond the too restrictive terms of Article 104, it did not shrink from recognizing the Organization's capacity to afford this protection even as against a nonmember State, holding that "fifty States, representing the vast majority of the members of the international community, had the power, in conformity with international law, to bring into being an entity possessing objective international personality, and not merely personality recognized by them alone, together with capacity to bring international claims."[116]

More particular and more burdensome are the treaty and special obligations of the host country to the international Organization. Respect for the privileges and immunities inseparable from the performance of an international function is incumbent on the local authorities even in relation to those international officers who are their nationals. A recent experience (1952) has shown how difficult it is for an organization founded on the principles of law and international cooperation to defend its prerogatives against the spirit of suspicion which at times of high political and ideological tension lays hold on public opinion.

§ 2. THE RESERVED DOMAIN

The doctrinal views propounded on the problem of the reserved domain ("matters which are essentially within the domestic jurisdiction of any State . . ."—Article 2, paragraph 7) are at times disappointing. Authors have usually approached the problem with the double intent of harmonizing its solution with their personal conceptions of the general relations between municipal and international law and of leaving no gap in the mechanism for the peaceful settlement of international disputes organized successively by the Covenant and the Charter. On this plane the debate easily degenerates into scholastic discussions that are as empty as they

[116] *ibid.*, p. 185.

are confused. Study of international practice, relying on concrete data, here as elsewhere yields more useful instruction.

When the Covenant of the League of Nations was being drawn up, the fear of authoritative intervention by the Council in a dispute on a matter which States in their traditional policy reserve for their own independent decision made itself apparent in the wording of Article 15, paragraph 8.[117] As everyone knows, the Article was designed to disarm opposition in the United States directed especially to matters (migration, customs tariffs) that form shifting frontier zones where international interests have not yet been adequately regulated. In the setting of compulsory mediation by the Council of the League of Nations, this text has a very definite procedural function. If the international organization intervened in a dispute already arisen and consequently always clearly individualized, it offered a means of defense, a "demurrer," which enabled the defendant State to prevent argument upon the merits by showing that the question was in its litigious aspect one of those which by international law are "solely within the domesic jurisdiction." The Covenant—and this is an essential point—left it to the Council to decide whether the plea was well founded.

Unlike the authors whose efforts to systematize often resulted in merely obscuring the problem,[118] the Permanent Court of International Justice had in 1923 pointed out the necessity of dealing with each case quite separately. In its Advisory Opinion on the nationality decrees, it had not only indicated that the content of the reserved domain "is an essentially relative question," being dependent on the development of international relations, but it had emphasized the impossibility of answering this question without taking into consideration the particular circumstances of each case. It observed that the "matter" to which the question in litigation relates is in no way decisive by itself, for "it may well happen that, in a matter which, like that of nationality, is not, in principle, regulated by international law, the right of the State to use its discretion is nevertheless restricted by obligations which it may have undertaken towards other States. In such a case, jurisdiction

117 "If the dispute between the parties is claimed by one of them, and is found by the Council, to arise out of a matter which by international law is solely within the domestic jurisdiction of that party, the Council shall so report, and shall make no recommendation as to its settlement."

118 L. Kopelmanas, *L'Organisation des Nations Unies*, p. 213: "Truly a singular method, seeking to resolve practical difficulties with the aid of still more uncertain theoretical conceptions."

which, in principle, belongs solely to the State, is limited by rules of international law."[119]

The distinction between "matters" and "questions" is accordingly of capital importance. An international convention on a "matter" which, in principle, is solely within the domestic jurisdiction takes out of this exclusive jurisdiction any "question" arising out of the interpretation or application of the convention.[120]

Moreover, it is not only the obligations occasionally assumed by the State in matters which are in principle solely within the domestic jurisdiction that make this individualization of the problem necessary. It is also and in fact more often necessary by reason of the almost infinite diversity of aspects in which the object of a dispute may be presented. There is hardly any matter which, looked at from a certain angle or at a certain level of generalization or specialization, may not raise now a question within the exclusive jurisdiction, now one subject to international regulation.[121]

There are, further, many rules of international law whose object is merely to contain within certain limits the exercise of powers belonging to the internal order, for example the delimitation by each State of its territorial waters. The rule of international law does not replace the internal norm and cover the matter governed by it; it relates only to the international behavior of the State in a particular aspect of the matter.[122]

All that can be said about the content of the reserved domain is that the problem of its demarcation arises most often in connection with matters which, owing to their projection into the international sphere or their repercussions there, are most likely to bring into play the interests of more than one State.

Finally, the formula in the Covenant, "matter which by international law is solely within the domestic jurisdiction," was accurate if it is taken to mean that the decision as to jurisdiction in each case belongs to international law and not to the unilateral discre-

119 Publications of the P.C.I.J., series B, no. 4, p. 24.

120 By adhering strictly to this distinction it is possible to avoid the controversy raised in France over the expression *compétence exclusive liée*, used to designate matters which, while remaining in the State's exclusive jurisdiction, have on certain points, by reason for example of a treaty obligation, ceased to belong to its discretionary jurisdiction.

121 See in this connection the judicious remarks of Maurice Bourquin, *Règles générales du Droit de la Paix*, *Rec. A.D.I.*, vol. 35 (1931), p. 154.

122 Cf. Gaetano Morelli, "La Competenza della Corte internazionale di Giustizia e la Giurisdizione Domestica," *Rivista Trimestrale di Diritto Pubblico*, 1952, p. 816.

tion of the interested State. It was misleading if it be interpreted as indicating that general international law contains a principle of demarcation enabling us to fix *in abstracto* and in general terms the configuration of the reserved domain. In the system of the Covenant, this configuration was to be worked out gradually under the control of the Council, enlightened, if need be, by the advisory opinions of the Permanent Court of International Justice.

The Court, having clearly found that a question governed by an international treaty was not solely in the domestic jurisdiction, took good care not to declare itself on a problem of which it was not seized and which is much broader and more complex. Can all the questions which international law leaves outside its regulation be regarded as lying solely in the domestic jurisdiction? Though all the dangers of an answer in the affirmative can be seen, it must be observed that the negative found no justification in the quasi-jurisdictional arrangement organized by Article 15 of the Covenant. But the Covenant, relying more on men's practical sense than on their theoretical speculations, enabled the League of Nations to meet the difficulty by the supple and quasi-diplomatic methods that Article 11 offered for the preservation of peace or good international relations. This movement from one plane to another was possible without too many shocks, for the Council usually tried even in performing this function of conciliation, where strictly speaking the reserved domain had no place, to treat with every consideration any argument based on the domestic character of the questions before it.[123] This explains why the notion of the reserved domain played far less part in the practice of the League of Nations than in doctrinal discussions.

The control of the plea of reserved domain, though essential to working out in practice so fluid a notion, was left totally unorganized in the United Nations Charter. We do not propose to dwell on the logical deductions that from other points of view might be drawn from a literal exegesis of Article 2, paragraph 7 (we are thinking here especially of those that have been drawn from the substitution of the words "are essentially within" for the words "by international law is solely within" which appeared in Article 15, paragraph 8, of the Covenant of the League of Nations), deductions that in any case are far from having been uniformly confirmed by experience. Suffice it to say that the demurrer of "domestic jurisdic-

[123] Cf. J. L. Brierly, "Matters of Domestic Jurisdiction," *B.Y.B.I.L.*, 1925, p. 15; C. B. H. Fincham, *Domestic Jurisdiction*, 1948, p. 70.

tion," pleaded by the interested State, is there conceived as a general and organic limitation on the activities of United Nations organs, though the authors of the Charter were unable to agree on designating an authority legally competent to pronounce upon the plea.

In practice, the organs of the United Nations, relying perhaps on the omission of the reference to international law in the Charter, have appeared to subordinate the legal to the political aspect of the problem. The frequent refusal to consult the International Court of Justice on the point, legally so delicate, is significant. In fact the principle—here most debatable—that every organ is judge of its own competence seems to have prevailed. This disposition of the United Nations to neglect the constitutional aspects of its own competence is the more deplorable in that there is, by unanimous admission, not a contradiction but latent opposition or tension between the very broad wording of Article 2, paragraph 7, and the obligations assumed by the States members in the precise provisions of the Charter (Article 13, paragraph 1; Articles 55 and 56).

This predominance of political preoccupations, and the absence of any control offering adequate legal safeguards, account for a confused legal situation which has more than once induced the international organs to take legally unjustified positions on the plea of reserved domain. As M. Charles Rousseau writes, "the retreat from the legal in this context is now an evident fact."[124]

In future perspective, as the Permanent Court of International Justice recognized, the delimitation of the two domains is a relative question closely linked with the development of international relations. A problem of change, this delimitation may have political aspects that do not always permit the use of legal criteria. In the context of Article 2, paragraph 7, of the Charter, it raises the question of the effects of exclusive domestic jurisdiction, more particularly the degree of acceptable intervention by international political organs in the development of those parts of international law which are on the border of municipal law. There is fairly general agreement that this development, which is political rather than legal, may take the line of recommendations by the General Assembly. But it would be a mistake to go no further here than the

[124] Report to the Institute of International Law (1952, Siena session), *op.cit.*, p. 156; G. Kaeckenbeeck, *La Charte de San Francisco dans ses rapports avec le Droit international, Rec. A.D.I.*, vol. 70 (1947), pp. 136 seq.

legal aspect of things, that is to say the absence of any compulsory force in recommendations. A General Assembly recommendation, when it relates to matters of exclusive domestic jurisdiction, may easily raise political passions and provide matter for propaganda. Though a general recommendation addressed to all States members seems reconcilable with the principle of nonintervention in the reserved domain, a particular recommendation relating to a litigious situation, though made only with a view to a procedure of settlement, is certainly acceptable only with the consent of the parties.[125] The contrary thesis might lead to discussion in the General Assembly of the United Nations, under the vague principle of national self-determination, of territories in which title has been established by one of the recognized modes of international law. This would rob international law of one of its fundamental guarantees of stability.

We can only observe with regret the effects of this state of affairs in the matter of jurisdiction. Certain States, as we know, have accepted the compulsory jurisdiction of the International Court of Justice subject to their own unilateral and final interpretation of "domestic jurisdiction." It is of course true that, being free to refuse any compulsory jurisdiction, States are also free to name the conditions under which they accept it; but this new restriction, which takes away from the international judicial authority the power to decide upon a reservation that naturally falls within its competence, can only be regarded as a retrogression. Such a reservation, becoming general, could not but accentuate the legal disintegration of international relations.

On one point, Article 2, paragraph 7, is happily precise. The plea of reserved domain is excluded in the situations contemplated in Chapter VII of the Charter where there is a "threat to the peace, breach of the peace, or act of aggression." Concern for the peace then takes unconditional priority over respect for national jurisdiction. Among responsibilities for the second world war, those of the authoritarian regimes were too recent to permit anyone at San Francisco to forget the clear danger to the peace involved in some forms of power concentration. When peace is threatened, there

125 Cf. the proceedings of the Institute of International Law, Aix-en-Provence session, *Annuaire*, 1954, vol. 2, pp. 169-173, 192-196, 292-293, together with the recent discussions in the U.N. on the competence of the General Assembly to pronounce upon information regarding the status of non-self-governing territories (Art. 73 of the Charter).

cannot be any closed frontier between the domestic organization of the State and the international order.[126]

§ 3. THE SO-CALLED "INTEGRATION AGREEMENTS." TREATY ESTABLISHING THE EUROPEAN COAL AND STEEL COMMUNITY (APRIL 18, 1951)

The legal problems raised by a treaty so new in type as that of the European Coal and Steel Community must be approached with caution.[127] Actual trial over a sufficient period of time will do more than the text to reveal the orientation and potentialities of this arrangement. But the text itself makes it clear that the surrender by the contracting States of certain sovereign rights in their mutual relations has withdrawn the interests regulated by the treaty from the class of "matters which are essentially within the domestic jurisdiction of any State." Much more than any ordinary treaty, the treaty of integration removes its subject matter from the reserved domain. Within a limited range of interests, the Community purports to superimpose upon the powers of States those of a new collectivity of the federal type.

On all counts this is a considerable innovation. In its supranational character the Community involves a true assignment of competences to the executive, regulatory, and judicial organs of an institutionalized entity. The notion of "competences" so often used in some doctrines to describe the subjective rights of States in the traditional relations of simple coordination was nothing more than an intellectual construction. Applied here to the powers of organs exclusively dedicated to purposes that are functional and consequently of general interest, the notion recovers its exact meaning and corresponds to a reality.

The Coal and Steel Community approaches federal organization again in the immediate or direct character of the High Authority's decisions in regard to enterprises belonging to the States members.[128] These decisions, as the application of a treaty itself regarded

[126] George F. Kennan, *American Diplomacy, 1900-1950*, p. 133: "In this way excess of internal authority leads inevitably to unsocial and aggressive conduct as a government among governments, and is a matter of concern to the international community."

[127] Cf. *La Communauté Européenne du Charbon et de l'Acier*, Institute of International Relations, Brussels, 1953.

[128] On "immediacy" as criterion of federal organization, see among others R. Pinto, *Eléments de droit constitutionnel*, 2d edn., 1952, p. 195. This "immediacy" makes the Coal and Steel Community a supranational community, whereas what results from certain provisions of the United Nations Charter is no more than a super-State community.

as the common law, are executory of themselves, each State member being under the obligation to assist in their execution as if they were taken by a national organ.[129]

In the internal order the surrenders of sovereignty upon which such a treaty depends could not fail to collide with constitutional rules of an old type to which they are manifestly foreign. On the other hand they were foreseen in the preamble to the French Constitution of October 27, 1946 and explicitly authorized by Article 24 of the Constitution of the German Federal Republic dated May 8, 1949.[130]

If it realizes its promoters' hopes, the Community may be called upon to play a unifying role in the economic order analogous to that played in the past by the Zollverein in Germany. More ambitious designs already assign it the mission of opening the way to a federal political organization of Europe.

129 "With immediacy every association of States is transformed." *ibid.*, p. 195.

130 See Paul De Visscher, *Les Tendances internationales des Constitutions modernes*, *Rec. A.D.I.*, 1952, pp. 515 seq.

CHAPTER III

INTER-STATE RELATIONS

Section I

International Recognition

§ 1. NATURE OF THE RECOGNITION OF STATES AND GOVERNMENTS

THE international recognition of States or new governments meets two primary social needs: the need not to exclude from international relations a human collectivity that combines the qualities required for admission to the advantages of independent political relations with foreign States; and the need to ensure the continuity of international relations by preventing a prolonged legal "vacuum" injurious to individual interests as to inter-State relations.

From a theoretical point of view, one might be inclined to believe that the recognition of a State is a strictly legal institution, governed by precise legal criteria, since it decides the participation of human collectivities in international relations. It would thus seem correct to speak not only of a right to recognition, but also of a duty of recognition binding on all States equally.

Observation shows that this is far from so and that the matter belongs, though in varying degrees, much more to politics than to law. In practice the recognition of a State has two aspects: objectively it takes note of the State's existence as a subject of international law; subjectively, it implies that the conditions under which the State established itself are not contrary to the rights or interests of the recognizing State. It is in this second aspect that recognition has political significance and is subject to the unfettered discretion of the government granting it.[1] This explains, on the one hand, why the existence of a new State, with all the associated legal effects, is not affected by the refusal of one or more States to recognize it, and, on the other hand, the special value for the new State of recognition granted by States that have been most interested in contesting its establishment.

[1] T. Perassi, *Lezioni di Diritto Internazionale*, pp. 42-43. Though well founded, the distinction does not spring from the practice of States. Recognition is in practice one act in which the two aspects merge.

In principle, effectivity is the criterion for recognition. Foreign States consider themselves justified in recognizing a new State when its independent organization appears to them solidly established; they habitually recognize a new government when the authorities that constitute it seem sufficiently consolidated to maintain themselves in power and show themselves disposed to observe international law. But practice offers examples of recognitions dictated by politics, some premature and designed to support a movement still engaged in the struggle for independence or for power,[2] others unduly delayed though the State is already firmly consolidated.

These precedents are hardly enough to justify speaking of an international duty of recognition as something based upon "a general practice accepted as law" (Art. 38 of the Statute of the Court of International Justice).[3] The most that can be said is that as a matter of principle political considerations are less admissible in the recognition of States than in the recognition of governments, because the facts that establish the organization of a human collectivity under a State regime are objective and notorious.

While the recognition of States, as an individual act, remains a matter of political judgment, the admission of a State into the United Nations, a collective act of the organs of that society, is a matter conventionally regulated by the Charter. The International Court of Justice drew the logical conclusion when it handed down the opinion that the conditions stated in Article 4 of the Charter must be regarded not only as necessary for admission but also as sufficient; that it is not lawful to superimpose political considerations independent of these conditions, since this would amount to recognizing an indeterminate and practically unlimited discretionary power in the States members; that the political character of the organs of the United Nations which must concur in admission

[2] A typically political act is the recognition *de facto* granted to a provisional government at a time when the new State whose existence is implied in recognition is not yet established. Cf. Charles De Visscher, "Les Gouvernements étrangers en Justice," *Revue de Droit international et de Législation comparée* (1922); and the observations of the Commission of Jurists in the Aaland Islands case, for which see above, Chap. II, Sec. I.

[3] Cf. the resolution of the Institute of International Law (*Annuaire*, 1936, vol. 2, p. 300): "The recognition of a new State is a voluntary act by which one or more States take note of the existence of a politically organized human society in a defined territory, independent of any other existing State, and capable of observing the rules of international law, thus manifesting their will to regard this society as a member of the international community."

does not release them from the obligation to observe the conventional rules governing them when these rules set limits to their powers or criteria for their judgment; and consequently that "a Member of the United Nations which is called upon, in virtue of Article 4 of the Charter, to pronounce itself by its vote, either in the Security Council or in the General Assembly, on the admission of a State to membership in the United Nations, is not juridically entitled to make its consent to the admission dependent on conditions not expressly provided by paragraph 1 of the said Article."[4]

The profound disagreement that persists in the United Nations on the admission of members in spite of the Court's opinion is a direct consequence of the political tension in international relations and not of any serious difference as to the legal character of the Charter's regulation of the matter. In fact the protagonists of the two opposing theses have been less concerned about conforming to the Charter than about fortifying their respective political positions in the Organization by recruiting new supporters.

Further, the admission of a State by the organs of the United Nations does not imply its recognition by the States members individually, any more than it entails any obligation on these members to recognize its government or to maintain diplomatic relations with it (see below). Neither Article 4 nor Article 78 of the Charter is any authority to the contrary. The scope of these provisions is limited to institutional relations regulated by the Charter; in the absence of any explicit provision they cannot be extended to cover the individual and strictly political relations of the States members. The contrary arguments drawn in the first sessions of the League of Nations from the obligations of the Covenant did not prevail.[5] In its fifth session the General Assembly of the United Nations adopted a resolution to the effect that the position taken by the Assembly on the representation of a State has, in itself, no bearing on the individual relations of the States members with the State whose representation has been the subject of a collective decision.[6]

The recognition of governments more frequently and in greater degree involves consideration of factors from which political aims

[4] Advisory Opinion of May 28, 1948, Reports, 1948, p. 65.

[5] Whether the admission of a State as a member of the United Nations can be accepted by courts and tribunals as evidence of general recognition by other States, is a different question. Cf. Quincy Wright, in *A.J.I.L.*, 1950, pp. 556-557.

[6] Cf. Yuen Li Liang, in *A.J.I.L.*, 1951, p. 689.

and ambitions are rarely absent. To recognize a government is to recognize in those who make it up an authority at once effective and stable as well as the will to maintain normal external relations. These criteria, well founded as they are, when applied to a regime or to the personnel of a government, lend themselves easily to the taking of political or ideological positions. Without so much interfering in the domestic affairs of a country, foreign States may be inclined to regard as unstable a government whose continuance in power is linked with a regime with which they are not in sympathy, or as unmindful of international law one that professes an ideology or employs methods that they disapprove.

The largely discretionary character of these evaluations explains the traditional nuances by which diplomacy tries to combine its acceptance of the fact with political reservations designed to leave the future uncommitted. Among these are semiofficial relations and the distinction between *de facto* and *de jure* recognition. These are expedients to cope with the diversity of factual situations, and against them the abstract dialectic of some doctrines keeps up a vain struggle.[7]

The discretionary and hence political character of recognition also explains the persistence of the controversy concerning its declaratory or constitutive effect. Legally, recognition is simply a declaratory act. Politically, it is not so. Recognition puts an end, for the recognized State, to an uncertain situation, and the positive advantages that it secures not only for the recognized but also for the recognizing State create a new situation.[8]

In periods of high tension in international relations, recognition is at times a mere instrument of power politics. States grant or refuse it as suits their rival policies in the regions for which they compete. The antagonism of the Western Powers and Soviet Russia in Asia offers contemporary examples. The United Kingdom's recognition of the Communist government at Peking, in itself completely in keeping with the traditional criterion of effectivity, was largely due to general British policy in the Far East, which was against open rupture with regimes of a communist tendency, and more

[7] On the political significance of these distinctions and the importance of their effects, see Ti Chiang Chen, *The International Law of Recognition*, London, 1951, pp. 288 seq.

[8] Quincy Wright, *op.cit.*, pp. 556-557. "Recognition is in principle declaratory but in practice it is constitutive." Cf. on the various politico-legal aspects of recognition, P. E. Corbett, *Law and Society in the Relations of States*, pp. 60-67.

particularly to the hope, which this policy still cherished at the time, of winning the Peking government's support in bringing about an end of hostilities in Korea. On the other hand, the United States' refusal to recognize Peking was part of a more intransigent policy in relation to governments sympathetic to communism. The difficulties regarding the representation of China in the United Nations that sprang from these opposed positions are well known. They were overcome only by a modus vivendi following Communist China's participation in the Korean war, and immediately reappeared with the armistice.

A refusal of recognition due to the unconstitutional or even violent origin of a government is generally considered unjustified, unless the government's position appears unstable precisely by reason of its origin or its behavior is such as to prevent any belief in its readiness to respect international law. Moreover, there is no doubt, especially since the second world war, that the required proof of stability is being reduced to the mere condition of exclusive possession of power and absence of internal resistance to its exercise. In our day we have got very far from what used to be a common enough condition, namely that recognition of a new government should depend upon the approval of the governed, expressed by popular vote. Today the balance indisputably swings toward confirmation of effective power. This can be regarded only as an expression of the need for stability in a period characterized by political upheavals.

At the opposite pole stand the doctrines, or more exactly the American policies, of nonrecognition, all more or less based on democratic constitutional legitimacy—the Tobar doctrine, incorporated in the Treaty of Washington, 1907, between the Republics of Central America; the still more radical doctrine embodied in the Treaty of 1923 between the same States; and the constitutional thesis propounded in 1913 by President Wilson. These express a political ideology bound up with a regional conception of order and security. They often invoked high principles, but they have lost their influence because their application involves a degree of intervention in internal affairs that is hardly compatible with the independence and legal equality of States.[9]

The claim of a political authority to represent a State in the

[9] On these various aspects of recognition, see the arbitral award rendered on October 18, 1923 (the Tinoco Arbitration) by Chief Justice Taft, between Great Britain and Costa Rica, *A.J.I.L.*, 1924, pp. 147 seq.

United Nations could certainly, when contested by another State, be judged in accordance with different criteria, which would include the tests proposed by the international Organization, especially the disposition to accept the obligations contained in the Charter and the fact that the authority soliciting its recognition had its origin in an internal change and not in an external aggression. These criteria, which tend in some measure to depoliticize the General Assembly's decision, were examined but not in the end adopted. The text actually accepted by the General Assembly of the United Nations merely declared in the most general terms that each case must be examined in the light of the aims and principles of the Charter and of its particular circumstances.

§ 2. POSITION TAKEN BY NATIONAL TRIBUNALS IN REGARD TO RECOGNITION

Despite established effectiveness, a government may be refused recognition or be recognized only *de facto* for reasons based on law.[10] This would be so in the case of a government established by a violation of international law, as after the Italian conquest of Ethiopia, when the Italian Government was recognized only *de facto* by some States members of the League of Nations.[11]

The Stimson Declaration of January 7, 1932, addressed to China and Japan, and the resolution by the League of Nations Assembly on March 11 of the same year to the effect that the members of the League should not recognize any situation, treaty, or agreement brought about by means contrary to the Covenant of the League or the Pact of Paris, belonged to the same order of ideas. The solidary responsibilities of the members of the international Organization may justify such a position as a matter of principle. It must be observed, however, that as a sanction for law breaking, nonrecognition is not effective even in law except insofar as it is the starting point for other sanctions sustained by collective action employing means adequate to prevent or reverse a situation of fact that is contrary to law.[12]

10 Defective terminology makes for confusion in this subject. In international relations one should speak of recognition *de facto*, not of government *de facto*. Cf. Herbert W. Briggs, "*De Facto* and *De Jure* Recognition: The Arantzatzu Mendi," *A.J.I.L.*, 1939, p. 689.

11 H. Lauterpacht, "De Facto Recognition, Withdrawal of Recognition and Conditional Recognition," *B.Y.B.I.L.*, 1945, p. 178.

12 On the tendency to use nonrecognition to imprint an objective or universal character upon the "illegality" of certain acts held contrary to a system of

The predominance of political factors nevertheless remains the characteristic of the present practice of recognition. It explains the development that has taken place in this matter in the relations between the executive power and the courts. Formerly the almost invariable position of the courts could be summed up in the two following propositions: it is for the political authorities charged with the conduct of foreign relations to decide, by recognition, whether a government is to be regarded as sovereign; the courts determine, according to the information received from those authorities, whether a foreign government may sue or be sued, and how disputes about the extraterritorial effects of the acts and decrees of a foreign government whose status is under discussion shall be resolved.

This theory could no longer be maintained in its entirety when international recognition became so dominated by political factors that the most respectable private interests were sacrificed, intolerable situations were created, and justice was actually denied. The prolonged refusal to recognize the Soviet government *de jure*, in spite of its obviously effective power, contributed much to the abandonment of the theory. Thus a number of judicial decisions, especially in the United States, tend to limit the effects of non-recognition to the sovereign relations between State and State, and in some degree to liberate courts deciding on private interests from the political considerations that determine the attitudes of governments. These decisions appear to be justified in cases where the effectivity and stability of the government concerned cannot reasonably be disputed. The Institute of International Law accepted this opinion when it adopted the following resolution at its Brussels session in 1936: "Even failing recognition, the extra-territorial effects [of the acts of a foreign government] must be admitted by the competent judicial and administrative authorities when, in view especially of the real power exercised by the new government, these effects are conducive to a good administration of justice and the protection of individual interests."[13]

---

law created by collective agreements, see J. Fischer Williams, *Rec. A.D.I.*, vol. 44 (1933), pp. 277 seq.; Arnold McNair, "The Stimson Doctrine of Non-Recognition," *B.Y.B.I.L.*, 1933, p. 65.

[13] *Annuaire*, no. 39 (Brussels session), vol. II, p. 305. See to the same effect the statement made in the Belgian Senate on April 6, 1933 by the Minister of Foreign Affairs: "If the Belgian courts, deciding in the plenitude of their independence, found that contemporary Russian legislation could have certain effects in Belgium, the Government would not regard this as opposition to its

It is again the influence, this time indirect, of political factors that accounts for the broad retroactive effect that the courts have generally attributed to the acts of a foreign government when it has been recognized by the authorities of their country, even to the point of holding that the acts (statutes, decrees, etc.) of such a government must be considered valid "as from the date of its first existence." Whatever may be said of it, this retroactivity does not follow either from the legal nature of the act of recognition or from any principle of international law; but the judicial authorities have found in this fiction the means of giving effect to legal relations which in their traditional dependence on the executive in this context they were obliged to ignore so long as recognition had not been granted by the government. It has been justly observed that retroactivity is a fiction devised to mitigate the defects of another fiction, the latter consisting in holding nonexistent a power which in fact exists.[14] In so acting, the judicial authorities are attempting to preserve the continuity and security of law, social values constantly threatened by the spread of revolutionary upheavals and by virulent ideological campaigns that fanatically deny all legal effect to the legislation of an enemy regime. They perform a stabilizing function.

In countries where the courts are accustomed to refer to the executive for information in doubtful cases on the international status of a foreign government, the fiction of retroactivity is quite generally reinforced by considerations of courtesy and of political expediency. It would diminish the value of recognition to call in question, for any but the most serious reasons connected with public order, the validity of the recognized government's acts since its establishment.[15]

---

policy of not recognizing the Government of the U.S.S.R." Cf. Philip Marshall Brown, "The Recognition of New States and New Governments," *A.J.I.L.*, 1936, p. 689, and, by the same author, "The Legal Effects of Recognition," *A.J.I.L.*, 1950, p. 617; Edwin M. Borchard, "The Unrecognized Governments in American Courts," *A.J.I.L.*, 1932, p. 261; John Bassett Moore, "The New Isolation," *A.J.I.L.*, 1933, p. 612; John Fischer Williams, *Rec. A.D.I.*, vol. 44 (1933), pp. 254 seq.; H. Lauterpacht, *Recognition in International Law*, pp. 145 seq.

[14] Ti Chiang Chen, *op.cit.*, p. 186. Recognition of a new government generally has effects retroactive to the time when its authority became effective in the whole country.

[15] A. M. Luther v. Sagor (1921), 3 K.B. 532. Cf. J. Nisot, "Is the Recognition of a Government Retroactive?" *The Canadian Bar Review*, 1943, pp. 627 seq.; J. H. van Roijen, *De Rechtspositie en de Volkenrechtelijke Erkenning van*

§ 3. RECOGNITION AND CIVIL WAR

A revolutionary movement may give occasion for a recognition of local government, of belligerency, or of mere insurgency. Neither insurrection nor revolution is condemned by international law. But this law does regard as irregular every form of foreign interference in the domestic affairs of a State and therefore condemns recognition that is premature, that is to say not justified by the course of events.[16] On the other hand, recognition of belligerency has a precise negative effect. The recognizing State may no longer dispute the existence of a state of war or, consequently, escape the duties of neutrality.

It is impossible to expound the practice of recognition in this context without at every step displaying the political character of the interests and the motives behind the positions taken by governments. These positions have been dictated by the very fluidity of events, by the interests of the governments concerned, especially by the demands of their maritime trade, and sometimes also by concern to limit the conflict and preserve the general peace.

The generally recognized absence of any right to this kind of recognition finds its explanation in the diversity and mobility of these extralegal factors. In the practice of States those factors have often outweighed what at times have been powerful considerations favoring a contrary decision, such as the reality of civil as well as military power over a portion of the national territory, or humanitarian reasons that make it difficult to treat regularly organized forces as rebels.

The Spanish civil war was a case where the internecine struggle, become part of a general political tension, threatened to start a world-wide conflict. From beginning to end, under the cover of the nonintervention agreement, the situation was dominated by the political and ideological antagonism that held the great European Powers at grips. Though the conditions that have traditionally justified recognition of belligerency were undoubtedly very early

Nieuwe Staten en De Facto *Regeeringen*, pp. 197 seq.; J. Mervyn-Jones, "The Retroactive Effect of the Recognition of States and Governments," *B.Y.B.I.L.*, 1935, p. 42; Charles De Visscher, "Les Gouvernements étrangers en Justice," *op.cit.*, pp. 162 seq.

[16] Recognition, especially *de jure*, granted to an insurgent government in order to facilitate supplying it with arms and munitions is a particularly dangerous form of interventionism. Granted by a great Power, it readily serves to sustain under cover of internecine conflict the wars "by proxy" that are characteristic of our time.

realized by the insurgents,[17] it is equally clear that these traditional criteria were perverted and rendered almost impossible of application by "a foreign intervention that threw the legal and political situation into utter confusion."[18]

The rights of belligerency were in principle denied to both sides in the Spanish civil war by the great Powers, who were concerned at once to prevent either from exercising rights on the high seas to their prejudice and to avoid finally destroying, to the sole profit of the navally much stronger insurgents, the delicate balance of their nonintervention policy. The recognition of partial belligerent rights conceded in the end by the Committee on Non-Intervention as *quid pro quo* for the withdrawal of foreign volunteers demonstrated the hybrid and highly political character of the arrangements adopted. It could not have been otherwise at the time, and it may be foreseen that much the same course would be taken in the future.[19] The practice of collective recognition, replacing for this occasion that of individual decision, altered the data of the problem; but the experience showed that this does not necessarily facilitate solution.

Notwithstanding some doctrinal reservations, recognition of insurgency must be regarded as approved by international practice. More limited in its effects, and still more elusive in its criteria, than recognition of belligerency, it is adjusted to a situation of fact and modelled on the course of events. It has been accorded by foreign States when, though admitting the existence of hostilities, they have not clearly conceded to the parties the status of belligerents with the relevant rights and duties, especially when the insurgents have been in effective control of what is still too small a part of the

17 In a statement in the House of Commons on November 8, 1937, Mr. Anthony Eden admitted that "it would be difficult to find a case in which the rights of belligerency had so long been denied."

18 Statement in the Belgian Chambre des Représentants by M. Spaak, minister of foreign affairs, on March 22, 1938.

19 Cf. Charles Rousseau, "La non-intervention en Espagne," *Revue de droit international et de législation comparée*, 1938, pp. 217, 473, 700; Arnold Raestad, "Guerre civile et droit international," same *Revue*, 1938, p. 809; Philip C. Jessup, "The Spanish Revolution and International Law," *Foreign Affairs*, 1937, p. 270; Norman J. Padelford, "International Law and the Spanish Civil War," *A.J.I.L.*, 1937, p. 226, and, by the same author, "The Non-Intervention Agreement and the Spanish Civil War," *A.J.I.L.*, 1937, p. 578; H. A. Smith, "Some Problems of the Spanish Civil War," *B.Y.B.I.L.*, 1937, p. 17; Hans Wehberg, *La Guerre civile et le droit international*, *Rec. A.D.I.*, vol. 63 (1938), pp. 101-102.

national territory.[20] Without the benefit of a definite legal status, the insurgents obtain, in addition to certain specified rights that vary from one case to another, a treatment in conformity with the demands of humanity. The political interest of foreign States generally has its part in the proceedings; for, unlike the recognition of belligerency, recognition of insurgency does not permit the insurgents to exercise the rights of visit and seizure on the high seas.[21]

There is finally a category of nonrecognition which has the specific object of protest against a violation of law or refusal to acquiesce in it. This nonrecognition may take the form of notification by a government that it will not recognize certain situations of fact or certain agreements that infringe or may infringe its own rights. Such a step is at the discretion of every State. Its political purpose is preventive; legally it is a mere reservation of existing subjective rights.

Different again is the declaration that takes the form of an undertaking by a government not to recognize certain situations, such as an annexation of territory, or certain treaties, because they are contrary to law or to some rules of conduct which this government considers itself bound to observe and in some measure to guarantee. Declarations of this sort are merely the fulfillment of pre-existing obligations.[22]

Section II

The Respect Due to Foreign Sovereignty

The extension of the powers of the State, and the political character that this imprints upon international relations, have more and more influence every day upon the attitude of governments and

[20] Hackworth, *Digest*, vol. I, p. 356; Arnold Raestad, *op.cit.*, p. 812: "In recognizing in one party to an internecine struggle the quality of insurgents, the foreign State merely takes note that according to international law civil war is in progress without further specifying the status of the parties." The nonintervention system in the Spanish civil war implied recognition of a state of insurrection; Norman J. Padelford, *International Law and Diplomacy in the Spanish Civil Strife*, 1939, pp. 3, 14.

[21] L. Oppenheim, *International Law*, ed. H. Lauterpacht, vol. I, p. 135; Pitt Cobbett, *Leading Cases*, vol. I, pp. 300-302; Charles Cheney Hyde, *International Law*, vol. I, § 50; G. Schwarzenberger, *Manual of International Law*, 1947, p. 105.

[22] See the resolution of the Assembly of the League of Nations, dated March 11, 1932, previously cited, and the Stimson declaration of January 7, 1932, notified to China and Japan.

national tribunals in questions touching the respect due to the person and the acts of the foreign State.

§ 1. IMMUNITIES OF THE FOREIGN STATE

There are few questions upon which national tribunals differ so widely and so persistently as upon the double immunity of foreign States from suit and from execution. To the traditional difference between the thesis of absolute immunity, very strictly sustained by the British and American courts, and that of limited immunity adopted by the courts of some continental European countries, there are added today new objectives and distinctions which on both sides have shaken convictions and called for reconsideration of the whole problem. There is no hope of reaching agreement upon it unless we start from an objective examination of some political, economic, and ideological realities upon which the solution must depend.

The concern to spare foreign sovereignty (*par in parem non habet jurisdictionem*), but without too completely sacrificing respectable private interests, is at the bottom of the problem of immunities. It is the weight to be assigned to these conflicting considerations that explains the fluctuations in judicial decisions, the imprecision and diversity of the criteria employed, and the obvious illogicality of some judgments. The practical interest of the problem stimulated some governmental action. Conventions were concluded before the second world war fixing the status of Soviet commercial missions, and recently the British Government set up a commission to examine the whole question of the jurisdictional immunities of foreign States and in particular to ascertain how far those recognized in England exceed those prescribed by international law and supported by the practice of other States.

The common concern of the courts in all countries to spare the susceptibilities of the foreign State, and thus to avoid embarrassing their own government, accounts for the immunities that they recognize in legal relations over which they normally have jurisdiction.[28] This concern emerges very clearly in the uniformity of decisions on claims to seize or levy execution on property belonging to the foreign State. Divided as they are on the justification, limits, or criteria of immunity from jurisdiction properly so called, the

[28] Thus immunity is conceded even to a State or a government recognized only *de facto*: *The Gagara* (1919), P. 95, and even in a suit brought by a government recognized *de jure*: *The Arantzatzu Mendi* (1938), P. 233.

courts are nearly everywhere agreed in dismissing such claims not only when they have forced execution as their direct object, but also when they cannot be passed upon without raising the question of execution, if only in the form of damages.[24] This observation is confirmed by the fact that the decision as to immunity finally rests with the foreign State: it is not granted if proof is brought that the State has renounced the privilege. In some countries the courts push prudence to the point of refusing to deduce from acceptance of jurisdiction a renunciation of immunity from execution.[25] These decisions can be explained only by the fear of obstructing the public services of the foreign State and causing diplomatic complications.

As for immunity from jurisdiction properly so called, grave doubts are now beginning to appear. In most countries the traditional solutions are being called in question. The concern to spare foreign sovereignty is visibly qualified here by apprehensions touching the invading propensities of some of the foreign State's activities.

Though the higher courts of the United States remain faithful to the doctrine laid down in the classic case, Schooner Exchange v. MacFaddon, which attached the immunity to the person of the foreign State and thus made it absolute,[26] there have been some quite recent dicta of the British high courts which discreetly but significantly[27] reflect new thoughts on the subject and which undoubtedly contributed to the British Government's decision to institute a fresh examination of the problem.[28]

No less interesting are the uncertainties about the criterion for immunity appearing now in those countries whose courts have long adhered to the thesis of limited immunity. It is certainly no longer

[24] Cf. in Dollfuss-Mieg et Cie. v. Bank of England, the decision of the English High Court of Justice (1950, Ch. 369). The French Court of Cassation's decision, February 5, 1946 (Sirey, 1947, 1.37), confirms rather than rejects the distinction.

[25] Cf. H. Batiffol, *Traité élémentaire de Droit international privé*, no. 706; and for American case-law the decision in Dexter and Carpenter, Inc. v. Kunglig Jarnvagsstyrelsen, *A.J.I.L.*, 1931, p. 360, and the note by Jessup and Deak, *ibid.*, 1931, p. 335.

[26] A recent step taken by the Department of State may cause a shift in the decisions. Cf. William W. Bishop, in *A.J.I.L.*, 1953, p. 93.

[27] House of Lords, *The Cristina* (1938), A.C., 485.

[28] H. Lauterpacht, *Observations on the Report of the Commission of the Institute of International Law Regarding the Immunity of Foreign States from Jurisdiction and from Forced Execution, Annuaire*, 1952, vol. I, p. 111, and, by the same author, "The Problem of Jurisdictional Immunities of Foreign States," *B.Y.B.I.L.*, 1951, p. 220; Carabiber, "Le Concept des Immunités de juridiction doit-il être révisé et dans quel sens?" *Journal du Droit international*, 1952, pp. 440 seq.

possible to cling to the idea that the State performs its proper function and acts in the public or national interest only so long as it does not engage in certain economic activities. The distinction that has been traditional in the jurisprudence of some countries between acts done by the foreign State *jure imperii* and those done *jure gestionis* in accordance with private law procedures is therefore no longer above criticism, though the new criteria to replace it are neither more precise nor more calculated to reconcile opposing views and interests. For the moment the only point clearly established—doubtless in virtue of the decisions about the Soviet trade missions—is the refusal of immunity in litigation arising out of commercial activities. But the considerations invoked to support this practice, as has been observed,[29] call for a fresh formulation of the distinction between the act of public power and the act of patrimonial administration.

Underneath these shifts and hesitations may be seen the fundamental and largely ideological antagonism between opposite conceptions of the role and functions of the modern State. The demarcation between State and private activity, which was easy to observe in the age of liberalism, has become more and more obscure as the public services have multiplied under the impact of directed economy. With the constant expansion of the activities of the foreign State, the tendency to attach conditions to immunity from jurisdiction has become more marked. The trend, which is already an old one on the European continent, is now appearing in England among the most qualified legal authorities.[30] If it is not more clearly apparent everywhere, the reason is to be found in the complex and fluid nature of the problem, and in the inclination of some great States to retain the benefit of very broad immunities while at the same time demanding a measure of reciprocity.

The history of the status of the Soviet trade missions in foreign countries seems to prove that as the foreign State's field of economic action expands certain ideological conflicts recede into the background to make way for practical regulation. Thus the U.S.S.R., while stoutly reasserting its own view that the monopoly of foreign trade belongs to the State and constitutes an attribute of its

29 H. Batiffol, *op.cit.*, no. 705.

30 See particularly the Observations of Sir Eric Beckett and H. Lauterpacht on the Report of the Commission of the Institute of International Law, *Annuaire*, 1952 (Siena session), vol. I, pp. 53, 111. For the trend in French doctrine, see, in addition to the authors already cited, M. Sibert, *Traité de droit international public*, vol. I, p. 268.

sovereignty, has in a series of commercial agreements recognized its responsibility for the transactions entered into by its representatives and accepted within these limits the jurisdiction of the local courts.[31]

§ 2. EXTRATERRITORIAL EFFECT OF THE PUBLIC ACTS OF A FOREIGN STATE

It is very generally admitted that legal relations established under legislation regarded at the moment as normally competent must in principle be recognized by foreign courts, since these have a duty to respect such legislation as the expression of a foreign sovereignty within the internationally recognized limits of its competence.[32] An exception to the principle is made where the absence of legal community prevents the judge of the forum from upholding rights flowing from the foreign law without offending his country's moral or political order. In this defensive function the exception, under different names (public order, public policy), is admitted everywhere, though the courts of some countries, France for example, make broader use of it than do those of the Anglo-Saxon countries. The frequency of its application in our day is explained by the coexistence of political regimes based upon different moral and social ideas, and by the often extreme legislative measures, as in some forms of nationalization, that mark the emancipation of certain peoples or their aspiration to found a new social order.

Such a state of affairs prevents unrestricted or unconditional international cooperation on the judicial plane. Thus, without arrogating the power to discuss the laws of nationalization or of expropriation without compensation enacted abroad, the judge of the forum has been able, either by invoking public order or by insisting on the strictly territorial character of such laws, to deny their international efficacy when their application would have seemed to him to conflict with the fundamental legal conceptions of his country in the matter of property.

Reciprocity in respect for law, which is the essential foundation

[31] A. Stoupnitzky, *Le Statut international de l'U.R.S.S., Etat commerçant* (1936), and by the same author, "Le Statut de l'U.R.S.S.—commerçant dans le droit conventionel soviétique," *Revue de Droit international et de Législation comparée*, 1936, p. 801.

[32] On the complication arising from the link between the recognition of a government and the application of foreign laws, see K. Lipstein, "Recognition of Governments and the Application of Foreign Law," *Transactions of the Grotius Society*, vol. 35 (1949), pp. 157 seq.

for all cooperation between States, might in some cases raise a still more serious problem, namely as to the international validity of the nationalizing State's title even to property which is normally subject to its law by reason of its situation. This could be the case when the refusal of compensation, the clearly discriminatory character of the nationalization, or the absence of jurisdictional safeguards justifies regarding the position taken by the State as a violation of international law. It would seem to be too much to ask the judge of the forum in such a case to apply unconditionally the principle of the international efficacy of the normally competent law.[33]

§ 3. ATTEMPTS ON THE SAFETY OF THE FOREIGN STATE

In few matters has there been such a rapid succession of different regulations as in this; and few have been so profoundly affected by the vicissitudes of politics and the shifts in public opinion.

The relations of simple coordination among independent States involve no mutual guarantee of their integrity or of the stability of their governments. The international duty of each of them, in terms of the common law, is merely to repress those subversive activities of private persons which by their collective character constitute a particularly serious threat to the external or internal safety of foreign States (organization of hostile expeditions, etc.).[34]

In the field of treaty relations, the organization of extradition attests the alternation of sometimes diametrically opposite political and legal conceptions. Under the old regime, extradition reached only political criminals; from 1830 on, most countries allowed it only for ordinary crimes. Revolutionary ideas separated power from its religious foundations. Liberal ideas, by emphasizing the contingent character of institutions and their merely relative value, destroyed the traditional solidarity of sovereigns. By the same blow they relieved the attempt against the State of its absolute criminality and excluded international cooperation in a domain where the moral law counts for less than the law of success.[35] With this change in

[33] For such reasons the Supreme Court of Aden, in its judgment of January 9, 1953 in the case of the Anglo-Iranian Oil Co. Ltd. v. Jaffrate and others, refused to hold valid the seizure of a cargo of petroleum under the Iranian nationalization law of May 1, 1951, and ordered its restitution to the owners.

[34] The Pan-American Convention of 1928 on the Rights and Duties of States in case of civil war makes it a duty for the contracting parties to use all the means at their disposal to prevent persons resident in their territory from taking part in the struggle. Cf. Hackworth, *Digest*, vol. II, § 156.

[35] On this development, see Maurice Bourquin, *Crimes et Délits contre la sureté des Etats étrangers*, *Rec. A.D.I.*, vol. 16 (1927), pp. 121 seq.; H. Donne-

political thought was joined the concern of governments not to lend aid to a regime whose fall would expose them to international complications.

Soon, however, a reaction set in, beginning with the generalization of the "*attentat* clause" in extradition treaties. Liberalism in decline was succeeded by nationalism imbued with a new *mystique* of power. The authoritarian regimes have no mercy for political criminals, whom they regard as dangerous malefactors. Their disappearance will be marked by a return to the liberal practice. The Italian legislation of 1930, of fascist inspiration, authorized the extradition of political offenders on condition of reciprocity. The present Italian Constitution (Art. 10) re-establishes the principle of nonextradition for "political acts."

But it was especially by way of qualification of the offense that limitations, often quite justified, were imposed upon political asylum. Though most treaties classify as unreservedly political for the purposes of extradition not only purely political offenses but also what are known as connected or complex delicts, there are some that reject this classification for crimes of a particularly odious nature (attempts upon life, for example) or that accept it only for those perpetrated in the course of civil troubles and closely connected with collective revolutionary action. The diversity of these criteria opens the way to regulation that differs widely in political motives. It seems impossible, in a time such as ours, when ideological conflicts are so sharp that they impress a political character on the very notion of asylum,[86] that general agreement could be reached on the limits of nonextradition for political crimes.

The same state of affairs reduces the practical interest of the clauses in the Geneva Convention for the prevention and international punishment of terrorism (November 16, 1937) that provided for extradition in some cases. International cooperation on a world scale in this domain is inconceivable at a time when fundamental human rights are brutally violated.[87] The legitimate attempt to exclude so-called "social criminals" from the privileged treatment

dieu de Vabres, *Traité de Droit criminel et de législation comparée*, 1947, no. 196 seq.

86 The constitutions of the U.S.S.R., Yugoslavia, and most of the people's democracies grant the right of asylum to foreign nationals wanted for their activities in the interest of the working class or of national liberation.

87 Cf. H. Donnedieu de Vabres, "La Répression internationale du Terrorisme: les Conventions de Genève (16 novembre 1937)," *Revue de Droit international et de Législation comparée*, 1938, p. 37.

of political offenders implies a minimum of moral and legal community.

Obstacles of the same nature now stand in the way of any agreement upon penal legislative competence in regard to crimes against the safety of the State committed by foreigners outside its territory. Such competence, disputed especially in England and the United States, is claimed in different degrees by most other States under the so-called protective principle. For thirty years this difference has been accentuated by political factors that became active in the period of ferment between the two world wars. Among these are the retreat of liberal traditions before a sensitive nationalism, the existence of States exposed to irredentist intrigue, and the establishment in some countries of authoritarian regimes which were incited by the sense of their own weakness to incriminate extraterritorial activities with a rigor which seems less necessary to States under normal regimes.[38]

The inadequacy of international cooperation in the repression of crimes against the safety of the State, and especially of terrorist attacks, was very generally admitted at the time. The Council of the League of Nations recognized it, following the assassination at Marseilles, by a resolution of December 10, 1934. But the fact remains that the laws of some totalitarian countries exceeded the reasonable limits acceptable to other States when they permitted the prosecution of aliens who in a foreign country engaged in attacks in the press declared dangerous or dishonoring to a people or its political regime. Such excessive claims cannot but engender ineluctable conflicts with countries where freedom of the press is guaranteed by law. From these claims to the famous demand for "neutrality of thought" is only a step.[39]

38 Cf. H. Lauterpacht, "Revolutionary Activities by Private Persons against Foreign States," *A.J.I.L.*, 1928, p. 105; Lawrence Preuss, "La Répression des crimes et délits contre la sûreté des Etats étrangers," *Revue générale de Droit international public*, 1933, p. 606.

39 See on this point a suggestion of the Harvard Committee: Draft Convention on Jurisdiction with Respect to Crime, 1935, p. 543. The comment indicates (p. 557) that the suggestion aims to reconcile the views of States "which have perhaps been oversensitive about their prestige or security, on the one hand, and other States which have probably been lax in providing the necessary minimum of protection for the interests of foreign States, on the other hand." Cf. L. Oppenheim, *International Law*, ed. H. Lauterpacht, vol. I, p. 300, note 1.

Section III

The International Treaty

The treaty is the essential regulator of international life, the principal instrument of the stability and adaptation of law. It owes this eminent role to the unique moral authority of the principle *pacta sunt servanda* and to its congruence with the present individualist structure of international relations. It is indeed the appropriate instrument of legal interchange between political entities which are naturally led by their passion for sovereignty to consider themselves bound only by undeniable manifestations of their own will. Usually directed to meeting concrete needs, the treaty adapts itself as precisely as possible to the diversity of particular situations which, as we have seen, is a predominant characteristic of the international sphere. Law for the parties, it normalizes their mutual relations. It tempers the play of political forces without stopping it, makes it indeed a factor of progress, since change is fruitful only when it is interrupted by stabilizations.[40]

But treaties do not escape the grip of the political. In varying degrees this may be seen in their conclusion, interpretation, and execution.[41]

§ 1. CONSTRAINT IN THE CONCLUSION OF TREATIES

Some treaties, particularly peace treaties, are concluded under pressure. Positive international law nevertheless holds them valid. This validity, which cannot be explained by the moral principle underlying agreements freely arrived at, is one of the most striking features of the international order, one of those that most emphasize its still primitive character.[42] It is explained by the place still occupied by force in the relations between States; it is justified up to a certain point by the needs of order.

[40] Fr. Russo, *Réalité Juridique et Réalité Sociale*, pp. 138-140.

[41] The stabilizing action of the treaty is limited by imbalances that no contractual foresight can quite eliminate. This aspect of the subject, being part of the general problem of peaceful change in international relations, will be discussed later (Chap. IV).

[42] Nowhere else is Hall's observation more justified: "There is no place for the refinements of the courts in the rough jurisprudence of nations." *International Law*, 7th edn., p. 395, note 2. For Montesquieu, princes are not free; they are governed by force and that is why treaties ratified under constraint bind them. *De l'Esprit des Lois*, xxvi, chap. xx.

The constraint suffered by a State—which is quite distinct from the defect of will due to the moral violence brought to bear upon the physical persons who represent it—could not constitute a cause of nullity in a law which, in spite of recent efforts, cannot yet claim either to distinguish clearly between licit and illicit resort to arms, or effectively to proscribe certain abuses of force. At the very most, all that can be said is that an international control which is still problematic would not permit the author of an aggression recognized as unjust to enforce by legal procedures the provisions of a treaty which he imposed by force on his victim.

Since there is still so much room for force in international relations, law cannot refuse to hold valid the so-called treaties of peace that are imposed by constraint. Their justification lies in considerations that take priority even over the legitimate interests of the parties. With all due reservations touching its necessary conformity, even for the sake of its own effectiveness, with justice, the victor's power is "potential order."[43] Because law, which has to reckon with force, sees in the person possessing it for the time being a power capable of establishing order, it sanctions a treaty that lacks the moral foundation of agreements freely entered into. The law anticipates the advent of a new order as the fruit of some moderation in the use of force and of the consolidation that comes with the passage of time. Here as elsewhere the notion of order forms the link between power *de facto* and power *de jure*.[44] But such treaties, being born of success, are more than any others subject to the law of success. The victor who is unable to establish a stable order remains exposed to the consequences of an inversion in the ratio of strengths. This is one of many cases where the legal institution tries, not always with success, to canalize the dynamism of political forces.[45]

[43] Maurice Hauriou, *Précis de Droit Constitutionnel*, 1929, p. 16.

[44] There must, it seems, be one exception to the rule that treaties concluded under constraint are valid. The treaty assumes two distinct wills, otherwise it loses even the external appearance of an agreement. If constraint takes the form of an armed intervention that so subjugates the internal institutions of a State that refusal becomes entirely impossible, acceptance, even in the established constitutional form, may lose all legal significance. The will that it is supposed to express is then a mere fiction disguising an enterprise of violence.

[45] Cf. Hold-Ferneck, *Lehrbuch des Völkerrechts*, vol. II, p. 151; Arnold McNair, *The Law of Treaties*, p. 129; L. Oppenheim, *International Law*, ed. H. Lauterpacht, vol. I, pp. 802-803; Fernand De Visscher, in *Revue de Droit international et de Législation comparée*, 1931, p. 513; Verzijl, in *Revue de Droit international* (Paris), 1935, vol. XV, pp. 324-327; J. L. Brierly, *Règles du droit de la paix*, *Rec. A.D.I.*, vol. 58 (1936), pp. 203-210.

§ 2. CONSTITUTIONAL LIMITATIONS ON THE TREATY-MAKING POWER

The problem of the international effect of constitutional limitations on the treaty-making power has for us a two-fold interest: it shows the decisive influence of the internal political structure of States on international practice, and it makes evident the weaknesses and the artificiality of a systematization based upon abstract ideas rather than observed realities.

The dualist school, proceeding from the separation of the international and municipal legal orders, does not admit that, apart from possible direct reference, a norm belonging to one of these orders can limit or condition the validity of a norm belonging to the other. It concludes that no failure by the Head of State to observe constitutional rules on treaty making, for instance the rule requiring approval by the legislature, can affect the international validity of treaty arrangements.[46]

This thesis rests upon a formal and theoretical conception of the systematic relations between international and municipal law, which asserts the exclusive control of each legal order over its own sources. It is refuted by the facts of practice and may now be regarded as very generally abandoned. It is now recognized that an international treaty concluded by the Head of State without observing the rules of the constitution on the procedure for formulating the State's will (extrinsic constitutionality) is not binding upon the State provided those rules, set out in a text, are sufficiently notorious. Modern law thus recognizes that this limitation of competence, an essential safeguard of the democratic regime in the internal order, is also a limitation upon international competence in the external order.

Against this the dualist theory in vain argues the purely logical necessity of conceptually separating the two legal orders, and up to a certain point the real need of confidence in the making of treaties. Practice decisively answers this argument—confidence in making treaties is not the only factor to be considered; still more important is confidence in their execution. A treaty accepted by the Head of State without regard for the constitutional rule of parliamentary approval has little chance of being observed by a country conscious of the fact that it never regularly gave its consent.[47]

[46] D. Anzilotti, *Cours de Droit international*, pp. 259-261.

[47] Paul De Visscher, *De la Conclusion des Traités internationaux*, 1943, pp. 237-276, and, by the same author, *Rec. A.D.I.*, 1952, p. 345.

If the development of internal politics has induced States to consider themselves bound only when the constitutional rules on competence have been followed, the uncertainties of international politics have sometimes led States, signatories of a multilateral treaty, to observe it in fact and as purely national law, in spite of failure to ratify, when observance meant an advantageous moral or legal position. A characteristic example was the acceptance of the Naval Declaration of London (1909) by the Allied Powers at the beginning of the war of 1914-1918. This acceptance, which was provisional and revocable by mere national decision, was made subject to important restrictions in violation of the principle of indivisibility stated in the Declaration. Nevertheless that instrument, on certain important points constituting what was thought a reasonable compromise within the framework of a sufficiently well-established customary law, had an authority which no belligerent in 1914 was inclined to ignore. In addition to this advantage, the belligerents saw some political interest in the arrangement. The Declaration, fruit of a still recent agreement among the chief maritime Powers, seemed unlikely to meet serious objections on the part of neutrals, in whose favor it would operate. Everyone knows how both these considerations were nullified by the pressure of developments in maritime war.[48]

§ 3. THE POLITICAL IN THE INTERPRETATION OF TREATIES

The interpretation of international treaties has its own logic, which is sometimes different from that of the contracts of private law.

Among the differences which more particularly reflect the persistence of State individualism are first those concerning the restrictive interpretation of clauses limiting sovereignty. There is no antinomy of principle between the notion of sovereignty and that of conventional obligation, the object of any obligation being to limit, on particular points, the normal liberty of action belonging to sovereign States. It is certain, however, that the individualism which still largely dominates the relations of States inclines the judge to admit the restrictive interpretation more frequently in international treaties than in private-law agreements, at least when there is real doubt of the sense and scope of a clause or in the

[48] Cf. J. Basdevant, *La Conclusion et la Rédaction des Traités*, *Rec. A.D.I.*, vol. 15 (1926), pp. 599-600.

absence of other guides to interpretation.[49] International case-law certainly tends in that direction. It seems probable that on this point there will always be a certain divergence between judicial practice, concerned with the living reality of concrete cases, and the more theoretical views which inspire some doctrines.

The mental reservations or political preoccupations of the contracting States explain the fact that they sometimes attribute to a treaty an efficacy so limited as to appear at first sight out of harmony with what seems logically to be its object. If in principle a treaty must be interpreted in such a way that it can achieve the purpose desired by the parties (principle of "useful effect," often expressed in the adage *ut res magis valeat quam pereat*), the search for this purpose must not degenerate into abstract reasoning about an end believed to be that aimed at by the parties when in fact the partial inefficacy of the treaty can be explained by their deliberate intention not to be bound beyond a certain point.[50]

In the right-of-asylum case (Colombia-Peru) and in the Haya de la Torre case that was its sequel,[51] the International Court of Justice found that the Havana Convention of 1928, which orders the surrender to the territorial authorities of persons charged with or condemned for ordinary crimes, contains no similar rule for political criminals and thus does not sanction with obligatory surrender asylum granted in violation of the Convention. The silence of the authors of the Convention on this point indicates the limit which they did not intend to pass. It is explained by the Latin American tradition in the matter of asylum, which exempts a political refugee from surrender. On this point the contracting States deliberately restricted the effect of their undertakings.

A similar legal situation presented itself on the occasion of the advisory opinion handed down by the Court on a point of interpretation in the Peace Treaties with Bulgaria, Hungary, and Rumania (second phase).[52] The question was whether the power conferred on the secretary general of the United Nations, failing agreement between the parties, to name a third member in the Commissions provided for by these treaties could be extended to the

[49] Publications of the Permanent Court of International Justice, series A, no. 23, p. 26.

[50] See H. Lauterpacht, in *Annuaire de l'Institut de Droit international*, 1950, vol. I, p. 420.

[51] Judgment of November 20, 1950, International Court of Justice, Reports, 1950, p. 266; judgment of June 13, 1951, Reports, 1951, p. 71.

[52] Advisory Opinion of July 18, 1950, Reports, 1950, p. 221.

case of one party refusing to name its own commissioner. The Court held that the sole source of the power in question was the will of the parties as expressed in the provision for the settlement of disputes; and that such a provision, being one of strict law, cannot be extended beyond the case explicitly mentioned. Politically and realistically speaking, both the refusal of cooperation marked by the failure to name national commissioners, and the absence in the treaty of a clause making adequate provision to remedy this defect, were due to generalized political tension between the Eastern States and the Western Powers. The tension that existed during the drafting of the treaties perhaps made it possible to foresee this eventuality; but to call attention to it in the course of negotiations would doubtless have been to exceed the limits of diplomatic prudence. In any case there was nothing to justify going beyond the natural and ordinary meaning of the words used on the pretext of efficacy or useful result.

It is the interpretation of multilateral treaties, particularly those negotiated under the aegis of the United Nations, that has recently attracted attention. The value and the utilization of preparatory work has again become a question of immediate practical importance. There are certainly cases where recourse to the preparatory documents—represented here by the minutes and reports of the organs (committees, commissions, plenary conference) that at various stages have taken part in drawing up the convention—may become necessary. But it is essential, even in the interest of conventions of this type, to emphasize the serious dangers to which they are exposed by too easy or broad recourse to a documentation which is often incomplete and heterogeneous.

The drafting of conventions in the United Nations is undertaken and proceeds under very special psychological and political conditions. It does not have the advantage of the firmness of position which the pursuit of well-defined national objectives brings to the negotiation of bilateral treaties, or the tried methods of legislative drafting. Usually it begins in the enthusiasm of a factitious unanimity. It goes on through discussions of which the essential phases are sometimes incompletely coordinated, and which bring out views that shift and change according to the demands of dialectic or publicity. It is unwise to rely too much on the statements of delegates who at times have only a very tenuous line of communication with their government, and who never fail to provide an advocate hard up for arguments with support for any thesis whatever. The impression often given is only the disappointing one that there has been no real agreement of wills—an observation confirmed by the large number of refusals to ratify that afflict these conventions with "infant mortality."

It is agreed that recourse to preparatory documents is justified only when the text is really obscure. But it is precisely at this point that politics comes into play. A text is not obscure because a contracting party, with a political interest in disputing it, maintains that it is, or because a politically divided assembly finds no other way of securing its application than by asking an interpretation from the International Court of Justice. An international tribunal must not expose the integrity of treaty texts to such accidents. This was the upshot of the Advisory Opinion rendered by the Court on May 28, 1948 regarding the admission of a State to membership in the United Nations.[53]

The free will of the parties makes of a text accepted by them the sole and final expression of their common interest. The interpretation that results from its natural meaning can only be set aside by proof that it does not correspond to this intent. The occasions will be rare indeed when this proof can be produced for treaties of important political content. In periods of high tension in international relations—periods always propitious to the least-founded contention—it is essential, as Max Huber says, to keep careful watch lest "the idea of a will of the parties float like a dim cloud over the solid earth of a contractual text.[54]

Observation of international practice shows that the content of treaties has some importance for their interpretation or application by the parties as well as for the possible reference of any dispute arising in this context to international justice. There are treaties which by reason of their specifically political content involve special tension between the legal point of view and political demands. These are much less often treaties which, though relating to clearly political interests (for example boundary treaties), confine themselves to establishing a well-defined settlement, than treaties which seek to fix some future course for the foreign policy of the contracting parties.[55] Most conspicuous among these are the great collective

[53] The political antagonisms that have since arisen out of the admission of new members merely reinforce this point.

[54] Max Huber's reply to the Report of the Twelfth Commission of the Institute of International Law, *Annuaire*, 1952, vol. I, p. 199.

[55] Paul Barandon, *Das System der politischen Staatsverträge*, seit 1918, pp. 183-184.

treaties setting up an institutional organization among States, such as the Charter of the United Nations. The specific aim of such treaties is to impose organic limitations upon the sovereignty of States, limitations that seek to discipline their political behavior to serve the higher purposes of the institution of which they are members. Though their interpretation is an eminently judicial function, it has been observed that it often confronts the judge with a difficult task.

A treaty of international organization like the Charter of the United Nations always produces some tension between the ends of the institution and the rights reserved to the States members. This tension accounts for most of the difficulties encountered in the interpretation of the treaty. Extensive interpretation relies on the spirit of the treaty and the higher demands of the organization. Dynamic in inspiration, this type of interpretation usually seeks in the so-called principle of "useful effect" support for a legal policy aiming now at expanding the institution's role, now at vindicating, under cover of the institution, the particular claims of certain States or groups of States. Restrictive interpretation usually entrenches itself in the principle, indisputable in itself, that only a precise text can establish exceptions to the "sovereign equality" of the Members (Art. 2 of the United Nations Charter).

But these general and often very subjective positions by no means account for the many processes necessary in the objective and precisely shaded interpretation of treaties of this type. In the first place it goes without saying that the initial relation established by the texts between the higher aims of the organization and the rights reserved to the States members must not be regarded as unalterably static. Since they create institutions and aim finally at some redistribution of political powers, these treaties are subject in their interpretation to the laws of evolution that all institutions obey. Long collaboration may gradually win acceptance for some extensive interpretations of the powers of the organization, and make less absolute the insistence of States members on their reserved rights. It is equally clear that the interpretation of treaties in this category is not subject to certain rules applied in the case of bargaining treaties of the traditional type and derived primarily from the contracting parties' search for personal advantages on a basis of reciprocity. Always of capital importance in the interpretation of such treaties is the master idea or fundamental conception that led to their conclusion, when this idea is beyond dispute. By way of example we may cite: on the universal plane of the United Nations, the protection of the independence and international character of the Organization's functions;[56] the primary demands of peaceful coexistence and more precisely the efficacy of coercive action against aggression;[57] and, on the regional plane, the narrower obligations necessary to more constructive cooperation for better defined objects.

The agreements, preliminary to a peace settlement, by which the High Contracting Parties fix their future line of conduct are liable to be inextricably involved in the political tensions which may arise among them before the settlement is reached. The Potsdam Agreements of 1945 are an example. Notwithstanding their legal character, neither the Western Powers nor the U.S.S.R. would take the initiative of referring to international adjudication the violations with which each side charged the other. Recourse to judicial settlement presumes a minimum of cooperation that would of course have been lacking here.

Always highly political are the treaties that purport to define the attitudes of the contracting parties in the event of war: treaties of alliance, guarantee, neutrality, nonaggression. Though these treaties should, like any others, be carried out in good faith, it must be admitted that their interpretation depends to a great extent upon entirely political contingencies which are not clearly defined until the moment of execution and which can only be evaluated by the contracting States themselves.

An example of the influence of such contingencies is to be found in the very different interpretations of their obligations by States parties to a guarantee of permanent neutrality or of territorial inviolability. Earlier discussions on this subject are well known, especially those relative to the guarantees given by the great powers to Belgium and the Grand Duchy of Luxemburg. Practice has shown that the execution of such undertakings depends largely on the nature and degree of political interest that each of the guarantor

[56] This consideration is the basis for the Advisory Opinion rendered on April 11, 1949 by the International Court of Justice, Reparation of Damages Suffered in the Service of the United Nations, Reports, p. 183.

[57] Permanent Court of International Justice, Advisory Opinion No. 12, Interpretation of Article 3 of the Treaty of Lausanne, p. 29. The development of this idea explains the absolute priority in the Charter of concern for the peace over domestic jurisdiction when there is a "threat to the peace, breach of the peace, or act of aggression" (Art. 2, para. 7, of the Charter).

Powers sees in it, and on the risks involved for each in a possible refusal on the part of its coguarantors to cooperate. The guarantee of the independence and neutrality of Belgium in the two treaties of April 19, 1839 was unconditional. It was more firmly interpreted by the British Government than was the later "collective" guarantee of the neutrality of Luxemburg in the London Treaty of 1867,[58] at least in the sense that the government in London never argued in relation to Belgian neutrality that it would have been automatically released by the mere fact of violation by one of the coguarantors or by the refusal of some of them to cooperate. It is clear, however, from the advice drafted by the Law Officers of the Crown on the interpretation of the guarantee given in the Treaties of 1839 that purely legal considerations by no means exhaust the question, and that other considerations, bound up with political contingencies often unforeseeable when the obligation is assumed, count for a great deal.[59] These considerations may lead to the conclusion that a guarantor Power, though it has the right to act alone in fulfillment of the guarantee, is not bound to do so in the event of a general failure of its coguarantors to take action. On the other hand, a majority of the guarantors might be considered bound notwithstanding the default of a minority.[60] Whether the guarantee be classified as joint only or as joint and several, political considerations rooted in the security and individual interests of the States guarantors will always have an important part in determining whether it is to be carried out.

These considerations also count in determining, in case of doubt, the duration of such undertakings. They can hardly be presumed to be perpetual; failing contrary indications, it will be readily admitted that any contracting party may terminate them unilaterally by advance notice.

Finally, it should be noted that though these treaties, in spite of their highly political nature, set up a legal bond between the parties that is clear and certain because willed by them, yet in fact the disputes that may arise in regard to their execution are not among those which the parties are generally disposed to refer to international justice or for which legal criteria provide a suitable settle-

58 Arnold McNair, *op.cit.*, pp. 275-276. Some statements on the effect of the Belgian guarantee made by Lord Derby in 1867 have been the subject of criticism; cf. Hall, *International Law*, pp. 401-402.

59 Arnold McNair, *op.cit.*, pp. 271 seq.

60 John Fischer Williams, in *B.Y.B.I.L.*, 1936, pp. 134-136.

ment. Such treaties lend themselves much less to judicial decision than to revision by the parties themselves.

Very different in spirit from the guarantees stipulated in particular treaties were those incorporated in the Covenant of the League of Nations and in the Locarno Treaty. Here the guarantee was mutual, not politically pointed against a specific State, directed only at a possible aggressor. In this generality, and in the international control of execution, such a guarantee represents a maximum effort to maintain contact between the political and the legal or institutional. For this reason its interpretation relies upon special criteria.

In general the great Powers have a much greater tendency than the secondary States to reserve a broad discretion in the interpretation of political treaties, especially those concerned with their mutual relations. That is the consequence of the present distribution of power among nations and of the fact that relations between the great Powers are the area of the most serious political tensions. The discretion claimed by these Powers is commensurate with the competition among them; it is due less to the vagueness of the obligations contracted than to the responsibilities and the political risks involved in their fulfillment. The tendency is particularly clear in great-Power interpretation of the political commitments made in the great collective treaties such as the United Nations Charter.

Finally, it must be pointed out that persistent political differences may lead to wording of which the conscious ambiguity really denotes the absence of common intent on a particular point. Instead of using the more current and more laudable device of mutual reservations, the contracting parties have simply put off to the future the problem of settling their conflict in some other way. As one author puts it, international law knows clauses which, politically, substitute for rather than express agreement of the parties.[61] These political *arrière-pensées* would not justify refusal by the judge to determine the meaning of such a clause in the unlikely event of its interpretation being regularly referred to him. He must set himself first to defining the relation between the clause under discussion and the treaty as a whole, then consider it in the light of the purposes and general spirit of this instrument; finally, he will invoke one after the other general international law and "the general principles of law recognized by civilized nations" (Art. 38 of

[61] H. Lauterpacht, "Restrictive Interpretation and the Principle of Effectiveness in the Interpretation of Treaties," *B.Y.B.I.L.*, 1949, p. 82.

the Court Statute). His decision will have a quasi-legislative character all the more marked in that it must rely less upon a search for the intent of the parties and more upon considerations of an impersonal and general nature.

§ 4. STIPULATIONS DEROGATING FROM THE COMMON LAW OF SOVEREIGNTY

We have already mentioned the political tensions to which treaties derogating from what may be considered the common law of sovereignty are exposed. These tensions depend at once upon the gravity of the discrimination, the resentment that it engenders, and the changes that have occurred since the conclusion of the treaty in the ratio of strengths. In such cases the grievances formulated are very apt to take the form of charges that the treaty clauses are incompatible with the sovereignty and independence of the State on which they have been imposed, sometimes even that they are too exceptional to permit the interpretation demanded by the natural meaning of the terms used. The conflict between the political and legal points of view here becomes sharply defined.

In the case of the "Wimbledon," the Permanent Court of International Justice decisively rejected the plea of sovereignty entered by Germany to prevent the exercise in wartime of the right of passage in the Kiel Canal. This right, understood as available in wartime, implied, according to the German thesis, surrender of a "personal and imprescriptible right" which constituted an element of sovereignty and which Germany neither could nor would have renounced in advance. "This contention," says Judgment No. 1, "has not convinced the Court; it conflicts with general considerations of the highest order. It is also gainsaid by consistent international practice and is at the same time contrary to the wording of Article 380 which clearly contemplates time of war as well as time of peace."[62] Doubtless the treaty obligation has the effect of prohibiting recourse by the contracting parties to the plea of sovereignty in the questions in which their liberty of judgment, decision, or action is limited by the treaty. But the State which has bound itself in relation to a given question does not thereby cease to be sovereign in the order of matters to which that question belongs; it merely ceases to be free in relation to that specific question in the sense that it may thereafter use its sovereignty only subject to the

[62] Publications of the Court, Judgment No. 1, p. 25.

conditions laid down in the treaty. "The Court," Judgment No. 1 goes on, "declines to see in the conclusion of any Treaty by which a State undertakes to perform or refrain from performing a particular act an abandonment of its sovereignty. No doubt any convention creating an obligation of this kind places a restriction upon the exercise of the sovereign rights of the State, in the sense that it requires them to be exercised in a certain way. But the right of entering into international engagements is an attribute of State sovereignty."[63]

The Austro-German customs union, submitted to the Permanent Court of International Justice for an advisory opinion in 1931, was another attempt by a State to escape the effects of treaty provisions derogating from the common law. Here it took the form of recourse to abstract notions, represented as the only relevant legal principles, against the consequences of stipulations of which the concrete and manifestly political tenor was quite apparent. The whole argument of the Austrian and German Governments sought to have the question decided by general ideas relating to independence and the customs union *in abstracto*, detaching it from the concrete and clearly political object of the relevant conventional instruments (the Treaty of St. Germain and the Protocol of 1922).[64]

Treaty provisions derogating from the common law of sovereignty often occur in history as the result of a collective settlement more or less dictated by a group of Powers. The authority derived from this collective action is entirely relative. True, the State subject to such arrangements must, to regain its liberty, obtain a plurality of consents; but it can often count on a supervening divergence of interests and views among the signatories.[65] This change in the political relations prevailing at the conclusion of a treaty is one instance of the termination of treaties by the advent of new circumstances.[66]

§ 5. POLITICS AND EFFECTS OF TREATIES AS AGAINST THIRD STATES

The effects in international law of what is called stipulation for a third party are still ill defined. This is especially so in the case of

[63] The dissenting opinion of Messrs. Anzilotti and Huber relied on the fact that in international conventions "the contracting parties are independent political entities." *ibid.*, p. 36.

[64] For further discussion, see below, Book IV, pp. 339 seq.

[65] Jean Ray, *Des Conflits entre principes abstraits et stipulations conventionelles, Rec. A.D.I.*, vol. 48 (1934), pp. 703-704.

[66] See below, Chap. IV, "Peaceful Change."

a bilateral treaty drafted in terms that seek to extend its advantages either to specified States or to an indefinite number of States. Failing a clause governing adherence, the effect of such a stipulation will depend largely on the state of political relations between the contracting parties and the beneficiary. For it is established that advantages stipulated for a third State do not belong to it in absolute right; they are conditional upon a subsequent agreement which alone gives rise to contractual rights.

The Hay-Pauncefote Treaty between the United States and Great Britain on the Panama Canal (November 18, 1901) stipulated that the Canal "shall be free and open to the vessels of commerce and of war of all nations observing these Rules, on terms of entire equality, so that there shall be no discrimination against any such nation. . . ." This clause did not prevent Elihu Root in 1914, and Secretary of State Hughes in 1921, from denying that third States had thus acquired actual rights.[67]

In the matter of the Free Zones, the Permanent Court of International Justice, while declaring that nothing prevents the will of sovereign States from creating such rights in favor of third States, and recognizing that Switzerland had them in the case before the Court, took care to observe that this intention must not be lightly presumed.[68] The right of a third State directly interested in the enforcement of a multilateral treaty which is the work of the great Powers cannot be regarded as merely contractual, at least when the arrangement based on the treaty is historically consolidated.[69] Such consolidation sets aside the principle of the merely relative effect of treaties. The situation is then an objective legal one with effect *erga omnes*, the outcome of prolonged political action supported by general agreement.

In exceptional cases treaties are binding upon States that had no part in drawing them up. This is so in regard to certain treaties by

[67] Hackworth, *Digest*, vol. v, § 491, pp. 221-222; Charles Cheney Hyde, *International Law*, vol. ii, p. 1467. The example is the more significant because it has sometimes been argued that treaties relating to communications *ipso facto* benefit third States. On the question as a whole, see P. Guggenheim, *Lehrbuch des Völkerrechts*, vol. i, pp. 88 seq., and his *Traité*, pp. 97 seq.

[68] Publications of the Court, series A/B, no. 46, June 7, 1932, pp. 147-148. A fortiori, third States cannot, in the absence of express provision, have a right to the maintenance of the treaty. See to this effect the individual opinion of Judges Sir Cecil Hurst and Altamira, *ibid.*, p. 185.

[69] For the same view, see the report of the Commission of Jurists (1920) on the effect of the demilitarization of the Aaland Islands by the Convention of March 30, 1856.

which the great Powers, acting "in the general interest of Europe" or "of all civilized States," established an agreed political and territorial status. Such stipulations, regarded as creative of objective situations, have sometimes been described as part of "the public law of Europe." We have mentioned the Treaties of 1815 and 1831, the first of which recognized the permanent neutrality of Switzerland, while the second established that of Belgium; and the clauses in the Convention of March 30, 1856 demilitarizing the Aaland Islands. A plausible legal case can be made for this "constituent role" of the great Powers, which finds its political limits in the necessity of a general agreement or "concert" among them.[70] It is clear, however, that in some cases it may conduce to political opportunism, leaving the great Powers liberty to invoke as they will the general interest to subject third States to a regime to which they have not subscribed or, on the other hand, to exclude them as having no interest.

The concept of the constituent role of the great Powers has been pushed far at times. In the matter of the European Commission of the Danube, brought before the Permanent Court of International Justice for an advisory opinion, the Powers invoked against Rumania the clause in the Treaty of London, March 10, 1883, that extended the territorial jurisdiction of the Commission from Galatz to Braïla. They relied upon a mandate alleged to have been conferred on them by the Treaty of Berlin, July 13, 1878. Could the Treaty of London be pleaded against Rumania, the territorial Power, which had taken no part in its conclusion? In its Advisory Opinion of December 8, 1927, the Court refrained from pronouncing upon this point.

Article 2, paragraph 6, of the Charter, which lays it down that "The Organization shall ensure that states which are not members of the United Nations act in accordance with these Principles so far as may be necessary for the maintenance of international peace and security," cannot be regarded as creating legal obligations for States having no part in the Organization. The text is purely political in effect.[71] It means only that collective action by the Organization shall be available in the service of peace even when it is

[70] Advisory Opinion of the International Court of Justice on the Reparation of Injuries Suffered in the Service of the United Nations, April 11, 1949.

[71] Article 17 of the Covenant of the League of Nations was a different matter. On the general problem of extending the obligations of the Charter to nonmember States, see J. F. Lalive, in *B.Y.B.I.L.*, 1947, pp. 72 seq.

threatened by the activities of States that are under no contractual obligation to observe the principles of the Charter. Even from the political point of view the practical value of this clause is minimal. Given the present distribution of forces in the world, the unanimous agreement of the great Powers will almost always be sufficient to prevent a nonmember State from seriously threatening international peace and security. Failing agreement among them, the aggressor will usually find in the dissenting Power a political support that will leave Article 2, paragraph 6, no possibility of effective application.

§ 6. POLITICS AND COMPATIBILITY OF SUCCESSIVE OR CONCURRENT CONVENTIONAL UNDERTAKINGS

The highly political character of some treaties renders especially delicate the problem of their bearing on other treaties dealing with the same subject, and in particular the problem of the compatibility or incompatibility of their stipulations with conventional obligations previously assumed.[72]

The more important precedents relate either to conflict between two multilateral treaties or to conflict between a multilateral and a particular treaty.

The question presents no special difficulty when the treaties both belong to familiar categories in which the scope of practical application has been fixed by experience. Here the interpreter has at his disposal generally adequate legal criteria. It is less easy when the treaties, or one of them, for example by reason of the novelty of their provisions, open up perspectives which are still ill defined. This was the case when in 1920 the admission of Switzerland into the League of Nations was on the agenda, and the question arose whether its permanent neutrality was compatible with the Covenant. At that time the compatibility of the two relevant instruments was admitted by the Council of the League (declaration of February 13, 1920) only in relation to participation in military sanctions; Switzerland would be bound by the other solidary duties attached to membership, including that of taking part in economic sanctions against a State guilty of violating the Covenant. Events proved the problematic character of this decision. In 1938, citing the League's abandonment of the sanctions system in the Italian-Ethiopian conflict and the secession of Germany and Italy, Switzer-

[72] On the more general problem of the validity of conventional rules set up by successive or concurrent treaties, see Charles Rousseau, *Principes généraux de droit international public*, pp. 765 seq.

land obtained from the Council, together with the assurance that it would not be asked to participate in any way in the application of the clauses relating to sanctions, unreserved recognition of the compatibility of its traditional neutrality with the Covenant.[73]

The difficulty is no less when a particular treaty, in spite of more or less exact technical conformity with a preceding multilateral treaty, shows a political orientation which it was the real object of the multilateral treaty to prevent. In the case of the Austro-German customs union this had been precisely the purpose of the Treaty of St. Germain and the Protocol of 1922. Austria had undertaken to abstain from any acts of a nature to compromise her independence, and it was from the point of view of its reasonably foreseeable effects on this independence, looked at in its concrete political reality, that the Court had to weigh the plan of customs union. The difficulties felt by the minority judges were due to their misgivings about entering a realm of ideas which was unfamiliar to them but which was clearly that in which the agreements submitted to the Court for interpretation had been drawn up.

On the other hand the question of the compatibility of two treaties, both with the declared object of establishing a system of mutual security but successively associating Powers divided by high political tensions, depends upon purely political criteria inaccessible to the judge. This was the way in which the problem of compatibility presented itself in connection with the Franco-Soviet bilateral Treaty of Mutual Assistance dated May 2, 1935, and the collective treaty of mutual guarantee concluded at Locarno in 1925 (the Rhine Pact).[74] In such cases the important thing is much less the new text than the calculation which it may reflect—the implied change of political orientation, which sometimes results from the mere fact of associating a great Power in relations too exclusive by nature to admit sharing. Legal argument can have nothing more than a subsidiary role in a discussion that will be dominated by political suspicions.

[73] It is assumed here that the incompatibility of the two instruments is real and not simply apparent. Often an attentive examination shows that the obligations contracted are complementary rather than contradictory. On the criteria to be employed, especially in connection with multilateral treaties, see the second report by H. Lauterpacht to the International Law Commission (July 1954), p. 35 seq.

[74] L. Reitzer, "Le Traité franco-soviétique est-il compatible avec le Pacte de Locarno?" *Revue de Droit international et de Législation comparée*, 1937, p. 545. It goes without saying that the mere assertion by the parties to the new treaty that it in no way derogates from their obligations under a previous treaty cannot be held decisive.

The annulment of a treaty concluded with a third State in violation of an earlier treaty, though this would seem the logical sanction of a duly established contradiction, is usually impossible or at least highly problematic in view of the individualist and still primitive structure of international relations. Where such a contradiction occurs between two bilateral treaties, the third State interested in the second treaty will usually insist upon performance, invoking the principle *res inter alios acta,* which it is entitled to do if it has not recognized the first treaty. The injured State, for its part, is justified in protesting and in reserving its rights. But protest and reservation will generally result in nothing more than a statement of the international responsibility of the State that has signed incompatible treaties, and in any event can at most lead to an award of pecuniary damages. It cannot but be observed that the handling of such situations, though it may have legal aspects, almost always depends on political factors.

It often happens that a multilateral convention abrogating and revising a previous multilateral convention is concluded without the participation of all the States who were parties to the earlier agreement. It is more and more clearly recognized that strict application of the rule requiring that all the original contracting parties shall take part in or adhere to the revision may be difficult or even impossible owing to changes in the political constellation, especially when the first multilateral convention, even though it created an objective situation good *erga omnes,* has itself a marked political character. There is some contradiction between the orthodox principle of unanimity among the contracting parties and a practice which more and more "regards as acquiescence anything less than solemn protest, overlooks resistances that are too weak to prevail, and if necessary ignores some governments to confront them with the accomplished fact."[75] Thus the great international acts of a constitutional nature have met the inescapable need of revision by sacrificing rather freely the contractual rule of unanimity. In this direction the United Nations Charter merely followed the example set by the Covenant of the League of Nations. The procedure of revision leaves to a dissenting minority only the choice, at times merely theoretical, between accepting amendments distasteful to it and seceding.[76]

When political considerations do not play so preponderant a part, the amendment of the original convention or the substitution of a

[75] See the noteworthy report by M. Georges Scelle to the Institute of International Law, *Annuaire,* 1948, pp. 11-12.

[76] For more detail, see below, Chap. IV, "Peaceful Change," Sec. v.

new one lends itself better to regulation established in advance by the parties, and it is easier for the judge to weigh the use that they have made of such regulation. The criterion will necessarily be provided by the effect of changes on the general object of the first convention. Though it certainly cannot be admitted that this object may be sacrificed, under the color of revision, to particular arrangements, it is no more possible to concede to one or two of the original contracting parties the power to prevent, without any real interest, a revision considered indispensable by the great majority of original signatories and justified by new circumstances.[77]

§ 7. RESERVATIONS IN MULTILATERAL CONVENTIONS

The legal problems raised by reservations were for a long time looked at only from the point of view of the contractual logic of the law of treaties, which makes the validity of any reservation conditional on acceptance by all the contracting parties, as it would have been if the reservation had been made in the course of negotiation. This is the concept of the indivisibility or integrity of conventions; it recognizes the power of each contracting party to exclude entirely from the relations set up by the agreement the author of any reservation whatsoever, even though it be compatible with the purposes of the convention. This concept attains its full value when the treaty, as is most often the case, is a bargaining agreement in which the contracting parties seek personal advantages on the basis of reciprocal claims. Such treaties have an internal equilibrium that is not to be upset by reservations. It is more debatable in relation to multilateral conventions in which the contracting parties seek ends superior to their particular interests. Such are the multilateral conventions concluded under the auspices of the United Nations when they take the form of real statutes designed to serve purely humanitarian, social, or civilizing purposes on a quasi-universal plane.[78]

The application and efficacy of such conventions depend upon various and sometimes almost irreconcilable exigencies. The great

[77] Harvard Research, *Law of Treaties*, p. 1016: "Two or more of the States parties to a treaty to which other States are parties may make a later treaty which will supersede the earlier treaty in their relations *inter se*, only if this is not forbidden by the provisions of the earlier treaty and if the later treaty is not so inconsistent with the general purpose of the earlier treaty as to be likely to frustrate that purpose."

[78] By reason of the same characteristic, conventions of this type generally escape the rule of interpretation *contra proferentem*.

number of contracting States, profoundly different in their traditions and institutions, makes unreserved agreement on all articles difficult. The end in view may prohibit sacrificing the essence and reason of the convention to the consideration of numbers. Finally, the authority of the convention in the world at large may not be compatible with limited participation, the abstention of certain States being in itself a threat or even an attack upon the principles and higher interests which the convention aims to serve. Under these conditions, and in the absence of any explicit stipulation of indivisibility, which the contracting parties are always free to make, it is difficult to admit that an objection, perhaps irrational or arbitrary, to a reservation of minor importance must necessarily exclude the State entering such a reservation from the convention.[79]

These considerations are reinforced by the new rule by which multilateral conventions are adopted by majority, and which, if it facilitates the conclusion of conventions, also inclines the contracting parties to multiply reservations. They call for recognition of the necessity of greater flexibility in determining the legal effects of reservations. Pan-American practice is one manifestation of this tendency. The Advisory Opinion of the International Court of Justice, dated May 28, 1951, on the effect of reservations in the convention for the prevention and punishment of the crime of genocide, though clearly limited to a specific case in which elementary considerations of humanity played a very important part, lends some support to the new trend. On the basis of an interpretation of the intention of the parties to this convention, the Opinion holds that a State that has formulated and sustained a reservation to which one or more parties object while the others do not can be regarded, the objection notwithstanding, as a party to the convention if the reservation is compatible with its object.[80]

The interest of the discussion on this subject does not lie in the solutions advocated on this side or that. These all exhibit different

[79] Cf. Guggenheim, *Traité*, p. 80 and note 3. The author rightly observes that the League of Nations Commission of Experts for the codification of international law (Fromageot-McNair-Diena Report) took a view on this point that was strongly influenced by the private law of contract and too absolute.

[80] Reservations to the convention for the prevention and punishment of the crime of genocide, Reports of Advisory Opinions, 1951, p. 15. The problem is broadly treated by the rapporteur of the International Law Commission, Professor H. Lauterpacht (5th session of the Commission, 1953), who, rejecting the opinion stated by the Commission in 1951, shows the impossibility of sustaining the rule of unanimous consent. *International Law Commission*, March 24, 1953, pp. 101-142.

degrees of weakness. The interest lies rather in the recognition of a differentiation, unavoidable to a certain point even in the domain of agreements, of the relations between signatories of multilateral treaties negotiated on the quasi-universal plane of the United Nations. The difficulties that sixty States may in all good faith experience, by reason of their particular legislation, mores, or traditions, in agreeing unreservedly to all the clauses of a multilateral convention of which the object is at times without precedent in the history of treaty relations, are the price of this almost universal participation. They constitute a political reality which cannot be shaken off by applying the traditional and oversimple rule of the indivisibility of conventions.

The problem is one of legislative policy. It is for the States parties to a multilateral convention to solve it by specifying, when the convention is adopted and in the light of its purposes, whether reservations are permissible, to what provisions they may be entered, and what their legal effect will be on participation in the convention and the mutual relations of the parties. In particular it is for them to judge whether and in what measure they should accept reservations in order to enlarge the circle of participants or reject them in order to preserve the unity of the system. True, this assumes that the contracting parties see clearly their object and that there is a complete agreement of wills—a condition not always realized in the negotiation of multilateral conventions in our day. Also, in such matters, time and experience teach more than do ready-made formulas or conjectures. The practice of multilateral conventions will soon draw a line between States whose agreement, though without reservation, may be merely verbal, and those whose participation, even with reservations, is real. Differentiation finds a place also in the domain of execution.

There are purely political reservations which, instead of expressing some particularism in the legal resources to be placed at the service of the convention, really destroy the conventional bond. This would be the case with a general reservation in favor of the "national" or "traditional" policy of a State, which would clearly subject the application of the convention to a potestative condition; and again with a reservation by which a State, while recognizing the convention as one of general interest, sought to free itself from any international control in applying it.[81]

[81] Cf. L. A. Podesta Costa, "Les Réserves dans les Traités internationaux," *Revue de droit international,* 1938, vol. I, p. 5. Cf. H. W. Malkin, "Reservations

§ 8. NECESSITY AND THE EXECUTION OF CONVENTIONAL OBLIGATIONS

The individualist character of international relations and the absence of any jurisdictional control also explain the difficulty of applying the notion of necessity as an excuse for nonfulfillment of contractual obligations. Indeed, in the very rare cases where necessity has been definitely pleaded, the excuse appeared frankly inacceptable; elsewhere it is likely to merge either in *force majeure* or self-defense.

The excuse of necessity leads to obstinate conflict wherever the essential or vital political interests of States are at grips. In municipal law, where social integration is largely complete, a concept of general interest governs a hierarchy of values and, in case of conflict, dictates the order of priority. There is nothing like this in the relations of States. The claim of one State to protect its vital interests at the cost of the essential interests of another is, in the present stage of international organization, a purely political claim, for it cannot be justified objectively and it is likely to exclude even the possibility of legal settlement. Germany's violation in 1914 of the Belgian neutralization treaties remains the best historical example.

It is true, where economic interests are the subject of contractual regulation, that a hierarchy of values is more easily conceived and established and, further, that the conflicting interests are not usually so vital and do not set up such high political tension. In his individual opinion in the Oscar Chinn case, relating to the application of the Convention of Saint-Germain, former President Anzilotti of the Permanent Court of International Justice pointed out that "necessity may excuse the non-observance of international obligations";[82] but the definition that he gave is more appropriate to *force majeure* than to necessity strictly so called. The excuse of necessity implies some freedom, in the sense that the party pleading it has made a limited but conscious and reasonable choice, holding that he could give preference to his own interests over the right of another. This involves a comparison of the respective values of the interests at stake. When Anzilotti defined necessity as "the impossibility of proceeding by any other method than the one contrary to law," he was really defining *force majeure*. This, by reason of its

to Multilateral Conventions," *B.Y.B.I.L.*, 1926, p. 141; P. Guggenheim, *Lehrbuch*, *op.cit.*, pp. 79-80.

[82] Judgment of December 12, 1934, Publications of the Court, series A/B, no. 63, pp. 113-114.

strictly objective character, is a justification that may be pleaded in international law as in municipal law. As such, it eliminates all responsibility. This was recognized as a matter of principle by the Permanent Court of Arbitration in the case of the war indemnity owed to Russia by the Ottoman Empire.[83]

Though it is not possible to state a priori that a qualified international organ cannot decide on the merits of the excuse of necessity, at least in questions where the essential political interests of States are not in conflict, it must be observed that this excuse is still in the domain of discretionary judgment and unilateral decision.

Notwithstanding these defects, the treaty remains international law's most powerful instrument of progress and diffusion. Much more than the other sources it calls for conscious and voluntary human action in the development of international law. It clarifies and rationalizes social relations in those still vast areas of interest where, owing to an insufficient sense of solidarity, general international law has not yet penetrated. Bringing together "parties," that is to say States already conscious of their interdependence, it gives them the opportunity to define, order, and develop that interdependence. It thus helps to identify the social phenomena that are susceptible of legal treatment and assimilation. In this way relations and oppositions, until then submerged in the amorphous mass of raw facts and inarticulate political tensions, are gradually clarified and given recognizable form.[84]

Finally, the treaty performs a truly innovating function when, without abandoning the firm ground where there is a real sense of solidarity, it succeeds in regulating by agreement matters or questions which general international law, lagging behind social needs, still assigns positively to the exclusive jurisdiction and thus to the discretionary decision of States. This innovating function is especially important and timely. The movement of customary law, which is of course surer, but is also too slow, is not adequate to the needs of a world that changes with unprecedented speed.

[83] Award of November 11, 1912. Cf. J. Basdevant, *Règles du droit de la paix*, *Rec. A.D.I.*, vol. 58, pp. 555-556.

[84] Cf. G. Schwarzenberger, *A Manual of International Law*, 1947, p. 58. "Though objectively speaking it is merely an unintentional by-product of the conclusion of treaties by States, not the least important function which is fulfilled by treaties is that they provide the humus in which international customary law grows."

Section IV

Diplomatic Protection and International Responsibility

§ 1. DIPLOMATIC PROTECTION

In the great majority of cases it is diplomatic protection that brings into play the international responsibility of States. For this reason the matter of responsibility—a subject very legal by nature and which it is one of the merits of contemporary doctrine to have systematized—has remained largely dependent on political factors.

Two chief factors have shaped the structure of diplomatic protection since the nineteenth century: capital investment in countries whose natural wealth or inadequate economic and technical equipment marked them out for foreign enterprise; and the strong concentration of power in the State, which, substituting governmental action for the archaic system of private reprisals, made this the exclusive mode of protecting national interests abroad.

A product of the industrial revolution, the flow of export capital helped to internationalize the currents of business without changing the national base of the peoples' economies. On the contrary, it soon gave a powerful impetus to economic nationalism. Associating political designs with economic penetration, nineteenth-century imperialism kept private enterprise and diplomacy in step, the dominant role passing from one to the other according to the needs of the moment. Thus tied to a conception of national interest in which calculations of prestige and power at times had a large part, diplomatic protection found itself charged with a high political potential.[85]

In the country of investment, the flow of private export capital demands conditions of order, security, and stability, failing which foreign enterprises cannot maintain themselves or prosper. In fact these countries were often politically and economically weak. Unsure of themselves and of the regular operation or stability of their institutions, they showed themselves particularly sensitive to foreign intrusion, and by various means sought to restrict it.

Anyone who fails to take liberal account of these factors risks

[85] Cf. Frederick Sherwood Dunn, *The Protection of Nationals*, chaps. 1-3. The examples cited by Eugene Staley, *War and the Private Investor* (pp. 360 seq.), are significant of the reciprocal support given each other by governments and the great banking and industrial organizations. Cf. Edgar Faure, *Le Pétrole dans la paix et dans la guerre*, p. 42: "If the State has a petroleum policy, the petroleum kings will have a policy for the State."

misunderstanding the character of the interests in play and the antagonisms that they arouse. They are the factors responsible for the opportunism that remains the law of diplomatic protection, and they explain the defensive legal positions by which States exposed to claims have sought to limit their responsibilities.

The history of diplomatic protection shows that it is always largely governed by considerations of political expediency. Protection being for governments merely a liberty, they use it in the measure that their intervention seems calculated to promote, or at least not to obstruct, the purposes of their general policy. Where this condition is not met, they abstain. Protection has been asserted with extreme energy where governments have associated certain forms of economic penetration with clearly defined political designs. It has been wanting, or reduced to modest pecuniary claims, when, notwithstanding patent injustices, governments have thought it likely to compromise either the pursuit of political objectives or simply the maintenance of normal relations with the accused State. In the latter case it has usually been argued that private enterprises seeking large profit abroad do so at their own risk and should not expect support from their government. "The same events which, in times of mounting ambitions, took on an aspect of extreme gravity, were at other times treated as minor misfortunes that might happen in any country."[86] Such opportunism does not of course exclude appeals to moral considerations of order and justice. States resorting to protection, especially armed protection, have very generally sought to justify it as part of their civilizing mission in relation to local authorities unable to fulfill their international duties.

The strong emphasis given in the nineteenth century to the personification of the State reinforced its protective role. Elevating private grievances to the plane of national affronts, and laying on the sovereign the duty to avenge the injury inflicted on a national, this emphasis accentuated the political tone of protection while at the same time providing it with a basis for technical systematization.

As for the countries of investment, their political and social structure left them badly prepared to meet the demands of their position. The instability of their public life, marked as it was by *coups d'Etat,* and by insurgent or revolutionary movements, often

[86] Frederick Sherwood Dunn, *Diplomatic Protection of Americans in Mexico,* p. 8. Definitions presenting diplomatic protection as "an institution of the law of nations" thus call for serious reservations.

impaired the normal operation of their administrative and judicial institutions. The frequency of damage to aliens in these circumstances, and the absence of adequate legal remedies, exposed their governments to numerous claims against which they tried to arm themselves by propounding various doctrines more consonant with their own interests than with the rules of customary law. This was the reflection of a special psychology adequately explained by historical differences—a political survival which has already been reduced by changes in the ratio of interests and forces, and which doubtless one day will be entirely eliminated.

At the bottom of these divergencies, which in 1930 brought about the defeat of the Codification Conference in the matter of international responsibility, is the thesis that the treatment of nationals is the measure of the rights which, internationally, the alien may claim. This thesis is contradicted by the practice of States as well as by doctrine. It is a fact that, whatever treatment they give their own nationals, States consider themselves internationally bound to observe certain principles limiting their power in relation to foreigners. The treatment of aliens is a matter directly subject to international law; it is not defined by reference to national treatment.[87]

The two devices, one direct and the other indirect, by which States exposed to claims have sought to defend themselves spring from a false premise. Some have proposed openly to exclude diplomatic protection, either by constitutional or legislative provisions, or by a clause of renunciation inserted in the concessionary contracts signed with foreign nationals (Calvo clause). Outside Latin America these various measures are generally considered legally inoperative. The so-called Calvo clause, in particular, cannot stand in the way of diplomatic protection, which is a governmental function, where there is a violation not only of the contract, but also of international law, as in the case of denial of justice.[88]

[87] Publications of the Permanent Court of International Justice, series A, no. 7, judgment of May 25, 1926, p. 33. Cf. A. Verdross, *Rec. A.D.I.*, vol. 30 (1929), pp. 442-443.

[88] Cf. Charles De Visscher, *Le Déni de justice en droit international*, *Rec. A.D.I.*, vol. 52 (1935), p. 431; Alwyn V. Freeman, *The International Responsibility of States for Denial of Justice*, 1938, pp. 469-490. The clause must be held valid insofar as it merely reaffirms the traditional rule on the exhaustion of local remedies. There is a characteristic exposition of the two theses in the decision of the United States–Mexico Commission in the North-American Dredging Co. of Texas case (1926), and in the opinion of the American Commissioner, Nielsen, in the International Fisheries Co. case (1931).

The denial of justice being, if not the sole, at least the most frequent basis of diplomatic claims for damage of private origin, some States, especially those of Latin America, have tried to impose narrow limitations upon this notion. This indirect device seeks at once to set aside claims and to minimize responsibilities. In general, it reduces denial of justice in international relations to the meaning given it by municipal law. Denial of access to the courts or unjust discrimination in the conditions of access, and the refusal of the judge to decide, would be the only relevant cases of denial of justice. As for judgment itself, this would be always and in every respect sovereign; even for reasons of manifest injustice it could never be the object of a claim or be submitted for review to any international authority.[89]

The thesis rests upon two postulates. According to the first, which we have already met, the judicial protection of aliens should in no case afford them facilities of access or recourse not open to nationals. Under the second, the judgment once rendered would be clothed, even in international relations, with the authority of *res judicata*. This view is very generally rejected: *res judicata* is decisive only in the internal order and, subject to reservations which a still hesitant international practice tends to confirm, it may entail international responsibility.

It is a traditional and solidly established principle that a government can give diplomatic protection only in cases of damage suffered by its own nationals. But there are great differences of opinion about the basis of the rule and its scope. The requirement of a bond of personal dependence between the claimant State and the injured individual was long supported, and up to a certain point is still supported today, by the argument that the injury done to an individual is an injury to the State of which he is a national. This thesis, revived from Vattel, was propounded for instance by the British Government in the Stevenson case submitted in 1903 for arbitration to the Anglo-Venezuelan Mixed Commission, and rejected by the umpire, Plumley; then it was expressly condemned in an administrative decision rendered by the umpire, Parker, in the

Claims Commission United States and Mexico, Opinions of Commissioners, February 1926–July 1927, p. 21; *ibid., October 1930–July 1931*, p. 225.

89 Some systems of law have attempted to give denial of justice a unilateral definition of this sort. Such definitions are without international effect. It is otherwise with definitions included in certain international treaties that seek to limit the notion of denial of justice.

German-American Mixed Commission (1924). The effect of these decisions, together with the judgments of the Permanent Court of International Justice in the Mavrommatis and Panevezys-Saldutiskis cases, is to attenuate the highly political virus of the so-called Vattel theory, which brings questions of national honor and prestige dangerously into play, and to put in its place a functional conception of the State's role in diplomatic protection.[90]

Though the political justification of the claim as based upon the injury to the State still survives in the instructions of some chancelleries, the recent practice of diplomatic protection has been marked by features that are not logically in harmony with it. Such is the requirement, confirmed by established usage, that the bond of nationality must continue from the occurrence of damage to the presentation of claim or even, according to a fairly widespread opinion, to the decision. If the wrong inflicted upon the national of a State was in itself an injury to that State, the right to intervene acquired at that moment could not be lost owing to a subsequent change in the nationality of the injured individual. The loss is on the other hand easily explained by the conception of the protecting State's role as merely functional. It is then simply a question of the State's title to perform a function which international law recognizes as belonging to it and at the same time subjects to specific conditions.[91]

It moreover seems that a juster conception of the protection due to human personality is beginning to appear in some recent treaties that lay down conditions for the admission of private claims in terms that supersede the somewhat uncertain criteria of earlier practice. In the Treaties of Peace with Italy, Bulgaria, Hungary,

[90] Administrative Decision No. v (October 31, 1924) of Parker as umpire: ". . . the generally accepted theory formulated by Vattel, which makes the injury to the national an injury to the nation . . . must not be permitted to obscure the realities or blind us to the fact that the ultimate object of asserting the claim is to provide reparation for the private claimant." In the well-known formula of the Permanent Court, the State intervenes not to obtain reparation for a personal injury, but to vindicate the right that belongs to it, namely "the right to ensure in the person of its nationals respect for the rules of international law." Publications of the Court, series A/B, no. 76, p. 16. It goes without saying that the same act may occasion private and public damage. Cf. Judgment No. 13 of the Permanent Court, September 13, 1928, p. 28.

[91] In its advisory opinion of April 11, 1949, the International Court of Justice declared, without further explanation: "even in inter-State relations, there are important exceptions to the rule, for there are cases in which protection may be exercised by a State on behalf of persons not having its nationality." Reports, 1949, p. 181.

and Rumania (1947) the notion of national is defined in terms that broaden the conditions for admitting claims.

A significant development in the institution is the granting of diplomatic protection to the shareholders of a company against the State of which the company bears the nationality. During the war of 1914-1918, in connection with the attribution of enemy character to companies, the unitary private-law conception, which entirely separates the company's personality from that of the units composing it, was for the first time broken down by the notion of control. Precisely adapted to the liberal economy and, besides, eminently favorable to the expansion of commercial operations, the unitary conception, as Lord Parker remarked in a celebrated decision, expressed "an ideal of profound peace."[92] Since that time it has had to give way, at least in some matters and for some purposes, to considerations of public law in which equity takes priority over a rigid application of private-law technique.

This evolution was bound soon to show itself in the field of diplomatic protection following upon damaging and at times discriminatory or confiscatory measures applied by certain States to companies which, though subject to their laws, had a share capital largely held by foreigners. The question assumes a particularly marked political character in cases where the local law has made any concessions granted to foreign groups conditional upon the establishment of a company subject to the legal system of the conceding State.

Diplomatic precedents, arbitral decisions still a little hesitant but tending to harden, and clauses in international treaties, especially in conventions that have set up mixed claims commissions, all go to prove the existence of a practice favoring the protection of the individual rights of the shareholders when the company itself is the victim of measures enacted by the State having jurisdiction over it and when, besides, local remedies have been exhausted.[93]

[92] House of Lords (June 30, 1916), Daimler Co. Ltd. v. Continental Tyre and Rubber Co., 1916 2 A.C. 307. Cf. a circular of the French Garde des Sceaux dated February 29, 1916.

[93] See Charles De Visscher, "La Protection diplomatique des actionnaires d'une société contre l'Etat sous la législation duquel cette société s'est constituée," *Revue de Droit international et de Législation comparée*, 1934, p. 624. Cf., with various distinctions: E. Borchard, *Rapport a l'Institut de Droit international, Annuaire* (1931), vol. I, p. 297; W. E. Beckett, "Diplomatic Claims in Respect of Injuries to Companies," *Transactions of the Grotius Society*, 1931, p. 175; J. Mervyn Jones, "Claims on Behalf of Nationals Who Are Shareholders in Foreign Companies," *B.Y.B.I.L.*, 1949, p. 225.

Thus behind the corporate veil of group personality, international law tends to protect the shareholders, providing them individually through the diplomatic channel with protection of which the company as such has been deprived by the absence of local remedies or by a denial of justice. As Max Huber has pointed out, "international law, which in this domain is based essentially on equitable principles, has established no formal criterion for granting or refusing diplomatic protection to national interests linked with interests belonging to persons of different nationalities.[94]

In such an approach to the matter, the protection of the rights of the individual deprived of any remedy figures as the primary object, and equity corrects the injustices that may result from applying technical rules established for and adapted to other purposes. It does not appear, however, that international practice has entirely adopted this approach or that it follows it consistently. The precedents show a tendency on the part of governments to rely now on the unity of the company's personality, now on consideration of the constituent individuals, according to their interests at the moment.[95]

It cannot be denied that, in its present state, diplomatic protection offers a disconcerting medley of heterogeneous elements. In particular, the absolute political discretion left to the State in the exercise of protection goes ill with the principle that the treatment due to aliens is a matter of international law. In this aspect the practice of protection very well illustrates the still semipolitical nature of many institutions of international law.

Despite its narrow scope and its gaps—these latter especially obvious in the matter of statelessness—diplomatic protection faithfully reflects the existing state of international relations, and therefore has the advantage of reality. Those are on the wrong track who would eliminate it in favor of an international system of protection in which man as such, without reference to any bond of nationality, would find the safeguard of his rights.[96] Such a suggestion is not only utopian; it threatens the effectiveness of interna-

[94] Reports on British claims in the Spanish Zone of Morocco (Ziat, Ben Kiran case), p. 185.

[95] Cf. Hackworth, *Digest*, vol. v, § 544, p. 831.

[96] This somewhat cloudy idea has found adherents in the countries traditionally hostile to diplomatic protection. See the suggestions along these lines offered to the Mexico Conference by the Interamerican Bar Association (1944), and the so-called Cárdenas doctrine. Cf. Alwyn V. Freeman, "Recent Aspects of the Calvo Doctrine and the Challenge to International Law," *A.J.I.L.*, 1946, p. 121.

tional law. A frontal attack of the sort on the principle of diplomatic protection, as Max Huber has emphasized, would lead to "unacceptable consequences; it would disarm international law in the face of injustices equivalent to denial of human personality, for that is what every denial of justice comes to."[97]

Various factors contributed not only to the abandonment of some particularly irritating forms of diplomatic protection, such as the so-called pacific blockade or naval demonstration, but also to the limitation of the object even of pecuniary claims for damages to the property of aliens. Individual coercive action, frequently practiced in the last century by various great Powers, came to an end at the beginning of the twentieth century at the same time as the preponderance of the European Powers, and more particularly the double naval and commercial hegemony of Great Britain, was diminishing in the world. In 1902 the Drago doctrine, combining the political substance of the Monroe theory with a legal thesis, emphasized the abuse of force to which armed coercive action lent itself. In 1907 the Second Hague Conference adopted the Convention on the use of force in the collection of contract debts. Making the resort to constraint conditional upon an offer of arbitration, the Convention subjected it to international control.[98] Since then, and especially since the second world war, the elements of the problem have profoundly changed. The notion and the protections of private property have weakened almost everywhere; while the more and more extensive practice of nationalization has made this the instrument of a State policy which can no longer be considered peculiar to certain countries. These changes, which have made foreign investment more precarious, have reduced the scope of claims for compensation for expropriation, withdrawal of concession, or nationalization.

§ 2. INTERNATIONAL RESPONSIBILITY

International responsibility, as a substantive problem, is not affected in the same degree as diplomatic protection by political factors. But it is far from escaping them entirely. Observation indeed shows that the operation and establishment of responsibilities largely depend on the organization of power and the effectiveness of the control maintained in its territory by the accused State.

[97] Reports, p. 53.

[98] On the affinity of this convention to the Drago doctrine, see H. Wehberg, *Rec. A.D.I.*, vol. 37 (1931), pp. 630-633.

This internal political element may be taken into account either to attenuate or exclude responsibility, or, on the contrary, to extend or increase it.

The control exercised by the State throughout its whole territory is the basis of the international responsibility that it may have to assume for acts contrary to international law committed there. The extent of this responsibility may then vary with the degree of effectiveness of control. This aspect of international responsibility loomed large in the measurement by the International Court of Justice of Albania's responsibility for the laying of a minefield in its territorial waters.[99] The Court rejected not only the manifestly exaggerated idea of a presumption of knowledge founded on the coastal State's mere control of its territorial waters, but also that of a prima-facie responsibility that would shift the burden of proof. On the other hand, it held that a State in whose territory an act contrary to international law has occurred may be invited to explain and that it cannot evade this invitation by limiting itself to the response that it knows nothing of the circumstances or authors of the act. Taking into account the double duty of prevention and of punishment, the Court also recognized that the accused State may, up to a certain point, be bound to show what use it has made of the means of information and examination at its disposal. Contrasting the facilities for information inherent in exclusive territorial control with the difficulty or even impossibility confronting the State against which a breach of international law has been committed of directly proving the facts, the Court held that this State must be allowed liberal recourse to the presumptions of fact and the circumstantial evidence which are accepted in all systems of law, and which may be especially cogent when they are supported by a series of connected facts that lead logically to one and the same conclusion.

It is very generally accepted that in cases where the revolutionary movement is finally crushed, the State is not responsible for damaging acts committed by insurgents or rebels.[100] Classical doctrine supports this view with two arguments. On the one hand, the insurgents or rebels cannot be considered organs or agents of the State against which they are in revolt and consequently cannot engage

[99] Corfu Channel case (Merits), April 9, 1949, Reports of Judgments, 1949, p. 18.

[100] On some correctives in the application of the principle, cf. award of the Mixed France-Mexico Commission in the G. Pinson case, *Annual Digest*, 1927-1928, no. 159.

its responsibility. On the other hand, the government can answer only for the acts of those whom it effectively controls, while the revolutionary events indicate temporary lack of effective control over part of the territory. Recognition of a state of belligerency or insurgency would naturally reinforce the case against responsibility.

In such cases, the responsibility of the State comes into play only if it is shown that it did not make use of its authority or of the forces at its disposal to prevent the damaging acts or to ensure the protection of foreigners, or, again, if it neglected to prosecute or punish those guilty when it was in a position to do so. These conclusions are based on the idea that the extent of responsibility is measured by effective power. They have been approved in a series of treaties concluded between European States and certain Republics of Latin America, as well as in a great number of arbitral awards.[101] It must be concluded, with the United States–Mexico Claims Commission (1923), that the nature and extent of the revolutionary movement count importantly in determining the duty of vigilance incumbent on the authorities.

It cannot be stated that these are definitely established rules. A more recent practice, influenced above all by considerations of order and security, is attested by the decisions of the United States–Mexico, Great Britain–Mexico, and France-Mexico Claims Commissions (Conventions of 1923, 1926, 1924). These decisions reflect two lines of thought. One, relating to acts of administration and current transactions of an insurgent government in the part of the territory which it controls, tends to break away from the principle that such a government ("local" government) is incapable of engaging the State's responsibility. Having at least temporarily performed the governmental functions in fact, this government cannot be considered completely stranger to the State.[102] Insofar as its acts amount to normal administration of the public services and not to revolutionary political activities on the part of the insurgent government, they can legitimately be imputed to the State.

[101] Haig Silvanie, *Responsibility of States for Acts of Unsuccessful Insurgent Governments*, and, by the same author, *A.J.I.L.*, 1939, pp. 78 seq.; Charles Cheney Hyde, *International Law*, vol. II, pp. 979 seq. Cf. J. G. de Beus, *The Jurisprudence of the General Claims Commission, United States and Mexico, under the Convention of September 8, 1923.*

[102] It has been justly observed that the classical theory on the subject represents the insurgents as enemies of the State because they are enemies of the government. Haig Sylvanie, in *A.J.I.L.*, 1939, pp. 78 seq.

Following the other line of thought, relating more particularly to illicit international acts (torts), the same Commissions have recognized—though only on the basis of the conventions by which they were established and, Mexico for her part contends, as an *ex gratia* measure—that Mexico had agreed to answer for damages inflicted on aliens by certain revolutionary forces at least during a specified period.

Without exaggerating the importance of these new ideas, especially in the matter last mentioned, they do manifest an indisputable tendency in international law to separate responsibility from any question of the legitimacy of the government and to attach it to effective control in a sufficiently important part of the territory. They also plainly reveal the thought that the State, being a permanent entity whose authority extends over the whole territory, cannot wholly escape the consequences of acts done in its name in part of this territory even by the mere *de facto* government which temporarily but effectively exercised power there.[103]

When the rebels have not risen to the dignity of insurgents, the responsibility for their damaging acts, which are most often the work of more or less organized bands, rests upon the State insofar as it has, by negligence or connivance, failed in its duty to prevent, or helped to bring about, a condition of general insecurity or anarchy in its territory.[104] This responsibility is, however, less severely measured where the acts of banditry occur in the course of warlike events which in themselves increase the burdens of the authorities and limit their means of action.

In spite of the accumulation of precedents, examination of the concrete cases reveals the impossibility of stating otherwise than in the most general terms the applicable legal criteria. Any systematization is to be avoided in a matter where everything in the final analysis depends on an exact and equitable weighing of factual circumstances which call for many and often very delicate distinctions.

Again, to understand the exact direction of international practice, account must be taken of certain considerations of political expediency by which it has often been guided. It will be observed, for example, that States have been willing enough to moderate their claims when the events from which their nationals had suffered,

103 Charles Cheney Hyde, *International Law*, vol. II, pp. 986-987.

104 See on this point the carefully differentiated conclusions set out in Max Huber's Reports, British Claims in the Spanish Zone of Morocco.

though they betokened a lapse of authority, were only of short duration or occurred in generally well-ordered countries. They appear to have been stricter where there was reason to believe that their abstention might put a premium on negligence or anarchy.[105] In this attitude, which is often the upshot of a purely political calculation of the safeguards that the claimant State proposes to secure for the future, the habitual or general diligence of the accused State counts for as much as its present responsibility.

The judicial evaluation of this form of responsibility at times reflects similar preoccupations. These can be discerned in certain decisions of the Claims Commissions condemning the failure to prosecute in cases of attack on the person and property of foreigners. Often the object was less to indemnify the victims or their heirs than to summon the local authorities to a stricter respect for their international duty to punish crime. Thus these decisions display a more or less avowed penal character.[106]

Still more clearly political are some treaty regulations and even some arbitral conventions which for various reasons make exceptions to the common law of responsibility. Among these are clauses mutually exonerating the parties responsible for damage caused to aliens in the course of revolutionary events; clauses providing for equitable settlement that sometimes extend the common law of responsibility; and reciprocal agreements for indemnification incorporated in a general diplomatic settlement. There are also numerous decisions, apparently unilateral and spontaneous, but often in fact negotiated, in which a State declares that, though not bound to grant indemnities, it deems it good to do so, either *ex gratia*, or from a desire to preserve good relations with another State.[107]

The classical theory of international responsibility rests on the distinction between acts of State organs, necessarily imputable to the State, and acts of a private character for which the State is not responsible unless it fails in its own duties by act or omission

105 Frederick Sherwood Dunn, *The Protection of Nationals*, pp. 159 seq.

106 Cf. the case of Laura M. B. Janes before the United States–Mexico Claims Commission, *Opinions of Commissioners*, November 16, 1926, p. 108; Charles De Visscher, *Le Déni de justice en Droit international, Rec. A.D.I.*, vol. 52 (1935), pp. 413-414; Herbert W. Briggs, *The Law of Nations, Cases, Documents and Notes*, 1938, pp. 642-643; J. Personnaz, *La Réparation du Préjudice en Droit international public*, pp. 276 seq.

107 G. Berlia, "La guerre civile et la responsabilité de l'Etat," *Revue Générale de Droit international public*, 1937, pp. 60 seq.

imputable to it. Certainly the application of this principle of imputation is an entirely logical operation, in the sense that it proceeds directly from a rule of law.[108] But rule and imputation are conditional upon the possibility of establishing between State and private activities a distinction that accords with the reality of things. The distinction is easily made in the case of States with liberal constitutions; but it has been obscured and perverted by the practices of totalitarian States. These practices have shown that unlawful acts might be the work of organizations closely associated with the political activity of the government, even at times organically connected with the government. It would appear difficult to exempt the State from the legal consequences of acts committed by a party which the law declares to be "indissolubly united with the State";[109] and still more difficult when a single party holds the real power, and the government, nominal seat of authority, is in fact subordinate to it.

.The question reopened by the anomaly of these relations is not that of the value of the traditional distinction as a principle; it is the conditions of imputation, given certain new political realities.

The question was raised in connection with the enterprises undertaken by national-socialist organizations in various countries, particularly Switzerland.[110] It also came to the fore in connection with the boycott organized in China against Japan in 1931-1932. The Japanese Government held the Chinese Government responsible, by reason of the close bonds between it and the Kuomintang (Chinese National Party).[111]

108 D. Anzilotti, *Cours de droit international*, tr. Gidel, p. 254; R. Ago, *Le Délit international*, *Rec. A.D.I.*, vol. 68 (1939), p. 450.

109 See, for the German National-Socialist Party, the Reich laws of July 14 and September 1, 1933.

110 Following the kidnapping of Berthold Jakob, where Switzerland's offer of arbitration was rejected, the federal authorities on June 21, 1935, enacted a decree aimed at official acts performed without right for a foreign State. This ordained punishment for any person who, without authorization, performed in Swiss territory acts that are normally the office of the public authorities. The interventions of the Nazi Party in Austria were the object of similar complaints recorded in the Brown Book published at Vienna in 1933.

111 The Lytton Commission's Report put the question clearly: "What is the responsibility of a government which is practically an organ of the controlling political party of the country?" Cf. C. L. Bouvé, "The National Boycott as an International Delinquency," *A.J.I.L.*, 1934, p. 19; Lawrence Preuss, "International Responsibility for Hostile Propaganda against Foreign States," *ibid.*, p. 649; W. Friedmann, "The Growth of State Control over the Individual, and Its Effect upon the Rules of International State Responsibility," *B.Y.B.I.L.*, 1938, p. 118.

These problems are new. They throw a bright line on the effects that differences in internal political structure may have on the application of international law, when they involve a displacement of the center of gravity of power. There is no doubt that they may result in a disequilibrium in the reciprocal relations of States, some of which, by reason of their totalitarian organization, assume responsibilities which are avoided by others. Along with an exceptional growth of internal power goes logically an extension of international responsibilities. Moreover, certain fundamental anomalies make it necessary to note the absence of any complete community of law.

There is no established practice clarifying the consequences of these structural differences or making it possible to state them in legal terms. They are charged with a high political potential which keeps them in the circle of general political tensions. Recent experience shows that the task of disentangling them becomes more difficult as these tensions grow in scope and gravity. They lose their individuality and their particular contours and escape all legal criteria.

The diffusion of political ideologies by propaganda conducted in more or less indirect or disguised forms by certain governments has provided matter for discussions of the same order. The problem is not new. It goes back at least to the beginning of the nineteenth century, when defense against the propagation of the French revolutionary ideology was one of the objects of the Holy Alliance.[112] But its elements have been drastically changed by the combination of two factors—one, the establishment of political regimes determined to spread their ideology beyond their own frontiers, and which at home control all expressions of opinion; the other, the technical progress of radio organized either as a monopoly or public service, or as an institution financed and supervised by the State.

A State whose constitution and liberal traditions forbid it to obstruct the free expression of thought will not incur the same political and legal responsibilities as a totalitarian State whose regime is on the contrary based upon the constant control of opinion. Further, responsibility will vary with the extent of control inherent in each mode of diffusion. In regard to the press, the liberty which is traditional in nontotalitarian countries generally relieves the State of any responsibility; but this is not so in regard

[112] On these precedents see Vernon Van Dyke, "The Responsibility of States for International Propaganda," *A.J.I.L.*, 1940, p. 58.

to radio communications, which in one way or another are everywhere under public control.[113]

What importance is to be assigned here to the excuse of necessity? Necessity assumes a collision of interests in themselves entirely legitimate and legally recognized, but which by a conjuncture of circumstances are in such conflict that one of them cannot be protected or preserved except at the cost of the other. Is international responsibility qualified by the excuse of a necessity that drives one State deliberately to sacrifice the right of another to the protection of its own interests when it regards these as bound up with its own preservation? The question, which is more prominent in doctrine than in the views officially expressed by governments, brings out with particular sharpness the conflict between the demands of politics on the one hand and law on the other.

In fact, the cases in which governments have specifically pleaded necessity in the proper sense of the term are not numerous. Necessity has often been confused with self-defense, for the distinction, though clear in theory, is at times very delicate in practice.

The theory of necessity is at bottom nothing more than the application of an old idea about a fundamental and absolute right of the State to self-preservation (*Selbsterhaltungsrecht*). For minds initiated in the immemorial traditions of the reason of State, there is nothing surprising in the fact that at moments of high tension politics finds in this idea justification for sacrificing to its demands the rights of the weak. From this point of view, the only condition required is an inequality in the ratio of strength sufficient to enable one who takes advantage of it to fend off a reaction that would rob him of the profits of his enterprise. This is something that should put men of law on their guard against a rehabilitation of the excuse of necessity, which, in spite of all their efforts, would lead to the confusion of politics and law.[114]

113 The States signatory to the Convention of September 23, 1936, on the use of radio in the cause of peace, assumed the obligation to prohibit in their territory the broadcasting of communications likely to compromise good international relations, to incite to war, or to endanger security and order. Cf. A. Raestad, "Le Projet de Convention sur la Radiodiffusion et la Paix," *Revue de Droit international et de Législation comparée*, 1935, p. 289.

114 In its judgment of April 9, 1949 (Case of the Corfu Channel, Merits), the International Court of Justice pronounced itself in very general terms against recourse to procedures of self-help. It rejected the defense in its application to territory, holding that between independent States respect for territorial sovereignty is one of the essential bases of international relations. For various

Here, as in many other matters, the false analogies of municipal law have helped to mislead some authors. In the municipal order the plea of necessity, admitted by way of exception in accordance with a legally recognized hierarchy of values, is sometimes authorized under the strict control of the courts. In the international order national individualisms are fundamentally opposed to the recognition of such a hierarchy of values, the more so as the stake in the conflict between them becomes more highly political. In the collision of truly vital interests, when the political or economic future of the State is really at stake, the present structure of international relations provides no legal justification for the claim of one State to prefer its own preservation to that of another State. Such extreme tensions between political interest and law cannot be judged in terms of subjective rights. So long as in these questions of vital interest international organization does not succeed in substituting for still primitive self-help the consideration of higher collective interests capable of expression on the plane of law, we must leave to politics what the law is powerless to regulate.

Seemingly more substantial, because it is linked with the quasi anarchy of international relations in their present configuration, is the consideration that, since States have the right to resort to war to preserve themselves, they must a fortiori have the right of recourse to less grave procedures; *in plus stat minus*. This reasoning, however, presupposes the liberty of States to go to war. Such a liberty is not regarded, even by the classical positivist school, as a faculty granted by the legal order, but rather as a consequence, implicit and independent of law, of the present structure of international relations. The error of those who defend the excuse of necessity is that they assign to this a positive legal quality, necessity figuring in their theory as a circumstance removing or attenuating international responsibility.[115]

Duly established, responsibility entails reparation or satisfaction. As distinct from reparations, measures of satisfaction may be indi-

---

views and further discussion, see Charles De Visscher, "Les Lois de la Guerre et la théorie de la nécessité," *Revue générale de droit international public*, 1917, p. 74; D. Anzilotti, *Cours de droit international*, tr. Gidel, p. 507; K. Strupp, *Völkerrechtliches Delikt*, p. 120; V. Borsi, "Ragione di guerra e stato di necessità," *Rivista di diritto internazionale*, 1916, p. 157; A. Cavaglieri, *Corso di diritto internazionale*, 1932, pp. 435 seq.; Robert Ago, *Le Délit international*, *Rec. A.D.I.*, vol. 68 (1939), pp. 540 seq.

[115] Cf. D. Anzilotti, *Cours de droit international*, tr. Gidel, pp. 511-512; Robert Ago, *Le Délit international*, *op.cit.*, pp. 542-543.

cated when there has been a direct attack, real or averred, upon the personality of the State as such. This characteristic explains the importance of political considerations in the context. The same facts which in a period of political tension will be taken as an attack upon the State's honor may be considered negligible between countries united by bonds of confidence and friendship. The concern of the injured State, moreover, is not limited to the reparation of the wrong suffered; it looks rather to the future, aiming to prevent repetition of the acts or practices complained of. For this reason the exemplary function of satisfaction often takes the foreground.[116] The sensitive political interests that come into play here explain the extreme difficulty, if not impossibility, of abstracting from these precedents any rules capable of uniform application.

The predominance of these political elements long withheld from arbitral or judicial settlement disputes arising out of illicit acts regarded as attacks upon the honor and dignity of the State. It also was the source of the most flagrant abuses in the direct settlement of such disputes, such as humiliating satisfactions made possible by the disproportion of strengths, and pecuniary reparations out of all proportion to the injury suffered.[117]

It is entirely different when the injured State agrees to submit the dispute to impartial decision by arbiter or judge, thus robbing it of sentimental virulence and political overtones. Without denying the psychological role of satisfaction in general, or excluding the mixed character—at once compensatory and penal—of some of its forms, and above all without making any claim to an exact proportion which could not be attained in this nonmaterial context, international case-law has sought to keep the demands of the wronged State within limits suggested by a sense of equity and by experience in international affairs. In the case of the "Carthage" and the "Manouba," the Permanent Court of Arbitration rejected the French Government's claim for a sum of 100,000 francs specified as sanction for the moral and political prejudice resulting from the violation of international law, and declared that the mere finding, particularly in an arbitral award, that such a violation had been committed was in itself sufficient sanction. This precedent was followed by the International Court of Justice when, in the Corfu

116 J. Personnaz, *La réparation du préjudice en droit international public*, p. 323.

117 Italy's demands on Greece in 1923 following the attack on the Tellini mission are a typical example.

Channel case, it dealt with the Albanian Government's complaint that the British navy had encroached upon its sovereignty.[118]

No branch of law reflects more clearly the transformations of power. Responsibility is the counterpart in the legal order of the enlargement of functions and expansion of powers of the modern State. Daily applications of the principle, now by governments themselves, now by arbitral and judicial tribunals, define the duties of the territorial authority in the direct relations of States and in the treatment of aliens. They contribute much to the progress of international law.

Section V

Recourse to Force. Armed Reprisals. War and Neutrality

Individual resort to force is the typical manifestation of the persistent individualism of international relations. The present impossibility of eliminating it results from the absence of an effective international organization and constitutes the major obstacle to the establishment of international relations ordered by law.

Politics long ago accommodated itself to this state of affairs. Doctrine has not been able to do so without falling into an internal contradiction. It is not possible at one and the same time to base international relations upon the independent existence of States and to concede to each State the sovereign right to take up arms to attack or destroy that independence. We must however distinguish individual resort to force in general from the legitimacy of its use in a given case. In this connection the positivist doctrine has professed an indifference to moral considerations which, even from the point of view of its particular method, which consists in the observation of facts, is by no means justified. Renouncing any attempt to adduce from the historical causes of wars a satisfactory principle of distinction, it has held it possible to treat recourse to war as a simple fact, as a neutral or extra-legal act. This is one example among many of the distortions produced by a shortsighted technique. Neither opinion nor governments are indifferent to the moral justification of recourse to war. Nothing is more striking than the constant care of governments to find moral reasons for such recourse—reasons that can excite in the masses that collective zeal without which any warlike enterprise is doomed to failure.

118 Judgment of April 9, 1949, Reports, 1949, p. 36.

Prevention of individual resort to armed force is the essential objective of international organization, and one cannot reasonably dispute the considerable place of moral factors in such a movement. But it is true that other forces move in the opposite direction; that these draw their strength from the age-old traditions of the nation-State; and that, to bring about the abandonment of a prerogative so closely bound up with the individualist conception of sovereignty as is the right of war will certainly require something more than the signature of conventions, however solemn they may be, between States. This will not be achieved without fundamental reforms of structure which in turn presuppose a radical change of mentality and postulate, in the last analysis, the abolition of national sovereignties.

§ 1. *MEASURES OF COERCION, MORE ESPECIALLY ARMED REPRISALS*

The historical evolution of armed reprisals reveals on the one hand the bonds that link the internal organization of States with the development of international law, and on the other the convergences and the tensions between politics and law in international relations.

Originally, even armed reprisals were in large part private. The individual, victim in a foreign country of an act contrary to law, and refused justice, could obtain from his sovereign letters of mark and reprisals which authorized him to indemnify himself from the goods of the foreigner who had caused him damage, and even indiscriminately from those of the wrongdoer's compatriots. A relic of private justice, reprisals were based upon collective responsibility, responsibility from which the group freed itself by rendering justice to the alien, but which it confirmed by denying him justice. The institution of private reprisals is thus seen to be closely linked to the weakness of the central authority. When, at the end of the eighteenth century, consolidation and concentration of political powers enabled the State on the one hand to assume the direct and exclusive protection of its nationals abroad and, on the other, to guarantee aliens the regular administration of an impartial justice, private reprisals lost all justification and disappeared.

Reserved thenceforth to the State, armed reprisals took on a double character in the course of the nineteenth century: they became separated from war, but they never lost their political quality.

The nineteenth century was the classic age of reprisals, as of all measures of so-called pacific coercion (blockade, embargo, boycott, occupation of territory, seizure of the property of aliens). In the practice of this period, armed reprisals were measures of constraint taken against a State, in time of peace, in order to induce it, by acts intrinsically hostile but not constitutive of a state of war, to bow to the will of another State. They were defended first as a manifestation, and after all a moderate manifestation, of a sovereign right, that of resort to armed force. Limiting the use of arms to a circumscribed objective, reprisals made it unnecessary to set up a real state of war which might inaugurate an era of unbridled violence and of indefinite demands. Also pleaded by way of justification was the real or alleged impossibility, by other means, of stopping practices contrary to the law or obtaining the satisfaction which the injured State could legitimately claim.

In fact, resort to armed reprisals was a matter of pure political opportunism, for it depended essentially on the existing balance of strength. Reprisals were par excellence the arm of the strong against the weak. The States resorting to them were those powerful enough not to have to fear a riposte that might lead to war. Even so, reprisals were able to retain the ambiguous label of measures of peaceful coercion (measures short of war) only so long as no sufficiently powerful third State challenged those employing them to choose between dropping them and instituting a regular state of war. That is the lesson to be drawn from the experience of the so-called pacific blockade, especially from the coercive action against Venezuela (1902-1903), where the transition from peaceful blockade to war blockade was decided wholly by the attitude of the United States.[119]

The use of armed reprisals implied not only this inequality of strength between the State resorting to them and the State suffering them. Politically, they could be continued only so long as the great Powers themselves regarded them as compatible with the state of their mutual relations. When, with the growing intensity of their rivalries in all parts of the world, they saw in armed reprisals a threat to their interests or to peace, they were led first to limit and then to proscribe them in the name of the law. Here again the reaction on the moral and legal plane coincided with a transformation in political relations which can be dated from the first years of the twentieth century.

The high political tensions that have marked the whole first half of the century have aggravated the dangers of war inherent in in-

[119] Cf. J. Basdevant, "L'action anglo-germano-italienne contre le Venezuela (1902-1903)," *Revue générale de Droit international public*, 1904, pp. 420 seq.

dividual recourse to armed reprisals and have, in fact, rendered this rarer. The procedure of limited-objective constraint has lost its attractions in the prospect of a world conflagration.

The impossibility of reconciling armed reprisals in time of peace with the regime instituted by the Covenant of the League of Nations became clearly apparent on the occasion of the coercive action taken by Italy against Greece. None of the reasons which might have justified them in the past had any place in the new legal order, and there could be little doubt that the reasons advanced on this occasion were irreconcilable with the precise obligations imposed by Articles 12 to 15 of the Covenant.[120]

However that may be, the United Nations Charter left no uncertainty on this point: it does not limit itself to prohibiting recourse to war; it requires the members in general to "refrain in their international relations from the threat or use of force" (Art. 2, para. 4).

It nevertheless remains true that reprisals, like other modes of individual coercion, will from the political point of view lose their significance and their *raison d'être* only when the international organization becomes capable of replacing them with appropriate collective action.

§ 2. WAR

War, in its principle as in its effects, is the supreme demonstration of the role of force as agent of change in international relations. Much less even than municipal law does international law pretend to eliminate the natural play of forces in social evolution. Every day the anonymous action of irrepressible and often pitiless economic forces molds the interests and modifies the position of States, and the resulting supremacies by no means always correspond to any moral superiority. But the generally slow and gradual changes thus brought about are compatible with a minimum of order. International law can either attempt to subordinate them, or tolerate them without belying itself. It cannot accommodate itself to war; it cannot treat it as an irrelevant or extra-legal fact, much less as an element of the legal order, without failing its essential mission,

[120] Cf. Charles De Visscher, "L'interprétation du Pacte au lendemain du différend italo-grec," *Revue de Droit international et de Législation comparée*, 1924, pp. 213, 377. As everyone knows, the answer given on this point by the Committee of Jurists set up by the Council of the League was inadequate. Cf. the resolutions voted by the Institute of International Law (1934), *Annuaire*, 1934, pp. 1-166, pp. 623-694, pp. 708-711; A. Verdross, *Rec. A.D.I.*, vol. 30 (1929), pp. 493-496.

which is to ensure order by regulating the social use of force, and without contradicting one of its fundamental principles, namely respect for the personality and independence of States.

Doctrine has taken cognizance of this capital function of law whenever wars, by their frequency or their scope, have taken on the aspect of a formidable threat to humanity as a whole. It was shamefully indifferent to it in the nineteenth-century era of calm, to the point of making no attempt to subordinate political decision to moral values. Adaptation to the fact was the final word of the positivist school. For it war was to be merely a fact. Indifferent to its causes, law was to concern itself only with the consequences that it attached to war, and these were to be considered independent not only of any declaration of war but even of the most solemn engagements prohibiting recourse to armed force. Nowhere can better ground be found for the reproach of insincerity (*Geist der Unwahrheit*) that von Gagern brings against international law.[121]

Fixed in this "defeatist" attitude,[122] international law, drawn along in the wake of the governments, found itself in a blind alley. The two Hague Conferences applied themselves to regulating hostilities, to enclosing in the rules of their conventions an enterprise of force that will never know any law but that of success or political interest. Thus they tied their fate to a military technique whose evolution was destined in a few years to annihilate the labored compromises of violence and humanity.

The two world wars scattered most of these illusions. They also threw light upon the character of total war and the changes that it works in the relations between politics and recourse to war.

The unlimited forces that it looses mean that total war has taken on the absolute form of which its nineteenth-century theorists, especially von Clausewitz, had foreseen the possibility. Made possible by the mastery of power over the moral and material resources of the nation, prepared for in peace by extending State controls to everything needed for the conduct of hostilities, characterized by a technique of mass destruction that excludes any distinction

[121] *Critik des Völkerrechts*, p. 181.

[122] J. L. Brierly, *The Outlook for International Law*, p. 51. At first sight it may seem paradoxical that international law should have sought to regulate such minor uses of constraint as measures of armed coercion and have remained so long not only inactive but apparently indifferent in regard to war. The explanation, which is wholly political, lies in the bond which, in men's minds, continues to exist between recourse to the supreme trial of strength and protection of the higher interests of the nation.

between combatants and noncombatants, three-dimensional war knows neither localization to a combat zone nor restriction on means of destruction. Atomic war provides the adequate weapon for this process of annihilation.

Where von Clausewitz's foresights have been outdistanced is in the relations between politics and war. It is no longer possible to regard war as a mere political instrument or as a continuation of political action "by other means." The unlimited character of the forces loosed is matched by the obscuration of political ends. Wars were formerly up to a certain point reasoned enterprises, with limited aims, with more or less foreseeable consequences. Preserving a certain control of events, governments occasionally were moderate enough to leave even to the conquered the strength necessary for a new peaceful order. Total war knows no measure; men gradually lose mastery of it. It no longer has a clear political objective, or any foreseeable end. Its demands mold the societies that it leads to ruin. The obsession it creates persists beyond victory. This expresses itself in military controls supported by constant inspection, if not by complete occupation of the conquered country, in the establishment of artificial regimes imposed on its structure, in "reparations" designed more to guarantee the victor's security than to compensate his losses, in the appropriation of human potential by the retention of prisoners long after the end of hostilities.

Experience shows that these prolonged struggles find their own logic and energy in the forces that sustain them. They displace political objectives, transform the alliances of yesterday into tensions symptomatic of new antagonisms. Spheres hermetically sealed against any suspect penetration; satellite States, subjected to a regimen of distrust and fear; financial and military assistance the more zealous the more likely the beneficiary appears to pass over to the enemy camp—never was it more true that war feeds war.[123]

As we write these lines the military high command has openly adopted the use of atomic and thermonuclear weapons as the basis of its tactical and strategic plans of operation. It is even said to have familiarized itself with methods of destruction the advantages of which it hopes to reserve to itself. This is a normal attitude for men who are exclusively concerned with forces in being. But the world has become anxious. It is seen that we are on the way to losing control of the forces so imprudently unchained. There ap-

[123] Cf. the work of Raymond Aron, *Les Guerres en chaîne*, 1951.

pears to be no effective defense against the thermonuclear weapon. As for atomic arms, which are already considered "classical" in military circles, their actual use will depend on the chances of war. For, despite what try to be reassuring declarations (the NATO resolutions of December 18, 1954), no illusion is permissible; the responsible governments reserve the right of further deliberation, but events will place the decision in the hands of the military.

Following the Franco-British Memorandum of June 11, 1954, the United Nations, acting for the first time in this context with the unanimous agreement of the five Powers that are the permanent members of the Security Council, declared their will not only to reduce effectives and conventional armaments, but absolutely to prohibit the use and manufacture of nuclear weapons as well as all weapons of mass destruction. This was to be accomplished by means of adequate international control. (Resolution of November 4, 1954.) There is reason here for unreserved congratulations. But we still have to learn what effective disarmament means in this order of ideas. "Anguish, the human motor,"[124] may serve to start the enterprise; but only mutual confidence can bring it to a successful conclusion. If the reduction of effectives and conventional armaments seems no longer to confront major obstacles, the interdiction of atomic and especially of thermonuclear weapons has a formidable preliminary condition to surmount, namely the establishment and installation of an effective international control system. Here the very nature of the new weapons makes it necessary to rethink every detail of the problem. From the military plane the discussion passes to the political, and the best reason for hope lies perhaps in the political significance that the Soviet delegation saw in the resolution of November 4, 1954. In the atomic and still more in the thermonuclear context, control at all stages involves nothing less than real collaboration: agreement on the functions of the control agencies; agreement on the permanent presence and the powers of inspection of control agents; and agreement on the authority of these agents to order on the spot the immediate and at least temporary stoppage of any forbidden manufacture.

So strict a control demands not only the elimination of present antagonisms, but a high degree of mutual confidence constantly stimulated by clear knowledge of the common peril. It must therefore be recognized that nothing effective will be done without a

[124] Jules Moch, *La Folie des Hommes*, New York, November 1, 1954.

general and rapid relaxation in the present international relations. In its essence the problem of control is wholly political. So much so that we may well ask whether the establishment of truly effective control does not in the last analysis presuppose the abandonment of the very concept of national sovereignty and an entirely new image of the relations between the peoples.[125] Will humanity, for lack of the elementary foresight to attack the problem at a time when the general anxiety makes its solution still possible, slip down the slope to destruction?

The new weapons of mass destruction have revolutionized all the data of war, and it is above all for this reason that the jurists will be well advised to waste no further time in what some of them still persist in calling the "restatement" of the laws of war. To try to adapt these laws to the new conditions is not only labor absolutely lost; it is an enterprise that in certain of its aspects may be dangerous, as was demonstrated by the indefinite extension given in the second world war to the notion of the military objective. There is better work to be done today than picking up the fragments of an obsolete body of rules. The only laws that preserve their imprescriptible authority are the unwritten ones dictated by respect for the principles of humanity. It is directly upon these that the safeguards of the future must be built.

No less problematic in these new perspectives is the role that the security mechanism established in the United Nations Charter may continue to fill. They were not mistaken who, even in 1945, regarded the Charter just signed as overtaken by events and insisted on the urgency of remedying its defects. It is only subject to these very serious reservations that the legal idea of collective sanctions, with the implied distinction between aggression and self-defense, still has substance.

The authors of the United Nations Charter deliberately abstained from defining the terms "armed attack" (Art. 51) and "act of aggression" (Art. 39). The question was left to the Security Council, and at the time it would have seemed improper to cast any doubt upon the cohesion and authority of that body. Since then, the Soviet Government has made itself the protagonist of a defini-

125 It is significant that in its very first Report (December 31, 1946), the United Nations Atomic Energy Commission stated the opinion that the use and development of atomic energy are not questions "which are essentially within the domestic jurisdiction of any State" (Art. 2, para. 7, of the Charter).

tion enumerating facts constituting aggression, while the International Law Commission, acting on instructions from the General Assembly, has chosen, though failing to reach agreement on any of the proposed formulas, to elaborate certain abstract or synthetic definitions, too vague to be useful, but having at least the merit of being drawn up in correlation with the idea of self-defense. Aggression, in the present state of international relations, is not a concept that can be enclosed in any legal definition whatever; the finding that it has occurred in any concrete case involves political and military judgments and a subjective weighing of motives that make this in each instance a strictly individual matter. The problem has been still further complicated recently by the proposal to include in the definition of aggression the notion of so-called ideological aggression.[126]

Besides, is a definition desirable? In particular, is it desirable to make the Security Council's finding depend on a definition when it is called upon under Article 39 of the Charter to determine the existence of an act of aggression, and especially to force into a definition the "right of self-defense" against "an armed attack" reserved in Article 51? This has been disputed, not without good reason. It has been pointed out that one enumeration which proclaimed itself exhaustive did not include what is now probably the most important form of aggression, namely the indirect form, internal subversion; and that, on the other hand, certain acts that would fall under the concept of aggression might in some circumstances be justified as self-defense or as the fulfillment of a guarantee of assistance under an international treaty.

Finally, it is not demonstrated that any system of definition whatever, especially since it would by no means imply automatic sanctions,[127] would facilitate the task of the Security Council, or that it would prevent the recurrence of certain abusive interpretations of the right of self-defense, on the pretext of "vital interests," that accompanied the conclusion of the Briand-Kellogg Pact.[128] On

[126] Cf. the observations by Mr. Fitzmaurice, delegate of the United Kingdom, in the Sixth Committee of the General Assembly, sixth session, January 9, 1952. The so-called ideological forms of aggression are most often really aspects of subversion. They were studied in the Report of the Special Committee of the United Nations set up to examine the definition of aggression (August 24–September 21, 1953).

[127] N. Politis, General Commission of the Disarmament Conference, May 24, 1933.

[128] Cf. Emile Giraud, *La théorie de la légitime défense*, *Rec. A.D.I.*, vol. 49 (1933), p. 738.

the contrary, it has become clear that certain definitions would provide the aggressor with the means of transferring the odium of aggression to the resistance offered by his victim. But the theme, inexhaustible in the food that it offers for the speculative spirit and for mutual suspicions, will not soon disappear from the assembly agendas.

Whatever may be the opinion on this point, one fact is clear: the notion of aggression is broader than that of aggressive or offensive war. The impossibility of limiting it to the traditional relations of belligerency was demonstrated in the Sino-Japanese conflict of 1931-1933, which, though marked by clear-cut military operations, was not represented by either party as constituting a state of war.[129] That the tolerance of which the aggressor took advantage at the time was promoted by the policy of certain great Powers as well as by the weakness of the existing collective organs, is of little importance; the paradoxical situation that developed was in flagrant contradiction with the principles of the Covenant as it would be now with those of the Charter. Such a situation may nevertheless reflect a clear-cut political reality, and the intentionally equivocal positions taken in the circumstances by some governments cannot be regarded a priori as senseless or irrelevant. Baffling as peace itself sometimes is, modern war, which tends to the absolute in its methods of destruction, is at times only relative in its political ends. Inversely, it may be limited in its field of operations and the arms employed without losing anything of the unlimited character of its final objective. The war in Korea is an example.[130]

The concept of aggression, which is wider than that of offensive war, is also better adapted to the multifarious processes of the ideologically inspired "cold war." This last has its peculiar ends, such as internal subversion; its own psychological instruments, for instance a message of national redemption or social regeneration addressed to masses disappointed by peace or terrified at the prospect of a new conflagration; its own technique, silent and insidious, adapted to the institutions and public spirit of each country as well as to the appetites of a society sick for revolution. More or less disguised participation in an internal struggle, economic war, ideological propaganda: the whole procedure, now so well known, leads to the seizure of power by the revolutionary party and forces

[129] G. Schwarzenberger, *Bulletin international des Sciences sociales*, vol. 1, no. 3-4, p. 64.

[130] Fritz Grob, *The Relativity of War and Peace*, 1949, pp. 189 seq.

opinion into conformity with slogans imported from abroad. It confirms everything said above about the increasing impossibility of drawing a sharp line between the internal institutions of States and their external relations and independence. In this aspect it is highly revealing of the evolution in the reciprocal relations between society and the State.

Limited in its means, subversion threatens the independence of the nation in its most fundamental possessions: its cultural, social, and political values. In this global objective it differs sharply from intervention as that was known in the nineteenth century; for even when its motives were political, intervention involved nothing more than occasional pressures for limited objectives.

The organization of collective defense against subversion is one of the objects pursued under pressure from the United States by the diplomacy of the Western Powers. The essential political problem that it presents is to make this organization really effective without slipping into a policy of constant intervention in the domestic affairs of the associated or of other States. The objections raised in the negotiation of the Southeast Asia Pact (S.A.C.D.T.), and the application to recent quarrels between Central American countries (Guatemala, Nicaragua, Costa Rica) of the directives issued by the Pan-American Conference at Caracas (1954), throw a bright light upon these contradictory aspects of the struggle against subversion.

§ 3. NEUTRALITY

Neutrality is closely bound to war; both have developed historically along the individualist paths of sovereignty.[131] Like war, traditional neutrality was left to the discretion of States; as in regard to war, international law confined itself to regulating the practice of neutrality without pronouncing on its legality. But since the right of war was undisputed, and its exercise in fact reserved to the strongest, nonbelligerents could never, in the name of neutrality, set up against them an equal right to complete immunity. In fact, primacy belonged to war; the precarious safeguards of neutrality were always subject to its demands.

Wars were formerly limited both in the means brought into play and in the number of States taking part. The rights and duties of neutrality tended to preserve this limited character. Individually,

[131] Cf. J. P. A. François, *Handboek van het Volkenrecht, Tweede deel*, pp. 475-476.

States sought in neutrality a safeguard against the risk of being drawn into hostilities. From a general point of view, neutrality was deemed to satisfy the interests of the neutrals' private commerce and facilitate localization of the conflict. Today, neutrality is impaired in its unity of status, and in the protection that it offers to neutral commerce. It is weakened to the core, sometimes even before the opening of hostilities, by submission to the imperatives of modern war.

1. The Wearing Away of the Legal Regime of Neutrality. Differential Neutralities. The legal status of neutrals remained ill defined, precarious, and generally subordinate to the claims of the belligerents until the moment when, at the end of the eighteenth century, there arose in the New World a Power sure enough of itself and far enough removed from European conflicts to make isolation, and hence strict abstention, the essential mark of neutrality. "It can be said that in its final form the regime of neutrality bears very clearly the American imprint."[132]

Because it was on the whole an era of relative tranquility when wars were infrequent and limited; because it was also an era of liberalism, profoundly attached to the distinction between State and private activities, and to the preservation of commercial freedoms, the nineteenth century was the golden age of neutrality. The First Hague Conference (1899), which reflected its spirit, did not limit itself to defining the rights and duties of neutrality; it assigned to "Powers strangers to the dispute" a truly international mission by recognizing their "right to offer . . . even during the course of hostilities," and on their own initiative, their good offices or mediation to the States at war, and by stipulating that the exercise of this right could not be regarded by either party to the dispute as "an unfriendly act." This was in the nature of a recognition of the moral vocation of neutrals, and at the same time a prototype of the procedures laid down in the Covenant of the League of Nations.[133]

This pacific vocation of the neutrals did not survive the test of two world wars. It may even be said that the conventional consolidation of the law of neutrality by the Conference of 1907 came at a time when political threats and the resources of military and naval technique had already robbed it of much of its efficacy.

[132] N. Politis, *La Neutralite et la Paix*, p. 45.

[133] First Convention, Art. 3. Cf. Philip C. Jessup, "The Birth, Death and Re-Incarnation of Neutrality," *A.J.I.L.*, 1932, p. 789, and, by the same author, "Neutrality, Its History, Economics and Law" (1936), vol. IV: *To-day and To-morrow.*

The last world conflict was marked by a desperate effort on the part of some States to cling to traditional neutrality and demonstrated the impossibility of practicing it according to the principles and in the spirit of the institution.

Generalized political tensions, after arraying the great Powers in opposing camps, drew them one after another into the war. Thus the forces which during the peaceful interlude of the nineteenth century had for an instant inclined towards neutrals turned back again towards the belligerents.[134] This is a fact of the first importance, which can no longer be regarded as accidental. Under the pressure of wars that were at once general in participation and total in the means employed, the neutrals saw the two primary interests of neutrality sacrificed—their territorial integrity and the maintenance of the commercial relations of their nationals. In 1914 the violation of a neutral State's territory had still called forth the world's reprobation. Before 1939 the European political tension had risen to such a height that the passage through and occupation of neutral countries had entered the expectations of the masses as well as the calculations of the chancelleries. They were no longer thought of as anything but an episode in a general war.

But above all, war, following the natural progressive tendency already pointed out by Clausewitz, attacks more than the military resources of the enemy. It aims at isolating the enemy economically, and on this terrain collides directly with the traditional liberties of neutrals.[135] On the economic potential made up not only of the commerce but also of the total national wealth of the neutrals, the belligerents put pressures which, especially in the case of contiguous and weak States, end in real economic dependence. Hence the adoption of new practices—sometimes renewed from the wars of the seventeenth and eighteenth centuries—that replaced the common law of neutrality with a mass of particular treaty regulations. Many neutral States, abandoning the terrain of law for that of political expediency, bowed to the demands of the belligerents by having their legislatures enact a series of measures that brought them in, indirectly but often effectively, as partners in the commercial controls of the belligerents. Others, by agreements painfully negotiated

[134] On the historical causes that explain the favor shown to neutrality in the nineteenth century and the consolidation of its legal regime, see J. L. Brierly, *The Outlook for International Law*, 1945, pp. 26-32.

[135] W. P. J. A. van Royen, *Analyse du problème de la neutralité au cours de l'évolution du droit des gens*, pp. 89 seq.

with the belligerents, contracted onerous obligations which on pretext of economic impartiality substantially changed the normal direction of their foreign trade. In the years preceding the second world war, the United States itself, notwithstanding its power and complete economic independence, was seen sacrificing to the fear of war its best-established traditions, thus bearing witness to its lack of faith that the legitimate interests of neutrality could be vindicated by law.[186]

Thus the homogeneous system which the Hague Conference thought that it had finally consolidated gradually crumbled. Nothing more starkly reveals the deterioration of a legal institution, to the advantage of political influences, than this replacement of a general body of rules by particular practices resulting from individual pressures.[187]

Recent practice has departed from the classical system of neutrality in other ways as well. The classical system was characterized by the strict impartiality which, at least theoretically, the neutrals were bound to observe in a conflict whose origins were held to be legally indifferent. As practiced under the League of Nations, on the basis of interpretations of Article 16 of the Covenant, neutrality tended to assume a differential character involving inequalities in the treatment of belligerents. Good will and partiality, excluded by the Hague Conventions, re-entered the law of neutrality. Though it is difficult to determine the respective parts of politics and law in this development, it is reasonable to think that there was too much haste in crediting the change with a clear-cut moral and legal meaning. For most States differential treatment was a product of the fear of war and invasion, historical affinities, or economic dependcncc.

By a singular irony, it was in a war expressly condemned by the League of Nations and marked by the application of collective sanctions that one of the last cases is to be found where the traditional rules of neutrality were more or less regularly applied. In the course of the Italian-Ethiopian war, third States, even some that were members of the League of Nations, observed in their relations

186 Cf. Charles G. Fenwick, *American Neutrality, Trial and Failure*, pp. 40 seq.

187 R. Cassin, *Présent et Avenir de la Neutralité*; *l'Esprit international*, 1940, p. 57: "Under a uniform denomination, neutrality now covers different situations, creating for neutral States rights and duties that are not identical. In Europe alone there can be discerned almost as many kinds of neutrality as there are neutral States."

with the two parties the rules concerning neutrality in war by land as by sea or by air.[188]

The failure of the sanctions ordered on this occasion was the reason for the rehabilitation of neutrality in Europe in the months preceding the second world war. This was a superficial movement, due in part to the disappointment of the hopes that had been placed in collective security and in part to the calculating intent of some governments to conciliate that one of the potential aggressors which seemed most to be feared. This neoneutrality, which in the most directly exposed States was at times very far from the practice of traditional neutrality, crumbled in contact with the realities of war no later than the month of May 1940.[139]

In the jurisdictional sphere, the failure of the collective security system was emphasized in a series of communications addressed early in September 1939 by the governments of the United Kingdom and the Commonwealth countries, and by the French Government, to the Secretary-General of the League of Nations. These governments informed the Secretary-General that their acceptance of the optional clause in Article 36 of the Statute of the Permanent Court of International Justice (compulsory jurisdiction) would not operate in regard to disputes arising out of events that might occur in the war. They defended the decision with the observation that their acceptance without reservation for wartime had been given in the hope that the Covenant of the League of Nations and the Pact of Paris would lead to a radical change in the old conceptions of war and neutrality. This hope had not been realized. The League of Nations had been forced to admit in 1938 the impossibility of replacing war with a collective-security system involving the compulsory settlement of all disputes, while on the other hand numerous States had from the beginning of the conflict proclaimed their neutrality in terms that implied a pure and simple return to the traditional status of neutrals.

188 See Charles Rousseau, "Le conflit italo-éthiopien," *Revue générale de Droit international public*, 1937, pp. 725 seq.

139 There is a significant instance of the division of minds at this time in the two drafts published by the Harvard Committee in 1939 on the rights and duties of States in the event of war. The first started from the classical idea that every war produces the same legal effects for belligerents and neutrals. The second sought to define *de lege ferenda* the rights and duties of States in case of aggression, which was defined as resort to force in violation of treaty obligations. In the spirit of the Covenant of the League of Nations and of the Briand-Kellogg Pact, it authorized third States to make broad use of discriminatory procedures against the aggressor. *Harvard Research*, pp. 167 seq., 823 seq.

2. Neutrality in Maritime War. The classical law of neutrality in maritime war was a compromise between the commercial liberty of the neutrals and the interests of the belligerents, a compromise which itself presupposed the distinction between public and private activities. Sea transportation to the enemy was considered a private venture, undertaken by the carrier at his risk and peril, abstention and impartiality being held State duties that were not incumbent on individuals.[140] The fact that the neutral State was not responsible for the operations carried on by its nationals protected it against the risk of being drawn into the war. It kept watch that the belligerents did not exceed the rights acquired by instituting a blockade or given for the control of contraband and unneutral aid. But the interests involved were limited, and even an energetic insistence on freedom of trade rarely exposed it to anything more than diplomatic argument which did not go to the length of imperiling its neutrality.

This balance, which was delicate enough, was compromised by the change in the relations between the individual and the State, by the gradual effacement of private enterprise by official controls. Neutral trade did not recover its traditional safeguards by the change, which on the other hand considerably increased the risks and responsibilities of neutral States.

This development in the first place took the form during the war of 1914-1918 of a gradual elimination, if not in law at least in fact, of the distinction between absolute and conditional contraband and an extension of the notion of continuous voyage or final destination of goods. It was essentially by taking advantage of broader State controls in both neutral and enemy countries, and of the correlative difficulty of distinguishing between goods destined for civilian populations and those destined for the armed forces, that the Allies gradually succeeded in depriving of all practical value the distinction between the two categories of contraband articles and in replacing it with a general economic encirclement characterized by the seizure of any article of enemy origin, ownership, or destination.[141]

140 "Neutrals who carry contraband do not break the law of nations; they run a risk for adequate gain, and if they are caught, they take the consequences." The "Prins der Nederlanden" (1921), Privy Council, B. and C. Prize Cases, vol. III, p. 951. Cf. the Privy Council's decision in the "Monte Contes" case (1943), Lloyd's Reports, Second Series, vol. I, p. 152.

141 Cf. *inter alia* the Note of February 17, 1915 addressed by Sir Edward Grey to the Government of the United States, and the opinion of Sir Samuel Evans in the case of the "Kim" (1915), Privy Council, B. and C. Prize Cases, vol. I, p. 405 and especially pp. 490-491.

These innovations, which robbed neutral maritime trade of most of its traditional protections, were defended as an adaptation of the rules to a new situation characterized by the broadening of official controls and the return of the belligerents to the armed-nation regime.[142] The adaptation was all the more legitimate, it was said, because great naval wars occur only at long intervals and between them profound changes may radically alter the factual conditions that determine the methods of war at sea. In this process of change technical factors have had their part, but there is no doubt that the extension of State controls has since 1914 been the preponderant factor.[143]

The most significant and most radical feature of the war of economic encirclement conducted by the maritime Powers against their enemies was the extension of the notion of contraband of war by the rationing of certain neutral countries. These were the neutrals which, by reason especially though not exclusively of their proximity to enemy or enemy-controlled territory, were considered able to reship to such territory in processed or unprocessed form part of the goods imported by sea. This method, introduced in the first world war, relies upon statistics, and starts from the idea that imports of conditional contraband that markedly exceed the needs of the importing neutral country, all circumstances being taken into account for each class of goods, are presumed to have an enemy destination. Supported by statistics alone, this deduction legalizes seizure, and, though by itself it is probably insufficient ground for condemnation, it reveals the bearing of the general movement of imports on the individual risk of the carrier or owner of the goods.[144]

142 "The crux of the whole matter lay in the question of the relations of the neutral national to his own Government." V. M. S. Crichton, "The Prewar Theory of Neutrality," *B.Y.B.I.L.*, 1928, p. 105. Cf. the memorandum of the British and French Governments, July 7, 1916, justifying the abandonment of the rules of the Declaration of London (1909).

143 Cf. H. A. Smith, *Rec. A.D.I.*, vol. 63 (1938), pp. 612 seq. It is well known that as soon as it entered the war in 1917, the United States adopted the practices begun by England. See, on this subject, the curious account in Burton J. Hendrick, *The Life and Letters of Walter Hines Page*, part II, pp. 264-266, of a conversation between A. J. (later Lord) Balfour and Frank L. Polk of the Department of State.

144 See, especially, the "Kim," *op.cit.* Cf. H. A. Smith, *Rec. A.D.I.*, *op.cit.*, p. 639; G. G. Fitzmaurice, "Some Aspects of Modern Contraband Control and the Law of Prize," *B.Y.B.I.L.*, 1945, pp. 89 seq., where the author identifies the factors which in the second world war reduced the importance of naval blockade properly so called and the number of prize cases. Among these were the development of the preventive control of contraband in the neutral ports

This places upon the claimant the burden of proving innocent destination of the cargo, a proof made difficult by a general suspicion which finds its support much more in the commercial policy followed by the neutral country than in the personal behavior of the carrier or owner of the goods. Here again, individual considerations have yielded place to the collective interests and anonymous factors inherent in State controls.

The system of undertakings not to re-export, guaranteed either by the neutral State itself or by agencies under its control, "navicerts" and certificates of origin, black lists—all these are devices that have associated neutral States, whether they liked it or not, in the economic war waged by the belligerents who command the seas. Doctrine has not always understood this development. It has often confined itself either to condemning the conduct of the belligerents under criteria which experience has proved obsolete, or to noting without any elaboration the almost complete disappearance of one of the parts of international law that it formerly took delight in systematizing to the last detail. Here, as everywhere else, we can get to the bottom of things only by a study of the factors, some of them political, the others technical, that caused the change of practice; such as total war, extension of State controls in belligerent as well as neutral countries, and the facilities for processing and reshipping to the enemy.[145]

As it became more difficult to preserve, neutrality became more timid. The legislation enacted by the United States in the years before the second world war shows to what concessions a very great Power stooped in its search for peace through neutrality. The case is uniquely significant, by reason as much of the supposed geographic remoteness of the United States from the probable scene of a new conflagration as of the means at that country's disposal to exact respect for the traditional rights of neutrality. As early as 1935, surrendering to the fear of seeing the country drawn into war by incidents in the exercise of the right of visit and capture, Congress embarked on a series of so-called neutrality laws that marked a sharp retrogression in the championship of freedom of the seas.

of shipment, and substitution of requisition for confiscation of the goods seized. For French practice see André Gervais, "La jurisprudence française des prises maritimes dans la seconde guerre mondiale," *Revue générale de droit international public,* 1948, pp. 88-160.

145 For a judicious weighing of these factors, see Charles Cheney Hyde, *International Law,* vol. III, pp. 2155-2158.

This legislation, consolidated in the statute of May 1, 1937, took revised and final form in the Neutrality Act of November 4, 1939. In substance it was an appeal to the State against the exercise of the commercial freedoms of which the great Republic had from the end of the eighteenth century made itself the interpreter and defender.[146]

The prohibition of the export of arms and munitions in 1937 had the support of a public opinion that was almost unanimous in its hostility to the arms traffic. It broke with the traditional idea expressed in Article 7 of Hague Convention XIII, according to which the manufacture, export, and transportation of arms and munitions were solely a matter of private economy. The Neutrality Act of 1939, insofar as it lifted the interdiction of export of arms and munitions, was from no point of view a return to this obsolete notion. Promulgated when the war was already in progress, in relation to belligerents now known, it was still less than the statute of 1937 a law of neutrality properly so called, designed to secure, in a spirit of strict impartiality, observance of the duties and respect for the rights of neutrals. It constituted a laborious compromise by which the advocates of aid to the Western democracies obtained repeal of the export prohibition, but in return accepted a series of restrictions having the common object of eliminating all American interest in the operation in order to avoid all pretext for diplomatic intervention.[147]

"To keep the country out of the firing line," American opinion in 1939 considered isolation a more effective safeguard than those that traditional neutrality had sought in the liberal distinction between public and private activities. The moment would soon come when isolationism itself would give way to a juster comprehension of the responsibilities of a great Power in the presence of aggression. By 1940 certain members of the Roosevelt administration were sketching out the thesis that the Briand-Kellogg Pact authorized its signatories to deny Germany, by reason of its aggression against Poland, the rights of belligerency and consequently the right to

146 This policy of renunciation or abandonment was not, however, without roots in the past. In the war of 1914–1918, Secretary of State Bryan had declared himself for it. Cf. Charles M. Chaumont, *La conception américaine de la neutralité*, pp. 107 seq.; Charles G. Fenwick, *American Neutrality, Trial and Failure*, pp. 40 seq.

147 Prohibition of transportation in American ships; prior transfer to an alien of all right, title, or property in the goods; designation of combat zones forbidden to American vessels.

demand that third States strictly observe the rules of neutrality.[148]

This was the point of departure for a whole series of measures which, notwithstanding official maintenance of neutrality, in fact constituted effective aid to the Allies. From traditional neutrality the United States passed in a few months to nonbelligerency with partiality, until the Pearl Harbor aggression, followed by German and Italian declarations of war, permitted it to deploy its full war powers against the Axis Powers.

§ 4. PRENEUTRALITY. NEUTRALITY OF THOUGHT

In the absence of an effective international organization, high political tensions, prophetic of great conflicts, naturally enough induce the small States even in time of peace to seek security in an attitude of rigorous impartiality between the future adversaries. Legally neutrality is born only with war; politically, there is a "preneutrality" which has a well-known influence on the behavior of States.

In this respect the attitude of several European States in the years immediately preceding the second world war was very significant. The defeat of the sanctions applied to Italy had demonstrated the impotence of the League of Nations. The political tensions of which it was the focus threatened to transform it into a coalition. The movement then witnessed confirms what has been said above about certain international reactions in the face of danger. The prospect of peril which strengthened internal solidarities disintegrated the League's structure.[149] The retreat was general; everywhere the tendency appeared to substitute for the so-called regime of "indivisible peace" the search for individual security in a policy of isolation.

In 1937, Belgium adopted its policy of "independence" and, confirming its purpose to defend its territory, obtained from the French and British Governments release from its obligations under the Treaty of Locarno, which had been denounced by Germany, and under the arrangements made in London on March 19, 1936. While renewing the assurance of its fidelity to the Covenant of the League of Nations, it reserved final judgment of the circumstances which

148 This was the view that a few authors were bold enough to defend as early as 1916 in regard to Germany as guarantor and violator of the permanent neutrality of Belgium. (Cf. Charles De Visscher, "La Belgique et les juristes allemands," 1916; and Grotius Society, vol. II: *Neutrals and Belgian Neutrality*). They collided at the time with the prejudices of the positivist school.

149 See above, Book II, Chap. II, Sec. I.

might oblige it under Article 16 of the Covenant to grant "facilities of passage in the event of common action being taken by the League against Germany."

Switzerland, given since 1920 the benefit of a differential neutrality that called for abstention from the military sanctions but participation in the economic sanctions of Article 16, secured from the Council of the League of Nations in 1938 restitution of her traditional complete neutrality. The shift was the result of public fears awakened by the collective action against Italy and by the withdrawal from the League of two great Powers neighboring on Swiss territory and closely allied with one another—fears that were sharpened by the new dangers to the country's external security resulting from the Austro-German *Anschluss*.[150]

The same desire to stand aside from the conflicts between great Powers appeared in the States of the Oslo Group at the Copenhagen Conference of 1938. The fears there entertained found expression in a "minimalist" interpretation of Article 16 of the Covenant. The same motive was already to be seen in the regional agreements of mutual guarantee and consultation set out in the Balkan Entente Pact of 1934.[151]

Under the influence of these centrifugal drives, the Covenant in its essential parts was gradually drained of legal substance. Even in cases where the loosening of League ties took place in a formally regular way, political pressures were manifestly the determining factor. The decision taken at Geneva in 1936 to adapt the mechanism of sanctions to the possibilities of the moment had been merely a resigned legalization of the *fait accompli*.

These same years of high political tension witnessed that other manifestation of "preneutrality" dubbed "neutrality of thought." This phenomenon is a function at once of the power of the modern instruments of thought diffusion and of the direction of opinion in the service of ideological propaganda. If it is true that the establishment of any State control in this domain, especially in radio, entails a corresponding extension of State responsibilities, it is equally certain that, in their desire to preserve themselves from war, weak States contracted obligations that went beyond their international duty or submitted to censure contrary to their liberal

150 D. Schindler, "La Neutralité suisse de 1920 à 1938," *Revue de Droit international et de Législation comparée*, 1938, p. 433.

151 C. G. Tenekides, "La neutralité en son état d'évolution actuelle," *Revue de Droit international et de Législation comparée*, 1939, p. 256.

traditions. Still more than ordinary neutrality, "neutrality of thought" worked in favor of the forces of intimidation and aggression. It promoted a regime of frightened control, designed solely to offer no pretext for invasion. It was pushed to the point of compelling some States to dissimulate their most legitimate anxieties and preventing them from obtaining in good time the external aid that could have saved them.

The future chances of so highly political an institution as neutrality are not to be measured by the texts, which have never expressed anything but the most respectable aspirations, too often frustrated by events. Optional neutrality survived the Covenant of the League of Nations with the help of minimizing interpretations of its rules about sanctions. Theoretically, it could just as well survive under the Charter, where failure of unanimity among permanent members is enough to paralyze the Council's entire security mechanism.

We must turn back to the facts. Once more the fate of neutrality is tied to the development of war. Today, in almost all the peoples, the ubiquity of the risks of war has destroyed confidence in neutrality. The condemnation of the so-called war of aggression is the projection into the legal and moral order of an irrevocable change in political and military realities. When the universality of the danger robs men of the hope of shelter in neutrality, the reprobation of the war of aggression and the organization of collective security take on in their minds the character of a moral imperative. The only ones who do not despair of the future of neutrality are those who still think to find in the well-understood interest of the belligerents, or in the remoteness of their countries from the lines of pressure in world strategy, a protection which they well know to be precarious.

In "cold war" on a world scale the need of undivided political direction grows with the duration and intensity of the tension. One after another the peoples align themselves with those who, on one side or the other, have the greatest strength. Even before total war has merged them in the combat formations, neutrality is morally and materially closed to them.

CHAPTER IV. PEACEFUL CHANGE

Section I

General Features of the Problem

THIS is a theme that the literature of the law of nations treated with conviction and abundance in the interwar period, to the point at times of making it the central problem of the system. Today it has been allowed to fall into complete oblivion. There has been contradiction and a want of comprehension on all sides, only to be explained by the course of events.

The very idea of peaceful change is inseparable from that of an established order. It was against the political and legal order imposed by the Peace Treaties of 1919-1920 that the "have-not" States directed their campaigns for revision. The twenty years that elapsed between the two world wars were dominated by the antagonism between these States, with their less and less peaceful demands, and the more and more divided defenders of the order established by the Treaties. No order whatever has succeeded the second world war; hostilities came to an end only to be followed by an unexampled political tension which permits the strongest at any moment to throw everything back into the melting pot. Further, it is now realized that the future of peaceful change is indissolubly linked with the progress of international organization. The fundamental conditions are a sense of community of interests deep enough to justify the sacrifices necessary for change, and the existence of adequate legal procedures. They are today too completely lacking to permit any hope of important achievements.

Often as it has been approached, the problem of changing international situations by peaceful means has never been sounded to its depths. This is to be accounted for largely by a sense of the present fragility of international situations; for there is a natural inclination to regard change not as an inevitable consequence of the evolution of things, but as an event likely to provoke crisis, or at least serious complications.[1] But especially the question has always been looked at from a too exclusively legal point of view. Confining their effort to the search for procedures (the machinery of peaceful change), authors have neglected the fundamental political obstacle usually thrown up against attempts to effect such change by a will to

[1] J. L. Brierly, *The Outlook for International Law*, p. 106.

power determined on altering to its advantage the established ratio of forces.

It is the mark of a consolidated legal system to combine, for the better satisfaction of social needs, suppleness of adaptation with the firmness indispensable to legal ordering. This double requirement is very generally met in the national order by a legally recognized hierarchy of values sustained by appropriate mechanisms of change.[2] There is nothing like this in the international order. Rigid in principle, authoritarian in method, sovereignty is naturally refractory to what Hauriou called "the slow and uniform movement of change in an ordered social system."[3] It asserts itself now in an unbridled dynamism that no legal order could satisfy, now in a shortsighted conservatism that in the end may prove equally dangerous to the stability of law. This being so, the aspiration to change easily takes on the appearance of a threat to the established order and to inviolable rights. Because change is not regarded and dealt with as a normal social need, the aspiration becomes charged with a political potential and results in inarticulate tensions or sharp fluctuations that escape the ordering action of law.

We may leave aside what are called general or impersonal situations, common if not to all States at least to a great number—situations subject to the general rules of international law. These represent balances of interest already largely integrated in law; change in them, proceeding largely by the process of custom, generally occasions no very serious political difficulties. It is different with change in particular or subjective situations, much the most numerous and most important politically, involving interests and rights of which States have in principle the free and exclusive disposition. Here the aspiration to change collides head-on with the individualist distribution of power among nations.[4]

This is lost sight of by those who denounce as an essential cause of the insecurity of international relations the excessively static character of international law, its inability to respond to economic

[2] It is well known that at times of crisis municipal law itself often enough bends under political pressures. A rapid succession of laws and their retroactive application are symptoms of this; they introduce instability and fragility into the law. Cf. G. Ripert, *Le déclin du Droit,* 1949; F. Russo, *Réalité Juridique et Réalité Sociale,* 1942.

[3] "Aux sources du Droit," *Cahiers de la Nouvelle Journée,* no. 33, p. 77 (1933).

[4] On the fundamental nature of this distinction, see Maurice Bourquin, *Stabilité et Mouvement, Rec. A.D.I.,* vol. 64 (1938), pp. 414-415.

and social demands and to redress the imbalances that are incidental to the development of human societies. It is of the essence of law to contain within its regulatory framework the moving and chaotic manifestations of social dynamism. The order that international law seeks to sustain among nations is inseparable from the state of possession that its rules have created. This state of possession, with all the elements of State power that it includes, cannot be submitted to revision except in one of two ways—either by the agreement of those concerned, or by the establishment of a federal organization strong enough to correct disequilibria by a constant redistribution of the elements of power. Meanwhile it is perfectly useless to blame law for the fact that it furnishes no support for demands that have no legal basis.

The jurists, for their part, go astray when, yielding to the fixed idea of the formal completeness of law, they seek to minimize the problem and dispute its dangers to international security and the maintenance of peace. The problem denoted by the vague idea of peaceful change is only too real, but it is wholly political. What it brings into question is not the legality of a state of possession; it is the political expediency of changing it in order to meet the real or pretended needs of dissatisfied collectivities.[5] This is the way the problem was looked at in League of Nations circles in the years before the second world war. There it figured as one element of a system of collective security that sought to eliminate in advance grievances that might provoke war.

Things are different when the situation is one of those of which the law has already to some extent taken cognizance, especially contractual situations. The imbalances of interests that after a certain time make their appearance here are generally subject to legal regulation. It is for this reason, and not by any means because it exhausts the problem of peaceful change, that treaty revision has always been the focus of discussion.

We must then, first of all, distinguish the change of legal situations from that of situations, not at present legally ordered, which are the subject of political grievances.

[5] D. Schindler, *Rec. A.D.I.*, vol. 46, p. 282: "The legally unassailable finding that each State may do as it will does not end the conflict, for the conflict springs precisely from this liberty. Such conflicts can only be eliminated in the measure that it becomes possible to replace the regime of liberty with a regulatory system of law providing an effective delimitation of interest. . . . The question is not one of applying the existing law, but of creating a new legal situation."

Section II

Change of Legal Situations

A situation that has been stamped with the approval of international law—though, like any other, open to alteration under the pressure of new forces—has nevertheless the benefit of the adage "Protection is due title."[6] From this flow two consequences: one who claims to change it must find legal support for his claim, and, legally, the change must lead to the creation of a new legal situation.

Only very rarely does the application of this principle raise difficulties in situations where customary rules are relevant, customary law being by definition eminently flexible and developing in direct contact with living needs. On the contrary, frequent and at times acute tensions are created where the interests at stake have been the object of treaty regulation.

Treaty revision finds no legal basis in the tacit clause *rebus sic stantibus* unless it is established that certain legal or factual circumstances have been regarded by the parties as presuppositions of the obligations assumed by them. Restricted to this hypothesis, the application of the clause does not rest upon a fiction of will; it is rather an a posteriori adaptation by a return to the *ratio* of the treaty. In fact, however, it is observable that the contracting parties usually had no intention whatever or at least no common intention about the points raised by the change that has occurred. The clause is therefore far from covering all the changes of circumstances that may make the revision or modification of treaties desirable or even necessary. Its application is therefore almost always distorted by a mixture of legal arguments that rely upon intentions more or less gratuitously attributed to the parties or, again, upon constraint or moral violence,[7] and political arguments that seek to break the treaty down by a more or less disguised appeal to the vital interests or fundamental rights of the contracting States.[8]

In international law the question of the effect of changed circum-

[6] J. Basdevant, *Rec. A.D.I.*, vol. 58 (1936), p. 590; Charles Rousseau, *Principes généraux du Droit international public*, vol. I, p. 591.

[7] In this connection we may cite the statement made by the Egyptian representative Nokrashi Pasha before the Security Council in 1947 in support of the thesis that the Anglo-Egyptian Treaty of 1936 was invalid.

[8] The politicians at times explain this without beating about the bush. Bismarck's pronouncement is familiar: "Any agreement between great Powers ceases to have obligatory force as soon as it is put to the test of a struggle for life."

stances on treaty obligations must be strictly individualized. In other words it is a matter in the great majority of cases of seeking, not in the light of principles but in the facts of each case, the relationship which the parties intended to establish between their obligations and the occurrence of new facts. This results from the fact that the vast majority of international conventions express no objective idea, but only the resultant "of subjective interests that have met on a middle line."[9]

But there may be serious difficulty in drawing a line between the strictly legal reasons and the political considerations produced in support of a demand for revision. It is so, for instance, in the revision of treaties that have established a regime of a permanent character between the parties, designed to meet not only their present but also their future needs, when the subject matter is one of those that are in some measure governed by general international law. It is not rare in such cases for the State seeking to have the treaty revised to invoke not only the changes that have occurred in the particular relations of the contracting parties, but also new tendencies in general international law, tendencies represented as being more in harmony with the spirit of justice or equity and with ideas of progress or international cooperation. Though there is no doubt that political interest may easily insinuate itself here behind the legal argument, it must be admitted that in matters already largely integrated in international law, as for example international rivers, the normal development of a treaty regime demands consideration of new ideas that have found general confirmation in international practice.

It has been pointed out that the objective discordance between the treaty and the new factual conditions brought about by the change explains, better perhaps than any real or presumed intent of the contracting States, the obsolescence of treaty obligations and the necessity of readapting them.[10]

The observation is exact and may provide useful hints for international tribunals. But it must not be forgotten that there are treaties owing their existence to force or constraint and that, although international law holds these in principle valid and obligatory, politically the temptation is great for the State that wishes to be free of them to represent a reversal of the ratio of strengths in

[9] Cf. W. Burckhardt, "La Clausula *Rebus sic Stantibus* in International Law," *Revue de Droit international et de Législation comparée*, 1933, pp. 5 seq.

[10] J. Basdevant, *op.cit.*, pp. 653-654.

its favor as being an objective contradiction of the purely political realities that gave rise to the treaties. Some jurists have been so conscious of this that they have proposed, against all reality, to exempt from application of the clause *rebus sic stantibus* treaties of highly political content, in particular those that affect the power relations among States.[11] It is clear, however, that it is precisely in this essentially fluid and shifting domain that the necessity of adapting law to fact comes most naturally to mind and commends itself most cogently in practice. The opposition between the legal and political points of view asserts itself sharply in these contradictory demands of stability and movement.

Treaty arrangements which derogate by marked inequality of treatment from the common law of sovereignty are especially vulnerable to the action of time and the political changes that it brings.[12] The neutralization of the Black Sea imposed on Russia by the Treaty of Paris was denounced by the Russian Government in 1870 as an "abnormal" regime to which no great Power could be bound to remain subject. Return to the common law was supported by an argument of force. In 1922-1923, Turkey obtained from the Lausanne Conference the abolition of the capitulations regime, arguing that, if at the beginning the capitulations were not in derogation of the common law of sovereignty, this was no longer so when sovereignty incorporated the principle of the territoriality of laws.[13] The objections raised by the German Government before the Permanent Court of International Justice against the consequences of what it declared to be a too literal interpretation of Article 380 of the Treaty of Versailles concerning the Kiel Canal; those that it subsequently lodged against the unilateral composition of the river commissions (Treaty of Versailles, Part XII); and the arguments of the minorities States in favor of generalizing the treaties providing international protection for minorities—all these revealed the same preoccupations. In every case the claim to equality concentrated upon an essentially political idea: the inviolability of sovereignty, the prestige of the State, national dignity. Experience has proved the precarious nature of conventional clauses of this type. Born of

11 Philip C. Jessup, "Modernization of the Law of International Contractual Agreements," *A.J.I.L.*, 1947, p. 401.

12 See the course given by Jean Ray at the Academy of International Law: *Des Conflits entre principes abstraits et stipulations contractuelles*, *Rec. A.D.I.*, vol. 48 (1934).

13 *ibid.*, p. 695: "It was from the day when it appeared like an exceptional regime that Turkey found it intolerable."

passing circumstances and tied to a certain balance of forces, they undergo tensions that expose them more than others to the risk of unilateral denunciation.

Section III

Political Grievances about the Distribution of the Elements of Power

The problems raised by aspirations to change in the political order, that is to say in the historical power relations of States, are purely political. Their character is not changed when, on the high plane of human solidarities and the search for peace, one tries to imagine the criteria of a more equitable redistribution of the resources and wealth which in concrete fact are today the elements of the relative power of States.[14]

The disequilibria that are complained of (inequality of access to raw materials or in their distribution, economic or social grievances arising out of demographic factors) pose problems that will remain inaccessible to law so long as the present individualistic structure of the relations between sovereign States persists. Always approachable as individual cases and in their particular conformation through diplomatic channels, these disequilibria are refractory by nature to the general criteria of equity and justice that could in the present state of international relations serve as basis for a legal decision.[15] Hence, as we have seen, the irrational character of the tensions that they set up, in which the issue will depend less on the justice of the

[14] It is because territory is so intimately associated in the minds of men with the possession of power that territorial claims have always been the most difficult to satisfy. This has been so even in connection with the territorial status of recently created States. Note this declaration by Beneš in the Chamber of Deputies at Prague, April 28, 1933: "To dispose of a territory was possible at the Peace Conference. Now that it is in the recognized legal possession of such or such State, it is utterly impossible to arrogate anew a right of disposition. That is the position we take and we will not change a word of it for anyone."

[15] George F. Kennan, *American Diplomacy, 1900-1950*, p. 98: "The national state pattern is not, should not be, and cannot be a fixed and static state. By nature, it is an unstable phenomenon. . . . The function of a system of international relationships is not to inhibit this process of change by imposing a legal strait jacket upon it but rather to facilitate it: to ease its transitions, to temper the asperities to which it often leads, to isolate and moderate the conflicts to which it gives rise, and to see that these conflicts do not assume forms too unsettling for international life in general. But this is a task for diplomacy, in the most old fashioned sense of the term. For this, law is too abstract, too inflexible, too hard to adjust to the demands of the unpredictable and the unexpected."

claims than on the more or less ordered state of the political relations among nations. Bound by the principles of the Concert of Powers, the diplomacy of the Second Empire invited the sovereigns to reconsider the bases of the European political order.[16] Locked up in himself, trusting only in force to deal with a frightened continent, Hitler raised unilateral action by war blackmail to the height of a system whose pacifying virtues he boasted.[17]

We touch here upon the critical aspect of the problem of change, the aspect so tragically illuminated by the Munich Settlement in 1938. No one will deny that the revisionist campaigns before the second world war were the work of regimes more inclined to use the threat of arms than to submit to peaceful procedures. Nor can it be disputed that the great efforts made in the period to achieve peaceful change were due less to the equity of the claims than to the fear inspired by the claimants.[18] The man of law, like the statesman, must distinguish situations that justify an earnest attempt at change from those that call for the mobilization of forces to resist aggression.

16 "Whenever profound disturbances have shaken the foundations and displaced the limits of States, solemn transactions have followed to coordinate new elements and to confirm, with revisions, the changes that have taken place. Such was the object of the Treaty of Westphalia in the seventeenth century and of the negotiations at Vienna in 1815. It is on this last foundation that the political edifice of Europe today stands; yet, as Your Majesty knows, it is crumbling in all its parts. If the situation of the various countries is attentively considered, it cannot but be admitted that on almost all points the Treaties of Vienna are destroyed, modified, ignored, or threatened. Hence duties imposed by no rule, rights without title, and unbridled claims. The danger is all the greater because the improvement brought by civilization, which has bound the peoples together in a solidarity of material interests, would make war still more destructive. This is a subject for grave meditation. Let us not delay in taking position until sudden and irresistible events cloud our judgment and drag us in spite of ourselves in opposite directions." Napoleon III to the Sovereigns of Europe, November 4, 1863.

17 "Whatever arguments may be advanced against my methods, it cannot be forgotten or disputed that I have succeeded without new bloodshed in finding, not for Germany alone, satisfactory solutions in many cases, and that I have also by this method freed the statesmen of other nations from the obligation, often impossible for them, to assume responsibility to their own peoples for this revision." Letter of Chancellor Hitler to the French President of the Council, August 27, 1939.

18 "Through successive stages in dealing with the Sudeten problem the Powers had proceeded from acts which were merely impolitic, to acts which were positively illegal and finally to acts which suggested panic—*facilis descensus Averno.*" Quincy Wright, in *A.J.I.L.*, 1939, p. 29. Cf. J. L. Brierly, *The Outlook for International Law*, pp. 126-127.

It has been observed that the problems created by economic disequilibria do not confront the same obstacles, the number of practically conceivable solutions leaving more suppleness and freedom of negotiation. Before the second world war an approach was being made in this spirit to "equal access" to raw materials and their "equitable distribution," the search for a better balance between population and arable land, and free access to colonial resources. But everything depends here on the possibility of sufficiently isolating economic desiderata from their political aspects. An economy directed by the State to a point verging on autarky automatically restates international economic problems in political terms. There can be no idea, for example, of separating the economic from the political motive where the obsession with war drives some States to make the race for raw materials an essential part of the race for armaments. In most of these problems the world seems to stand before the following alternative: either a supervised return to the free play of economic laws which would gradually resolve the existing tensions by emptying them of the State controls which every day intensify their political character; or a progressive advance towards authoritarian planning, on a world scale, in the hands of a universal federal organization, which implies at least in some domains the establishment of a supreme political as well as economic power.

Section IV

Emancipation Movements

Among the problems of peaceful change, the movement for the emancipation of important human communities in Asia, the Middle East, and Africa, independently of the trusteeship system (Chap. XII of the Charter), is the most pressing and vast. The destruction of the Ottoman Empire was the signal for the movement; the second world war gave it a precipitate course. It extends today from Indonesia to the Atlantic coasts of North Africa. A proliferation of new States or autonomous communities marks the stages of this reawakening of nationalisms whose aspirations, often complicated by ideological subordination, today constitute, along with the East-West tension, the most striking feature of international relations.

As we have seen, these are claims for which there is no sufficiently precise legal criterion to provide a clear-cut principle of legitimation. Their progress, which formerly depended entirely on the unregulated play of historical forces and the laws of effectivity, is today subject to the generally ill-informed criticism of a public opinion which is itself kept in ferment by currents of ideas and opposing interests. What is usually lacking in dealing with these problems is the long view, the ability to seize the precise moment when a freely consented transfer of powers may replace an era of subjection with one of fruitful collaboration.

The Charter here sowed the seed of a controversy in the background of which may be discerned the fundamental opposition between the legal principle that excludes United Nations intervention "in matters which are essentially within the domestic jurisdiction of any state" (Art. 2, para. 7), and a political ideology that seeks to impair this jurisdiction by setting up against it the so-called interventionist aims of the Organization. The contradiction is nonexistent. Article 2, paragraph 7, is the rule for the relations of the United Nations with its members. Good exegesis does not permit us to invoke the interventionist character of a few marginal provisions against so fundamental and strict a rule. The grandiloquence of such provisions habitually exceeds their legal significance. The safeguard of Article 2, paragraph 7, was precisely intended as protection against the political deductions that their extreme generality might warrant.

Moreover, the legal discussion once more fails to touch the substance of the problem. Though protected on the procedural terrain against undue intervention by the United Nations, the State responsible for the administration or protection of territories not under the international trusteeship system has nevertheless two duties inherent in its mission. The first is to promote the capacity of the inhabitants to govern themselves and to guide them in "the development of their free political institutions" (Chap. XI of the Charter), and its fulfillment is exclusively a matter of the State's internal order. The second is to guide this gradual change in such a way as not to compel the United Nations to resort to coercive measures reserved for threats to the peace and breaches of the peace (Chap. VII), but applicable under the final provision of Article 2, paragraph 7.

No general formula applies here. For particular situations, constantly shifting and each profoundly different, only practical experience and the sense of the possible can find suitable adjustment.

Section V

Precedents and Procedures

Though peaceful change has occupied a large place in the deliberations of international organizations and in doctrinal thought, international practice offers few examples of change, by appeal to the clause *rebus sic stantibus*, of situations established by convention—the only hypothesis which in fact confronts the governments concerned with a truly legal problem. By "situations established by convention," let us understand situations that result from executed treaties, for example a frontier treaty, and those that impose continuing obligations (executory treaties) upon the party seeking revision. Let us also understand the legal relations that result from a multilateral or general convention designed to set up a regime or a legal status (law-making treaty), as well as those that arise out of a contract treaty. In the present stage of international relations, it is a purely intellectual construction that limits to the last-mentioned the requirement of some equality of burdens and of reciprocity in execution.

The influence of political factors on the possible scope of revision varies according as the conditions of revision have or have not been stipulated and organized in advance by a clause to this effect in the original instrument.[19] In the first case, which occurs frequently in connection with general conventions of nonpolitical content (legal, social, cultural) concluded by international organizations or under their auspices, revision has a distinct legal character and under some conditions would be subject to control by international justice. The revision clause is usually lacking in treaties of definitely political content; not that these are any less exposed than others to the vicissitudes of time, but on the contrary because the parties, conscious of the frailty of the bonds that unite them and of the indeterminacy of the factors that may affect these bonds, deliberately abstain from specifying the circumstances that might terminate them.[20]

[19] Cf. H. J. Tobin, *The Termination of Multipartite Treaties*, 1933; G. Scelle, *Annuaire de l'Institut de Droit international*, 1948; S. Engel, "Les clauses de révision dans les traités multilatéraux," *Revue de Droit international et de Législation comparée*, 1939, pp. 529, 708; C. W. Jenks, in *B.Y.B.I.L.*, 1945, pp. 65-68.

[20] True, there are political conventions equipped with clauses for revision. But these are cases—and the exception proves the rule—of agreements designed to mitigate political tensions, or agreements which, though they have an at

In these cases the chances of revision depend largely on the state of political relations between the interested parties at the moment when the question is raised. The change which in 1936 substituted the Convention of Montreux for the Straits Statute in the 1923 Lausanne Convention is cited freely and with some reason as a happy example of the revision of a political treaty. We should not, however, overlook the political circumstances which at the moment when Turkey entered her claim so greatly facilitated her task. The inadequacy of the international arrangements designed to prevent or stop the enterprises of force that were then following one another in Europe was already manifest; and the Turkish Government could not be gainsaid when, pleading recent political crises and the bankruptcy of the institutions responsible for collective security, it demanded liberation from a territorial obligation that had ceased to have any object.[21] Even so, the Powers represented at Montreux took care not to count upon the repetition of such favorable circumstances. On the contrary, Articles 28 and 29 of the new Convention (July 20, 1936) show an interesting but still very exceptional attempt to organize a procedure of revision in the political domain.[22]

The preponderance in the nineteenth century of political factors in the revision of treaties regarded as of permanent and general political interest (the public law of Europe) has often been emphasized. It asserted itself in the convocation of conferences of revision that met on the initiative of the great Powers or with the support of some of them; in the view that the participation of all the great Powers was a matter of right, while the invitation of other States parties to the original instrument was usually left to the discretion of the great Powers; in the representation at these conferences of States not parties to that instrument but which, in the interval, had risen to the rank of great Powers; and in the unequal participation or mere liberty of accession permitted to some of the original contracting parties.[23]

times considerable political interest for some signatories, regulate a matter of common interest to States as a whole. In the first case the right of revision is generally set out in a safeguarding clause (Treaties of Washington, 1922, and London, 1930, on the limitation of armaments). An example of the second type is the Montreux Convention on the Straits, July 20, 1936.

21 F. De Visscher, "La Nouvelle Convention des Détroits," *Revue de Droit international et de Législation comparée*, 1936, p. 670.

22 C. W. Jenks, "The Montreux Conference and the Law of Peaceful Change," *The New Commonwealth Quarterly*, 1936, p. 247.

23 Tobin, "The Role of the Great Powers in Treaty Revision," *A.J.I.L.*, 1935, p. 487; Charles Dupuis, *Le Principe d'équilibre et le Concert européen*, 1909.

Examples abound of collective political treaties being revised by those Powers alone which at the time of revision formed the dominant constellation. The more or less resigned acquiescence of those original signatories who were not strong enough to offer opposition was taken for granted.[24] Article 31 of the Treaty of Versailles, which stated the principle of replacing the 1839 regime for Belgium by new agreements, entrusted the mission of drawing these up to a group of Powers whose composition remained uncertain. The result was the exclusion of Russia and the inclusion of Japan—an arrangement that emphasizes the role, passing though it may be, of the powerful of the hour in the enactment of a collective statute of general interest.[25]

Similarly the Powers signatory to the Treaty of Versailles and Switzerland did not think it legally indispensable but merely politically desirable, in the abrogation of the clauses relating to the neutral zone of Savoy (Art. 435, Treaty of Versailles), to obtain the consent of those States signatory to the Treaties of 1815 which were not parties to the negotiations of the 1919 Peace Conference.

From this point of view, one cannot criticize those decisions of the Concert of Europe that in the nineteenth century brought about the transformation of a political order which it was responsible for maintaining.[26] It is more difficult to justify the process in the case of treaties which, despite some political interest, aim chiefly at establishing a system of international collaboration. The question was discussed on the occasion of the judgment rendered on December 12, 1934 by the Permanent Court of International Justice in the case of Oscar Chinn.[27] Was it competent to certain Powers,

[24] See the already cited Report of G. Scelle, *Annuaire, op.cit.* The application of the best-conceived revision clauses may be defeated by the unforeseeable entry of these political factors.

[25] Article 31 imposed the obligation on Germany "to recognize and to observe whatever conventions may be entered into by the Principal Allied and Associated Powers, or by any of them, in concert with the Governments of Belgium and of the Netherlands. . . ." The Report of the Commission on Belgian Affairs of the Peace Conference specified, on the subject of collaboration in the revision of the 1839 Treaties: "The great Powers with general interests represented at the Peace Conference should also participate." Cf. A. Moscato, "Le sorti della neutralizzazione belga dopo la guerra," *Rivista di Diritto Internazionale*, 1931, especially pp. 203-215.

[26] To the same order of ideas belonged various provisions of the Treaty of Versailles assigning a special role to the Council of the League of Nations in the revision of Clauses relating to communications or to economic interests.

[27] Publications of the Court, series A/B, no. 63. The question was put with special clarity in the individual opinion of Judge van Eysinga, p. 131.

parties to the General Act of Berlin, February 26, 1885, revised by the General Act of Brussels, July 2, 1890, and by the Declaration of the same date, to abrogate the Berlin Act *inter se* and replace it also *inter se* with a new convention, in this case the Convention of Saint-Germain of September 10, 1919, without the agreement of the other States parties to the earlier Acts? The Court abstained from dealing with this problem, which had not been raised by the parties in the case before it.

It is easier to justify from the political than from the legal point of view the position taken by the Powers signatory to the Convention of Saint-Germain.[28] Doubtless the revision of the regime set up by the Berlin Act was desired by the Powers with possessions in Central Africa who had not found in that regime just compensation for the heavy burdens of their colonizing mission, and it is equally true that to make revision conditional on general agreement tends to impress upon collective statutes a rigidity out of harmony with the need for change.[29] But the Berlin Act, which had explicitly provided for the possibility of periodic revisions, had made these strictly conditional upon the "common accord" of the contracting parties (Art. 36). On the other hand the Act itself could not be analyzed into a simple treaty contract generative only of individual relationships between its signatories. Designed to secure the interests of peace, the protection of the natives, and freedom of trade and communications, and to fix the legal rules regarding the occupation of *terrae nullius*, it was manifestly a collective and normative act, establishing a highly internationalized legal regime.[30] Will it be said that the necessity of providing for such lofty interests justified certain Powers in taking immediate charge of them without the concurrence of all the original signatories? The argument would be

[28] See the individual opinions of Sir Cecil Hurst and Judges van Eysinga and Schücking. Cf. J. Verzijl, "La validité et la nullité des actes juridiques internationaux," *Revue de Droit international*, Paris, vol. xv, 1935, pp. 320 seq.

[29] The author (H.L.) of a note published in this connection in *B.Y.B.I.L.* (1935, p. 166) justly observes that failing an express provision of this sort, "the approach must . . . be a pragmatic one," that is to say taking into account the interest, direct or indirect, immediate or more remote, but in any event real, of all the parties.

[30] The eminently civilizing aim of the Berlin Act is moreover expressly recognized in the Preamble to the Convention of Saint-Germain. It is essential to distinguish from the case of abrogation contemplated in the text that of particular agreements having it as their sole object to clarify *inter partes* and thus better to secure the principles stated in the general statute.

valid only if it had been established that this concurrence was unattainable.

From the political point of view, the situation looked quite different. The States signatory to the Berlin Act and not parties to the Convention of Saint-Germain did not attack the validity of the latter; it even seems that, without using the right of adherence given them by Article 14, they in fact accepted certain consequences of the regime established by the Convention. The truth is that the Convention of Saint-Germain, strong in the support of the five great Powers that had signed it, was politically consolidated.

In the same line of thought, reference may be made to the approaches made by the Soviet Government to the Government of Turkey (Notes of August 8 and September 24, 1946) in an effort to induce the latter to revise the Montreux Convention on the Straits. This was an attempt to substitute for a statute of general international interest, based on a collective treaty, a particular arrangement inspired by the political views of certain Powers. The part immediately taken in this discussion by the United States, a Power not signatory to the Montreux Convention, emphasized at once its general interest and its highly political significance.

These questions have attracted little attention in legal doctrine or judicial decisions. The reason is not that they are new, but that for the most part they are essentially political.

The contractual organization of a procedure of revision for multilateral nonpolitical conventions contrasts happily with the rudimentary arrangements connected with political treaties. International practice, profiting by the experience gained from accumulated precedents, here presents a great variety of clauses. These aim at regulating in advance, and allowing for the particular nature of each convention, the principal points touching revision—the initiation of proceedings, scope and limits, conditions of acceptance, effects as against States that ratify and against those that refuse or delay ratification.

This technical development is easily explained. Unlike changes in the relations regulated by political treaties, which almost always occasion conflicts of interest and new differences of view, those made in relations governed by nonpolitical treaties usually leave a surviving and substantial community of mind and interest that is demonstrated by the disposition of the parties to preserve their work by adapting it to new needs.[81]

[81] Progress has been especially noteworthy in conventions drawn up by the

Section VI

Revision under the United Nations Charter

Article 14 of the Charter gives the General Assembly the authority to recommend "measures for the peaceful adjustment of any situation, regardless of origin, which it deems likely to impair the general welfare or friendly relations among nations." This provision attributes to the international Organization some part in the peaceful change of international relations. It occupies a place corresponding to that of Article 19 in the Covenant of the League of Nations. It differs from Article 19 by the intentional omission of any specific reference to treaty revision. Its wording may be justified by two considerations. Without going so far as to say that the revision of treaties is incompatible with respect for them, one can well understand that, in a world exposed to every kind of upheaval, too direct an instigation to States to call in question the authority of treaties should have seemed inexpedient. Besides, what really matters is less the treaty itself than its effects, direct or indirect, foreseeable or unforeseeable, on international security and the preservation of peace. In this light the very comprehensive formula of the Charter appears satisfactory.[82]

From the political as from the legal point of view, the chief obstacle to the power thus lodged in the General Assembly lies in the state of confusion in which the United Nations today stands regarding the scope of the reservation of domestic jurisdiction (Art. 2, para. 7). Indisputably some of the gravest political problems arise in fields of interest still left by law to the discretion of governments, though they now call for international collaboration. The political sense recognizes that these cannot all be indefinitely kept within the confines of a debate on jurisdiction as defined by a text, however decisive this may be in the legal order to which it belongs. Where law declares a sharp separation, the facts suggest transitions towards new structures or reveal inevitable conflicts.

Of all the functions devolving on the international Organization, peaceful change is politically the most important, but also, unfortunately, the one which it is today least able to perform. There is

International Labor Organization. Cf. C. W. Jenks, *Les instruments internationaux à caractère collectif*, *Rec. A.D.I.*, vol. 69 (1939), pp. 530 seq., and, by the same author, "Some Constitutional Problems of International Organizations," *B.Y.B.I.L.*, 1945, pp. 65-68.

82 Cf. H. Kelsen, *The Law of the United Nations*, 1951, pp. 211-215.

none which more imperatively demands a deeply felt and accepted international solidarity, a fundamental revision of the prerogatives of sovereignty, and an impartial supervision that cannot be expected of assemblies that are today an arena for the passionate violence of nationalisms. As everyone knows, Article 19 of the Covenant of the League of Nations was a dead letter. Its wording had nothing to do with this; the reason was that the function which it tried to organize was beyond the strength of the League. There is small chance that the new provision in the Charter will be more effective. The resounding defeat of the United Nations in its attempt to divide Palestine stands witness.

BOOK IV

THE JUDICIAL SETTLEMENT OF DISPUTES

BOOK IV

THE JUDICIAL SETTLEMENT OF DISPUTES

Section I

General Bearing of the Political on International Justice

THERE was a time when the possible contribution of international tribunals to the maintenance of peace was exaggerated. At the end of the nineteenth century, the anxieties aroused by changes in the European balance, combined with some discrediting of the diplomatic methods employed to sustain it, led some minds to look to the development of the jurisdictional function, and more particularly to the extension of obligatory arbitration, for the most effective safeguards to peace. At the same time the somewhat confused ideal of "the primacy of law over force" promoted the view that the establishment of a permanent international tribunal of fixed composition must be the principle and center of all international organization.

Yet nothing in the past history of arbitration justified such hopes. Rare in all ages were wars arising out of pure disputes as to rights. In the immense majority of cases, wars sprang from conflicts of interest. Their motives were political, even though a legal discussion furnished the pretext for recourse to arms. Arbitral decisions, though in fact more and more numerous, did not always have the importance that the pacifist movement liked to assign to them. Most of them related either to claims of private origin or to disputes of which the political significance, even when it was substantial, was not comparable to the tensions that characterize contemporary international relations. If on the American continent more serious disputes, relating for example to the line of a frontier, were settled by arbitration, this was not always from devotion to peace but because, in vast and still very sparsely populated countries, such disputes were less important than elsewhere.

History shows that generalized political tensions really dangerous to peace, such as those that began to develop at the end of the nineteenth century, have their origin in profound changes which occur within States and which, in domains that States hold vital, alter their mutual relations of interest and strength at the cost of the established legal order. The absolute primacy that the theorists assign to the jurisdictional function artificially inverts the terms of the problem. It must be observed that so long as the individualistic distribution of power among States persists, with the major political tensions that it engenders, peace will serve justice better than justice will serve peace.

The provisions of the Covenant of the League of Nations bore witness in this respect to an exact sense of realities. The obligation which they prescribed for States members to settle their disputes by peaceful means could be fulfilled in two different ways—by legal procedures applicable to disputes recognized as "generally capable" of settlement by law, and, subject to agreement of the parties, leading to compulsory settlement; failing these, a procedure of compulsory investigation by the Council, leading however to a mere recommendation, a procedure suitable for disputes which, because they are politically acute, bear directly on the preservation of peace. These provisions were wisely conceived and perfectly adapted to the state of international relations.[1] Subsequently, yielding to the impatience of "legal perfectionism," the League of Nations set itself to the artificial task of expurgating from the texts the reservation of the political, which cannot be banished from the realities of international relations.

The obstacles to the broadening of the international judicial function spring directly from the distribution of power among States and the eminently political character of the relations that it engenders. The result is that the settlement of disputes between States, for all that has been said of it, is never comparable to the settlement of disputes between individuals. For these last the judicial decision is the impersonal application of the law, which is itself an expression of deeply inculcated disciplines, and which embraces virtually the whole of social relations. This state of affairs disposes individuals generally to limit their claims to what is legally defensible and to formulate them in terms of law.

It is not the same in relations between States. There is here neither hierarchic order embracing the totality of interests or values, nor superior power capable of controlling effectively the play of competing forces. Not only have States, especially when they are

[1] Max Huber, "Die Konstruktiven Grundlagen des Völkerbundvertrages," *Vermischte Schriften*, vol. III, p. 212.

powerful, ways other than legal ways of enforcing their claims, but they retain in a vast number of matters a liberty of action to which international law, which is itself founded on the principle of the individualistic distribution of power among nations, gives its approval. This is the case with the very numerous decisions that States may legally make without leaving what is known as the "reserved domain"—those for instance, so charged with international consequences, that economic nationalism induces governments to make in regard to immigration, customs tariffs, quotas, and export or import prohibitions. Yet there is no doubt that the damage which these measures may inflict on a foreign State is often much greater than that which may result from a violation of law. This is an area of inordinate struggles between interests, struggles that generate unrelenting international competitions which governments are little inclined to end by submitting to regulations that could furnish the judge with criteria for a legal decision.

These individualist tendencies are observable, as we have seen, even in the inter-State conflicts that arise in the borderland between politics and law on such matters as naturalization, immigration, nationalization and respect for acquired rights, the international recognition of States and governments, and international responsibility. Even here governments, jealous above all of their liberty of action, prefer to retain for their relations and the disputes that may arise out of them an individual or particular, hence political, character.

Resistance to judicial settlement is most intense in the political oppositions that set up "tensions," especially what are called "diffuse tensions." These, having no definite object and being above all incapable of legal formulation, bring into play the constituent elements of State power. Such tensions are the resultant of political rivalries between States; they can be appeased only concurrently with these rivalries themselves. Arising out of a will to power, the generally unavowed aim of which is to substitute a new balance of interests and forces for an existing balance momentarily guaranteed by law, they usually offer no opening to judicial action.

Such a state of affairs obstructs the judicial resolution not only of the tensions themselves, but also of the secondary disputes to which they give rise, so long at least as the generality or intensity of the underlying tension makes it impossible to separate these from it and to deal with them on their own merits in accordance with legal norms.

But political tensions may be interrupted by periods of calm and relaxation. They may also, instead of increasing in scope and intensity, be dissipated in minor disputes. Governments then recover some freedom of action in regard to these; it becomes possible to detach from a diminishing tension some elements that are more clearly justiciable and sufficiently circumscribed for submission to legal settlement. This is the time when recourse to international justice has a definitely pacifying effect and provides grounds for the dictum that "for the preservation of peace the *compromis* is more important than the award."[2]

Many conflicts between States can be compared to those which within the State from time to time set the workers' organizations in opposition to the legal operation of power. Very generally, the demand here is not for the application of the existing law but for its adaptation to new situations. Social peace calls for adjustments of interests for which the mediating action of the executive is more appropriate than any exercise of the judicial function. It is often so in the relations of States. Justice here follows a regular course only when a basic political settlement has re-established among directing powers a minimum of order and stability.[3] Treaties of peace once performed this ordering function. The grave and incessant political tensions that have followed one another in Europe for twenty years, and the chaotic condition of the world since the second world war, have been hardly propitious to international judicial activities.

Notwithstanding these weaknesses inherent in the present state of international relations, judicial settlement offers—if not always, at least very generally—the advantage of "depoliticizing" disputes more completely than other modes of settlement because, more than any other, it implies the voluntary renunciation by the parties of their individual power of decision and submission to the impersonal criteria of law. It is this freely consented renunciation, and the limits which it sets to political action, that give the international award its truly unique authority. This observation is as valid for the International Court of Justice as for other international tribu-

[2] N. Politis, *La Justice internationale*, p. 49.

[3] *ibid.*, p. 253: "It is thought that justice will bring peace, because it is believed that it can kill war. The contrary is rather the truth: the reign of justice presupposes peace. In an atmosphere saturated with passions, rivalries, and the spirit of war, the judge is powerless, for the law which is his arm loses all its virtue in the presence of force."

nals. If some of its decisions have helped to reduce political tensions between States, this is due to the voluntary acceptance of its jurisdiction. Any attempt to constrain States to submit to this jurisdiction either directly, or indirectly by the roundabout way of advisory opinions, can lead only to impairing the authority of the Court by multiplying refusals to respect its decisions.[4]

The systematic refusal of a government to submit to arbitral or judicial settlement a dispute which in its object indubitably falls under international law, even though no universally accepted rules have been formulated, must be regarded as eminently political. This is the case today with the Soviet Government's rejection of Sweden's proposal to submit two disputes arising out of the unilateral Soviet decree extending territorial waters to twelve marine miles. Such an attitude reveals the political will to accept no restriction of the State's freedom of decision.

Section II

Nonjusticiable Disputes. Relativity of This Notion

As we have seen, the notion of justiciableness is a relative one. It has not the same meaning for the man of law as for the man of politics. For the first, justiciableness depends on an objective criterion: it is the fitness of a dispute for settlement on the basis of legal principles. In the eyes of the politician, a dispute appears justiciable or not according as its more or less intimate connection with State interest permits or forbids the State to surrender its personal and discretionary decision in regard to it. From a political point of view, a government may refuse to submit a dispute to judicial settlement without disputing the existence of legal rules binding on the judge.

International practice demonstrates the reluctance of governments to submit to compulsory decision conflicts of high political significance, not because it would be impossible for the judge to decide them, but because his decision would not satisfy the grievances out of which such conflicts spring. They hold a conflict to be politically nonjusticiable when they know that satisfaction of their

[4] The same must be said of the attempt to introduce a new category of compulsory jurisdiction based upon a recommendation from the Security Council that the parties submit their dispute to the Court. Corfu Channel case (Preliminary Objection), Judgment of March 25, 1948 and the individual opinions of seven judges; Reports, 1948, pp. 15 and 31.

claims can be found only in a change in the legal position protected by the law in force. "A declaration of their legal rights when States are quarrelling about something other than their rights is not in any true sense a 'settlement' of their dispute."[5] In such conflicts the judgment may well reject the claim and close the case; it cannot liquidate the political tension between the parties. In pronouncing itself under these conditions, the international tribunal will do its judicial duty; but it will be unable to perform its pacifying mission, which is to bring to an end conflicts between States. These distinctions too often escape the man of law, whose particular view of things inclines him to find a place for every dispute on the plane of legal debate.[6]

The notion of the political, as everyone knows, has nothing fixed about it. It is essentially fluid, being linked with the highly variable relations existing from time to time between some questions and State interest as this is conceived by the rulers. The result is that, failing a provision for settlement, disputes of the same type are regarded as justiciable or nonjusticiable according to circumstances. Does this mean that justiciableness is a wholly subjective thing and that it depends exclusively, as has been argued, on the good or ill will of States? This would be a manifest exaggeration. There are disputes in which the very absence of recognized norms reveals interests regarded, rightly or wrongly, as too closely connected with the State to be removed from its discretionary decision. There are others which, in spite of their undisputed international interest, are still retained, under the existing law, in this discretionary domain.

In all these cases, the real obstacle to international jurisdiction lies in the individualistic character of the existing distribution of power among nations, the subjective attitude of governments in regard to judicial settlement being merely a reflection of the present structure of international relations.

It is thus an exaggeration to say that what makes a dispute political is simply the refusal of the State to submit it to judicial settlement. Apart from the fact that a dispute may be largely

[5] J. L. Brierly, *The Law of Nations*, 4th edn., p. 265.

[6] There is no room here for the sterile arguments of the schools over the thesis of the plenitude of international law. There is no reconciling either ideas of justice or the exigencies of international relations with this entirely formal and static notion which is content to describe the law as "complete" while recognizing that it is seriously "imperfect." In the recent work of Julius Stone, *Legal Controls of International Conflict* (pp. 146-152), will be found views very similar to those expressed in the text.

"depoliticized" by recourse to other modes of peaceful settlement, this view overlooks the relations that often exist between a dispute over a specific matter and a more general conflict or a pre-existing state of political tension which in fact overshadows it. When a dispute, though it has a particular and legally definable object, is not detachable, politically speaking, from a serious political tension —when, for instance, it arises between States precisely by reason of this tension or comes to represent the tension to the point of being its manifestation or symbol—it becomes clear that resistance to judicial settlement finds its real explanation in the political tension and not in the refusal to submit to the judge the dispute *in se*.

Though it is generally true that readiness on the part of States to detach a dispute from an existing tension and refer it to the international judge indicates some relaxation in their political relations, it has been observed, inversely, that such a tension may make itself felt even in the arbitral procedure itself. This was so in the arbitration of the Wal-Wal incident during the Italian-Ethiopian conflict.[7] Here again the matter at issue is the general structure of international relations and the antagonisms to which it gives rise much more than the parties' opposition to the exercise of arbitral or judicial jurisdiction in relation to the immediate object of a specific dispute.

This was the meaning of the refusal by the governments of Bulgaria, Hungary, and Rumania to name their commissioners in the mixed Commissions stipulated in the Peace Treaties (1947) for the settlement of disputes relating to the interpretation or execution of these Treaties.[8] In the specific instance the cause of this attitude, which implied a complete refusal to cooperate in the arbitral procedure, was much too broad for the category of disputes contemplated in the settlement clause; it was to be found in the fundamental political opposition which even while the treaties were

[7] *United Nations Reports of International Arbitral Awards*, p. 1660. Cf. D. Schindler, *Die Schiedsgerichtbarkeit*, p. 114, and the reflections of Hans Morgenthau, *Politics among Nations*, pp. 343 seq. This was already made plain in the clear-sighted reflections of Funck-Brentano and A. Sorel, *Précis*, p. 461: "If there is to be arbitration, the object of the litigation must be real and sharply defined. If States are in conflict over a matter of general policy, . . . especially if they are struggling for preponderance, they find it very difficult to submit their dispute to arbitration. Elements too complex and too diverse enter into these problems; man can hardly explain them even after history has solved them."

[8] See the Advisory Opinion of the International Court of Justice, July 18, 1950, Reports, 1950, p. 221.

being negotiated existed between the three ex-enemy States and certain allied and associated Powers. It was a mistake to generalize the elements of the problem and to see in this incident a grave threat to the future of the very numerous arbitral clauses drafted after the same model. Those who have drafted such clauses have frequently been concerned about the difficulties that might be encountered in the designation of a third arbiter, but it is to be noted that they have almost always refrained from making any provision for the refusal of a party to name its own commissioner. The risk of such refusal is entirely exceptional, for each party normally has an interest in making this nomination. If the risk showed itself to be a real one in the case referred to the Court in 1950, this was because the sharp political tension between the U.S.S.R. and the so-called satellite States on the one side and the Western Powers on the other, even during the negotiation of the treaties, prevented the contracting parties from setting up a more effective mechanism for the settlement of disputes. The history of the negotiations in 1946 proves beyond debate that the cause of the relative weakness of this provision did not lie in a defect in the mechanism which the signatories failed to notice. It lay rather in their purely political will not to bind themselves beyond a certain point and therefore to draft an only partially effective settlement clause.[9]

Experience shows, on the other hand, that the parties do not always empty a dispute of its political content by referring it to the international judge. This is so when their cases depend on a conventional text in which the intention was to reserve to the contracting parties a liberty of decision guided by considerations of mere convenience or political expediency. One example was the asylum case (Colombia–Peru), which the International Court of Justice had to decide in 1950-1951. The Havana Convention of February 20, 1928 on asylum, which was the only law applicable to the circumstances, had nothing to say on the manner of terminating asylum irregularly granted to political criminals. This was an intentional silence, the Latin American tradition being definitely against handing a political refugee over to the territorial authorities. This surrender was nevertheless the nub of the dispute. By putting

[9] This was a case where the so-called principle of "useful effect" as a canon of interpretation was excluded by an indication of contrary intention in the parties (see above, Book III, Chap. III, Sec. III, §3). In such a case we should not speak of a divergence between the texts and the aim of the parties; the parties had agreed to a limited effect.

the problem of asylum on the too narrow plane of the Havana Convention, the parties got themselves into an impasse from which a judicial decision manifestly could not extricate them.[10] In a case where very special extra-legal factors played so large a part, an agreement of the parties to submit their dispute to a settlement *ex aequo et bono* would have been more conclusive proof of their sincere wish to "depoliticize" it.

A dispute can also be nonjusticiable from the point of view of the tribunal seized of it. The tribunal, unless it derives all its powers solely from the agreement of the parties, cannot ignore the limits that the judicial character of its function sets to its activity when it comes to adjudging claims on any basis other than law. A claim which, without disputing the existence or effect of the law in force or even raising the question, left this aside and sought thus to substitute for a legally protected situation a new legal situation based only on a different adjustment of the interests involved, would not initiate litigation in the proper, that is to say legal, sense of the term. The demand for such a change springs from a conflict of interests in which settlement is a political task, for it is a matter of constructing for the future rather than rendering judgment on the past. This amounts to saying that we here find again some of the characteristic features of political discussion noted above, such as the habitual broadening of the scope of the debate provoked by the initial claim; the consideration of larger interests, leading possibly to a general compensatory settlement; and the preponderance of considerations of expediency.[11]

This approach is that of amiable composition or mediation. The settlements so reached are adapted to the political relations of the States concerned, not dictated by established norms. They are not the only conceivable settlements and it is generally possible to propose alternatives. Finally, since they are formulated for a future necessarily uncertain, experience alone decides their value.

Judicial settlement in equity, on the basis of a clause *ex aequo et bono*, is another question. It has been complicated by confusion

10 The Act of Lima (August 31, 1949), upon which the procedure was based, was only an agreement on settlement, not a real *compromis*. The plenipotentiaries expressly recorded in it their inability to agree on the terms in which they could jointly submit the question under discussion to the Court. The reticence of the parties' pleadings in both parts of the case on the question of the surrender of the refugee was equally significant.

11 Cf. Decencière-Ferrandière, "Réflexions touchant le règlement des conflits internationaux," *Revue générale de Droit international public*, 1929, p. 441.

resulting from inadequate analysis of the role of equity, and this must be cleared up at once.

Article 38, paragraph 2, of the Statute of the International Court of Justice reads as follows: "This provision shall not prejudice the power of the Court to decide a case *ex aequo et bono*, if the parties agree thereto." Of this provision, about which there has been so much argument, only one thing can be said with confidence: it was intended to authorize the Court, given special agreement of the parties, either to decide in equity instead of basing its judgment on the rules of law flowing from the sources enumerated in the preceding paragraph (absolute reliance on equity), or to draw upon equity to fill the gaps in these rules, the recourse to equity being here only subsidiary to the application of legal rules.

Equity can be something other than an independent basis of decision, as when, in a decision which in other respects is founded on positive law (*intra legem*), the judge chooses among several possible interpretations of the rule the one which appears to him, having regard to the particular circumstances of the case, most in harmony with the demands of justice. In this merely interpretative role, equity is inherent in all sound application of the law and is to this extent imperative for any international jurisdiction. Clearly the requirement of special agreement between the parties does not refer to this necessary function of equity.

On the contrary, equity plays a part which manifestly transcends the sphere of law and becomes a political task when, with the consent of the interested States, the search for it extends to values, properties, or interests which under the law in force are not legally in debate, with a view to distributing them by other principles, according to the demands of a better-conceived or broader social justice. This extension of the search to all factors that might contribute to a better balance in the relations between States, whether they are legally relevant or not, is characteristic of the political function. Since it postulates a state of affairs "which is in no way predetermined by the existing law,"[12] it takes place on a plane foreign to law, and the views which confront each other there do not give rise to a legal dispute. Equity here adjusts not law but interests based on mere facts.[13] Such adjustment could not be the work of an organism whose functions are strictly judicial.

[12] Max Huber, in *Annuaire de l'Institut de Droit international*, 1934, pp. 234-235.

[13] *ibid.*, pp. 234-235.

Intermediate situations can however be imagined—and it was precisely these that Article 38, paragraph 2, of the Court Statute had in view—where the search for equity, without ignoring the existing law, attempts to fill the gaps in that law (decision *praeter legem*) or to procure for the parties either a more supple application of law, or an adjustment of their contractual relations which they had not provided for. Equity does not here cease to operate as an adjuster of law. A decision of this kind has a mixed character. Though it remains an act of jurisdiction in virtue both of the quality of the person rendering it and of the search for a justice more precisely adapted to the peculiarities of the specific case, it is also, in the scope of the factual elements that it embraces and utilizes and in the search for an adjustment of the parties' interests on a new basis, a creative or legislative, and to this extent political, act.[14]

Two consequences follow from the character of such an assignment. Notwithstanding the provision in the Statute of the Court, the task ill befits an agency whose functions are essentially judicial. Apart from the fact that it calls for a mentality and knowledge that the judge only exceptionally possesses, the execution of decisions in equity, especially when they bring important political interests into play, often depends on the existence of adequate political force ready to give support.

As we know, the International Court of Justice has shown itself very circumspect in recourse to considerations of equity.[15]

[14] In equitable settlement so conceived, the ethical considerations brought to bear are not always separable from considerations of social utility or from the more particular considerations of convenience or expediency. On the politico-legal character of certain gaps resulting from the imperfections of legal regulation judged by social needs or ideas of justice, see Max Sörensen, *Les Sources du Droit international*, pp. 199-200.

[15] The Permanent Court, it is true, first referred more particularly to the fact that it could not take into account considerations of pure expediency. The Order of December 6, 1930 reads as follows: ". . . even assuming that it were not incompatible with the Court's Statute for the Parties to give the Court power to prescribe a settlement disregarding rights recognized by it and taking into account considerations of pure expediency only, such power, which would be of an absolutely exceptional character, could only be derived from a clear and explicit provision to that effect . . . ," and, further on, "although the Court, being a Court of Justice, cannot disregard rights recognized by it, and base its decision on considerations of pure expediency. . . ." Publications of the Court, series A, no. 24, pp. 10, 15. More absolute is the Judgment of June 7, 1932: "Such questions (depending on the interplay of economic interests) are outside the sphere in which a Court of Justice, concerned with the application of the rules of law, can help in the solution of disputes between two States." Series A/B, no. 46, p. 162.

Today, the International Court of Justice is not in exactly the same situation in regard to this question. The insertion in Article 38 of its Statute of the words "in accordance with international law," without excluding the possibility of a settlement *ex aequo et bono*, which is still expressly provided, seems nevertheless to have been designed to make it easier for the Court to deny its jurisdiction on the ground that the task which the parties would assign to it would be more political than legal.

The quasi-legislative character of the equitable settlement has also the effect of limiting the possibilities of its practical application to disputes that have actually arisen and turn upon a subject defined by special agreements. When in these circumstances the contracting States submit to equitable settlement, they can up to a certain point anticipate its scope and their risks. It can hardly be imagined that a State could in general terms assume the obligation to permit its legally protected interests to be put in the balance with claims of another State that have no legal foundation.[16] Such an attitude would presuppose a social milieu whose structure and distribution of power would be organized quite differently from that now existing.

Settlement *ex aequo et bono* is most naturally the office of an arbiter whose powers are all fixed in the *compromis*. It moreover implies not only great confidence in the arbiter but also and especially some degree of political detachment in regard to the matter in dispute. Such detachment is exceptional when really important interests are to be adjusted on a new legal basis. Besides, the States concerned rarely have an equal interest in requesting a settlement *ex aequo et bono*. Advantageous for the party conscious of the weakness of his claims from the point of view of the existing law, it usually offers few attractions to his opponent.

To facilitate agreement between the parties on a change in the law applicable to their particular relations, the proposal has been made to precede either diplomatic negotiations or a decision in equity *lato sensu* with a judicial trial in which the opposing legal theses would be judged exclusively on the basis of the positive law.[17] It has been argued in particular that a discussion of the legal rules in force is quite often obscured by the political tendency of a gov-

[16] Cf. J. L. Brierly, in *B.Y.B.I.L.*, 1930, p. 132. See also M. Eugène Borel's Report in the *Annuaire of the Institute of International Law*, 1934, pp. 218 seq., 285 seq., 295 seq.

[17] Decencière-Ferrendière, *op.cit.*, pp. 416, 439 seq.

ernment to interpret them to its advantage. A judicial decision, by clarifying the situation in this respect, would prepare the ground for an equitable settlement. This suggestion is of some interest so long as we are concerned only with minor conflicts, those for instance that turn merely on administrative, financial, or technical matters.[18] It makes little sense in reference to really serious political conflicts where it would serve merely to harden opposing positions. Experience shows that States discontented with their situation under an international treaty which they consider contrary to their prestige or their vital interests usually avoid legal decision. Supported by a public opinion which they keep on the alert, they have the tendency, on the contrary, to claim an out-and-out revision on principles sufficiently general and vague to promote their political aspirations—equality of States, ethnic unity, free access to the sea, etc. Here again, everything depends finally on the nature of the political relations between the parties and the importance of the interests at stake.

Section III

The Political in the Judicial Interpretation of International Treaties

International treaties make use of terms like "sovereignty" and "independence," the meaning of which can be determined on the level of concrete reality only by taking into account the prospects of future political development. It was in this light that the Permanent Court of International Justice looked at the question of the compatibility or incompatibility of the proposed Austro-German Customs Union (March 10, 1931) with Article 88 of the Treaty of Saint-Germain and with the Geneva Protocol (October 4, 1922) which had forbidden Austria to take, without the consent of the Council of the League of Nations, any action that might impair her independence.[19]

The difficulty did not lie in the abstract definition of the term "independence." All the judges agreed that in the judicial interpretation of a treaty the notion of independence, the normal condition of States, could not be treated otherwise than as a legal

[18] In the case of the Serbian Loans before the Permanent Court of International Justice, such a procedure was provided for.

[19] Advisory Opinion of September 5, 1931. Publications of the Permanent Court, series A/B, no. 41.

notion, despite its political implications. But must the reply to the request for an opinion limit itself to expounding the relevant texts, interpreted and compared in accordance with the principles of literal exegesis and exclusively from the point of view of their immediate bearing on the independence of Austria? Or should it take into consideration elements which depended at least in part upon future contingencies and which could therefore represent nothing more than reasonable expectations?

The problem was clearly put and solved with exactitude in the dissenting opinion of the former President of the Court, D. Anzilotti. The acts from which Austria was bound to abstain were not only those that implied alienation, that is to say actual loss, of her independence. The texts meant that this duty of abstention extended to any act of a kind to "compromise it directly or indirectly" and, consequently, to threaten it, to expose it to a danger. By this prescription the High Contracting Parties had clearly placed the question in the perspective of the future and accordingly made it dependent upon future political development. As Anzilotti emphasized, it was a special case, and one which derived all its significance from the fact that the relations affected by the projected Customs Union were the relations between Germany and Austria, and from the political design of the Powers to ensure the independent existence of Austria against the danger of incorporation in the German Reich. Austria's general right to enter into a customs union was not in question; it was this particular customs union, and this alone, that was under discussion. This analysis perfectly delineated the characteristic features of political situations. For a sharply individualized case a particular regulation had been designed; its effects were a question of fact and could be the subject only of reasonable expectations.

An important minority of the Court refused to follow this line of thought. "The Court," it argued, "is not concerned with political considerations nor with political consequences. These lie outside its competence."[20] And it may well be thought that it would have been better to seek the solution of such a problem before the Council of the League of Nations rather than before an institution of such strictly judicial character as the Court. But the complaint against the majority of the Court, that on this occasion it abandoned its proper function, is not well founded. An international court is not

[20] *ibid.*, p. 75.

acting politically when it takes political considerations into account insofar as these have found expression in a convention of manifestly political content. Though clearly it must not judge by its personal sentiments, which would lead it to conclusions of a speculative kind, it cannot be absolved from considering the normal political consequences of an act when these have been covered in the convention which governs the act and when, besides, they are reasonably foreseeable on the basis of "facts well known to all and established in the present proceedings."[21]

In cases of this kind the international judge cannot be forbidden the foresights that such facts dictate to practical reason and good sense.[22] But it is true that, particular or individual situations being much more numerous than general situations in international relations, the international judge is bound to show more reserve than the national judge when he takes into account the "normal and ordinary course of things" or the "results of experience." Finally, the inability of the Permanent Court of International Justice to give a more impersonal and more rigorous character to its reasoning in this case is explained by the relative rarity of precedents, the insufficiency of generally recognized criteria, and, in the last analysis, by the present structure of international relations.

The international judge is in a different position when he is called upon to interpret a treaty which, like the United Nations Charter, has the specific object of limiting the exercise of sovereignty or the liberty of decision or action of States in a well-defined sphere. Here the institutional character of the norms provides the judge with more precise criteria.

By resolution of November 17, 1947, the General Assembly of the United Nations asked the Court for an opinion on the question whether a member of the United Nations voting on the admission of a State to membership is legally entitled to make its consent to admission depend upon conditions not expressly mentioned in the first paragraph of Article 4 of the Charter. The consultation raised the point whether the admission to membership had been made the subject in the said article of a truly legal regulation or whether, on the contrary, States members were free to add other conditions to

[21] Individual opinion of. D. Anzilotti, p. 70. Cf. Manley O. Hudson, *The Permanent Court of International Justice, 1920-1942*, § 574.

[22] Cf. Philip C. Jessup, in *A.J.I.L.*, 1932, pp. 105-110. For the contrary view and an example of incomprehension, see the comments by Edwin M. Borchard in *A.J.I.L.*, 1931, pp. 711-716.

those prescribed in the text and, more generally, to superimpose on them the most broadly political considerations. The Court's opinion (May 28, 1948) recognized the limitative nature of the list of conditions in Article 4, not only in the sense that the absence of these conditions makes admission impossible, but also in the sense that admission cannot be made to depend upon circumstances other than those that can logically and in all good faith be subsumed under the conditions mentioned in the text. The Court said that any other interpretation would tend to give the members a practically unlimited power, incompatible with the character of a regulation which "by reason of the close connexion which it establishes between membership and the observance of the principles and obligations of the Charter clearly constitutes a legal regulation of the question." The Court took care to emphasize that the political nature of the organs called upon to decide cannot absolve them from observing the treaty provisions by which they are governed, when these are conceived as limits set to their powers or criteria established for their judgment.[28]

The minority opinion emphasized the political nature of resolutions regarding admissions, and the political character and responsibilities of the deciding organs, to conclude that, subject only to the requirements of good faith and respect for the purposes of the Charter, these organs are legally entitled to make their consent to admission conditional upon any political consideration which may in their opinion be relevant. The whole interest of the debate lay in the difference in points of departure—regulated liberty or discretionary judgment.

Although the question was in itself a legal one and the General Assembly subsequently recommended that the States members comply with the answer given by the Court, experience has shown that a consultation on such a subject is devoid of practical interest. For nothing compels States to explain their votes, and unexpressed motives escape all control. Finally, the implications of the problem looked at in its total reality were broader than the question put.

[28] Reports, 1948, pp. 63, 64. The effect of Article 4, paragraph 1, is exactly defined by M. G. Berlia when he says that the article can be understood as establishing "a criterion of legality" (since the problem is to determine whether the conditions enumerated in the text, excluding all others, are or are not fulfilled), together with "a large measure of discretionary power," since, in the absence of a sure test by which the fulfillment or nonfulfillment of some of these conditions can be judged, such judgment can only reflect a personal conviction. In *Revue générale de Droit international public*, 1949, p. 496.

Section IV

Resistances to Compulsory Jurisdiction

It is naturally in regard to compulsory jurisdiction that the political preoccupations of States become most palpable. The obligation assumed in advance to submit to judicial decision disputes not yet arisen involves in its vagueness a large unknown, and consequently risks, against which governments have always sought in various ways to forearm themselves. In the first arbitration treaties, of which the Franco-British Treaty of 1903 was the prototype, these political preoccupations were openly expressed. Though the principle of obligation was there stated, its effective application was made subject to the express condition that the dispute did not affect the vital interests, independence, or honor of the signatory States, or, finally, the interests of third States. Reservations so general and left so entirely, in fact, to the discretion of the contracting governments for their practical application weakened the obligation to such a point that they soon appeared irreconcilable with a compulsory and organized system of arbitration.

From that time on, and especially after the League of Nations had opened new vistas of development for arbitral or judicial settlement, the cautious reserve of governments in the matter of a general jurisdictional obligation, without much diminution in substance, found expression in new forms.

The concern to exclude certain disputes by reason of their political nature manifests itself in texts which, though they state an obligation in principle, tend to retain the requirement of a special agreement for valid submission to the designated tribunal. This is the case with treaties that limit compulsory settlement to "legal" disputes without otherwise specifying their object, or without conferring on a tribunal unilaterally seized the power to decide, in the event of debate on the point, whether the dispute is a legal one as belonging to one of the categories mentioned in the clause giving compulsory jurisdiction.[24]

The history of the German-Swiss Treaty of December 3, 1921 offers an interesting example of a bold attempt to give the judge power to decide upon the plea that a dispute is a political one.

[24] Acceptance of the compulsory jurisdiction of the Court under the conditions mentioned in Article 36 of the Statute has, on the contrary, the effect of rendering the disputes covered, within the limits of the obligation assumed, compulsorily justiciable whatever the importance of the interests involved.

Article 4 stated a double reservation. On the one hand it foresaw the possibility that the validity of the plea of "independence, territorial integrity, or other extremely important vital interests" entered by one party might be contested by the other, and authorized the tribunal to decide this difference by simple majority. Foreseeing next the case where one party, without entering such a plea *in terminis*, should demur on the ground that the dispute was "of a primarily political character" and for this reason "would not lend itself to decision on exclusively legal principles," it gave the same power of decision to the tribunal, but with the proviso this time that the demurrer could be judged valid only "by a vote that was either unanimous or unanimous less one."

These texts invited the judge to determine the nature of the dispute by taking into account not exclusively the terms of the claim and their relation to facts belonging to the past, but the whole of the political relations of the parties, considered in all the elements, sometimes imponderable, of their present reality and their future development. They made allowance for the undeniable fact that a dispute prima facie legal may take on a political character by reason of the consequences that a judgment in accordance with law may involve for one of the parties.[25] But it was possible to reproach them with having "carried over the notion of political dispute into the domain of legal disputes."[26]

This attempt to transfer to the compulsory decision of the judge an appraisal which in the present state of international relations necessarily belongs to the sovereign power, had to confess itself fruitless. A Protocol of August 29, 1928 abrogated Article 4 of the German-Swiss Treaty of 1921.[27]

The proposal of the United Nations International Law Commission to make the obligations assumed in arbitration conventions more effective calls for similar observations. The Commission's draft (1952-1953) would have submitted to judicial control the objections by which a State party to such a convention might, before an arbitral tribunal was set up, seek to escape its obligation to arbitrate either by denying the existence of a dispute, or by claiming that the dispute is not one of those covered by the convention. The judicial organ exercising this control, in default of another tribunal designated by the parties, would be the International Court of Justice,

25 Cf. D. Schindler, *Die Schiedsgerichtsbarkeit*, p. 78.

26 Eugène Borel, *Arbitrage et Sécurité*, pp. 22-23.

27 D. Schindler, *op.cit.*, p. 88, note.

and its decision would be final. Further—and this was the heart of the problem—by refusing to distinguish between legal and political disputes, the draft convention sought to eliminate the political considerations that usually account for a unilateral refusal to fulfill the arbitral obligation. Legitimate as were these legal designs, the draft on this point altered the traditional characteristics of arbitration, robbing it of the suppleness which in the eyes of governments is one of its most definite advantages. Arbitration rests on the agreement of the parties. In the present state of affairs, obligatory judicial control cannot be constituted for that agreement in relation to questions so essential as the existence of a dispute and its fitness for arbitration. This could only be done with any chance of success given a change in the present very conservative attitude of States towards acceptance of the compulsory jurisdiction of the International Court of Justice. In trying to enclose arbitration in too rigid a legal framework, there is the risk, as some governments have pointed out, of fettering the institution itself and thus doing a definite disservice to the cause which such efforts seek to promote.[28]

Conscious of political resistances, the International Court of Justice, like its predecessor the Permanent Court, looks with scrupulous care for the foundation of its powers in the assent of the parties to its jurisdiction. Less concerned to enlarge its jurisdiction than to fix its indisputable limits, it finds in this assent the just measure between the sovereignties that it recognizes and the law that it is called upon to apply.[29] In the Corfu Channel case (Preliminary Objection) the Court's concern to leave no doubt subsisting as to the voluntary basis of its jurisdiction in a contentious matter was most strikingly displayed in the collective decision of seven judges rejecting the United Kingdom Government's argument that the Charter had created a new case of compulsory jurisdiction. This declaration was the more significant in that it was

[28] Report of the International Law Commission, Fifth Session, June 1–August 14, 1953. Cf. Julius Stone, *Legal Controls of International Conflict*, pp. 732-738.

[29] The interpretation of Iran's declaration on the compulsory jurisdiction of the Court (case of the Anglo-Iranian Oil Co., July 22, 1952) is a new proof of this circumspection. Having to deal with a text in which a purely grammatical interpretation left some doubts, the Court sought the intention of the Iranian Government at the time of its declaration. In this connection it took into consideration Iran's general policy in relation to its capitulation treaties, a policy that had induced it to draft "in a very restrictive manner" its declaration accepting the compulsory jurisdiction of the Court. Reports, 1952, p. 105.

not strictly necessary to the decision of the question, the Court's jurisdiction having been established by the Albanian Government's recognition.

On the other hand, where the agreement of the parties appears to it established, the Court asserts its jurisdiction without letting any purely formal objections stand in its way.[80] Whether the question is one of applying the rule of preliminary diplomatic negotiations, or of deciding upon the form that the defendant's consent to the principle or to the extent of its jurisdiction must take, the Court always, under appearances and forms, seeks the real intentions of the governments.

If the absence of a purely formal condition does not prevent the Court from exercising jurisdiction, neither is it bound to a particular form to the exclusion of others. Here the Court invokes a consideration that indicates an exact sense of the relations between States: the suppleness, the flexibility which these relations must preserve and which the Court cannot ignore without obstructing recourse to its jurisdiction.[81] This breadth of view must certainly not be taken as meaning that the Court has adopted the maxim *boni judicis est ampliare jurisdictionem.* This would be a gross misinterpretation of its thought. What is true is that in making its jurisdiction dependent on sovereign wills, the Court, faithful to its Statute, concedes that this jurisdiction should be limited, never that it should be evaded.

It is natural that resistances to the acceptance of compulsory jurisdiction should increase at times of high political tension. States assume more rigid positions, asserting their rights in more absolute terms. They have a sharper sense of the risks involved in the compulsory settlement of future disputes on indeterminate issues. True, recent reservations in the acceptance of the Court's compulsory jurisdiction do not take the form *in terminis* of an unqualified return to the purely political reservations current at the beginning of the century, and it may be thought that this, in spite of everything, marks some progress. But some of them, for all their legal style, are drafted in such a way as to make real fulfillment of the obligation dependent on the unilateral and sovereign judgment of the signatory State.

80 "The Court, whose jurisdiction is international, is not bound to attach to matters of form the same degree of importance which they might possess in municipal law." Permanent Court of International Justice, Judgment No. 2, Mavrommatis Concessions case, p. 34.

81 *ibid.*, p. 15.

In this connection, the form recently given by some States to the reservation excluding compulsory jurisdiction of disputes relating to internal affairs or "matters which are essentially within the domestic jurisdiction" marks a retreat to earlier practice. Before the second world war, none of the States making a reservation of this kind had claimed the right to decide by itself and without appeal the question of its legitimate application. The texts of the period, modelled at once on Article 15, paragraph 8, of the Covenant of the League of Nations, and on Article 39 of the Geneva General Act, 1928, explicitly referred the question whether or not a dispute related to a matter within "the exclusive jurisdiction of the State" to international law, interpreted, in case of debate, by the Court. This solution favored progress in international law since it opened the way for the rules of that law into questions left until then to the discretion of the State.

Some recent reservations to the acceptance of compulsory jurisdiction, based on Article 2, paragraph 7, of the Charter, are conceived in a different spirit: they expressly refer the definition of domestic jurisdiction to the personal and sovereign decision of the State making the reservation. Doubtless such freedom of decision must be understood as limited to questions in regard to which the vagueness of the rules of international law delimiting the reserved domain leaves room for reasonable differences of view.[32] These would be only marginal cases; and so interpreted and applied the reservation would not too seriously reduce the value of the obligation assumed. It remains true, however, that it weakens the obligation by introducing a new discretionary element and constitutes a regrettable precedent, calculated to encourage political resistances to the exercise of international jurisdiction.

There is some truth in the observation that the general adoption of the clause on obligatory jurisdiction has had the frequent effect of concealing under artifices of the legal technique resistances which formerly were openly expressed in the refusal to submit to the

[32] In fact, the passage in the Report to the President of the United States relating to the omission of the reference to international law in Article 2, paragraph 7, reads as follows: "The present text omits reference to 'International Law,' found in the Dumbarton Oaks Proposals. . . . This deletion was supported by the argument that the body of international law on this subject is indefinite and inadequate. To the extent that the matter is dealt with by international practice and by text writers, the conceptions are antiquated and not of a character which ought to be frozen into the new Organization."

judge disputes of real political significance.[33] But it must be admitted that an unreserved undertaking to submit all disputes without exception to judicial settlement would hardly accord with the present structure of international relations, which favors leaving to the individual decision of States those of their interests which they consider inseparable from their personality or their power. The observation applies particularly to the mutual relations of the great States, exposed as they always are to the fluctuations of what is called power politics.

The political preoccupations of States do not manifest themselves exclusively in reservations to the acceptance of compulsory jurisdiction. They are discernible also in the very frequent recourse to preliminary objections against unilateral citation. The Permanent Court of International Justice rejected all of these pleas that appeared to it to be directed by the desire to evade, under cover of technical objections, an undertaking for which good faith commanded respect. Its decisions were in this respect remarkably consistent. They had reference to the denial by one of the parties of the very existence of a dispute, condition of recourse to international jurisdiction. Avoiding any too formal a position which would have led it into complex definitions, calculated only to foster the spirit of pettifoggery, the Court reduced the notion of dispute to the simplest elements: "A dispute is a disagreement on a point of law or fact, a conflict of legal views or of interests between two persons."[34] The Permanent Court took a similar position on the requirement of previous diplomatic negotiations as proof of the existence of a dispute and as an obligatory preliminary to recourse to international jurisdiction. Recognizing the importance of such negotiations for a precise definition of the subject of the dispute, the Court declared that in appraising their adequacy account must be taken of the fact that "the question of the importance and chances of success of diplomatic negotiations is essentially a relative one," and that the Court itself could not fail to take into consideration "the views of the States concerned, who are in the best position to judge as to political reasons which may prevent the settlement of a given dispute by diplomatic negotiation."[35]

[33] Hans J. Morgenthau, *Politics among Nations*, p. 224. Some reservations, by reason either of their great generality or of their excessive legal technicality, have been an unfailing source of the preliminary objections so frequently pleaded before the Court.

[34] Judgment No. 2, Mavrommatis Concessions case, p. 11.

[35] *ibid.*, pp. 13, 15.

Section V

Politics and the Exercise of the Advisory Function of the International Court of Justice

Article 65 of the Statute of the International Court of Justice lays it down that "The Court may give an advisory opinion on any legal question at the request of whatever body may be authorized by or in accordance with the Charter of the United Nations to make such a request." The meaning of the term "legal question" is clear here. It means any question that can be answered in terms of law. Bound in principle to fulfill its advisory function and therefore to answer any such question, the Court would refuse to do so where the answer depended on considerations foreign to law, especially political considerations. The general criterion that determines the Court's position is thus objective, but it is for the Court to apply it; the Court alone is entitled, for instance, to decide whether the answer that it is requested to give is in fact compatible with the judicial character of its functions. In its opinion on principle of March 30, 1950, the Court clearly asserted that "There are certain limits, however, to the Court's duty to reply to a Request for an Opinion. It is not merely an 'organ of the United Nations,' it is essentially the 'principal judicial organ' of the Organization (Art. 92 of the Charter and Art. 1 of the Statute). . . . Article 65 of the Statute is permissive. It gives the Court the power to examine whether the circumstances of the case are of such a character as should lead it to decline to answer the Request."[36]

It may happen that the request for an opinion relates to an existing dispute or to a legal question actually pending between two or more States. The hypothesis is mentioned in Articles 82 and 83 of the Rules of the Court. In that case, opposition to the exercise of the advisory function by a State interested in this dispute or question may well assume a political character, especially when the State does not belong to the United Nations Organization. The Covenant of the League of Nations contained an explicit provision (Art. 17) to the effect that a non-member State could be invited to accept the obligations of membership for the purpose of settling a dispute. The invitation could be freely accepted or refused. It was chiefly on the basis of Article 17—which has no counterpart in the Charter of the United Nations—that the Permanent Court of

[36] Opinion of March 30, 1950, Interpretation of Peace Treaties, Reports, 1950, pp. 71-72.

International Justice refused to comply with the request for an opinion addressed to it on April 21, 1923 by the Council of the League of Nations in the matter of Eastern Carelia. Faced with the absolute refusal of the Soviet Government to take part in the examination of this question by the League of Nations or the Court, the Court refused to render an opinion, declaring first in general terms that acceptance of the methods laid down in the Covenant for settling a dispute between a State member and a State non-member must depend upon the latter's consent, and then stating specifically that the question put to it touched directly upon "the essential point" in dispute, and that to answer it would in substance amount to deciding this dispute between the parties. "The Court, being a Court of Justice, cannot, even in giving advisory opinions, depart from the essential rules guiding their activity as a Court."[87]

The request for an opinion voted by the General Assembly of the United Nations on October 22, 1949 had a very different object. Its sole concern was the applicability of a procedure of settlement established by the Peace Treaties to disputes that had arisen between certain Allied and Associated Powers on the one side and Bulgaria, Hungary, and Rumania on the other. The answer to such a request could not in any way touch the merits of these disputes. Nor could it prejudice the decision on objections that might be raised to the jurisdiction of the arbitral commissions provided for in the Treaties, when they came to examine each dispute. Holding consequently that the legal position of the parties to these disputes could in no degree be prejudiced by the answers to the questions put, the International Court of Justice decided that it had the power and duty to answer them.

Thus it was in a legal analysis of the particular features of each case that the Court found the criteria that must determine its attitude, refusing to be influenced by the more or less political considerations or motives that filled the background of the picture.

It goes without saying, finally, that when it can give a legal answer to a question regularly submitted to it, the Court cannot refuse on the ground that the request for an opinion was inspired by political motives. In its opinion of May 28, 1948 on the conditions for admitting a State to membership in the United Nations (Art. 4 of the Charter), the Court declared that it could not impute a political character to a request formulated in abstract terms

[87] Series B, Advisory Opinion of July 23, 1923, p. 29.

which, in referring to it the interpretation of a conventional text, invited it to perform an essentially judicial function, and that it could not be prevented from complying by any consideration of the motives that might have prompted the request. Nor could a political character be imputed to such a request by reason of the political consequences that might or must follow a legal response. The contrary view would rob the advisory function of much of its interest and practical usefulness.

Still in the advisory field, political opposition to the interpretation of treaties by the Court took the form of a complaint of improper interference by the United Nations in the application of a multilateral convention, in this instance the Convention for the prevention and punishment of the crime of genocide. Having found that the General Assembly had not only taken the initiative for such a Convention, fixed its terms, and opened it for signature and adherence by all States, but had also been given an intimate part in its application, the Court held that definition of the conditions of participation constituted a particular and permanent interest of the United Nations which was sufficient to justify the request for an opinion addressed to the Court.[38]

Section VI

Judicial Settlement and the Development of International Law

Much more than the establishment of peace, the development of international law is the essential function of judicial settlement and more particularly of the International Court of Justice. The gradual elaboration of the law through the accumulation of a body of reasoned and homogeneous decisions is a condition of order and stability in international relations. A more precise knowledge of the law enlightens States in the daily business of their mutual relations, promotes their recourse to justice itself, and in particular facilitates acceptance of compulsory jurisdiction.

The present inadequacy of the norms of international law for certain kinds of disputes is a fact that weighs heavily on the attitude of governments towards international justice. It is to be satisfied with a superficial view to protest, as is sometimes done, the rarity of recourse to *non liquet* in the practice of international tribunals.

[38] Opinion of May 28, 1951, Reports, 1951, pp. 19-20.

Governments are not accustomed to refer to international jurisdiction disputes in no way open to settlement by some rule of international law. The small number of those submitted is not to be wholly explained by the political importance that they attach to the others; the uncertainty of the law is partly responsible. The resources of legal logic, which can indeed always provide a formal answer to any question whatever, foster doctrinal complacency on the subject of what is called the "plenitude" of international law.

The priority of legal settlement was already recognized in the Covenant of the League of Nations. In its concern for peace, the Covenant required mediation by the Council in disputes serious enough to lead to a breach, but in its respect for law it nonetheless gave preference to arbitral or judicial settlement of all disputes, however grave they might be, that in the opinion of the parties could be settled by reference to law.

As a judicial organ whose duty it is to declare the law, the International Court of Justice, like its predecessor the Permanent Court, has not disappointed the hopes entertained of it. The interest of its jurisprudential achievement has been heightened by the negative results of the efforts to codify international law.

Yet we cannot overlook the fact that the contribution of the Court's decisions to the development of international law depends largely on the general state of political relations. There is no doubt, for example, that the Permanent Court was able to do more for the development of the law in the first years of the League of Nations, a relatively quiet period, than in the years following Hitler's advent to power. The observation holds as well for the advisory activity of the Permanent Court as for its contentious jurisdiction. Too many requests for an opinion recently addressed to the International Court of Justice bear the mark of the political conflicts or compromises in the United Nations from which they spring.[39]

The international judicial function has one aspect that cannot be

[39] The General Assembly's resolution asking the Court for an opinion on the legal effect of reservations to the Genocide Convention (November 16, 1950), and at the same time inviting the International Law Commission to present a report on the general problem of reservations to multilateral Conventions, was the result of a compromise liable to impair the prestige of the Court. Besides, the purely abstract form of the questions put to the Court regarding a sharply individualized convention was prompted by political preoccupations; it put the consultation in a false light and prevented the Court from giving a wholly adequate answer.

too strongly emphasized: it is the great difference in some respects between the judge's application of the law in this domain and its application by national tribunals.

From the point of view of the adequacy of the norms to international realities, relations between States suffer, as we have seen, from a lack of solidarity and regularity which is accounted for now by natural differences, now by the strictly political and individualistic operation of power. This state of affairs becomes manifest in the predominance of particular over general situations. Typical relations, capable of being compared and assembled in common categories by processes of abstraction, are definitely rarer here than in the more evolved disciplines. These features are ill suited to the habitual methods of legal logic, which is generally concerned to fortify the authority of the decision by setting it, through some norm or institution, in a predetermined legal framework.

Thus, from the beginning and in much greater degree than the national judge, the international judge is faced with a fundamental question: On what level of generalization or individualization must the actual case before him be approached?[40] An objective analysis of the details of the matter in dispute, preceding any recourse to technical construction, guides this first confrontation of the case with the norms. It is made particularly delicate in international law by the frequent want of an exact adaptation of norms to the variety of cases. The influence of this initial orientation, though it is at times only implicit in the text of the judgments, is of considerable importance not only in the decision of the concrete case, but also in the development of case-law by the establishment of judicial precedents.

When the circumstances of the concrete case include elements which prima facie connect them with typical situations already ordered by law, the judge will endeavor by some process of abstraction to find a solution along the lines of generalization by classification. When, on the contrary, the case, looked at in its reality, evades any such effort because its elements are sharply particularized or individualized either by their material incidents or by the will of the States concerned, he must respect its particular configuration without yielding to the charm of generalizing abstraction or to teleological considerations, and without being led astray by objec-

[40] On the classification of concepts, their meaning, and their limits, see J. Dabin, *La Technique de l'élaboration du Droit positif*, pp. 166-168.

tions based on the anomaly of the case or the relative inefficacy of the regulation to which he brings his sanction.[41]

The importance of the international judge's role, already strongly marked in this initial interpretation of the litigious situation, is still clearer in the delimitation of his jurisdiction and the application of the substantive rules by processes which the judicial technique puts at his disposal. It is at this stage, as we saw above, that the political resistances to judicial settlement assert themselves in contentious matters. Most frequently they take the form of the plea of sovereignty.

The spirit that animates the delimitation of the jurisdiction of the International Court of Justice is again evident in the search for and application of substantive rules. From its beginnings the Court understood that, in the application of the law as in the establishment of its own powers, sovereignty would be the center and symbol of resistance, the critical element that it must seek to contain without provoking dangerous reactions, and must respect without subordinating to it the law which was in its keeping. If the positions that it has taken in this connection have attracted less attention than those by which it defined its jurisdiction, this is simply because the rules of international law which it has the duty of applying already largely represent in themselves a compromise between law and power. The Court has therefore felt less often the need to explain itself.

The problem raised by the deficiencies of international law over against sovereignties naturally prone to accentuate their independence may be stated in terms of politics as in terms of law. From a political point of view, it may be said that the limitations on sover-

41 Advisory Opinion No. 7 of the Permanent Court of International Justice, Acquisition of Polish Nationality, p. 20: "The Court's task is clearly defined. Having before it a clause which leaves little to be desired in the nature of clearness, it is bound to apply this clause as it stands, without considering whether other provisions might with advantage have been added to or substituted for it." Examples of generalization by classification abound in international judicial decisions. Among examples of the inverse process of particularization, we may cite: the celebrated individual opinion of President Anzilotti in the case of the Austro-German Customs Union, and, among the recent decisions of the International Court of Justice, the Advisory Opinion of July 18, 1950 on the interpretation of the Treaties of Peace with Bulgaria, Hungary, and Rumania (second phase), Reports, 1950, p. 221; the Advisory Opinion of May 28, 1951 on Reservations to the Convention for the Prevention and Punishment of the Crime of Genocide, Reports, 1951, p. 15; Judgment of December 18, 1951 in the Fisheries case (United Kingdom–Norway), Reports, 1951, p. 116.

eignty may not be extended by interpretation or that such limitations must be interpreted restrictively. Speaking more legally, it may be said that international law does not authorize extending by generalization, or more particularly by analogy, the norms restricting the liberty of States.[42] These are the two faces of one and the same problem, which for the international judge turns essentially on the question up to what point and by what steps he has the power and the duty to dictate to sovereign States by way of interpretation a concrete solution which does not stand in necessary logical relation to the norm.

The processes of legal logic, those for instance which help to coordinate the application of norms or to interpret international acts by examining the intention of the parties, occupy an important place in the drafting of international judgments, and undoubtedly their role here appears greater than in national judgments. The international judge is naturally concerned to reinforce with logical apparatus the application of rules that are often far from precise. But the significance of these processes must not be exaggerated. The rules of reasoning are not the rules of law. It has been justly observed that those relating to the interpretation of international treaties, for example, are not generally the determining cause of the decision, but rather the clothing in which the judge dresses a solution that he reached by other paths. There are scarcely any, rigid as they may appear, that can prevent the judge from standing on his interpretation of the intention of the parties according to his idea of the object and aim of the treaty.[43]

Quite distinct from logical reasoning are certain considerations based on practical experience of international affairs and connected with the particular nature of relations between States. Expressed or not, these play an important part in international judgments. By

[42] D. Anzilotti, *Cours de droit international*, tr. Gidel, p. 116. In its political expression the idea figures in the Judgment rendered on August 17, 1923 by the Permanent Court of International Justice in the "Wimbledon" case, p. 24, in the Judgment of September 7, 1927, in the "Lotus" case, p. 18, and in the Judgment of June 7, 1932 on the Free Zones, p. 167. In its Judgment relating to the Oder Commission (September 10, 1929), the Court sharply limited the scope of the argument by stating (p. 26) that "This argument, though sound in itself, must be employed only with the greatest caution . . . it will be only when, in spite of all pertinent considerations, the intention of the Parties still remains doubtful, that that interpretation should be adopted which is most favorable to the freedom of States."

[43] H. Lauterpacht, in *B.Y.B.I.L.*, 1949, p. 53; Henri Rolin, *Rec. A.D.I.*, vol. 77 (1950), p. 418.

way of examples we may cite the deductions drawn from the more or less notorious character of some international situations and the extent to which States are held to have knowledge of them; the behavior of States in relation to facts that may affect their interests, particularly their abstention or their silence; the facts which in the matter of territory constitute historical consolidation;[44] the considerations of order and stability which incline the judge not to adopt without decisive reason interpretations that would create confused or ambiguous situations likely to promote or prolong inter-State conflicts,[45] or lead him to avoid as far as possible altering an existing and long-established state of affairs (*quieta non movere*);[46] and, finally, the concern of the judge not to adopt an interpretation which "would discourage conciliatory diplomatic transactions and encourage the assertion of extreme claims in their fullest extent."[47]

If we go on from these as it were "innominate" forms of judicial reasoning to the sources of law enumerated in Article 38 of the Statute of the Court, we observe that these, while doubtless more precise, are far from offering the firm contours that ensure uniform application of municipal law. The most fundamental, international custom, is often made up of elements of unequal density or value, some more or less essential or basic, others more or less accidental and as it were detachable from their context by adaptation to a particular case. It is well known that the International Court of Justice made an important application of this idea in the Fisheries case (United Kingdom v. Norway).[48]

When they included in the list of applicable sources of law "the

[44] Judgment of the International Court of Justice, December 18, 1951, in the Fisheries case (United Kingdom–Norway), Reports, 1951, pp. 138-139.

[45] This consideration had its influence in the Advisory Opinion of the Permanent Court of International Justice, December 8, 1927, Jurisdiction of the European Commission of the Danube, pp. 62 and passim, as well as in the passage of the Judgment of August 11, 1932, Interpretation of the Statute of Memel, on the definition of the sovereign powers of Lithuania and the autonomous powers of Memel.

[46] Permanent Court of Arbitration, October 23, 1909, Grisbadarna case (Norway v. Sweden), in J. B. Scott, *The Hague Court Reports*, Carnegie Endowment for International Peace, 1916, pp. 121 seq. This consideration was not without influence on the judgment of the Permanent Court of International Justice in the Eastern Greenland case, where Norway's thesis would have opened an era of competition between States incompatible with the stability of established situations.

[47] Award of the Permanent Court of Arbitration, September 7, 1910, North Atlantic Fisheries case, in J. B. Scott, *The Hague Court Reports*, *op.cit.*, p. 186.

[48] See above, Book III, Chap. I.

general principles of law recognized by civilized nations," the drafters of the Court Statute intended to extend as far as possible the domain of international law judicially applicable, "to push to the last limit," as has been said, "the productivity of its sources."[49] They thought of these principles as a source of law independent of convention and custom, as belonging in virtue of their rational character to a common legal fund, but as having acquired through recognition *in foro domestico* by the civilized nations that positive character which makes them rules of law and which forbids including among them what has been called the "ideal element" or mere aspiration, more or less widespread, to a legal organization deemed desirable.[50] It must also be observed that recourse to such principles by the international judge is possible only by a process of abstraction which, stripping off the particular adaptations received in the municipal order from a much more developed technical elaboration, reduces them to their most general and only truly universal aspects. In this connection it is significant that in the very rare cases in which members of the Court have expressly invoked "the general principles," they have done so under cover of some of the most elevated and most general categories of the legal order, such as "justice" or "equity," much more than as the result of a comparative and systematic study of the rules of municipal law.[51]

The fact reveals clearly enough the spirit in which the Court might have recourse to the general principles. Theoretically, such recourse seems to leave much room for subjective judgment, since it leaves the judge free to limit his examination to systems of municipal law of his choice, as well as to decide the level of generalization which he should adopt for their application. In practice, however, a tribunal made up as the International Court of Justice is would probably rely in effect only on principles which are too universally recognized to give grounds for any complaint of subjectivity.

[49] D. Anzilotti, *Cours de droit international*, tr. Gidel, p. 117.

[50] Gény, *Science et Technique*, vol. II, no. 170.

[51] It is because the idea expressed in the maxim *inadimplenti non est adimplendum* corresponds to a principle "so just, so equitable, so universally recognized," that President Anzilotti considers it applicable in international relations. It is because "equity" does not permit a party to demand fulfillment of a contract which he himself is not ready to fulfill or which he has violated, that an international tribunal may, according to Judge Manley Hudson, be led to apply a principle "of such obvious fairness." Judgment of June 28, 1937, Case of the Meuse Canals, Publications of the Permanent Court of International Justice, series A/B, no. 70, pp. 50, 77.

This observation is confirmed by the considerable number of cases in which the Court, without reference to Article 38 of the Statute, and without demonstrating the proposition, simply asserted the existence of a general principle. As examples may be cited: for substantive law, the Judgment of July 26, 1927 in the Chorzow case, where the Court declared that "It is, moreover, a principle generally accepted in the jurisprudence of international arbitration, as well as by municipal courts, that one Party cannot avail himself of the fact that the other has not fulfilled some obligation or has not had recourse to some means of redress, if the former Party has, by some illegal act, prevented the latter from fulfilling the obligation in question, or from having recourse to the tribunal which would have been open to him;"[52] for the admissibility of evidence, the Judgment of the International Court of Justice, April 9, 1949, in the Corfu Channel case, where the Court said: "This indirect evidence is admitted in all systems of law, and its use is recognized by international decisions."[53]

The arbitral tribunals have sometimes displayed more boldness in this context than the International Court of Justice, and it is interesting to observe that they have taken a particularly firm position on considerations of order, stability, and peace. Following the lead given in 1925 by the Institute of International Law,[54] several decisions by mixed arbitral tribunals and claims commissions have approved the general idea of the extinctive prescription of debts as founded on the needs of security and stability in human affairs, or as occupying an essential place in any legal system, and therefore meriting application in international law.[55]

Before a clearly new legal situation the International Court of Justice has not, however, recoiled from new solutions. The request for an advisory opinion on reparation for injuries suffered in the service of the United Nations provided an occasion for demonstrating this.[56] It is true that the Court was able to apply here two

[52] Publications of the Permanent Court of International Justice, series A, no. 9, p. 31.

[53] Reports, 1949, p. 18. In this case the Court based the territorial State's duty of vigilance on "certain general and well-recognized principles, namely: elementary considerations of humanity, even more exacting in peace than in war; the principle of the freedom of maritime communication; and every State's obligation not to allow knowingly its territory to be used for acts contrary to the rights of other States." *ibid.*, p. 22.

[54] *Annuaire*, 1925, pp. 558-560.

[55] G. Schwarzenberger, *International Law*, vol. I, pp. 229-230.

[56] Advisory Opinion of April 11, 1949, Reports, 1949, pp. 174 seq.

principles of interpretation which, converging in a given case, are almost always enough to convince the interpreter: the object and aim of the treaty (the Charter in this case) and full effect for its provisions. On this double basis and despite the Charter's silence, the Court held that on the one hand the Organization has personality even in the international order and, on the other, the functions assigned to it by the Charter necessarily imply the power to present both to States members of the Organization and to States not members claims arising out of the performance of its functions, even—and on this point the Opinion is definitely new—for personal injury suffered by the victim.

Only very rarely, however, does the Court find such clear grounds for so progressive a decision.

Among the most fruitful leads are those provided in contractual material by the method sometimes called logical interpretation. This presumes in the contracting parties a unity of views which justifies either regarding a treaty as a coherent unit, free of contradictions, each of whose provisions, seen in the light of the general economy of the text, must if possible preserve its useful effect and agree with the others;[57] or interpreting or completing it on certain points, by invoking the "principles which in general govern" the matter and enquiring what position the treaty under discussion took in regard to those principles.[58] The method has its limits; but applied with the necessary discernment, it promotes gradual and reasoned development of international law.

Understood as the expression of an assimilating tendency, analogy, under which some have wished to classify application of the general principles of law, can hardly play the creative part in judicial decisions which it plays in doctrinal expositions, and which doctrine must expound in full independence and a broad spirit of coordination and synthesis. For the Court, analogy must remain what it in essence is, a process of reasoning which, on the subordinate plane of legal technique, consists in extending the application of a rule to a case not covered by it, but bordering or analogous. It must moreover be recalled that the frequent inadequacy of the

[57] Advisory Opinion of the International Court of Justice, July 11, 1950, International Status of South-West Africa; dissenting opinion of Charles De Visscher, Reports, 1950, pp. 186-190.

[58] Judgment of the Permanent Court of International Justice, September 10, 1929, Territorial Jurisdiction of the International Commission for the Oder, pp. 26-27.

norms—a consequence of the predominance of particular situations—considerably reduces the field of application of analogy in international law. Clearly the Court's mission is to declare law, not to make it.

When everything has been said of the principles, criteria, methods, and various reasoning processes that may guide international justice, it becomes apparent how impossible it is to include in any formula the infinitely supple and diversified mental operations that point the judge towards what he can regard as a just decision. As Max Sörensen has well said, "the pursuit of a reasonable and equitable goal is certainly one of the essential elements of all interpretation, and the fact that this element rarely appears in the stated reasons for a judgment is no denial of its presence."[59]

Much more marked, or at least more apparent, than the concern to extend the field of application of norms is the Court's concern to assert the unity and coherence of its own decisions. This becomes obvious on a mere reading of its judgments. The Court frequently refers to its earlier decisions, either to corroborate the one now being rendered or to point out the difference between the cases and to forearm itself against a reproach of illogicality or contradiction. It does this in one context simply to find the elements of a legal construction that it is developing, in another and more firmly to present those elements as a doctrine from which it does not propose to stray.

This constant concern of the Court to build gradually a body of homogeneous case-law is in line with the expectations of governments justly interested in greater legal security, and contributes effectively though indirectly to the development of international law.

Much more than the judgments of national courts, those of the International Court of Justice demand for a correct understanding an exact knowledge of the written procedure and the oral pleadings of the parties. The student there discerns the nature of the collaboration which from the point of view of the development of international law is set up between the Court and the governments represented before it; the amount of a generally abundant and recondite documentation that the Court makes use of; the arguments that especially hold its attention; and the order in which it places those that it finds it possible to accept. This side of its judicial

[59] *Les sources du droit international*, p. 236.

activity is rich in instruction and for every reason deserves to be better known.

Doubtless, long years must still pass and many more judgments be rendered before the Court's decisions can be synthesized in a systematic body of principles or rules. To tell the truth, this question depends less on the Court itself than on a change of structure in international relations which would make recourse to justice no longer an expedient conditional on political contingencies, but the normal mode of regulating interests in an organized community.

CONCLUSION

Rerum cognoscere causas.

THE relations of law and power are the object of singular appraisals in recent publications. Some writers, diametrically opposed to the legal theorists who shut themselves up in a purely legal image of the world, give way in these days to the intoxication of political totalitarianism. To believe them, international law is nothing but a tissue of abstractions, fit only to distort the real relations between States, dominated as those are alleged to be by the search for power. Such ideas have always had their disciples. Everything is reduced to force and ends in the national interest. This neorealism, visible already in 1945 as a reaction against the ideology and methods of the League of Nations, could not but flourish in the highly political atmosphere produced by the East-West tension. Realism has its limits. Inclined towards action, guided by an ideal, human nature refuses to accept these distorting simplifications as the final goal of thought.

Much richer in new insights are the perspectives that the study of international relations opens up to international law. This offers a fund of data of all kinds gathered from the direct observation of their concrete influence on the relations between States. The problem here is not one concerning the expediency of research about the utility of which there is no doubt, but one of integrating the results of research in international law.

It must be agreed that in this respect little progress has been made. Efforts to bring together the study of law and the study of international relations have been obstructed by the traditional differences in point of view between jurists and sociologists. There is matter for instruction even in the examination of these differences. In this work we have amply emphasized the inclination of the jurist working in the field of international law to exaggerate the autonomy of his discipline. The specialist in international relations sins on his side by failure to understand the particular requirements of law. Law is a normative discipline; who says law says precept, and precept is never to be confused with fact. This explains that selection of social elements which at the very outset of any elaboration of law gives a construct, and so specifically legal, character to the matter submitted for legal ordering.

Only those elements are selected which are conceived as answering certain purposes and which a group of characteristics (external prominence, generality, regularity) marks for the legal technique—a technique dominated by the search for effectiveness and consequently inclined towards simplicity, precision, and security. The selected elements will therefore always be socially differentiated ones. That is where the dividing line runs between the study of international relations, which has observation and explanation for its object, and the essentially teleological orientation of the normative disciplines. The observation of the data of international life furnishes the indispensable material for legal elaboration, the function of which is to shape certain of these data, by an appropriate technique, to the ends towards which it is directed. The sociologist errs when he reproaches law for this measure of formalism, which is inseparable from its normative ends.

Being distinct in their object, the two disciplines thus have their own requirements and methods. Contact between them is nonetheless necessary. Neither free scientific criticism of public international law, nor its sound interpretation by the arbiter or judge, can overlook the realities in which rules have their origin and which fix their meaning. And it is primarily to legal policy that the vast enterprise of international organization belongs—a decidedly creative task, involving choice and hierarchic ordering of values, in which there can be no question of separating from their moral and social ends the institutional structures to which the man of law brings his constant collaboration.

Various suggestions concerning the teaching of international law follow from this broadening of horizons. They spring at least in part from the discussions of projected reforms in legal studies that have gone on in various circles, especially in the French faculties. In a general way they propose a closer association of the specifically legal training with the study of the social sciences. For international law it is a matter of more completely digesting the data, now so rich, that the young science of international relations can provide.

The idea is a good one. On the pedagogical plane it demands much closer examination. Doubtless a truly scientific study of international law would require an introduction of international sociology, of which Max Huber's work, already old but still precious, and the course given at The Hague by the lamented D. Schindler, have furnished excellent models. Beyond this point, a distinction would seem imperative between preparation for the administrative careers offered by international institutions and the more specifically legal training appropriate for the professor, the governmental legal adviser, and the advocate who in various ways collaborates in the settlement of international questions.

The first, which indeed would involve several specializations, calls both for an extension of the programs of study corresponding to the principal activities of the international Organization, and for an initiation into the special techniques of its various institutions. The second is less a matter of program than of spirit and method. What it categorically demands is personal contact between teacher and student, and consequently the reduction of "master courses" and of dogmatic and formal instruction in favor of seminar courses and of practical work which permits the student to grasp directly the underlying reasons for legal positions or, on the contrary, their inadequacy for social realities. This is not a matter, as is sometimes said, of reconstructing international law out of sociology—a fallacy that leads to nothing but confusion. It is rather one of submitting to a more realistically informed criticism the rules and practices of international law observed in their living application, and of identifying the political, economic, and demographic factors that shape, sustain, and develop them, as well as those that help to distort or destroy them.

All that, certainly, may lead to excellent results. But let us not forget that a general culture, nourished with the teachings of history and philosophy, is still the secret of that degree of intellectual detachment which, on the borders of different disciplines, perceives their limits and presages their convergence. Choice of data that can be put to legal use, delimitation and refinement of concepts, supple adaptations of method—here is an order of problems which, even more than a quantitative enlargement of knowledge, calls for an informed critical spirit, experience of the peculiar exigencies of international life, and a profound sense of the law's mission.

Such is the general direction of this work and above all of those parts of it which seek to set forth in their living and changing reality the present conditions governing the elaboration and application of international law. An inquiry conducted in a terrain still restricted, it is true, but large enough to warrant even now some general conclusions, has enabled us to put a finger on the dangerous gap that the growing politicization of international relations is opening between precept and practice, between formal conceptions and realities. A devitalized law is the product of doctrines that cut institutions off from their two essential sources: moral inspiration strong enough to raise them gradually above their positive and contingent forms, and exact observation keeping them in firm contact with nature and life.

The hour is not one for doctrinal generalizations moving in the rhythm of a transcendental logic, or for brilliant systematizations in which intellectual ingenuity often counts for more than respect for the facts. It is rather one that challenges us to recognize the limits which in our day the dependence of international law on the historical forms of power distribution sets to its effectiveness, and to seek in the human ends of power the moderating principle that may develop aspirations to international collaboration. Every renewed recognition of the foundations of power stimulates a renewal of values; every return to the realities holds promise of effectiveness.

In the same spirit, the individualistic distribution of power among nations has appeared to us to be, if not the sole, at least the primary cause of the present deficiencies of international law. In fact, every attempt to organize international relations is an attempt to redistribute power, and there can be no doubt that this is the way of progress. Some forms of federalism can certainly provide the framework. But among these attempts it is essential to distinguish those for which a spontaneous process of integration ensures a firm foundation and a mission of order and peace from those which owe their inspiration to a political conjuncture or simply to deductions of the systematizing spirit. Federalism, as a new form of power distribution in international relations, must reckon with the social laws that govern all transformations of power. It must reckon with time, which has no respect for what is done without its aid. No more than any other mode of organization has it any value in itself. Partial federations, especially those which it is proposed to create from the ground up, in the very heart of a generalized political tension, without adequate spiritual affinities or independent economic and military resources, are liable to be nothing more than instruments of the antagonisms that divide the peoples.

A redistribution of power has no moral and universal significance save in the safeguards that it offers to order and peace. To be a force for order in a system of peace, it must proceed from solidarities profoundly enough felt to generate new disciplines. It must above all be inspired by ends broader and higher than those which have traditionally guided the political action of national sovereignties.

INDEX

GPSR Authorized Representative: Easy Access System Europe - Mustamäe tee 50, 10621 Tallinn, Estonia, gpsr.requests@easproject.com

www.ingramcontent.com/pod-product-compliance
Ingram Content Group UK Ltd.
Pitfield, Milton Keynes, MK11 3LW, UK
UKHW021827280926
475585UK00003BA/15
* 9 7 8 0 6 9 1 6 4 9 3 3 7 *